W9-CAW-799

government by and for the people, at least in theory. With Adams as her fulcrum, Schiff vividly returns us to the streets and halls where it all began."
—Chris Vognar, *USA Today*

"Riveting, suspenseful, and even laugh-out-loud reading, as Adams outflanks the British at every turn...A vivid and evocative writer, Schiff excels in her portrayal of Boston in its agony and anger...Superb."
—Mary Ann Gwinn, *Minneapolis Star Tribune*

"The inimitable Stacy Schiff, author of utterly captivating books, returns with a biography of one of the most pivotal and oddly neglected of all the U.S. Founding Fathers: Samuel Adams, cousin to the more famous politician (and second president) John. Schiff's book finds the real man behind the Revolutionary mythos."
—*Christian Science Monitor*

"This enthralling biography is a persuasive exercise in rehabilitation. Making her case through stylish prose and a close reading of Adams's career as a canny propagandist and syndicated news service provider, Schiff suggests that he may have done more than any other of America's founding fathers to prime colonists for armed rebellion and is undeserving of the neglect in which his post-Revolution reputation has often foundered."
—*New York Times Book Review* (100 Notable Books of 2022)

"A new book from Pulitzer Prize–winning, powerhouse historian Schiff is always an event."
—*Booklist*

"Schiff masterfully chronicles the myriad twists and turns of Adams's life as protests against the British grew and the streets of Boston became choked with soldiers, spies, and whispers of war...Schiff understands how to translate even the most knotty history into quick-paced narrative. There is something about Samuel Adams that seems especially compelling today. 'He set more store in ideas than institutions,' Schiff writes, 'he encouraged an allegiance to principles over individuals.'...We forget him and his ideas, it seems to me, at our peril."
—Kate Tuttle, *Boston Globe*

Extraordinary Acclaim for
Stacy Schiff's

THE REVOLUTIONARY: SAMUEL ADAMS

Winner of the Colonial Dames of America Book Award
Finalist for the George Washington Prize
Finalist for the New England Book Award in Nonfiction

"With incomparable wit, grace, and insight, Stacy Schiff narrates the birth of the American Revolution in Boston and the artful, elusive magician who made it all happen: Samuel Adams. For too long, Adams, hiding behind his many masks and stratagems, has evaded historians, but Schiff draws him from the shadows into the spotlight he so richly deserves. A glorious book that is as entertaining as it is vitally important. This is a time for Americans to meditate on the fate of their republic and no better place to start than here, at the beginning, with this book."

— Ron Chernow, Pulitzer Prize–winning author of
Alexander Hamilton and *Washington: A Life*

"Step aside, Thomas Jefferson; let's talk about the man whose devotion to resistance behavior makes him, for some, the most essential figure in the American Revolution. Samuel Adams comes to electrifying life through this Pulitzer Prize–winning historian's meticulous research and dynamic storytelling as a man of principle and persuasion. There was also Adams's devotion to stealth and secrecy, which may be why it's taken so long to tease out his unusual story." — Bethanne Patrick, *Los Angeles Times*

"A tour de force...With her exquisite, fast-paced prose...Stacy Schiff has produced a delightfully enthralling and insightful account of an elusive Founding Father. Samuel Adams 'did not preen for posterity,' but we now know him much better than we did. Perhaps even better than he'd want us to." — Mark G. Spencer, *Wall Street Journal*

"Any book from the Pulitzer Prize–winning Schiff is reason for excitement. Her previous subjects, including Véra Nabokov, Antoine de Saint-Exupéry, and Cleopatra, have established her as one of the most talented and creative biographers at work today. Readers interested in the American Revolution or the ability of individuals to destabilize political institutions will find her new book rewarding. This brisk narrative of the outsize role that Adams played in colonial Massachusetts during the 'messy, anarchic, provocative years' before the Revolution places the reader at the center of the action, while dramatic events, including the Boston Massacre and Tea Party, unfold anew in the light of Adams's involvement. Schiff writes beautifully and lyrical passages provide a great deal of reading pleasure...Readers will likely find themselves agreeing with John Adams, who said, 'Without the character of Samuel Adams the true history of the American Revolution can never be written.'" —Amy S. Greenberg, *New York Times Book Review*

"A wildly entertaining exploration of the roots of American political theater. Unreliable rumormongering, slanted news writing, misleading symbolism, even viral meme-sharing—it was all right there at the start." —Adam Gopnik, *The New Yorker*

"A beautifully crafted, invaluable biography...Schiff ingeniously connects the past to our present and future, underscoring the lessons of Adams while reclaiming our nation's self-evident truths at a moment when we seemed to have forgotten them." —*Oprah Daily*

"This book, at times brimming with drama, carefully sifts through the remaining materials to build a robust portrait of an important patriot." —Laura Zornosa, *Time*

"Schiff is a master biographer...These pages contain great drama and constant motion...To read this book is to immerse oneself in a very particular and thrilling time and place. Boston in the years leading up to 1776 was a wild and often dangerous city, with violent protests and brawls and raucous meetings of the people. This is how a democracy was born, a

"Schiff, who won a Pulitzer for her 1999 biography of Véra Nabokov, not only has a gift for crafting narrative out of freshly interpreted history but also has a wicked sense of humor. All her talents are in evidence in this story of Founding Father Samuel Adams, a Harvard-trained businessman's son who went rogue to fight the British, using his genius for strategy and propaganda to outwit Boston's oppressors at every turn. Schiff paints an indelible portrait of colonial Boston and places Adams at the center of it all."   —Mary Ann Gwinn, *Los Angeles Times*

"Schiff is one of the most formidable nonfiction writers working today."
                              —Liberty Hardy, *BookRiot*

"After I put down *The Revolutionary: Samuel Adams*, I wanted to pick it up and read it over again from the beginning, if only for the pleasure of the prose...Read this book if you wish to know how, historically speaking, thirteen English colonies became the United States."
                              —Robert Knox, Medium.com

THE
REVOLUTIONARY

Samuel Adams

STACY SCHIFF

BACK BAY BOOKS
LITTLE, BROWN AND COMPANY
New York Boston London

For Nancy Faust Sizer

Back Bay Books / Little, Brown and Company
Hachette Book Group
1290 Avenue of the Americas, New York, NY 10104
littlebrown.com

Originally published in hardcover by Little, Brown and Company, October 2022
First Back Bay paperback edition, October 2023

Little, Brown and Company is a division of Hachette Book Group, Inc. The Little, Brown name and logo are trademarks of Hachette Book Group, Inc.

The publisher is not responsible for websites (or their content) that are not owned by the publisher.

The Hachette Speakers Bureau provides a wide range of authors for speaking events. To find out more, go to hachettespeakersbureau.com or email hachettespeakers@hbgusa.com.

Little, Brown and Company books may be purchased in bulk for business, educational, or promotional use. For information, please contact your local bookseller or the Hachette Book Group Special Markets Department at special.markets@hbgusa.com.

ISBN 9780316441117 (hc) / 9780316441094 (pb)
Library of Congress Control Number: 2022941865

Printing 1, 2023

LSC-C

Printed in the United States of America

CONTENTS

TRULY THE MAN OF THE REVOLUTION

Omissions are not accidents.

— MARIANNE MOORE

SAMUEL ADAMS delivered what may count as the most remarkable second act in American life. It was all the more confounding after the first: he was a perfect failure until middle age. He found his footing at forty-one, when, over a dozen years, he proceeded to answer to Thomas Jefferson's description of him as "truly the man of the Revolution." With singular lucidity Adams plucked ideas from the air and pinned them to the page, layering in the moral dimensions, whipping up emotions, seizing and shaping the popular imagination. On a wet 1774 night when a group of Massachusetts farmers settled in a tavern before the fire and, pipes in hand, discussed what had driven Bostonians mad—reasoning that Parliament might soon begin to tax horses, cows, and sheep; wondering what additional affronts could come their way; and concluding that it was better to rebel sooner rather than later—it was because the long arm of Samuel Adams had reached them. He muscled words into deeds, effecting, with various partners, a revolution that culminated, in 1776, with the Declaration of Independence. It was a sideways, looping, secretive business. Adams steered New Englanders where he was certain they meant, or should mean, to head, occasionally even revealing the destination along the way. As a grandson acknowledged: "Shallow men called this cunning, and wise men wisdom." The patron saint of late bloomers, Adams proved a political genius.

His second cousin John swore that Samuel was born to sever the cord between Great Britain and America. John also believed Samuel an original; he mystified even his peers. Committed, as he termed it, to "the cool voice of impartial reason," Samuel Adams breathed fire when fire-breathing was in order. Serene, sunny, tender, he seemed instinctively to grasp what righteous anger could accomplish. From four feckless decades he emerged intensely disciplined, an indomitable master of public opinion—a term yet to be coined. In a colony from which, as a Crown officer observed, "all the smoke, flame, and lava" erupted, Adams seemed everywhere at once. If there was a subversive committee in Massachusetts, he sat on it. If there was a subversive act, he was somewhere near or behind it. "He eats little, drinks little, sleeps little, thinks much, and is most decisive and indefatigable in the pursuit of his objects," noted a Philadelphia colleague, unhappily. His enemies, insisted Adams, came in handy: "Our friends are either blind to our faults or not faithful enough to tell us of them." He knew that we are governed more by our feelings than by reason; with rigorous logic, he lunged at the emotions. He made a passion of decency. He was a prudent revolutionary. Among the last of his surviving words is a warning to Thomas Paine: "Happy is he who is cautious."

Deeply idealistic—a moral people, Adams held, would elect moral leaders—he believed virtue the soul of democracy. To have a villainous ruler imposed on you was a misfortune. To elect him yourself was a disgrace. At the same time he was unremittingly pragmatic. Adams saw no reason why high-minded ideals should shy from underhanded tactics. Power worried him; no one ever believed he possessed too much of the stuff. His sympathies lay with the man in the street, to whom he believed government answered. A friend distilled his politics to two maxims: "Rulers should have little, the people much." And privilege should make way for genius and industry. Railing against "the odious hereditary distinction of families," Adams fretted about vanity, foppery, and "political idolatry." He did his best to contain himself when John Hancock—who traveled with "the pomp and retinue of an Eastern prince"—appeared in a gold-trimmed, crimson-velvet waistcoat and an embroidered white vest. In 1794, Adams was inaugurated as governor of Massachusetts. To maintain ceremonial standards, a benefactor produced a carriage. Adams directed the coachman to drive his wife to the State House, to which he proceeded, at seventy-one, on foot.

On no count did he mystify more than in his disregard for money. "I glory in being what the world calls a poor man. If my mind has ever been tinctured with envy, the rich and the great have not been its objects," he wrote his wife of sixteen years, who hardly needed a reminder. At a precarious point she supported the family. Having dissipated a fortune, having run a business into the ground, having contracted massive debts, Adams lived on air, or on what closer inspection revealed to be the charity of friends. A rarity in an industrious, hard-driving, aspirational town, he was the only member of his Harvard class to whom no profession could be ascribed. Certainly no one turned up at the Second Continental Congress as ill-dressed as Adams, who for some weeks wore the suit in which he dove into the woods near Lexington, hours before the battle. It was shabby to begin with. Alone among America's founders, his is a riches-to-rags story.

There was an elemental purity about the man whom Crown officers believed the greatest incendiary in the king's dominion. Puritan simplicity never lost its appeal. Afflictions invigorated. Adams handily beat Ben Franklin at Franklin's thirteen-point project for arriving at moral perfection. On meeting Samuel Adams in the 1770s, a foreigner marveled: It was unusual, in life or on the stage, for anyone to conform so neatly to the role he played. Here was what a republican looked like. "A man wrapped up in his object," Adams disappeared into the part, from which it is difficult to pry him, identical as he was to his ideals.

In July 1774, newly arrived in London and reeling still from seasickness, the royal governor of Massachusetts was whisked off for a private interview with George III. For two hours Thomas Hutchinson briefed his sovereign on American affairs. The king seemed as eager to show off his knowledge as to learn what was happening in the most unruly of his American colonies. He asked about Indian extinction and the composition of New England bread. He had heard of Samuel Adams but had not grasped that he was the cause of so many royal headaches. Hutchinson revealed that Adams was "a great man of the party." What gave him his influence? inquired the king. "A great pretended zeal for liberty, and a most inflexible natural temper," explained Hutchinson, adding that Adams had been the first to advocate for American independence.

Making the same point differently, Thomas Jefferson called Adams "the earliest, most active, and persevering man of the Revolution." For many years it was possible to assert that he ranked with, if not above, George Washington. His fame spread alongside New England obstreperousness, which he hoped to make contagious. "Very few have fortitude enough," he wrote, neatly summarizing his life's work, "to tell a tyrant they are determined to be free." Various patriots made their mark as the Samuel Adams of North Carolina, the Samuel Adams of Rhode Island, or the Samuel Adams of Georgia. "The character of your Mr. Samuel Adams runs very high here. I find many who consider him the first politician in the world," reported a Bostonian from 1774 London. John Adams met with a hero's welcome when he arrived in France four years later to solicit funds for the war. He hurried to clarify: He was not the renowned Mr. Adams. That was another gentleman. (No one believed him.) "Without the character of Samuel Adams," declared John, "the true history of the American Revolution can never be written."

And yet it was, for various reasons. Adams engaged in a delicate, dangerous business. As the font of "thoughts which breathe, and words which burn," he was in the eyes of the British administration for years a near-outlaw, ultimately an actual outlaw. Had events turned out differently he would have been first to the gallows. Much of his work depended on plausible deniability; he covered tracks and erased fingerprints. He made no copies of his letters. (One example: Adams and Paul Revere must have been in frequent touch. Two notes between them survive.) John Adams watched helplessly in 1770s Philadelphia as his cousin fed whole handfuls of papers to the fire in his room. Was he perhaps overreacting? asked John. "Whatever becomes of me," Samuel explained, "my friends shall never suffer by my negligence." In the summer he had no fire; with scissors, he cut bundles of letters to shreds and scattered the confetti from the window, sparing his associates if stopping the biographer's heart. A portion of what he did not manage to destroy met with some shameful mistreatment, of which we have only hints.* Even a complete record would neither adequately answer the king's question nor illuminate Adams's tactics. He operated by stealth, melting into committees and crowd actions, pseudonyms and smoky back rooms. "There ought to be a memorial to Samuel Adams in the CIA," quips a modern historian, dubbing him America's first covert agent. We are left to read him in the twisted arm, the borrowed set of talking points, the indignation of America's enemies. We know more about him from his apoplectic adversaries than from his friends, sworn to secrecy.

Unlike his contemporaries, Adams did not preen for posterity. He wrote no memoir, resisting even calls to assemble his political writings. He consigned the history to others, with predictable results, the more so as his ideas diverged from those of post-Revolutionary America, leaving him intellectually homeless. Sometimes history blossoms after the fact — where a Massachusetts boulder or a Virginia cherry tree might suddenly insert itself into the record — and sometimes it evaporates. Adams escaped the golden haze that settled around his fellow founders, as if it were too extravagant for him. He hailed from the messy, anarchic, provocative years. It would not help that he would be confused with John, who collected his letters, wrote prolifically for the record, and, since adolescence, had rehearsed for greatness.†

Adams was rare for his ability to keep a secret, any number of which he took to the grave, including the backstory of the Boston Tea Party, which he knew as well as anyone. (Dryly he noted that some individuals

---

* "I would mention here or elsewhere Mr. Farley's discovery of the papers behind the wainscot," noted Adams's grandson, sounding like Agatha Christie. There are various allusions to letters having been lost, suppressed, or sanitized — their radicalism extracted — for posterity.
† A Philadelphia package destined for Mrs. John Adams might be delivered in error to Mrs. Samuel Adams, leaving the first, on an afternoon visit, to envy a gift that was rightfully hers.

enjoyed every political gift except that of discretion.) He freely discussed his limitations, reminding friends that he understood nothing of military matters, commerce, or ceremony, though Congress charged him, at various times, with all three. Most of America's founders became giants after independence. Adams began to shrink. A cloud of notoriety survives him; the fame does not. He would be minimized in any number of ways. He was called many names in his life but one thing he was never called was "Sam." He is the sole signer of the Declaration of Independence to come down to us as an incendiary, and a beer.

A PHILADELPHIA MERCHANT who would soon sign the Declaration of Independence raved of Adams: "All good Americans should erect a statue to him in their hearts." Two generations later, John Trumbull exhibited his massive painting of the Declaration in Boston. Thousands flocked to Faneuil Hall, crowding close to the canvas. Trumbull had aimed for "absolute authenticity" but the sublime depiction left some heads spinning. Where was Samuel Adams, who had played the central role in this illustrious history? Barely discernible in the crowd, he was upstaged by Elbridge Gerry, blotted out by Richard Henry Lee, "pilloried in a manner between the shoulders of the two gentlemen beside him." He seemed literally to have fallen out of the picture.* Reactions divided along party lines. Old Whigs fumed to see "their Moses thrust almost out of sight." One suggested that Trumbull rework the painting. The character of Samuel Adams must be restored; it was unfair for laurels to be "stripped from his brows to decorate the heads of those who by his labors have glittered in the sunshine of popular applause." Tories countered that Adams preferred

---

* There were any number of reasons to cry foul. Fifty-six men had signed the Declaration. Forty-seven figured in the painting. Trumbull omitted individuals who had signed the document and included those who had not, two of whom had violently argued against it. When in 1818 the painting was exhibited in Carpenter's Hall, on its way to Washington, where it hangs today in the Capitol, it did not match the room it was meant to depict. Nor does the likeness of Adams, although Trumbull painted him from the flesh. Already the Revolution had come a long way since 1776.

the background. Trumbull had treated him as Adams treated himself. Others sputtered at the mere mention of his name.

He would make nearly as much trouble for historians as he did for the British. His biographers have turned him into a neurotic, a Socialist, a mobster. One profile consists solely of blistering contempt. Another whitewashes him to the point of anemia. Even when historians acknowledge his influence he disappears between the lines. Garry Wills identified Adams as the most influential member of the first two Continental Congresses. "Probably no American did more than Samuel Adams to bring on the revolutionary crisis," contended Edmund Morgan. "No one took republican values as seriously as Adams did," writes Gordon Wood. He was "the premier leader of the revolutionary movement," "as astute a politician as ever America has produced." All echo Thomas Hutchinson in their outsized claims—"the whole continent is ensnared by that Machiavelli of chaos," groaned the royal governor—but the superlatives then slink off, headlines without articles, as if fearing the envy of John, the disapproval of Samuel, or the need to dislodge a man from behind over thirty pseudonyms. When he does not get enough credit, he gets too much. He single-handedly directed the Stamp Act riots and the Boston Tea Party in some accounts, the battle of Lexington in others.

Before his first inaugural address, Thomas Jefferson asked himself: "Is this exactly in the spirit of the patriarch of liberty, Samuel Adams?" Would he approve of it? To understand why the new president hoped to channel Adams's spirit is to discover not only where a daring revolutionary came from but where a revolution did. His curious career explains how the American colonies lurched from "spotlessly loyal" to "stark, staring mad" in fifteen dizzying years, how a group of drenched, pipe-smoking Massachusetts farmers, fifty miles from Boston and thousands from London, might reason that they should act sooner rather than later if they did not care to be "finessed out of their liberties." Adams introduced them into the political system, persuading them their liberties were worth the risk of their lives. To lose sight of him is to lose sight of a man who calculated what would be required to upend an empire and who—radicalizing men, women, and children, with boycotts and

pickets, street theater, invented traditions, a news service, a bit of character assassination, and any number of innovative, extralegal institutions—
led American history's seminal campaign of civil resistance.

Adams banked on the sage deliberations of a band of hard-working
farmers reasoning their way toward rebellion. That was how democracy
worked. He dreaded disunity. "Neither religion nor liberty can long subsist in the tumult of altercation, and amidst the noise and violence of
faction," he warned. There was nothing feigned about his zeal for liberty,
"the best cause," he assured his wife, "that virtuous men contend for." In
his case it was bred deep in the Calvinist bone. Adams could not live in
the house with a slave and arranged for the one who arrived on his doorstep to be freed. He refused to believe that prejudice and private interest
would ultimately trample knowledge and benevolence. Self-government
was in his view inseparable from governing the self; it demanded a certain asceticism. He wrote anthem after anthem to the qualities he believed
essential to a republic—austerity, integrity, selfless public service—qualities
that would become more military than civilian. The contest was never
for him less than a spiritual struggle. It is impossible with Adams to
determine where piety ended and politics began; the watermark of Puritanism shines through everything he wrote.* Faith was there from the
start, as was the scrappy, iconoclastic spirit, as were the daring, disrup-
tive excursions beyond the law.

Much of the maneuvering Adams kept out of sight while practicing it in
plain view. He bobs and weaves, vanishing around corners and behind Richard Henry Lee—who also believed him to be the author of the Revolution.
At times Adams amounts to little more than a flicker and dash, a vapor trail.
Even in his letters he seems to have one foot out the door. The clock strikes
midnight; he cannot linger; he hates to leave us hanging (or so he says). He
will tell us more next time. He is forever slipping from grasp, as a rider gal-
loping from Boston late on a warm spring night is about to urge him to do
again, as swiftly as possible, as if the future depended on it.

---

* To some religion seemed a stalking horse. "Scripture is brought in to cover treason
and murder," howled a Boston customs officer in 1770.

A VOICE IN THE DARKNESS,
A KNOCK AT THE DOOR

Everything in American affairs happens contrary to probability.
— THOMAS HUTCHINSON, 1779

A GLIMMER, a gleam, the hurry of hoofs: a sturdy, square-jawed man speeds through the night, with an urgent message, on a borrowed horse. His topcoat flaps behind him. A bright moon hangs overhead. Within days he will know he has participated in some kind of history, though he will hesitate to attach his name to it for decades and is never to know that his own account will be obliterated—the adrenaline alone enduring—by verse, leaving him trapped in tetrameter, a mythic figure, eternally jouncing his way toward Lexington.

It is just after midnight. Despite a near-encounter with a pair of British officers, Paul Revere has made excellent time. Only two hours earlier he had rushed through town to the home of the last remaining patriot leader in occupied Boston. On previous occasions Revere had stood at hand while Dr. Joseph Warren wrote out secret messages for him to carry; already in advance of this evening, Revere has devised a system. Friends await him on the north side of town, where they have hidden a boat in which to row him to Charlestown. From there, he will ride twelve miles west. He knows he has minutes before British regulars lock down Boston. He knows, too, that Warren has dispatched an earlier rider, by a longer route, with a similar message. Both speed toward Samuel Adams and John

Hancock, in Lexington. What the newspapers would later term Revere's "secret and speedy intelligence" was simple: British regiments are on the move. Adams and Hancock are their quarry. Revere gallops off to warn of imminent arrest if not outright assassination.

Minutes after he has pulled on his riding boots, British officers circulate through fetid Boston barracks to lay hands on sleeping backs, whispering to their men, in the gentlest of military awakenings. It is time to march, unwelcome news at 10:30 p.m., "a soldier's hour to be in bed," as one light infantryman later put it. Furtively the men file from their barracks, through rear doors, in small parties. They dodge their own sentries; in silence they pick their way through the late-night streets. The dog who opts to announce them meets with a bayonet. Regimental officers are not privy to their destination; their men know less about their expedition than does Revere. By the time some eight hundred British regulars finally assemble in east Cambridge, soaked to the waist after a long trudge through freezing marsh, stalled as they wait for the supplies that should have preceded them, word of their clandestine sortie has already reached Lexington.

Adams and Hancock had retired for the night when Revere galloped into town, which was not to say that either the messenger or his message was entirely unexpected. Two days earlier Revere had made the same ride, in daylight and at a more relaxed pace, to confer with the patriot leaders. Both had recently fled Boston, where they no longer felt safe. Adams had made a hasty exit with only the clothes on his back. Even he judged them threadbare. He fled as well without his papers, destroyed later by a fast-thinking friend. Having attended the last session of a provincial congress that Saturday, Adams and Hancock were poised to ride to Philadelphia for a more momentous gathering. The two lodged temporarily in the comfortable, clapboard Lexington parsonage, guests of the Reverend Jonas Clarke, a gregarious man, a Hancock relative, and a firm friend of American liberty. The Bostonians shared a wallpapered room on the ground floor. Hancock's fiancée lodged above.

On the earlier visit Revere would have revealed what many in Boston had noticed: the regulars had hauled their longboats out of the harbor.

General Thomas Gage had relieved his elite troops, his prized grenadiers and light infantry, from duty, ostensibly for training. The feint fooled no one. Twice already Gage's men had ventured into the Massachusetts countryside to confiscate munitions. Twice already the countryside had known to expect them. British itineraries had surely been evaluated that Sunday at the Lexington parsonage, along with precautions. Adams had neither respect nor sympathy for Gage, whom he considered "void of a spark of humanity." It was on the return from that ride that Revere had arranged for signals from the North Church steeple; a single lantern would indicate that the British intended to march by land. Two lights would indicate that they proceeded by boat. It was imperative that word reach the countryside even if a messenger could not; all depended on provincial readiness. We cannot control events, Samuel Adams liked to say. The trick, he revealed that summer, "is to foresee as far as we are able, prepare for, and improve them."

He could not have been surprised to learn that friends believed him the object of Gage's expedition. He had made himself more obnoxious to the colonial authorities than any man in British North America. For the same reason, advertisements ran that spring for poster-sized portraits of him. For half a dollar—well below the price of a primitive brand of toothpaste—one could acquire a fine mezzotint likeness, printed in Rhode Island, of "that truly worthy patriot, S. A." (The printer anticipated robust sales.) Panegyrics circulated, lauding Adams's genius and predicting immortal fame. What qualified from one vantage point as sterling patriotism appeared from another as bare-faced treason. For the better part of a decade, Adams had, as General Gage saw it, churned irritations into insults, poisoning the minds of Americans, ripening them for insurrection. "I doubt whether there is a greater incendiary in the King's dominions," sputtered Thomas Hutchinson, the previous royal governor, whom Adams had done all in his power to sabotage; whom Gage had arrived, with four regiments, to replace; and who could never sufficiently excoriate "the black art of Adams."

Color rushed to the Tory face at the mention of Adams's name. So "thorough a Machiavellian," he would stop at nothing to accomplish his ends—assumed, despite his early disavowals, to be American independence. He employed every dirty trick along the way, including, one Crown officer fumed, "such arts as an oyster wench disdains to lower her reputation to." From the imperial descriptions, Adams can sound like Marx, Lenin, and Robespierre rolled into one. Over and over he had sent British legal authorities scrambling to review case law on treason. He distinguished himself as the most wanted man in the colonies; peace could not be restored in America until someone made an example of him. When a Tory sympathizer threw an anonymous letter into an encampment of the Boston troops, he offered up a roster of those who had instigated the Massachusetts madness. Were rebellion to break out, they should be executed. Adams topped his helpful list. Already Gage had attempted by other means to eliminate the problem that was Samuel Adams. He had sent a British colonel to call on Adams, at home. The two were acquainted: the officer asked if he might speak in confidence and without interruption. Adams's conduct left him vulnerable to a treason conviction. Might he rethink his stance? He could both make peace with his king and expect a handsome reward. Adams listened in silence to the elegantly packaged bribe. He rose when the colonel had finished. "Tell Governor Gage," he glowered, "it is the advice of Samuel Adams to him no longer to insult the feelings of an exasperated people."

Second only to Adams's talent for persecuting royal governors was his equanimity. He read plenty of cheerful doggerel about his hanging. Oaths and insults were hurled steadily in his direction, as in that of his associates. A friend might be greeted with: "You are an incendiary, and I hope to see you hanged yet in your shoes." Dr. Warren, Adams's closest confidant, had been informed that he was headed soon for the gallows. Printer friends were threatened with tar and feathers. John Hancock was physically assaulted. British officers jeered that his magnificent Beacon Hill mansion would soon be theirs. That spring Adams heard from another Samuel Adams, on Cape Cod. He was honored "to share the name of a great patriot," though it exposed him to a fair amount of abuse. Adams seemed only invigorated by rumored plans to seize the prominent troublemakers—the colonists were not yet rebels, still peasants, ragamuffins, "mad fanatics," or "low dirty rascals"—and transport them, in chains, to Great Britain.

With the arrival of General Gage in June of 1774, the situation deteriorated. Friends admonished Adams. Why had he no nighttime security at his doors and windows? Was he fully alert to traitors and informers? Had he forgotten the Ides of March? With difficulty they convinced him to stay home: twelve days after a large quantity of tea plunged into Boston Harbor, he was blocked—or as he saw it, forbidden—from attending a party to which he had looked forward. Weeks before Revere hastily borrowed his Cambridge horse, Adams had faced down a British officer who challenged him to a duel. Colleagues agonized when he failed to materialize on time. One engaged in a bit of gallows humor. "I hear nothing from you of late," he complained in January, "more than I should if you was apprehended, transported, tried, and executed." Even his most unflappable friends—and Samuel Adams had many friends—cowered a little. One had it on reliable Tory authority that Adams was to be arrested before he could make his way to Philadelphia for the Continental Congress, scheduled to begin on May 10.

Meanwhile his enemies snickered. Samuel Adams quaked, they taunted, at the sight of hemp. Indeed, Adams trembled often, on account of a mild palsy that intensified over the next years, and with apprehension for the fate of the American colonies, oppressed and insulted by the mother country. But nowhere does the record convey a syllable of fear. He nonetheless took a few precautions. He desisted from signing his letters. He began to carry a pistol wherever he went. He removed most of his family from Boston. By April 18, 1775, the majority of his associates had slipped out of town as well, some in disguise; others with bare possessions; one by water, at midnight, with his printing press. Still Adams remained unintimidated. Crown officials in Massachusetts attempted all in their power to overawe, "endeavoring," Adams wrote, "to terrify the people with strange ideas of treason and rebellion." They labored in vain. And they had their terms backwards. The right-minded were those who insisted on colonial liberties. Treason, he held, consisted of the failure to defend those liberties.

Adams had an additional reason for equanimity. Revere belonged to a Boston surveillance team that scrutinized every military move. Its thirty members patrolled the streets nightly, swearing on a Bible to confide their observations largely to Warren, Adams, and Hancock. Even Gage was impressed by the results. "The people get very early and good intelligence," the British commander in chief alerted London. Everyone seemed to know his instructions before he did. He had been mystified by the mad exodus of rabble-rousers. His orders to arrest them arrived only on April 14, by which time, regretted Gage, "They had received notice of their danger, and were fled." He too had his spies, but the advantage went handily to the provincials. It was an odd thing about Boston, Crown officials observed. A confidential, early-morning insinuation could blossom into common knowledge by evening. Yet when 342 crates of tea immersed themselves in water, no one had seen a thing. Military stores tended to vanish hours before Gage arrived to confiscate them. Cannon burrowed their way under piles of coal or loads of manure. Powder kegs secreted themselves under beds. As soon as red-coated backs turned, the woman who appeared to be brewing tea well after midnight picked up where she had left off, melting pewterware into bullets.

As royal governor and military commander, Gage's task was to subdue an obstreperous community that he believed should have been subdued long before. It was an unenviable assignment. Gage was simultaneously to "quiet the minds of the people," to close Boston's port, and to prosecute the leading radicals. For weeks he had attempted subtly to make his presence felt outside Boston; he hoped he might encourage the countryside to relax its guard. He needed to exercise his men, moldering in town. In February he had dispatched two officers, disguised as surveyors, to reconnoiter eastern Massachusetts. Red bandanas around their necks, sketchbooks in hand, they managed to observe a militia exercise. Even the waitress in a local inn penetrated their disguise, however. The only people the officers seemed to fool were Gage and his aide-de-camp, who failed to recognize them on their return. The sorties effectively trained no one better than the Massachusetts farmers, now "eagle-eyed and alert," as the faux surveyors reported. From his spies Gage learned of secret stockpiles of munitions. He also heard, on March 26, of something Adams already knew. Believing itself in Gage's sights, the town of Concord had carted off cannons and barrels of flour. It buried its musket balls.

Early in the evening of April 18, a group of some eight British army officers had been spotted milling about near Lexington. A gust of wind revealed pistols under their heavy blue overcoats. British officers did not saunter about the New England countryside, armed, after sundown, without reason. Given the frequent threats, the immediate assumption was of "some evil design" against Adams and Hancock. The local militia sergeant assigned a ten- or twelve-man guard to the Clarke parsonage. If Dr. Warren's informer and most of the Massachusetts countryside that evening believed Gage poised to apprehend Adams and Hancock, there was additional cause for suspicion: his orders were to do precisely that. London had long believed colonial unrest a localized affair. The American contest could be reduced to a few malcontents on the one side "and the whole people of England on the other." Gage's instructions were explicit. "The first and essential step," Lord Dartmouth, secretary of state for the colonies, enjoined him, was "to arrest and imprison the principal actors and abettors." Adams's name figured first on that list as well. The order would recur in every communication from Dartmouth, who made no mention of rounding up military stores, at least until a dispatch that reached Gage long after April 1775. The sole question seemed to be whether, once captured, Adams and Hancock should be transported to London for trial or hanged in Boston.

Few understood Gage's hesitation. Why, vented one of his officers in February, had they not already seized the "impudent rascals"? It could easily be done. It begged to be done. A lieutenant colonel dropped hint after hint. It was time to pursue harsher measures, in particular "against that most artful clever fellow Adams, who has nothing to lose." Another fulminated that he hoped before long to see Hancock, Warren, and Adams strung up "by the hands of the hangman." Standing them before firing squads — or suspending them from trees — was the only corrective now. If a respectable force could be assembled, the most subversive individuals seized and the rest pardoned, colonial order could surely be restored, the sovereignty of Parliament upheld.

By 1775 the reality was very different. To apprehend the popular leaders was by spring to trigger hostilities, something Gage intended at all costs to avoid, in part because he was not actually void of humanity, in part because he was woefully outnumbered. An arrest would prove Great Britain the aggressor and make martyrs of the colonists. The optics mattered, as Adams understood better than anyone. "I would wish," he asserted, "to have all the impartial and reasonable world on our side." Specific though they were, Gage's orders also came with a caveat. The Massachusetts ringleaders had subverted a government. But Gage was to arrest only if he could secure a prosecution. There was no reason to disgrace the king or invigorate the opposition.

If Adams managed any sleep at all on the evening of April 18 — if Revere actually woke him when finally he galloped, splattered with mud and spewing adrenaline, into Lexington — it was in part for that reason. It was too late for Gage to attempt arrests. As he glumly conceded, Adams and his accomplices trusted in their immunity. They scoffed at deportation threats. They made it their business to menace, provoke, and wear him down. Gage explained to Lord Dartmouth that his hands were tied. Should he arrest Adams, "that would be the last letter they would ever receive from him, for he should be knocked on the head."

Adams enjoyed one additional comfort. Over and over he had demonstrated an uncanny ability not only to second-guess Gage but to anticipate events. History is that thing that, in hindsight, one always saw coming; a few seem able to glimpse it before it has settled on its destination. Among Adams's shrewd predictions was how critical the man with whom he shared a Lexington bedroom would prove to America's cause. Their wainscotted parlor was familiar to Hancock; orphaned young, he had spent his early years in the Clarke parsonage, built for his grandfather, the previous town minister. Hancock had moved to Boston at seven when adopted by an uncle, whose fortune he inherited, making him, at twenty-seven, one of the richest men in New England. He took to gold waistcoats and lilac suits. He traveled with liveried servants. Even in the estimation of an indulgent biographer, Hancock presented, in eighteenth-century Boston, as "a foppish pseudo-aristocrat." It was Adams who recruited him, correctly surmising that Hancock would revel in glory as he did in frivolity, proving an essential ally and opening his coffers. It was Adams who consoled the thin-skinned Hancock when a wayward comment left him bruised; Adams who coaxed Hancock back when he attempted to sulk off; and Adams who propelled Hancock into the spotlight, his preferred address.

How much of a coup Adams had scored could be read in the indignation of Boston's Tories. They compared his seduction of the rich young merchant to the devil's seduction of Eve. With an ambition disproportionate to his aptitude, Hancock had proved easy prey. Occasionally he managed to liberate himself, but then Adams, "like the cuttlefish, would discharge his muddy liquid," disorienting Hancock all over again. Events would prove that Hancock could indeed be coaxed in any direction. Already bribes had been distributed to poison the friendship, which lurched along uneasily, over slights and recriminations, by way of pauses and lapses, and—much later—past a bitter, thirteen-year hiatus, when the two men could not bring themselves even to be cordial in public.

In New England it had been clear for months that the time for reconciliation between the mother country and North America had passed. Goodwill had evaporated, outrage congealed. Massachusetts had endured what it believed was a decade of affronts. The two sides glowered at each other, incomprehension heaped upon incivility. British regulars could barely contain their disdain for the ragtag colonists. "Such a parcel of poor mad Quixotes were surely never scraped together since the time of the Crusades," one sneered. The redcoats came in for similar treatment. One newspaper contributor reduced the regulars to "mercenary, hackneyed, tattered regiments patched up by the most abandoned and debauched of mankind, the scum of the nation, the dregs of Irish and Scottish desperadoes." On the other hand, posturing went a long way. As late as March 1775, outright confrontation struck most as unthinkable. Which left Gage and the patriot leaders at a standoff, refusing to relinquish ground while sidestepping any measure that might detonate a crisis. As Thomas Hutchinson wrote in London, days before Revere flew to Lexington: "I cannot yet believe Mr. Adams will be able to persuade our people to so irrational a step as to form themselves into a body to oppose the King's troops."

Here it became difficult to pry eerie prophecy from artful planning. "One cannot foresee events," Adams had written an intimate in November 1773, "but from all the observation I am able to make, my next letter will not be upon a trifling subject." Within weeks, a smile playing on his words, he submitted a remarkable report: in under four hours, 342 chests of tea had slipped into Boston Harbor. For at least a decade, whenever the British used the loaded word "preconcerted" in connection with American affairs, fingers pointed directly at Adams. In March he warned that the people of Massachusetts restrained their acrimony yet would not hesitate to restrain tyranny. Should Gage march into the countryside, his men could expect a warm welcome. "Are your letters, my friend, designedly oracular?" an associate asked. Times being what they were, he turned out to be a British spy.

PAUL REVERE CLATTERED up to the parsonage around 12:30 a.m. He had not yet attained legendary status; the guards around the house barred his way. Might their muddy visitor create a bit less commotion? The reverend, his wife, eight of their ten children, Adams, Hancock, Hancock's fiancée, and his elderly aunt had retired for the night. They were trying to sleep. A bluff man cradling a time bomb, Revere was not easily deterred. "Noise! You'll have noise enough before long," he reportedly huffed, adding, "The regulars are coming out," the closest he came to announcing that the British were coming. The Lexington guard relented; Revere banged on the parsonage door. From an upstairs window Reverend Clarke called down. Who was this late-night caller? Without identifying himself, Revere asked for Hancock. Clarke was some way into a speech about preferring not to receive strangers in the middle of the night when Adams and Hancock appeared at their downstairs window. "That is Revere; you need not be afraid of him," Hancock assured their host. Clarke descended his handsomely carved staircase to greet Revere, who, after delivering his message, presumably to a household in nightclothes, asked if they had heard from

Warren's earlier messenger. Though he had a two-hour lead, he had not yet been seen. Revere feared that William Dawes—intrepid enough to have recently smuggled two cannon from Boston—had also met with, but not managed to outride, a British patrol.

. Dawes materialized a half hour later, when refreshments appeared. The men then walked to the nearby tavern to concert a plan of action. If indeed Gage had dispatched several hundred soldiers, he did not intend merely to arrest Hancock and Adams. There was some discussion with the town militia, immediately on guard, though the regulars were at that moment still shivering, soaked and miserable, in the briny Cambridge cold, their officers arranging them into formation by company and seniority. At least on paper, Gage ordered his men to destroy the Concord munitions, something London had not yet mentioned. Emphatic and specific, the most recent instructions he had received also carried a note of reproach. The king's patience was exhausted. Even if Gage could not prosecute the troublemakers, they would stir up less mischief from prison. He was to proceed immediately, taking every precaution to keep his mission secret. "You can hardly fail," the British secretary of state assured him, "and you should be able to accomplish this without bloodshed." Lord Dartmouth did not address the question of what Gage might do were he to encounter armed resistance.

Of the commotion at the parsonage we have only a later account; we can be more certain of the degree to which Revere set eastern Massachusetts in motion. He made it his business to rouse household after household between Boston and Lexington. Church bells tolled across the countryside in his wake. Shortly after leaving the parsonage, midway between Lexington and Concord, Revere, Dawes, and their companions rode into an ambush. "God damn you! Stop! If you go an inch further you are a dead man," shouted a British officer, maneuvering the riders into a pasture. Revere attempted to escape into a nearby wood; from it emerged six additional officers, pistols pointed at his chest. One seized his bridle. Another asked his name. The answer caused much consternation. Unlike the Lexington militia, the British officers knew precisely who Paul Revere was. The appearance in Lexington of the best patriot messenger confirmed that Adams and Hancock were in the vicinity. It also suggested that someone was expecting them.

The officers peppered Revere with questions: What time had he left Boston? Where exactly were Adams and Hancock? Between questions his captors discharged insults, which made it difficult for cool-headed Revere to resist informing them that their troops sat stalled in Cambridge. He had guessed their mission. They would not succeed. He attempted too a marvelous bluff: he had alarmed every household in the country. The regulars should expect five hundred Americans to descend upon them any moment. Taken aback, the ranking officer rode off to confer with his commander, who galloped down to examine the prisoner himself. Clapping a pistol to Revere's head, the major announced that he was going to pose a few questions. Revere replied that he did not need to be threatened to speak the truth. Ordered to dismount, he was frisked. He carried no gun.

More specific questions followed from a less even-tempered interrogator. Revere was then returned to his horse, its reins entrusted to a British officer. "We are now going towards your friends," he was informed, "and if you attempt to run, or we are insulted, we will blow your brains out." The redcoats formed a tight circle around him, reminding Revere, as they rode, that he was "in a damned critical situation." He admitted that he had noticed. As they neared the Lexington meetinghouse a volley of guns sounded, a blast that seemed to confirm his warnings. He was asked to interpret. Revere thought every bit as swiftly as he rode; he assured his escort that they had just heard an alert to the countryside. A companion merrily chimed in: the British, he added, were all dead men. To the ominous tolling of the Lexington church bell the officers conferred. How far was it to Cambridge? Was there any other road? Minutes later they galloped off, a sergeant astride Revere's horse, a particularly fine one, never to be seen again.

By foot Revere hurried through pastures and a cemetery to Reverend Clarke's. He had tangled with the British officers nearly a half mile from the parsonage. The wind was up; the night had turned raw. It was nearly 2:30 a.m. The Lexington militia had mustered; as no redcoats had appeared, they had been dismissed, to reassemble at the beat of a drum. Several men now dozed in their chairs at the tavern at the edge of the Lexington Common.

Revere met with a livelier scene at the parsonage, where it would have been difficult to say who was more surprised to see whom. Though thrice urged to flee, Adams and Hancock had not budged. Elegant Hancock had been aflutter since Revere's departure, "cleaning his gun and putting his accoutrements in order." He seemed intent on impressing his fiancée and on personally facing down the regulars. At least once he headed out to the Common on a reconnoitering mission. It was dark. There was not a redcoat in sight.

By candlelight Adams labored—with an assist from Clarke, an animated man, rarely given to a few words when more would do—to impress upon his younger colleague that their place was not on the battlefield. One account has Adams clapping a hand on Hancock's thin shoulder as he reminded him: "That is not our business; we belong to the cabinet." The two remained at loggerheads; under any circumstances they made for a study in contrasts. Excitable Hancock was given to the grand gesture. Imperturbable, Adams preferred to set the stage for others to occupy. He was rarely present even in his own version of events; it was easier to gauge his presence by the temperature of a room. It reliably rose when he entered. In their physical bearing too they made for an odd couple. About the same height, one was lean, the other, at fifty-three, athletic and stout, with thick brows and dark blue eyes. Hancock walked with a slight stoop. Barrel-chested Adams carried himself erect. One man was highly susceptible to flattery, the other impervious to the stuff. "The delight of the eyes of the whole town," Hancock had also by 1775 long been its most eligible bachelor. Among Samuel Adams's talents was an especially rare one: he knew the limits of his own expertise. Hancock seemed to believe himself to possess none. Their middle-of-the-night debate raged amid a panic-stricken household. Hancock's aunt wrung her hands. His fiancée helped the Reverend Clarke bury the family valuables in the potato patch.

It was by now close to 3:00 a.m. The regulars had begun their march past stone fences and rolling pastures, square-toed boots beating a regular rhythm on unpacked ground. They advanced through the starry night as well to the faint clang of country bells. It looked increasingly unlikely that Gage's covert mission would be accomplished under cover of darkness. Disconcerted officers had already sent word to Boston: They would not surprise anyone. Reinforcements would be necessary. With Revere's return came an end to the parsonage tug-of-war. He could after all report that British officers had stood, pistols loaded, within striking distance of Adams and Hancock. In Hancock's heavy coach the two rattled toward Woburn, some five miles away, Hancock complaining that it was not his style to turn his back on the enemy. Revere accompanied them part or all of the way. He could later not remember exactly. With Hancock's secretary he then returned to Lexington, "to find what was going on."

By 4:30 a.m. streaks of orange and pink glinted in the east. Still there was no sign of any regiment. Hancock profited from the quiet to send to Lexington for his aunt and fiancée. Might they bring with them the excellent salmon on which he hoped to breakfast? It was the first of the season. If Revere's intelligence could be believed, the redcoats were hopelessly late. Indeed, they had squandered four hours; Adams must have doubted they were actually coming. He would be spared the sight, as dawn broke, of a gleaming quarter-mile ribbon of red coats, snow-white linen flashing, a short distance from Lexington and moving through the pale morning light, in perfect order, at an impressively brisk pace.

Adams would be deprived as well of the company of Revere, sent to Lexington a third time that evening to retrieve Hancock's trunk of papers. By the time Revere arrived on the village green it was daylight. From the rooms above the tavern he watched the regulars approach at a near-run. Downstairs he and Hancock's secretary, the leather trunk between them, passed through the fifty-odd militiamen. Their commanding officer ordered them to let the redcoats pass peaceably unless they fired first. Yards from the meetinghouse, Revere spotted a British officer on horseback; minutes later he heard — but did not see — the "continual roar of musketry." Nor would the two Woburn fugitives manage their salmon breakfast. They sat down to it just as a frantic Lexington farmer arrived with word that regulars approached, bayonets gleaming. The coach was hastily stashed. Adams and Hancock dived into a swamp, where they remained for some time. (They fared better than a fellow delegate to the provincial congress, who earlier that morning landed face-down amid damp corn stubble, in his nightclothes, as the troops passed.)

After a hike through the woods Adams and Hancock finally break-fasted, several towns north, on salt pork and potatoes. They neither heard a shot nor caught the peppery bite of gunpowder in the Lexington air. It would be some time before either man knew precisely what had happened. Neither would know—as no one ever will—who fired first that morning, a question with which Adams would contend later. Facts were facts but could always stand a little polish. Of the weight of events he had no doubt. He believed independence should have been declared that bright spring day. For his purposes it essentially had been. At some point in those harried hours, despite having spent a damp night outdoors, unguarded and under-dressed, his spirits swelled. "O! What a glorious morning is this!" he exulted. Mistaking his meaning, John Hancock looked searchingly to the sky—or so Adams, or an Adams friend, later recalled.

Of the three, Paul Revere alone wound up with a pistol aimed at his head that evening. He would wait twenty-three years to reveal the full story of his arrest. For their own reasons, General Gage and Samuel Adams left only cursory accounts of the most written-about day in American history. At some point before the Reverend Clarke found seven bodies of his parishioners slumped on the ground, before he discovered that a cannonball had punctured his meetinghouse, as the column of redcoats thudded toward Concord, amid the "confusion and distress," as Clarke had it, Adams did something else at which he was expert: the most conspicuous man in Massachusetts vanished from the scene, slipping through Gage's fingers and out of a picture he had done as much as anyone to compose. Events had caught up with him after eleven laborious years. As the curtain rose on what he would term "this important glorious crisis," the opening act of what qualified for some weeks still as a civil war, he could just be glimpsed, triumphantly exiting stage left.

LATE THE FOLLOWING Monday Adams and Hancock arrived in Worcester, where they were to join their fellow delegates for the trip to Philadelphia. No colleague or message awaited. Nor was there any guard for the bedraggled travelers, who still had only anecdotal reports of what had transpired thirty-two miles away, five days earlier. Adams could not have been far off when Hancock sat down to write a blistering letter to the committee charged with provincial militias, a committee on which he sat. He and Adams would need depositions for the journey south. It was essential to certify the Lexington assault unprovoked; her sister colonies had insisted that Massachusetts act only on the defensive. Already the roads were thick with overloaded carts of furniture and howling children. Town records were secreted underground. Women sat in parlors behind barricaded doors. There were "a thousand uncertain and different reports." Amid the confusion it seemed difficult to believe that the regulars had suffered a stinging defeat at the hands of the minutemen who—from over forty towns, with old French firearms and family flintlocks—had sped to meet them.

Word went out that Adams and Hancock had escaped Lexington half-naked; that the house at which they eluded capture was instantly surrounded by the king's troops; that, unable to find the two men, the "inhuman soldiery" had turned the parsonage upside down, murdering the women and children in cold blood, setting fire to the house, and afterward proceeding to Concord, "firing at, and killing hogs, geese, cattle and everything that came in their way." Lunging through its windows, soldiers had fired into the meetinghouse, claiming three fatalities. Paul Revere was reported missing, in some versions slain. The commotion extended to New York, where business came to a standstill. Yale students jettisoned their studies. In the Worcester tavern Hancock wrote imperiously and breathlessly, his page streaked with dashes. He hoped the fighting spirit would persist. But where *was* everyone? He could abide neither the chaos nor his meager circumstances. He appeared a deserter, which was unacceptable. He preferred to head off without the rest of the Massachusetts delegation if he was not to travel with dignity.

An escort arrived the next day. With a few detours, in the constant company of Hancock and for some time still without a decent wardrobe, Samuel Adams turned up weeks later in Philadelphia, where he would continue to do all in his power to prove Thomas Hutchinson right: everything in American affairs indeed happened contrary to probability.

THE GREAT TOWN OF BOSTON

Security and leisure are the parents of sedition.
— SAMUEL JOHNSON, 1775

JOHN ADAMS swore that his cousin had been born a revolutionary. If so, the symptoms were slow to manifest. John—thirteen years younger and a country relation, little acquainted until adulthood with his more worldly cousin—was more likely extrapolating backwards. Everything about Samuel's early years promised a public-spirited, tradition-upholding member of the New England establishment, in which his father, Samuel Adams Sr., a fourth-generation Massachusetts man, was firmly entrenched. As early as 1650, in England and America, Adams men had made their living as malsters, steeping, drying, sweating, and kilning barley to be fermented into beer. It was a messy, exacting, labor-intensive business at which Samuel Adams Sr. had splendidly succeeded. At the time of his son's birth, the family occupied a stately home on what is today Purchase Street, with a commanding ocean view, an observatory, a wharf that bore the family name, various outbuildings, and an orchard. The estate fronted Boston's sparkling harbor; a garden sloped to the shore. Even a non-admirer was impressed. Samuel Adams Sr. had—in an intricate business, practiced on a modest scale, supplying Boston housewives with the malt with which they brewed beer—"accumulated a surprising amount of money."

On another front the family fared less well. The fourth of his mother's children, Samuel Adams was born at noon on September 16, 1722. The daughter of a prosperous ship captain, Mary Fifield Adams would give birth no fewer than twelve times. Already she had lost two children in infancy. The family would bury seven more. A second son, Joseph, arrived in 1728, just before Samuel enrolled at Boston Latin, the forming ground of the Massachusetts elite. It was the same establishment that Benjamin Franklin had briefly attended some thirteen years earlier and in which John Hancock would enroll sixteen years later. To gain admission to the old wooden building across town, behind the Anglican chapel, Samuel read a few verses aloud from the King James Bible. The test constituted a bit of false advertising: for the next years, from 7:00 to 11:00 in the morning and again from 1:00 to 5:00 every afternoon, under a hard-driving schoolmaster, from a seat along the oak benches that lined the walls of the room, Adams would be steeped in the classics. Rote memorization absorbed his first three years. Soon he began to fit Aesop's fables into Latin verse. Afterward came translations of Erasmus, submitted in English and rendered, at week's end, back into Latin. A steady stream of Ovid, Cicero, Virgil, and Homer followed, a reading list that imprinted itself, stylistically and substantively, in its accents and allusions, on the literature of the American Revolution.

On a summer afternoon in 1736, thirteen-year-old Samuel Adams submitted to the Harvard College entrance exam. Administered by the college president and several tutors, it might involve the translation of a lengthy passage of Virgil from Latin, the New Testament from Greek. Part oral, part written, the performance could be nerve-wracking. In his best clothes, Samuel would have taken the ferry with his father the short distance across the Charles River to Cambridge, to a campus that consisted of three redbrick Georgian buildings set around a desolate quadrangle. An orchard stood at one side, a row of outhouses at the other. The July 1736 return was a triumphant one: Adams left Cambridge with a summer writing assignment and an invitation to join the student body of about one hundred in mid-August. The majority of his classmates were several years older, though one was twenty-one, and a fourteen-year-old was by no means unusual at the college.

Of greater import in hierarchical Massachusetts was class rank, determined by one's father's status, from the sons of governors and the Governor's Council down. The adult Adams reared from displays of superiority, but such distinctions extended across the board in eighteenth-century Boston, where every laborer knew that a cabinetmaker stood superior to a shoemaker, a tailor to a seaman. Harvard rank prescribed the size of your room, whether you prayed at the front of the chapel, when you claimed your serving at mealtimes, and where you took your place in a scholarly procession. It could also be recalibrated. The theft of a hat might cost you a rung. For a more serious offense you proceeded directly to the bottom of the class.*

As the child of a justice of the peace — Samuel Adams Sr. could append a weighty "Esquire" to his name — his son ranked a prestigious sixth among his 23 classmates. Outfitted in dark gowns, subsisting on a miserable diet of baked beef at midday and meat pie and bread with milk in the evenings, the boys returned to the classics. Over the course of a twelve-hour day, beginning at 5:00 a.m. with prayers, and ending at 5:00 p.m. with prayers, Adams studied Euclid and learned to compose a syllogism. He memorized passages of Homer, which he recited for his tutors. He submitted to mandatory Hebrew, the language understood to be spoken in heaven if a course reviled by the undergraduates. He peered through the campus telescope and inspected a model of the solar system. As an upperclassman, he prepared a series of public declamations.

Enlightenment thinkers were as well represented in the curriculum as classical ones; the Harvard president at the time was a liberal thinker, eager to merge the ideas of John Calvin with those of John Locke. Adams knew his Cicero, Sallust, and Livy. He was soon on familiar terms with Montesquieu and Hume, as in a matter of years he would be with Rousseau. Locke's *Essay*

---

* Rank by social standing survived until 1769. Even at the time there were some who railed against it. In the year of Adams's birth, another Boston Latin alumnus mocked any institution that based admission on parents' purses rather than students' merits: the system, he argued, meant that the college turned out graduates who were every bit "the dunces and blockheads" they had been on entry, having in four years learned only to carry themselves with more self-importance. That malcontent was sixteen-year-old Benjamin Franklin, who would have ranked at the bottom of any Harvard class.

Concerning Human Understanding essentially served as a textbook in ethics; Adams seemed to swallow the work whole. Neither history nor politics figured in the curriculum. For the eighteenth-century American the heroes were classical ones; there was a reason why it would be said that Adams made his way to the Whigs and Tories by way of the Greeks and Romans.

At a time when Harvard students distinguished themselves as much for insubordination as for academic excellence, Adams did not stand out. He figured nowhere among those fined and suspended for planting snakes in tutors' beds, for drinking stolen rum in church, for singing in his room after midnight, for carousing, criticizing the government, or defacing the library copy of Montesquieu. His brother would be remembered for "contemptuous hallowing" on a late winter night, when he broke down a classmate's door. (He suffered a public reprimand.) Thomas Hutchinson was fined and scolded for cheating, having secreted a page of the original Greek into the Latin text he was to translate. A future Massachusetts chief justice was punished for stealing a goose and a turkey and roasting them over the fire in his room. John Hancock got a slave dangerously drunk. Samuel Adams's future father-in-law, a minister and Harvard College overseer, broke his share of windows. John Adams was far from alone in overstaying a vacation, for which he paid a fine. Samuel Adams's sole infraction seems to have been once oversleeping, for which he was reprimanded and which, as an adult, he seems not to have attempted again.

Perhaps the most remarkable aspect of his adolescence was how invisible were the qualities for which he later distinguished himself. Nothing about the early years presaged a future likely to set a colony ablaze. "It is my fate to be always in a hurry," Adams wrote an intimate just after Lexington and Concord, but the impatience was years in announcing itself. Little set his apart from any number of other privileged New England childhoods except, over the first decades, how little he did with it. Having graduated in 1740, having received the best education available in Massachusetts—it was also the best education in colonial America—he stalled. He seemed to be saving all the ingenuity for later.

He left few details of his early years. Only from a 1726 newspaper account do we know of the mountain lion that turned up at the Adams household, where it was briefly exhibited. (His mother arranged to ship it abroad.) There would be no mention of the deafening earthquake that rocked Boston, rearranging furniture in living rooms, when Adams was five; of the visits of George Whitefield, the English evangelical preacher, who electrified Boston and raised hackles at Harvard shortly after Adams's graduation; or of the diphtheria epidemic that delayed that graduation by two months, leaving Adams to collect his diploma in late August. He volunteered neither enduring parental admonitions nor family lore. He did allow that it was "a happy young man who has had an elder sister upon whom he could rely for advice and counsel in youth." Though he had decades in which to offer it, he spared us the eminently sensible, after-the-fact account, the kind that—bright with enameled anecdote—aligns beginnings with ends and causes with effects, lending a specious integrity and inevitability to the whole.

Adams would proudly claim that he never troubled himself with plans for his future. All evidence corroborates that approach, one not everyone could afford. Certainly it is impossible to imagine him either as the kind of child who, like Thomas Hutchinson, preferred to stay home to read history rather than play in the street, or who, like John Adams, rehearsed Ciceronian orations before a mirror. The classics similarly quickened Samuel's pulse. They reverberated always in his voice, like harmonic progressions. There would be no grandstanding before a mirror, however. What can be said of him is this: if everyone has an age when he is most himself, young adulthood was not his. It is difficult to improve on the summary of the chronicler who delivered up Adams's first years in a single storm cloud of a sentence: "He read theology and abandoned the ministry, read law and abandoned the bar, entered business and lost a thousand pounds."

Religion played a central role in his life and his thinking, as it would in the Revolution. It was no accident that so many Boston town meetings were conducted in houses of prayer, or that republicanism, as envisaged in Massachusetts Bay, traced the independent-minded, egalitarian, community-based lines of Puritanism. Men who preferred a church without a bishop came naturally to the idea of a state without a king. Adams's piety would be made to sound dangerous, as in some respects it was: natural rights and principled defiance resonated deeply with his faith. As Gordon Wood has suggested, republicanism is in its essence a secular, more relaxed form of Puritanism. Or in the words of a British major, having pried a book of prayer from Massachusetts prisoners in 1775: "It is your God-damned religion that has ruined your country. Damn your religion!"

At the time of Adams's Harvard graduation, it was also true that an American intellectual was, by definition, a clergyman. Adams seemed fleetingly headed in that direction; it was the traditional career for the gifted, book-loving New England son. The families of both Ben Franklin and John Adams hoped their sons would enter the ministry. Adams either abandoned or rejected the idea early on, displaying an indifference to expectation that would bloom into an indifference to reputation. We know his mother almost entirely on account of one objection and of her son's response to it: she preferred the newly minted Harvard graduate avoid the law, a profession toward which he also briefly gravitated. It suited him; he could debate a point of logic, cordially and unflaggingly, for hours. (To the dismay of the British Ministry, deductive reasoning was the mainstay of the Harvard curriculum.) For a few years still New England would think lawyers vaguely suspect, however. Massachusetts courts had operated for years without them.* Which did not stop Bostonians from suing one another with abandon or from discoursing at length on legal issues, evidently a New England birthright. Massachusetts seemed a place, bleated General Gage, "where every man studies law, and interprets the laws as suits his purposes."

Samuel Adams Sr. prevailed on a friend: for a brief period his son found work in the counting house of a prominent merchant. Thomas Cushing was the Speaker of the Massachusetts House of Representatives and a generous-minded, cool-headed South End neighbor, among the most popular men in town. He had a son nearly the same age as the recent graduate. The fit was not a natural one for Samuel; as the family put it, the work was "not consonant to his feelings and disposition." His father suggested that he make it so. He failed to improve. John Adams supplied a clue that may

---

* Two generations earlier a call had gone out to London. Could they send over a few honest attorneys, if such a thing existed in nature?

illuminate his cousin's unpromising early years: Samuel, he claimed, had an unrivaled understanding of liberty, something that in a young adult looks suspiciously like free-spiritedness. No hints survive either of bruised family feelings or burning ambition. Cushing's office attempted to accommodate its new employee. Adams was in every way a perfectly capable young man, explained Cushing, but "his whole soul was engrossed by politics." He could think of nothing else. He lasted several months.

He seems briefly to have ventured into business on his own, opening a shop. Again he met his defeat in the practical details. The passion for politics interfered with his attention to ledgers—or, as he seemed to believe, the opposite. He was stupefied by financial details, as he hastened to admit. He may have squandered his father's thousand pounds in that enterprise, or he may have entrusted part of the sum to a friend and lost the rest. It cannot be traced. In some accounts, the money—Boston mansions sold for less—landed in Samuel's hands for safe-keeping, which sounds unlikely. A well-connected son of the establishment, he strained to find his place, loitering his way toward his future.

In 1743 Adams earned a master's degree at Harvard, a straightforward endeavor that involved no residency in Cambridge, where his younger brother would soon enroll as an undergraduate. The advanced degree was largely a rite of passage, for which nearly all of Adams's classmates returned. The summer proved a joyous one for the family: the master's was conferred weeks before his older sister bore a son, also named Samuel. The sole academic requirement for the degree was a thesis; in Latin, a master's candidate answered a theoretical question drawn from the realms of philosophy, ethics, religion, or science. Two or three of the most adroit graduates argued their cases on commencement afternoon. Samuel did not figure among them, although he was presented formally to the college president and tutors at the exercise. Harvard commencement was the closest thing Boston knew to carnival, a much-anticipated July Wednesday that combined Latin and Hebrew orations with jugglers and acrobats, tents, peddlers, and food stalls. Families banded together for the outing. Alumni returned with dates. Long-lost relatives turned up, as did runaway apprentices and the Massachusetts governor.

Businesses closed throughout the province. The festivities began with a traditional psalm and ended with late-night singing in the streets, littered the next morning with watermelon rinds and peach pits.

The flavor of New England can be read in the thesis subjects, which offer a crisp snapshot of early America. Both before and after Adams's graduation it was argued that agriculture constituted the most honorable of secular pursuits. Some propositions seemed self-evident. Others located colonial America a great distance away. In 1769, by which time Adams had found his stride, a master's candidate contended that "the reptiles of America originated from those preserved by Noah." It would later be posited that gold could be produced chemically, that the sun was inhabitable (in 1772, by a future chief justice of the Massachusetts Supreme Court), that the Native Americans descended from Adam, that the pope was the Antichrist (three times between 1695 and 1762). Some topics recurred. As early as 1724 and regularly over the years, it would be asserted that it was unlawful to sell Africans. Other questions—Is capital punishment just? Will we meet our friends in heaven? Do ends justify means?—were eternal. There was much attention to ethics (it was repeatedly demonstrated that a good intention did not alone produce a good action), a preoccupation with certain theological riddles (the existence of angels was a favorite), and—between the 1740s and the 1760s—a steady march from the theological toward the professional, by way of the patently political.

As his subject Samuel Adams chose: Is it lawful to resist the supreme magistrate if the republic cannot otherwise be preserved? He had plucked the query from a 250-page Latin sourcebook that grouped together questions of logic, ethics, and the sciences. At least four other classmates consulted the volume, which provided a reading list and arguments on both sides of each question, their pertinent passages highlighted. It directed Adams to Algernon Sidney, John Locke, and Thomas Hobbes, to thinkers who had defended the divine rights of kings and those executed for conspiring against them. The class of 1743 produced no other great revolutionaries. One turned Tory. Several went on to become ministers, two merchants, two judges, one a distiller. There is all the same some truth to the allegation that—as one intimate put it—the American Revolution could be blamed on the Harvard College library.*

Though Adams had not himself formulated the thesis question, he did select it from among four hundred others, ignoring queries about whether all men are naturally equal and whether vegetables breathe. It resonated with him. Nor was there anything controversial about the proposition in 1743, when the college president approved both Adams's choice and his line of reasoning. Few others asked at the time—when George Washington was a child, Thomas Jefferson months old, and James Madison yet to be born—if resistance to a king might be justified. Twenty-year-old Adams answered the question in the affirmative. Man enjoyed no greater blessing, he argued, than civil government. It protected him both from his neighbor's self-interest and his own "propensity to superiority." To resist a ruler was treason. Adams rejoiced in the security their sovereign extended to his subjects. His power and their liberties stood in graceful balance. It was "the duty of every subject, for conscience's sake, to submit to his authority, while he acts according to the law." Should he imperil the natural right and liberties of his subjects, however, "he overthrows the very design of government, and the people are discharged from all obedience." Adams may have come to those conclusions on his own. Or he may have had an assist from events, his family having that spring sustained a catastrophic collision with royal authority.

ADAMS'S EARLY YEARS seem at first glance nearly to belong to someone else, so discordant are they with the career that follows. On closer examination certain qualities emerge that at least elucidate the lack of urgency. He had neither any use for despair nor much patience with it in others. He believed all was ordered for the best; he was not put out when things failed

---

* All five of the Massachusetts signers of the Declaration of Independence graduated from Harvard. John Adams would claim it had been the college—and Samuel Adams's town meetings—that had set the universe in motion. Hancock declared that Harvard could be considered "the parent as well as the nurse of the late happy revolution."

to proceed exactly as he liked. "By fretting at unfortunate events we double the evil," he admonished a friend. Enemies repeatedly discovered that you could not get a rise out of him. Flattery, he held, was "always great in proportion as the motives of flatterers are bad." He heard only the sensible and the honest. "The censure of fools or knaves," he would remind his wife, "is applause." Untroubled by perfectionism, he counseled friends not to overthink the details. He invoked a favorite analogy: Did it truly matter if the turkey arrived on the table boiled or roasted? He did not too much inquire into peevish humors, difficult to explain and generally not worth the trouble. He excelled at friendship, which at its best he termed "thinking aloud together." Acknowledging a letter in which an intimate sounded notes on which Adams had harped for years, he wrote: "You therein speak, as you ever have done, the language of my soul."

Indifferent at the table, even-tempered and sweetly obliging, patient in the extreme, he was fussy when it came to words, which he buffed, buffed again, and afterward refined. Meaning mattered. With swift precision, he reduced the convoluted to the essential, shaking an argument upside down until the nonsense tumbled out. He recoiled from those who, as he put it, made a show of looking down on their equals. Though he bore the same name as his exemplary father, he invested little in bloodlines. When traced far enough back, one bumped up against the inevitable horse thief. Neither wisdom nor virtue was hereditary. "The cottager may beget a wise son, the noble a fool," he noted, adding that only one was capable of improvement. (This lesson he formulated for his cousin, a provincial farmer's son who was then vice president of the United States.) He proved the only downwardly mobile of the Founding Fathers.

Pride and vanity kept their distance; Adams nearly needs to be drafted into starring in his own biography. He found ambition suspect. It arrived at his address belatedly, then all at once. He thought the best of people until he could no longer. He shrugged off their opinions. "I am *in* fashion and *out* of fashion, as the whim goes," he airily informed his family. Physically he was indefatigable. As affable in his manner as inflexible in his principles, he was at ease with everyone he met. Most gravitated toward his corner of the room. With a bit of effort, you might manage to resist his appeal. But you had to concede: Samuel Adams was the kind of man you like to believe exists and rarely meet.

While he dithered about the future, he was firm in his convictions. It is clear how he felt about his associates ("What is life without friendship!" he asked at an emotionally raw moment); about matrimony ("designed to complete the sum of human happiness in this life"); about the equality of its parties (the line between authority and subordination should remain perforated); about happiness (too easily squandered on the road to our destination). He knew what motivates and how to approach any audience. "He could see," observed a friend, "far into men." The list of things to which he seemed immune included small-mindedness, boasting, doubt, frustration, art. He left no record of the sullen, pewter-gray light of a New England winter afternoon or—it was the stuff of colonial diaries—the blazing snow-glare after a storm. When he waxed rhapsodic it was about liberty and the rights of man.

Never in his life would he make a wise financial decision. Poverty was not so disagreeable a companion, he held, as the affluent seemed to believe. He rarely missed an opportunity to proclaim the value of a sound education for young men and women. Essential to a republic, it was the requisite partner to virtue. His own studies yielded the expected results: when he applauded Bostonians for their forbearance, he commended their reprise of "the spirit of Rome or Sparta." A colleague displayed "as much of the stern virtue and spirit of a Roman censor as any gentleman I ever conversed with." His contemporaries would return the favor, applauding his "Roman-like firmness." Nothing would have made Adams happier than to have learned that an eminent minister declared him out of step with his time, more in keeping with "one of Plutarch's men."

Though no portrait survives of the young Samuel Adams, it is possible to picture him as he made his way around mid-century Boston, a town cooled by a salty sea breeze, laced with hints of wax and woodsmoke, coffee, fish, and lye. He was of medium stature and muscular build. The carriage was that of a good middleweight fighter. His lips were thin, the chin slightly dimpled, the nose straight and Roman, the complexion polished, fresh, and pink. The features left him just short of handsome, with an open countenance and—under thick brows—piercing, unexpectedly deep blue eyes.* When excited he raised himself on his toes, bouncing, for emphasis, at the end of a sentence. The portraitists arrived only after he had gone gray; Boston was, however, a fair-haired city, and the coloring suggests he had been a blond youth. Known to all whose path he crossed as the son of Deacon Adams, the grandson of an earlier Deacon Adams, he was, as Henry Adams phrased it generations later, distinctly branded. He wielded a great deal of charm, to his enemies "vast insinuation and infinite art."

We will not hear him distinctly for another decade, but we have a fair idea of how Adams sounded. There was a sort of rasping scrape to the New England voice. Words rolled off the tongue differently in Boston than they did elsewhere in North America; in the hurry to the end of a sentence, short syllables collapsed into one. "Necessary" shrank to "neccary," "continuous" to "kontinoss." Consonants flattened in the rush. The letter "r" floated about, vanishing for long spells and emerging in unexpected places. "Sort" sounded in Boston like "sought," but the Caucus Club—to which Adams's father belonged, and which used its influence to settle town appointments in advance of elections—was the "Corcass Club." The "g" at the end of a sentence went missing, so that Thomas Cushing became "Thomas Cushen." Adams had a crystalline singing voice and a fine ear for music, of which he was fond. He entertained friends' children with song. At one time he led the church choir, a role not easily held against a man. His enemies pounced on it all the same. They charged—it is the only hint we have of the practice, which may never have been practiced—that Adams presided over "singing societies" of tradespeople, embracing the opportunity to foster sedition.

Otherwise Adams sounded like an Englishman; there was a reason why two British army officers in disguise did not raise suspicions in Worcester the minute they opened their mouths. As one foreigner noted, the colonists "speak better English than the English do." And it was to London that the New Englander looked as home, London to which all was compared, London from which Boston imported the books it

---

* John Adams would report that Samuel looked much like William the Conqueror. If so, every extant portrait of him is inaccurate.

consumed by the crate. Culturally and politically, the colonies felt closer to the mother country than to one another. Adams grew up celebrating the king's birthday and coronation; as late as 1773, the first toast went to the king. As any Massachusetts colonist could tell you and as Adams did repeatedly, the British government was the best government on earth. He rejoiced in calling himself an Englishman. The oversized, elaborate Adams family Bible — an embossed, brass-clasped volume that Samuel inherited from his father and in which he inscribed family records throughout his life — bore, on its title page, a view of London.

A Bostonian not only spoke and thought but hoped to dress as an Englishman. Thomas Hutchinson engaged in a lively correspondence with his tailor, inconveniently located an ocean away. The three-month time lag left Hutchinson second-guessing what might be in style. "Tell me what outerwear is now worn and whether of cloth and what color," he demanded one summer. He ordered lace to match the king's. He longed for a rust-colored suit, of the deepest hue, but only if London fashion permitted. Boston owed its preeminence in part to the fact that it was the closest port to Great Britain. And it was on England that Boston — itself nearly an island, with 16,000 people packed into fewer than four square miles — was modeled.

At the time of Adams's birth the town was less than a century old, yet the dress, the conversation, the furnishings, the fine linens and wines could prove as splendid as those of a prosperous London tradesman. A particularly opulent residence might bear a crown of Great Britain over every window and busts of the king and queen in the entry, as did Hutchinson's childhood home. Given the architecture, the fare, the customs and conversation, a Londoner felt immediately at ease in Boston. It was, a visitor noted, pale, white, and graceful, its buildings neat and handsome, like its women. While cows still grazed in the center of town, while swine ran at large, Boston counted — with its smooth, pearly clapboard facades, its well-swept, airy interiors — among the most civilized of addresses. "This is the most beautiful country I ever saw in my life," announced the British officer who in 1775 would lead reinforcements to Concord — and who only wished the people were more like it. On the first count he spoke for countless others. Visitors thought the town stunning, its food superb. The pork was without rival, the lobsters colossal, the poultry ludicrously affordable. Boston hosts did not stint on delicacies like venison, salmon, or turtle. One rarely went to bed without oysters.

When Adams walked out his front door on the less populated, less fashionable side of town, he found himself amid pastures, fields, and orchards. To his back were the wharves. To the west and north stood ropewalks, where long hemp cables were laid out on the ground, their fibers twisted into ships' rigging. Hot tar waterproofed the ropes; the smell pinched the nostrils. The New South Church, which Samuel Adams Sr. had helped to found, stood, with its elegant Ionic steeple, a few blocks north. To Adams's left was the slim ribbon of causeway that connected Boston to the mainland. About the same distance to his right stood Griffin's Wharf, where East India Company tea would eventually land. A few blocks north, Adams passed along pebbled streets — one walked always in the smooth center — into the congested center of town, a knot of crooked alleys and narrow turns, where the acrid fumes of tanners, candlemakers, and distillers bit into the sea air. The chic lived in the North End, in splendid homes that rose among a clutter of warehouses, bakeries, blacksmiths, barns, and shipyards. At Boston's center, raised above pavement level on a small green, stood its stately Town House, where Adams was to spend countless hours. At its base was a covered walk; its upper floors divided into meeting rooms. Booksellers clustered around the three-story structure. Adams could easily walk from one end of town to the other in a morning, as had a minister years earlier, in search of his lost cow.

No one approached Boston without remarking on its superb harbor, a majestic crescent bristling with masts. Shops and handsome storehouses lined its wharves, the longest of which extended a half mile into the ocean. A forest of steeples rose above the low-lying town; beyond them spread a ribbon of velvety hills. It was a vantage that Adams probably never himself enjoyed. In his long life he would cross many rivers — including the Rubicon, countless times — but never an ocean. Boston echoed not only with the clatter of industry but with its unsynchronized daily bells, and, after sundown, with the calls of the watch, delivering the time and the weather. The general impression was one of unremitting activity. The town won higher marks from a Parisian or Londoner than it did from a Braintree farmer's son. John Adams found the bustle of chimney sweeps and oxcarts, wood carriers and coaches—the percussive tin-hammering and cart-trundling, the jangle of ships' tackle—bewildering. He lost his way from the beginning of a thought to its end amid the thunderous "rattle gabble" of it all.

In Samuel Adams's writing there is barely a nod to the aesthetic. He was forthright about his affection for his hometown, however, an affection that—once he found ground for comparison—tilted into chauvinism. It was not difficult for Boston, throughout Adams's youth the largest town in the colonies, to flirt with a superiority complex. Rarely had a people given so much thought, so early on, to education. Boston won the American awards for literacy and sophistication. As a visitor observed: "Knowledge is probably more universally diffused here than in any other considerable town in the world." With its seventeen churches, genteel Boston was no less remarkable as a place that went entirely silent on Sunday, where a barber could be fined for performing a shave on the Sabbath.

Adams's Boston was a town in which you had your pick of harpsichords, where you could acquire a fine umbrella tipped with ivory or brass; a box of fresh Malaga lemons; a set of false teeth (designed by Paul Revere, goldsmith); silkworm eggs; a "ripe, delicate pineapple"; French lessons; *The Complete Woman Cook*; or "as fine a pleasure boat for sailing or rowing as perhaps ever was built." Plenty of families kept coaches; a select few rode out accompanied by servants in scarlet livery. The incursion of those superfluities was surveyed with some alarm. "Luxury and extravagance," the adult Adams would fret, "are in my opinion totally destructive of those virtues which are necessary for the preservation of the liberty and happiness of the people." Nor was he the greatest of killjoys. Clucked a friend in 1779: "In short we are arrived to that stage of civilization and polished manners which I think incompatible with public or private virtue, and therefore worse than barbarism."

In Adams's expostulations his opponents heard the resentment of a man without fortune. They were correct about the poverty, mistaken about the envy. They tended to lose sight of an essential fact: Samuel Adams would wind up a poor man who had not been a poor boy, a different creature altogether, especially in a country where upward mobility set records. It was said to take three centuries to breed a gentleman in Great Britain. In America the miracle could be accomplished in three generations. Adams came of age, too, at a time when the Massachusetts economy was markedly on the skids. Plenty of other young men stumbled in finding their footholds. On leaving Harvard shortly after Adams, a future colleague would try his hand as a schoolmaster. Miserable, he sailed off as a merchant, later as a whaler. He was soon back in Boston. In a patched gown, he served briefly as a chaplain. Out of options, he turned to the law. "A wretched condition this town is with regard to people who have their living to earn," he squawked in 1758, when Adams, having sidestepped each of those careers, had begun to sell off his father's estate.

BETWEEN THE TIME Adams earned his undergraduate degree in 1740 and the July afternoon in 1743 when he and his parents celebrated the conferral of his master's, the ground shifted dramatically under the family's feet. This earthquake went well recorded. Massachusetts trade had fallen off precipitously. It would decrease by half in the decade after 1735, when prices soared and the value of currency plunged. Industries decamped to less expensive ports, eroding Boston's role as the colonial shipbuilding capital. Faster ocean crossings undermined its geographic advantage. The dry goods businesses, the cod fishery, and the town distilleries suffered acutely. As unemployment rose and the population declined, the cost of supporting Boston's poor doubled. The town found itself crushed by taxes. For any but the most wealthy, the lust for luxury had been curtailed already.

Further exacerbating the matter was the acute shortage of currency in New England. The trade imbalance left most specie in Great Britain. Without gold or silver at its disposal, with currency, like industry, restricted by the Crown, the Massachusetts economy limped along in beaver skins and lumber. By the 1740s it stood in need of a more sophisticated medium. Bills of credit had been introduced as a substitute for government-issued specie; by royal edict, those bills were to be withdrawn from circulation in 1741, a redemption that would deprive Massachusetts of the bulk of its already scarce currency.

As that deadline loomed, the Massachusetts House appealed to the citizenry for ideas. An elegant solution presented itself in the form of a land bank. New England was poor in hard currency but rich in property. Why not issue paper money secured by land? The idea had been under consideration for some time. And the Massachusetts governor, Jonathan Belcher, endorsed it. Near the end of Adams's undergraduate career, a prospectus was submitted to circulate notes worth 150,000 pounds. Nearly four hundred men, in sixty-four towns, pledged their properties as capital, against which the Land Bank issued loans at a modest rate of interest. The bills would be redeemable in twenty years, either in notes or in a long list of domestic commodities; the new institution would both ease the monetary pinch and stimulate American manufacturing. Samuel Adams Sr. figured among the Land Bank's nine directors. His fellow board members did not count among the wealthiest men in Massachusetts, an intermarried circle of merchants who held a monopoly on trade. Shipbuilders, mill owners, and iron manufacturers, the directors were, however, all individuals of stature. One was an admiralty judge, another a militia captain. Six sat in the House of Representatives. All but one were justices of the peace.

To great enthusiasm, the bank issued its first bills in the fall of 1740. Over the following months more than a thousand subscribers from all over Massachusetts took out loans with which to improve farms, enhance ironworks, or outfit glassworks. The liquidity problem had been resolved, but a new issue emerged. The bank's popularity with provincial towns was matched by its unpopularity with Boston's merchant elite. It did not care to settle debts in an untried currency, worthless to English creditors. Nor did it care to invite tavern keepers, bricklayers, or blacksmiths into the mercantile community. How, they protested, could such an institution even be legal? Surely any scheme that pumped thousands of pounds into the economy would induce inflation! Many had pinned their hopes on a competing enterprise, endorsed by the Hutchinsons. As early as September 1740, some 135 merchants warned that they had no intention of accepting Land Bank bills. They urged their concerns on Governor Belcher.

Startled by the intensity of those objections, Belcher moved to suppress a venture he had earlier encouraged. The bank offered further proof, he decided, that the colonists had been deranged for two decades, in which time they "seemed to study how they could provoke the King and his Ministers." He appealed to the House of Representatives to prohibit the issue of Land Bank bills. It refused. The colonial legislature consisted of two bodies: the House and an upper chamber, the twenty-eight-man Governor's Council, historically a more conservative, more prominent group. The Council took its affluent governor's position. In July, Belcher warned against either accepting or extending Land Bank notes. He upped the ante in the fall, forbidding anyone who held a royal commission from doing business with the bank. Justices of the peace who subscribed to it should consider themselves relieved of duty. Samuel Adams Sr. resigned several weeks before the governor summarily dismissed him.

Hastily reversing course, Belcher enlisted every method at his disposal to destroy the bank. He chastised the House. He warned taverns that accepted bills that they should expect to lose their licenses. He instructed militia officers to purge miscreants from their ranks. He forbade lawyers associated with the bank from pleading before the Council. And he dispatched an urgent missive to Parliament: Would they formally dissolve the Land Bank? He pitched the request feverishly, invoking the South Sea Bubble of 1720, a speculative venture that had decimated investors, reputations, and a national economy. The Land Bank, Belcher warned, could prove yet more pernicious. What could stop twenty other such concerns from issuing millions of pounds of paper currency? Were Parliament not to intervene, he foresaw "the total subversion of this government and the ruin of the country."

For neither the first nor last time a Massachusetts economic issue mutated, nearly overnight, into a political one. Governor Belcher complained that the bank had raised "a malignant spirit." Though the greater part of the province supported the venture, it left its critics fuming. One called in the *Boston Evening Post* for the bank's directors to be prosecuted. Were it not for the fact that they would leave their creditors high and dry, they should be carted off to London to be tried for "their high crime and misdemeanor." The author took an additional swipe at the directors, noting that "this would ruin them in their small fortunes." It was the kind of high-handed comment that suggested something other than inflationary fears were at stake. Despite the fury with which Belcher railed against "an affair so destructive to all good order and to the liberties and properties of the King's subjects," there was nothing remotely illegal about the bank. By supplying individuals excluded from the economic system with a currency, it threatened the social order.

In a long letter to his political protégé, Belcher fumed that the Land Bank infected every Massachusetts effort and address. Were it not "speedily and effectually crushed," he cautioned, it would topple a government. For twenty-five years the people of Massachusetts had done their best "to treat the Crown with all possible rudeness and ill manners." He would have preferred to suppress the wicked scheme on his own but did not believe his efforts sufficient. The colony had grown brazen; the insubordination was breathtaking. The Massachusetts House seemed to think itself on par with the Parliament of Great Britain! London could not intervene quickly enough. Belcher had no hope for any assistance from the current House, which he "wouldn't trust for a pair of old shoes." (He had cause to feel beleaguered. Belcher was up against two-thirds of the Massachusetts populace and at war with the House, plump, after the May 1741 elections, with additional Land Bank supporters.) He warned his young correspondent to steer clear of a government that seemed to have gone rogue. The protégé—who would have ample reason to remember the warning—was Thomas Hutchinson.

Parliament complied with Governor Belcher's request, as Massachusetts learned shortly after the May elections. While no one moved to ship the Land Bank directors abroad for prosecution, Parliament did opt for severity. Extending the Bubble Act, it declared illegal any money-raising ventures not endorsed by the Crown or an act of Parliament. Parliament moreover deemed the bank directors jointly and severally liable for the bank's obligations. The loans were to be redeemed immediately in gold or silver. The penalty left the directors dumbfounded; the sums were colossal. Late in September a bare majority of directors agreed to dissolve the bank. Others argued for defying the act of Parliament, a colonial first. Why should a far-off authority quash a popular venture? As his family saw it, Samuel Adams Sr. was singled out in particular. Certainly the London edict left him the most exposed. Having invested all of his political capital and most of his fortune in the bank, he was effectively ruined.

In part for his clumsy handling of the crisis, Governor Belcher was recalled weeks later. Having neglected to suppress the scheme, he had exacerbated the matter. A "bad spirit" now animated the colony. Meanwhile, the Massachusetts treasury remained empty. London replaced Belcher with William Shirley, a nimbler and more amiable administrator. He met with "consternation and distress" among the Land Bankers, over a third of whom remained stubbornly delinquent. Recovering funds proved slow going. Shirley prepared to prosecute the outliers but could, months afterward, at least assure London that they were in the minority, their bills largely eliminated. "And I think I may now assure your Grace," the governor wrote his London superior, "that this scheme will have been so timely destroyed that not one honest man will suffer much by it." Resistance had been formidable, but he had headed off a crisis.

The Land Bank survived for sixteen months. Its dismantling consumed decades. Some of the fallout made itself felt immediately. Samuel Adams Sr. found himself in court, where he would remain for the rest of his life, appealing a penalty that struck him as of dubious legality and of governmental overreach. (He could only have winced that his home stood on Belcher's Lane.) The financial catastrophe translated into political popularity: in 1744 Boston voted him a selectman and, two years later, sent him to the House of Representatives. The following year the House elected him to the twenty-eight-member Council. As was his right, Governor Shirley rejected Samuel Adams Sr., along with nearly half the elected Council members, Land Bankers all.

The controversy did nothing to revive Boston's fortunes. By 1760 New York and Philadelphia had overtaken it in terms of population. But the collapse hollowed out a little room for resistance. It raised thorny questions: Who was in charge of Massachusetts—its own House of Representatives, or a Parliament thousands of miles away? The long arm of London had rarely before seemed so brutally intrusive, so arbitrarily flexed, or so hostile to colonial ingenuity. Did the interests of the two countries coincide or were they perpendicular? Not for the first time, the Land Bank set a Massachusetts governor bitterly against his House. Very much for the first time, it led a group of men to contemplate defying Parliament. Legacy served as augury: the bank left a royal governor, his back to the wall, manufacturing disorder to elicit assistance from London, help that came in a form disproportionate to the crisis at hand. It created a constituency at odds with London. As Samuel Adams would later complain, those who questioned authority soon saw themselves "represented as a rude, low-lived mob."

The bank's borrowers had been printers and locksmiths, millers, hatters, and schoolmasters. The collision exacerbated a class divide, preserved in the first published Massachusetts history. That account fell to Thomas Hutchinson, whom Belcher had looked upon as a son. Hutchinson knew his Massachusetts history better than any man alive, though was, when he composed his pages, unaware that he was about to be steamrolled by it. Of the rancor he was acutely aware. Writing twenty-five years afterward, he hinted at a political power play: had Parliament not intervened, the Land Bank directors would have taken over the government. He issued a heartfelt defense of his mentor. He immortalized the bank's subscribers as men "of low condition among the plebeians and of small estate and many of them perhaps insolvent." The venture had set the needy against "men of estates and the principal merchants." And the votes of the former, groaned Hutchinson, who had begun to amass his fortune even before his Harvard graduation, counted as much as those of the latter!

The Land Bank proved simpler to relegate to the history books than to unwind. Over and over hands flew up in frustration. The task became more daunting after a Town House fire destroyed its ledgers. Committee would be piled upon committee, in the Massachusetts way, the bank's affairs strangling the court system for years. Careers and families would be shipwrecked in the process. A generation afterward, penniless sons, grown old, petitioned still for dead fathers. Delinquent debtors were impoverished, deceased, or far off. How equitably to allocate losses? The issue remained on the House agenda until the end of 1770, when the commission assigned to resolve the affair submitted their expense account, the bulk of it an astronomical liquor bill. The decision to reimburse was postponed until the next session, when events the debacle so neatly forecast obliterated the matter.

For all parties, the Land Bank fiasco provided a convenient gauge by which to measure future unrest. Relying on the memories of others, John Adams would insist that it caused greater ferment than would the Stamp Act, decades later. Hutchinson took the opposite tack. The Land Bank had been "a peccadillo compared with the combinations now afoot in so many colonies," he reported in 1769, when the melody of two decades earlier was revived, scored for a full orchestra. Left upon the death of his father with a massive debt and a larger grievance, Samuel Adams spoke more obliquely. He expressed a sentiment that may well have preceded the Land Bank but that its collapse reinforced. In his sixties, Adams would say that vigilance in civic life had been inculcated in him at an early age. "Let the people keep a watchful eye over the conduct of their rulers," he explained, "for we are told that great men are not at all times wise. It would be indeed a wonder if in any age or country they were always honest."

John Adams and Thomas Hutchinson fully agreed on another point: the collapse of the Land Bank ushered Samuel Adams in from the wings. Eager though John was to make his cousin a political instrument from birth, he dated Samuel's political involvement specifically to 1741. Hutchinson described his debut on the Massachusetts stage with an uncharitable review of a ferocious performance: Samuel Adams enters roaring, pursued by creditors. After his father's death, the family estate was put up for auction to settle his debt. Hutchinson tells us that Adams "attended the sale, threatened the sheriff to bring an action against him, and threatened all who should attempt to enter upon the estate, under pretense of a purchase; and, by intimidating both the sheriff and those persons who intended to purchase, he prevented the sale, kept the estate in his possession and the debt to the Land Bank company remained unsatisfied." The unflinching account probably differed little from what Adams himself would have reported. And it could only have gratified, falling as it did in the censure-by-knaves department.

IV

THE VERY HONEST
SAMUEL ADAMS, CLERK

*The blessed work of helping the world forward happily does not
wait to be done by perfect men.*
— GEORGE ELIOT

IN MARCH 1747, Adams accepted election as a Boston market clerk. The position provided a modest salary and aligned him more closely with his hometown; an underemployed Bostonian proved an oddity well into the next century, when it was observed that "a man who is not believed to follow some useful business can scarcely acquire, or retain, even a decent reputation." The clerkship sent Adams out into the bustling streets, among bakers, butchers, and oystermen, to confirm that all was fresh, orderly, and in accord with town regulation. He was to prevent bread and butter from turning up at fictitious weights or inflated prices. Boston would be hailed as the best governed of colonial towns, its laws enforced by fence-viewers, overseers of the poor, measurers of boards, and a surveyor of hemp. For an idealistic, gregarious twenty-four-year-old, the clerkship was a perfect fit. In his element among worsted caps and leather aprons, Adams more or less invented retail politics as he went; early on he had read that the opinions of the man in the street should never be neglected, an assertion that stayed with him. The post—a first step up a well-polished ladder—was not unusual for a promising young Bostonian. Several Harvard acquaintances figured among the town's dozen clerks. An uncle performed a similar service at the larger

Faneuil Hall market. Samuel Adams Sr. had served as a 1727 market clerk, afterward as tithingman, constable, assessor, selectman, and fire warden.

Adams no doubt heard a certain amount in the streets about the veto that excluded his father from the Governor's Council. Massachusetts differed from its sister colonies in that its House selected its Council. Only rarely did it meet with opposition. To some, the rejection qualified as a badge of honor. At home it rankled. The veto could be exercised without a hint of a reason. It had, Samuel pointed out, no parallel in England. The king himself could not reject a member of the House of Lords! Adams would eventually work to reconfigure the Council, so that it acted not as a check on the legislature, as intended, but on the executive. The events of the 1740s left him, in his late twenties, with firm convictions and several strong aversions. It is not difficult to guess where his sympathies lay in the fall of 1747, when Admiral Charles Knowles arrived in town with a squadron. Knowles's crew deserted; the admiral saw no reason why Boston should hesitate to supply replacements. He performed a sweep of the wharves. While forced recruiting was standard practice in London; in Boston sticks and clubs appeared. Bricks flew through Town House windows. Governor Shirley decamped after his house was nearly stormed. Carted off by the mob, a deputy sheriff wound up in the stocks. Knowles's officers were taken hostage, held prisoner for two days, then paraded through the streets. The squadron sailed two weeks later for the West Indies, its ranks in no way supplemented by Bostonians.

The riot provided Adams with his first taste of violent resistance. It hinted that detours around authority might prove both necessary and effective. Boston had been restive before but had not convulsed as it did in 1747, when several thousand took to the streets. Shirley called in the militia, only to discover that the mob and the militia—officially every man between the ages of sixteen and sixty—were one and the same. To salvage the town's honor, he submitted, the militia had only to disperse the mob and deliver up its ringleaders. Though he assumed the House of Representatives complicit in the uprising, he acted throughout with the same cool dexterity that he had demonstrated in the Land Bank crisis. For his part, Captain Knowles regretted he could not simply bombard Boston.

A week afterward, a pseudonymous pamphlet appeared that some attribute to Adams. The style is not his though the substance is. "A Lover of his Country" appealed to the inhabitants of Massachusetts Bay on the occasion of the "late illegal and unwarrantable attack upon their liberties." Boston had met a wrongful act with an exercise of natural rights. It was especially justified in doing so as those affected were of modest station, "full as useful as their neighbors, who live at ease upon the produce of their labour." The author touched on an issue that would poison relations over the next decades: Massachusetts had borne more than her share of expenses in expelling the French from North America. Her men had been killed and captured in great number. Her trade had been decimated. Decades of military expeditions translated into ruinous taxes. If anything, the colony should now be singled out for the king's protection. The author explained that he would have published his remarks sooner save for "an unexpected and unprecedented restraint upon the press."

For that there was a solution. With friends, Adams began to mull the idea for a newspaper, a time-honored way to shrink a fortune. The *Independent Advertiser* debuted in January 1748, when the bulk of the edition went to the Knowles tumult. It is unclear who provided the paper's funding as it is largely unclear who wrote which of the weekly's columns. While the *Advertiser* made no "pompous promises," its readers could expect the best and freshest intelligence. When news was slow—as it would be that January—the paper pledged to print selections from "our most celebrated writers, which may be most likely to improve or entertain our readers." The *Advertiser* professed no agenda and represented no party. The paper took as its mission simply to defend the liberties and rights of mankind, to inspire New Englanders "with a just and proper sense of their own condition, to point out to them their true interest, and rouse them to pursue it."

From the start came attacks on Governor Shirley. Opting to overlook November's flying bricks, the *Advertiser* insisted that the people were all calmness and resignation. Massachusetts struggled under multiple hardships. Boston had in three years lost nearly a fifth of its men. Small wonder that a "haughty commander" should meet with resistance when he attempted further to eviscerate the town. Would a wise governor not protect his constituents against such an affront? The people were hardly disposed to riot, as Shirley seemed to think. But they had met with aggravations. If the State did not care to defend their rights, they had no choice but to assume the task themselves. Along with previews of coming attractions came a deft bit of recycling. A lead piece in January 1748 served up a reminder that civil government counted as the greatest of God's blessings. Men regularly invaded one another's lives and property. Government existed to keep them in check. As for the form of that government, the best was one in which the rights of individuals and the prerogatives of power stood in equilibrium. Such was that enjoyed by English subjects. Anyone who resisted such a monarch committed treason. By the same logic, a people owed no allegiance to a ruler who trampled their rights. If the piece was not a reprint of Adams's Harvard thesis, it grew out of the assignment. He was clearly its anonymous author.

Claims of impartiality aside, the *Advertiser* proved itself deeply partisan at a time when most papers delivered straightforward reporting. It sparked much interest; speculation began immediately as to who stood behind its pieces. Its contributors remained anonymous, but for the next years the *Advertiser* offered a steady stream of excerpts from Locke and attacks on the royal governor, a smattering of foreign news, headlines from New York and Philadelphia, occasional verse, and plenty of local color, from the visiting contortionist to the linen stolen from the clothesline to the advertisement for a camera obscura. A few columns stand out as Adams's; he had not yet perfected his prose style, but he had found his voice. He is calm, deliberative, and precise. He is unassailably logical. The sentences are long; the embrace of the semicolon ardent. He did not revert, as did his contemporaries, to the exclamation point, or to long ribbons of capital letters. He trusted muscular reasoning to stand on its own.

In the close-cropped columns of the *Advertiser* he also found his subjects. The anthems began early. "There is," he wrote, "no one thing which mankind are more passionately fond of, which they fight with more zeal for, which they possess with more anxious jealousy and fear of losing, than liberty." The very word liberty emitted a "charming sound."

Yet liberty was a commodity more often admired than enjoyed or under-stood. Men happily extolled it when they meant nothing by it save their own well-being. They unfurled tributes when they intended only "to oppress without control or the restraint of laws all who are poorer or weaker than themselves." Instinctively, we work to distinguish ourselves. That was laudable, so long as our ambitions did not impinge on those of our neighbors and so long as inequality met with limits. Adams stressed an equation on which he could never sufficiently insist: A corrupt people would not long remain free. "He therefore is the truest friend to the lib-erty of his country who tries most to promote its virtue," he concluded.

While he shared neither Ben Franklin's whimsy nor his gift for mim-icry, Adams seems to have written several essays in the guise of a poor cobbler. His prose, the shoemaker assured readers, in no way interfered with his trade. He had concealed his name, he wrote, even from the print-ers themselves. Though he considered venturing out from behind the curtain—the reception of his essays left him puffed with pride—he opted to labor in obscurity. He knew "the great and affluent" had little regard for him but held that in public affairs the opinions of "the more artless and less interested" mattered more than those devoted to party schemes and pri-vate gain. (Cobblers figured at the bottom both of the social scale and the tax rolls.) He pitied the man who could not think for himself, "whose soul is enslaved to the passion of ambition—whose life and happiness depend upon the breath or nod of another." The honest, unlettered shoe-maker also quoted liberally from Tacitus, Cicero, and Milton.

Adams took over the entire front page of a March 1748 issue to denounce "lawless avarice and ambition," two hungers of which he would never be accused. Susceptible as they were to disease, states had life spans. One that especially threatened the health of the body politic was any disruption of its balance of power. A state in which the power of the government and the liberties of the governed stood in equipoise, where no man stood above the law nor any man below it, was "a most lovely and beautiful sight." Adams wrote off the love of money, which led men to upend the state. The people owed it to themselves to monitor those who governed. The dangers of complacency could not be stressed often enough. "The foundation of a people's ruin is often at first laid in small, and almost imperceptible encroachments upon their liberties," he warned. No people—the idea is central to modern civil resistance theory—should forget their own power. He was watchful before any cause for alarm had yet materialized. He seemed to be listening for something no one else could yet hear.

He had additional cause that spring to reflect on his political inheritance. The same issue of the *Advertiser* announced the death of fifty-nine-year-old Samuel Adams Sr. the previous Wednesday. In a notice that his son may have drafted, the malster was remembered as "an honest patriot." The obituary paid tribute not only to the deceased but to his generation, those New Englanders who "well understood and rightly pursued the civil and religious interests of this people." The death had not been sudden; Adams's father had signed his will the day before. As executors he named his elder son and namesake; Samuel's brother, Joseph Adams, set to graduate that summer from Harvard; and their sister's husband, a tailor. What remained of the estate went to Mary Adams. Adams forgave the 1,000 pounds with which he had attempted to launch Samuel and that his son had misspent.

With emotions that left no recorded trace, Adams took over the malt business, assuming his place among what the *Advertiser*'s shoemaker termed "the middle industrious sort." For at least a few hours a week he concerned himself with kilns and cisterns, drying schedules and deliveries. As did most in the malt business, he kept pigs, raised on spent grain. The Hancock family, to whom Adams's father had sold bacon and pork cheeks, counted among his customers. Along with the business, Adams inherited the Land Bank debt. It dominated dinner table discussion for some time, as it would affairs throughout the province. When Joseph Adams prepared his Harvard master's thesis in 1751, he chose as his subject a question in no manual. Did the confiscation of a dead parent's property, he asked, constitute an unjust penalty for his innocent children? With an assist from Locke—"the miscarriages of the father are no faults of the children"—Joseph argued in the negative.

From the evidence on the page, all of Samuel Adams's youthful longings seemed to have been for ideas. At some point before he turned twenty-seven, a young woman caught his eye. She could never have been far; she lived two streets away. And Adams had known Elizabeth Check-ley as long as he could remember. She was the daughter of Samuel Check-ley, the New South Church minister. Her father had baptized them both. A family intimate, Checkley owed his position in part to Samuel Adams Sr., who had lobbied for his appointment. Elizabeth's brother, a minister in a prestigious pulpit across town, had overlapped at Harvard with Adams, who had likely attended his 1748 wedding. Samuel and Eliza-beth's ceremony took place at the Checkley home on the evening of October 17, 1749. The match may have been in the works well before the death of the groom's father. We know nothing of the courtship. Where love entered the picture is unclear, but the union was a deeply happy one. Adams found Elizabeth "as sincere a friend as she was a faithful wife." Her in-laws admired her greatly. Modest and pious, she shared her new husband's equanimity, put to the test over their years together. Soon pregnant, twenty-four-year-old Elizabeth bore a son the following fall. Named Samuel, he was baptized by her father. He lived eighteen days. Nearly a year to the day later she bore a second son, also named Samuel, also baptized by her father. He survived. The couple would bury another son and daughter by the time their daughter Hannah arrived in 1756.

No edition of the *Independent Advertiser* appeared the week of the Adams wedding; the paper published only irregularly over the winter. Some felt liberated. "There is hardly any character that deserves less envy," noted a contributor, "than that of a political writer, especially if he writes from principle and is perseveringly honest." That contributor—if not Adams, he could have been speaking for him—announced the end of the journalism experiment with relief. It cleared the way for a trial Adams knew would be coming. Before long the *Advertiser* however reconstituted itself as the *Boston Gazette*, in the pages of which Adams would make his mark, if never under his own name.

IN 1750, SAMUEL Adams climbed to the second floor of the Town House, the inner sanctum of Massachusetts politics. At twenty-eight, he appeared before the committee meant to settle the Land Bank debts, a task that would have been no easier had the company's ledgers, deeds, and mortgages survived the 1747 fire. (As Adams saw it, having been invalidated by an act of Parliament, the bank had been reduced to ashes by an act of God.) The directors' integrity had been questioned. While their reputations survived, their accounts remained unsettled.

As requested, Adams had deposited his records with a clerk. They showed a considerable credit; the family had reimbursed more than their share. To his surprise, he discovered that his accounting had found its way to a larger House committee. He now appealed to those men with a humble proposition: "If they had a right to audit my account," he maintained, "I might have the opportunity of being heard upon it." The chair cordially agreed. Adams paid his respects and left, confident that he would be summoned when convenient. That moment never arrived.

A new committee was instead appointed in 1751, when the debt-allocating resumed. This time the committee summoned Adams, who appeared that winter alongside several other Land Bankers and their heirs. Each fielded the investigators' questions. This meeting ended less cordially. When the visitors were dismissed, Adams lagged behind. He had a few questions for the chair. The banking misadventure may have reinforced a belief in the sanctity of property; it certainly reinforced Adams's conviction that no individual should hesitate to inquire into the mysteries of state. Did the committee have his ledgers, submitted earlier? he asked. They did not. Had they, he asked, any intention of reviewing them? They did not. The requests met with some consternation. The committee, explained its chairman, had no authority to delve into individual accounts. Their mandate was to settle the collective one, instructions the chairman offered to share with Adams. Adams reminded his examiners of what they presumably knew: he had no funds at his disposal, as he offered to swear on oath. The commission demurred, sending him on his way. Adams left the Town House with a sinking feeling.

The investigators afterward assigned charges to each party at their discretion. Adams quibbled with the allocations—why was he on the line for 219 pounds and another family for 10?—and pointed up the absurdity of the exercise: How could the examiners devise an equitable settlement without examining each investigator's ledgers? Had the committee not overstepped? They had assessed amounts in secret, after which their report became law. Somehow his favorable balance had mutated into a sizeable debt. In no year of his life would he earn 219 pounds. And in 1751 the Massachusetts legislature authorized sheriffs to seize the estates of Land Bank directors who failed to satisfy their creditors.

"It will easily be imagined," he noted tartly, "that I was in some surprise to receive an account which in my apprehension was totally an error—to have so pressing a demand for immediate payment of a large sum, and to be told of the frightful consequences which would follow upon my refusing to comply with such a demand." He requested an accounting. None materialized. He refused payment, respectfully, or at least gesturing in that direction: "Unwilling to fall under the odious imputation of resisting authority," as he gloriously put it, he submitted a petition to the House of Representatives. He and his father had complied with every demand for records. He sought only "the inestimable privilege common to all British subjects" of defending himself. How had the committee arrived at its assessments? No one could in good faith have answered his question. The accounting was gnarled beyond recognition.

Adams demanded a pause in the proceedings. Privately several members of the commission acknowledged that he had cause for complaint: the case consisted of error compounded upon error. They would not however publicly oblige him. The request was denied. He allowed himself a little stab; he pitied men who carried out measures they knew to be unjust. The sheriff was directed to seize and auction not a part of Adams's estate but all of it, worth over five times the contested sum. Were the estate worth fifty times as much, Adams remonstrated, the sheriff would follow the same procedure. For all his affability, Adams did not shy from confrontation. He was mulish or principled, depending on your perspective. And others shared his qualms. The sheriff himself conceded that the law had its defects. They dissuaded some from bidding on the embattled property.

At thirty-three Adams was left, the father of a five-week-old and a four-year-old, nominally still a malster, to hold off homelessness. By 1756 he had no hope of family assistance. His brother, now married, had become a doctor, having served an apprenticeship that Adams presumably underwrote. (No one evinced much interest in malt-making, a profession Samuel Adams Sr. seems to have urged on neither son.) Adams took out a loan that March for Joseph with a shipyard owner. The brothers found themselves unable to repay it a year later, when the lender sued them. Their sister's husband had mortgaged and remortgaged his home. Generous in extending credit, he wound up regularly in court, chasing payments from delinquent customers. Already the siblings had begun to sell off pieces of the family estate, including a parcel of land south of Boston. Adams transferred his case to the only court remaining: that of public opinion. Though far from the only party battered by the Land Bank fiasco, he was the sole debtor who chose to publish the details of his odyssey.

In the year-old *Boston Gazette* Adams presented himself as an injured innocent, a guise he wore more comfortably than that of moonlighting cobbler. His account of the "extraordinary transactions" ran in two parts, the second splashed across most of the front page. Though it affected only one family, he believed the ordeal would be of interest to all; already he excelled at inflating a small issue into a larger one, of salvaging radiant principle from a slag heap of detail. He squared off against the sheriff charged with confiscating his estate. (He was the sheriff mauled in the Knowles riot.) "His treatment of me," Adams conceded, "has been with all that politeness and humanity which could be expected from one touched with true sympathy, and conscious of the severity of the precept he had to execute." It was a cool statement in what would become a familiar tone; Adams could sound at once stinging and submissive. He had applied for no favors. He merely demanded justice, "and God be thanked, in an English government we have a right to expect it."

It is not impossible that his defiance increased the assessment. Either way, finances weighed on Adams heavily, which may or may not explain what followed. A week after the public complaint, he was elected one of Boston's six tax collectors. It would be difficult to name another position for which Samuel Adams was so spectacularly unsuited. Nor was tax-collecting a position Bostonians eagerly embraced. It was nearly as difficult to draft a collector as a constable, a post Adams had declined in 1744. Most paid a fine to avoid service. Incumbents regularly begged off.* On at least one occasion the town amused itself—or vented its frustration—by electing as collectors several slates of rich merchants, Hutchinson among them. All avoided service.† Prominent men, and Harvard men, did not collect Boston taxes, a task that fell instead to keepers of taverns and layers of brick. Over the next decade Adams's colleagues would be a shipbuilder, a candlemaker, a baker, a shop owner, and a brewer.

He would no doubt have been elected sooner or later. Well respected, he turned up as a referee in court cases. He lent a hand with the town census, inspected the schools, and served on various church committees. In 1758, he served as a proprietor's clerk for a group establishing a town in present-day Maine. A collector earned a premium on the revenue he collected, in Adams's case a sum of roughly 135 pounds a year, or a schoolmaster's salary. There was, however, compelling reason not to serve. Adams was responsible for his assessment whether it materialized or not. His share was backed by a bond, guaranteed by two friends. Together the three appeared before the town treasurer, where Adams swore to "well and faithfully collect" all town, county, and provincial taxes. A hint of desperation hangs around the decision, given what a well-meaning relative termed the "natural aversion he had to details of pecuniary calculations." The family assumed that he accepted the office at the urging of friends. He had yet to meet the one whose counsel would have been most valuable. Musing later on town governance, John Adams noted: "Collecting taxes has laid the foundation for the ruin of many families."

Adams would be deprived of another confidant that summer. On July 6, 1757, Elizabeth gave birth to a stillborn son. His father would remember him

---

* Some appointments seem to have been intended as revenue producers. It was fairly obvious which young husband would choose to pay rather than to leave the side of his new bride for a night policing chilly Boston streets.
† Based on property assessments, all men over the age of sixteen paid taxes. The sole exemptions were the governor and lieutenant governor, the clergy, teachers, and anyone connected with Harvard College, including its students. Ben Franklin would not have been pleased.

as their fifth child, though he was in fact their sixth. The grief was compounded by alarm. The delivery was difficult, leaving Elizabeth to languish for days. She wound up in bed, if ever she left it. Early on a Monday morning, three weeks after the birth, she breathed her last. She was thirty-two. The couple had been married for nearly eight years. No letters between them survive. None may have existed, the two having seldom strayed from each other's side. Nor have we any account of the funeral, presumably a well-attended, deeply moving affair. Adams's father-in-law presided at the New South Church, his brother-in-law at the Old North. At once brusque and sentimental, the Reverend Checkley wept freely in the pulpit. By the 1750s he had cause to be shattered: Elizabeth was the tenth child the Checkleys had lost.*

Adams reached, as always, to his faith. "She ran her Christian race with a remarkable steadiness and finished in triumph," read his epitaph for Elizabeth. In the family Bible he added: "She left two small children. God grant they may inherit her graces!" He exerted himself to see that they did. Boston parents were known to be attentive to the point of idolatry. Still, the extended family marveled at the tenderness with which Adams cared for his son and infant daughter, whom for some time he raised on his own. He displayed no impatience on that front either. Given the wartime casualties, given the dangers of the maritime trades, Boston practically blossomed with widows. Where friends barely paused between wives, Adams would wait seven years to remarry. Paul Revere would be a widower for all of five months.

It was at the end of his first year of widowerhood that the showdown Hutchinson immortalized—with Adams sending the sheriff packing—occurred. In and out of the Town House chamber, he continued to fend off attempts on the family estate, advertised for auction no fewer than six times. A public call-and-response ensued. Sheriff Greenleaf would announce an auction for the following Tuesday at 3:00 p.m. Adams would publish a letter on the legal irregularities, so that "any gentlemen who may be inclined to purchase may be aware of the difficulties that will

---

* The expectations may have been low all around. Adams never forgot that his father had sired twelve children, of whom only three survived him. Even for the times, the math was harrowing.

unavoidably arise." It was in fact likely, he asserted, that "every step leading to it may be deemed strange and unwarrantable by the Constitution
and Laws of Great Britain." (At one point he inserted an additional barb:
an earlier sheriff had hesitated to pursue the matter so as not "to subject
his own estate to danger.") Adams acknowledged that he raised a considerable fuss. Some doubtless felt he had gone on long enough about the
rights and privileges of British subjects. He was only getting started.

If Adams wrote with certainty it was, he explained, because he had
consulted the most eminent legal authorities around. Lest he be thought
unreasonable—a charge he labored all his life to avoid—he would clarify: After fourteen years the case had still not been adjudicated. He had
never been granted a hearing. There was some "dispute whether the
estate is indebted to the Land Bank Company or the Company to the
estate." Were any balance due, he would happily pay it. The commissioners themselves had expressed sympathy for the proceeding, and, after
more than a decade's wrangling, presumably knew of what they spoke.
Various contrivances had been attempted to snatch the estate from his
hands. They had been foiled. They would be again. Meanwhile should
anyone attempt to purchase the estate, he should count on contending
with owners who would defend it "with the whole strength of law."

Three years later, a widower, he was every bit as disagreeable as
Hutchinson suggested in defending the roof over his family's head. Again
the property—the home, the malthouse and outbuildings, the garden, the
wharf, the docks, the flat—was advertised for sale. Adams reminded the
sheriff intending to conduct the auction the following afternoon that his
predecessor had abandoned the effort. "How far your determination may
lead you," Adams darkly warned, "you know better than I." He was fortunate in his adversary; Greenleaf was neither particularly resolute nor principled. In his first career he had accepted bribes for selling confidential
government materials. As sheriff, he preferred paths of least resistance. By
fits and starts, the Land Bank untangling proceeded. Greenleaf never again
advertised the Adams property for sale.

THE TENACITY WITH which Adams held off Greenleaf should have served him well as a collector of taxes. He did not deploy it. Mostly he seems to have offered dispensations. He may have been elected for that reason; the popular tax collector was the inefficient one. Assuming Adams accepted the post for the income, his timing was poor. The economy deteriorated further. Military expenses lay heavy on the town, its commerce interrupted by the French and Indian War. Reports of bankruptcies swelled the papers. It was not unusual for a prosperous distiller to find himself in duress by the late 1750s, when—having auctioned off his furniture and carpets, his sugar-boiling utensils, his silver-hilted sword and his slave—he might apply for a tax abatement due to "his very considerable losses in his trade and business."

The office sustained Adams through a difficult time. He lost his mother, most likely in 1758, and nursed both children through the measles early in 1759, when his brother died as well, leaving an estate worth a negligible ninety-one pounds. The catastrophes piled up. On March 18, 1760, Adams would have been startled by a thunderous blast on the wharfs; it could be heard in New Hampshire. Two days later a fire raged blocks from his front door, roaring from Griffin's Wharf to a nearby arsenal, where it met with a powder reserve. Flames leapt across town, consuming hundreds of homes and warehouses. Friends escaped with nothing. The smell of charred wood hung in the air for days; the ruin evoked comparisons with the burning of Rome under Nero, or the destruction of Lisbon by earthquake. Smallpox swept afterward through Boston. Drought, a violent, waterfront-wrecking storm, and an earthquake followed. There seemed no end to the travails. The only plague missing, it was observed, seemed to be witchcraft.

The 1760 fire wreaked particular havoc on Adams's ward where, he noted, "it raged with great desolation." Already the collectors were at their wits' ends; the town was pious and well managed but no more eager to part with hard-earned wages than any other community in history. Nor was Adams alone in his difficulties. Plenty of collectors took years to close accounts. In 1750 one labored valiantly to collect his 1734 sums.

Collectors resorted often enough to legal action, as did Adams, who took ropemakers and widows, blacksmiths and innkeepers to court, sometimes for as little as eight pounds.

Others saw the problem differently. As a committee formed to rectify the situation put it, the muddle had been "occasioned by the neglect of the collectors, or some of them, and the backwardness of the inhabitants to pay owing to the great lenity of the collectors." All felt they were extracting from stones, though some met with more success than did Adams. He fell steadily behind. Confusion in accounts came naturally to him, but here he surpassed all expectation. By 1764 he had accumulated a debt of 8,000 pounds, more than twice that of the second-most dilatory collector. For the same sum, he could have built two buildings at Harvard.

Ineptitude seemed the obvious explanation; a collector had, after all, the power to seize and sell delinquents' properties, an option Adams may have found unappealing in light of his own ordeal. Two other possibilities presented themselves. It was baffling that someone who browbeat sheriffs could not manage to winkle eight or nine pounds out of chairmakers and truckmen. Was something more pernicious than carelessness with public funds at work? Was Adams indulgent, or was he corrupt? Many on his list had absconded; were his bond called, Adams would be ruined. However great his legal jeopardy — the treasury sued the collector rather than the taxpayer — his negligence cost him no friends. In 1765, after eight years of spotty collecting, he finally refused reelection. The following year a well-wisher established a private collection to settle his debt. More than half Adams's benefactors were Harvard men, deacons, doctors, and judges. Several were very rich. One — "a gentleman of distinction" — preferred to donate anonymously. Among them they raised nearly 1,100 pounds. The largest donor by far, having contributed nearly a quarter of the sum, was John Hancock.

Repeatedly Boston attempted to sue its three tax-collecting underperformers. Adams proceeded from six-month extension to six-month extension. On the morning of March 22, 1768, he appeared before the town meeting. A petition was read to grant him an additional six months. A counterpetition surfaced, signed by, among others, Thomas Hutchinson's brother. It advocated prosecution. After a warm debate, a large majority rejected Adams's appeal. The question somehow reappeared on the afternoon agenda, when close associates arranged for a reprieve. A year later, Adams had still not produced the funds. His home stood again in jeopardy.

In 1769 he submitted a new petition, read aloud at a town meeting. He had served his fellow citizens for eight years. Despite his best efforts, he had failed to collect the sums due. "Poverty and misfortune," he explained, had intervened. The fire and epidemic had not helped. The demands of the town's treasurers "were continually more pressing upon him than were the abilities of those, upon whom he depended, to enable him to answer them." Against his better judgment, he had applied funds received in the new year to deficiencies of the previous one. (It was a common practice.) But he had got off to a flying start, having paid his first years in full. And in all he had collected over 51,000 pounds! He submitted his accounts. To the best of his knowledge they were accurate, though he conceded that his numbers might be approximate, marred by "unavoidable errors which may happen on so large a sum and in so great a number of hands." For a partial sum he hoped that he might be released from his obligations and someone else appointed to pursue the outstanding monies. Tongues clucked. After a sustained debate—no one cared for the list of Adams's debtors to be read aloud—the meeting replaced him with his bondsman.

The debt would be forgiven. The missing funds trailed Adams for years, when he took his place among what friends of government termed a "rebellious herd of calves, asses, knaves, and fools," and when he could be written off, sneeringly, as "the very honest Samuel Adams, clerk." Naturally a man who pilfered from the Massachusetts treasury would lead a charge against imperial taxes! That, anyway, was the view among some people. It was not the prevalent one. After nine years of tax-collecting, between summonses to explain his accounts, Adams was elected to the House of Representatives, which suggests something about how Bostonians felt about taxes, Samuel Adams, or both. He sported an additional qualification. Some contended that the rich were best suited to occupy public office, least liable as they were to corruption. Was a man intimately acquainted with poverty not a wiser choice, immune as he was to such temptations?

Adams did his enemies one additional favor. It was never easy to pin him down, careerless as he was. When a Tory derided a group of Bostonians, identifying each by his trade, he could find none to assign to Adams. He could however be designated—in a snide borrowing of the Roman term for taxmen—"Sam the publican," dismissed as someone who had "forfeited the good opinion of his fellow citizens, by his peculation and abuse of a public trust." London heard of him soon enough as "a man of superior cunning" who "in a most notorious manner, cheated the town of a sum not less than 2,000 pounds sterling." Within a decade he would be credited with having set the 1747 blaze that had gutted the Town House. By the time royal governors found themselves obliged to explain to their superiors who precisely Samuel Adams was, they had two careers at the ready. He was a notorious embezzler. Or he was a geyser of sedition, a canny, commanding writer, famed above all for "his cheating in the Land Bank scheme and burning the books."

V

NOTHING COULD HAVE GIVEN GREATER DISGUST

No great thing happens suddenly.
— REBECCA WEST

HERE COMES Samuel Adams then, a graying widower, inexpensively and unremarkably dressed, familiar with nearly everyone who crosses his path. He is all loose ends and blighted promise. He has held off his father's creditors, but his house is in disrepair. He has run the malt business into the ground. Charges of financial impropriety cling to him; a potential prosecution stubbornly follows him around. He could be embarrassed by his brushes with bailiffs but, cheery and congenial, has elected not to be. He has time to talk. Suffused in and affirmed by his faith, he offers up religious wisdom for any occasion. He carries himself with the serenity of someone on intimate terms with another world. He is devoted to his children, whom he arranges to have inoculated this spring against smallpox. He is a favorite of his friends' children. If you look closely you notice that a quiver has crept into his hands. He appears to be shambling his way to obscurity. His fortunes will not improve but events are about to meet him halfway; the House of Commons is on course to blast him from his aimlessness. Hutchinson would gripe that—having miraculously escaped the wreckage of his tax-collecting—Adams's improbable ascendancy began now, in 1764. Soon he will preside over Boston by, as one woman deemed it, falsehoods and subterfuges. He is forty-one years old.

Where is he headed, or where does he think he is headed? True to his word, he appears allergic to plans. We know that by the 1760s he had found his way to various political back rooms, including the garret of a bricklayer's spacious home, where a tight group gathered, the heirs to the Caucus Club frequented by Samuel Adams Sr. Mugs at hand, pipes lighted, they settled Boston appointments and contemplated the news of the day, enjoying "the little tattle of the town." Insofar as Adams has a mentor in those smoke-filled quarters, it is round-faced, almond-eyed James Otis Jr., another well-born son of a justice of the peace. Three years behind Adams at Harvard, portly Otis is as impulsive as Adams is even-keeled. Only one of them has ever complained of "miserable, despicable, and arbitrary government" at Harvard College. Adams would have heard Otis deliver a valedictory address at his graduate commencement, also Otis's undergraduate ceremony. Already a colorful orator, Otis was to become a fluorescent one. As Adams drifted over the post-collegiate years, Otis read deeply, immersing himself in the law. He established a reputation as a brilliant practitioner of a profession creeping out, by the 1750s, from its years of ill repute. Otis thought with an intensity that left his muscles twitching. He could speak extemporaneously for an entire afternoon and did, on February 24, 1761, without interruption, for nearly five hours.

On behalf of sixty-three Massachusetts merchants, Otis argued that Tuesday against the newly fortified writs of assistance, open-ended warrants that allowed Crown officials to enter and search premises for contraband. The writs had been issued with cause. Smuggling was dear to Bostonians; from it derived many of the greatest New England fortunes. In a rousing discourse, Otis contended that the newly authorized writs were unconstitutional. He touched on sensitive issues and crystallized a number of free-floating ones. For years the relationship with the mother country had remained ill-defined, the Massachusetts charter—a document that predated a population surge, the French and Indian War, and the emergence of American industry—vague and outdated. Otis contended that Parliament might well have the right to regulate American trade but did not enjoy the power to tax it. Swerving from law to

principle, he delivered a tirade. An unlimited writ invited abuse, expos-
ing a private citizen to the mercy of a petty officer. Not only was a man's
house his castle, but every man enjoyed an uncontested right to his life,
liberty, and property. Fundamental to the British Constitution, those
rights were inherent and inalienable. No colonist could be cheated of
them by a "fiction of law or politics or any monkish trick of deceit and
hypocrisy." Before five scarlet-robed justices, Otis lost his case but made
an indelible point.

He argued his case before Thomas Hutchinson, presiding for the first
time as chief justice of the Superior Court. Nothing could have been
more galling to Otis. A year earlier the sitting chief justice had died. Even
before the burial, Otis had called on Hutchinson, then lieutenant governor. Might he exert his influence to see that Otis's eminently qualified
father ascend to the bench? Or had Hutchinson himself an eye on the
office? Hutchinson swore that he harbored no such ambitions. He was
not a lawyer. The appointment came his way all the same. Swallowing
his reservations, he accepted only after every assurance that the governor
had no intention of considering the senior Otis.

By the spring of 1763, a newly elected member of the Massachusetts
House, Otis had taken to snapping publicly at Hutchinson. The lieutenant governor prided himself on his candor and disinterest. Why then
had he claimed he did not want the appointment? The hectoring earned
Otis enemies. One parody of him occupied the entire front page of the
March 28, 1763, *Boston Evening Post*. To some he seemed at war with the
whole human race. Adams may have flinched at the excesses: Otis
expressed himself in torrents and tantrums while Adams wrote some of
the most tightly reasoned prose in North America. One man was foulmouthed, the other decorous. Adams counted all the same among Otis's
staunchest defenders. Otis had filed several tax cases for him; over the
next years Adams would serve as his lieutenant, wingman, accomplice,
ghostwriter, and editor. Briefly, they sounded interchangeable notes. As
pertinently, they shared an aversion. Otis set his sights on destroying the
lieutenant governor, an agenda that by no means disturbed Adams. John
Adams would say that he and his cousin agreed from their earliest

acquaintance in their commitment to American liberties—and in their conviction that those liberties had more to fear from Thomas Hutchinson "than from any other man, nay than from all other men in the world."

Already tensions had made themselves felt. Days after the *Boston Evening Post* skewered Otis, Adams wrote Andrew Oliver Jr., the friend who, alongside his father, had underwritten Adams's tax-collecting. Adams enclosed a certificate from the town. The bonds for which Oliver had posted security were now canceled. Adams could not thank him enough for the "unremitting friendship." He also warned of swirling rumor and noxious innuendo. Oliver should disregard what he might hear. "We are fallen into such perilous times that a man must even break off all social connections to avoid being embroiled in a party, and there are some who are industriously sowing the seeds of jealousy among friends," sighed Adams. He sounds like someone caught uneasily between loyalties and obligations, as he may well have been. Andrew Oliver Sr., then the provincial secretary, was Thomas Hutchinson's brother-in-law. By the 1770s the two families would be joined four times in marriage.* Adams closed on a cryptic note. He could be less opaque, he hinted, at a future date.

Throughout 1763 Otis glared at a three-story, pilastered brick mansion on the north side of Boston. The fireballs he launched in that direction likely accounted for Adams's abashed note. Boston was a small town; there was awkwardness all around. Otis had sworn, Hutchinson took it upon himself to inform the public, "that he would do all the mischief he could to the government, and would set the province in a flame." The papers brimmed with Otis's snarls and the ripostes of Hutchinson's friends. Otis's zeal was all well and good. But the objects of his resentment stood far beyond his reach. He was "but barking at the moon."

Hutchinson found himself baffled. Otis buried the hatchet, dug it up, buried it again. He flattered Hutchinson to the skies at every public gathering "and as soon as he goes home sits down," Hutchinson wrote,

---

* The extended family enjoyed a lock on political offices. For one critical stretch of the 1770s, all Massachusetts lieutenant governors and chief justices were Hutchinsons or Olivers.

"to libel me."* He attempted to shrug off the attacks; they were not worth mentioning, he stoutly insisted, after mentioning them. Instead he contemplated some writing of his own. He had in mind a history of the Massachusetts Bay Colony. The timing made sense: it was a moment for taking stock. The French and Indian War had ended in 1763, burnishing Great Britain's glory. The colonies had come into their own, secure in their borders and focused on their industry, though in London there was some disagreement as to whether they flourished on account of Great Britain's care or Great Britain's neglect. Hutchinson anticipated a roseate future. Over the year that followed he devoted his leisure time to the project, rarely managing more than two pages in a single sitting, composing in fits and starts, stealing a few minutes in the morning and at night, neglecting the work for weeks on end. The press of business interfered: Hutchinson was at the time lieutenant governor, chief justice, judge of probate, and a member of the Council. He was also the perfect man for the job.

Not only did he love New England deeply, but by 1763 he was its most prominent and popular citizen. His family had prospered along with the colony they helped to found. Active in public affairs, they had, over five generations, supplied Hutchinson with plenty of documents. All contests with authority seemed to have ended with his great-great-grandmother Anne, banished for her heretical convictions. Thirteen years before Adams, Thomas Hutchinson had received the same education. It took him in a different direction. For starters, he turned a healthy inheritance into a substantial fortune. Titles seemed to gravitate toward him. Most in Massachusetts took him, sniffed John Adams, to be the first man on the continent.† There was a reason why a colonial governor might appoint Hutchinson to the bar despite his lack of expertise. He read deeply, unraveled problems patiently, understood, or felt he understood, New England

---

* Others shared his mystification. Otis might resign his seat in the House one day and appeal for its return the next. His genius seemed to enable him to argue either side of an issue with equal conviction.
† Oxenbridge Thacher, whom Adams replaced in the House, nicknamed Hutchinson "Summa Potestatis," or "Most Powerful." He referred to him as "Summa."

instinctively. (Once appointed chief justice, Hutchinson engaged in a crash course in the law. He came to relish the appointment.)

It helped that—in his brand-new, pinkish-red corduroy waistcoat, or the French suit with the gold stitching and gold basket buttons— Hutchinson looked the part. Nearly six feet tall, fair-skinned, well spoken and well connected, he was mannerly if unexciting company. He carried himself with easy authority. Half the women in the colony and more than half the men were said to be under his spell. Sober and modest, he genuinely believed that he had neither sought nor solicited any position. Had anyone else intended to write on New England, he would, he held, never have attempted the task himself. History thrilled him. In a statement that could as easily have originated with Adams, he explained: "I found no part of science a more pleasing study than history, and no part of the history of any country more useful than that of its government and laws."

Hutchinson found it difficult to understand why exemplary public service should strike others as "ambition and covetousness." The disfavor wore on him. He felt that he suffered more than anyone for all of the "foolish internal quarrels." In his history he stuck largely to the facts as, he confessed, "I have no talent at painting or describing characters." The line hinted at something of the trouble of the years ahead: People remained always opaque to Thomas Hutchinson. He tended to gloss over the things that got under their skin as they did not burrow under his.* He tried to serve to the best of his abilities yet met with criticism when engaged purely in the public good. It left him exasperated, sounding, in private, highhanded. "I hate the unholy rabble!" he exclaimed that winter.

Hutchinson had worked with every Massachusetts governor since the hasty departure of his mentor, Jonathan Belcher. He was named lieutenant governor in 1758. In 1760, as the town cleared the wreckage from the devastating fire, he served as acting governor. He became lieutenant governor again that August after Boston arranged a majestic welcome for its newest chief executive. Sheriff Greenleaf marched at the head of the

---

* That did not mean he failed to savor the prospect of revenge in his *History*, as, in a light moment, he teased Otis.

detachment of guards that met Francis Bernard south of Boston and escorted him into town amid a parade of coaches and chariots. Bernard was fifty-eight, a deeply cultivated, Oxford-educated lawyer and the father of ten. He had fine taste in music. He considered himself an amateur draftsman. He knew all of Shakespeare by heart, or said he did; no one in America could have tested him. As a friend put it, Bernard "told a thousand good stories, and everybody was pleased and happy in his society." He had neither the finesse nor expertise of his predecessors but was steeped in colonial affairs, having served as New Jersey governor. Though he had hoped to land either in New York or Pennsylvania, he was happy to find himself in Massachusetts, where he looked forward to the refined conversation and music that had evidently been lacking in Perth Amboy. With his family he moved a few blocks north of Adams, to the edge of Boston Common, settling in for what he could see would be "a quiet and easy administration." He intended to steer clear of provincial debates. His predecessors had intervened at their peril. "This people," Governor Bernard assured his London superiors, "are better disposed to observe their compact with the Crown than any other on the Continent that I know."

IN SEPTEMBER 1763, the prime minister of Great Britain, George Grenville, conferred with a trusted friend. It seemed the Crown extracted revenue from the North American colonies of between one and two thousand pounds, which cost seven or eight times as much to collect. What, asked Grenville, could be done to correct the equation? In the course of the American wars British debt had ballooned. Reports of colonial prosperity circulated freely. The mother country maintained troops in North America at great expense. Should the colonies not contribute to their own protection? New to his position, eager to prove himself, Grenville solicited ideas from his peers. Not for the first time, it was suggested that the duty on molasses imported to America be lowered, to discourage smuggling, and enforced, as it had not been previously.

What became known as the Sugar Act presented itself as a means to raise monies for "defraying the expenses of defending, protecting, and securing" the colonies. Great Britain had spent much in America, Grenville reasoned. "Let us now avail ourselves of the fruits of that expense." With few objections and little attention, Parliament passed the Act on March 9. It was difficult to oppose: Grenville had halved a duty. He attempted merely to bolster efforts to collect it. A little austerity was in order. With the king's signature, the Sugar Act became law on April 5, 1764.

Nearly a decade earlier, well before Samuel Adams discovered the joys of extracting funds from his neighbors, another Boston native had explained the dangers of raising an American revenue. It was understood to be the right of Englishmen to be taxed only by their consent. The colonies had no representative in Parliament. To compel payments under the circumstances amounted to "treating them as a conquered people, and not as true British subjects," explained Benjamin Franklin, outlining the multitude of ways in which the colonies already paid British taxes. Trade was strictly regulated in favor of British merchants, whom the Americans enriched, and who in turn filled British coffers. Was that not tantamount to taxing the colonists themselves? Franklin added a reminder that royal governors—often planted in America to make fortunes, with which they returned to Great Britain—had no particular concern for colonial welfare. Nor did they tend to report accurately on American affairs. Were taxes to be levied, Franklin warned, pandemonium would result. Especially when it came to imposing burdens on people, he observed, it was wise to consider what they were inclined to think as well as how they ought to think.

As word darted around the colonies that some kind of revenue act headed their way, alarms began to sound. Hutchinson raised a question that seems to have been little deliberated in London: Was this not taxation without representation? Massachusetts enjoyed the most independent administration in the colonies; imperial reform was likely to sit especially poorly there. Hutchinson had no more interest in opposing authority than he had in resisting the dictates of London fashion. But the concept grated: anyone who held that duties were to be imposed for the sake of regulating trade was fooling himself. They were levied to raise revenue. As for additional taxes, in his mild-mannered way Hutchinson

opposed them. The province would be drained. The colonists were entitled to every privilege of the mother country. Given what they had contributed to the territory and wealth of Great Britain, was it not fair that
they continue to enjoy those rights and liberties? Humoring and cherish-
ing the colonies made more sense than taxing them.

Before official word of the Sugar Act arrived, a committee was
appointed to prepare instructions for the Massachusetts House. How
should they reply to London? A town meeting drafted Adams to prepare
the response. For some time he had been honing his style along with that
of Otis, who submitted his pages so that Adams might "polish and burnish" them. That May he supplied a sample of the "simplicity, purity, and
harmony of style" that was said to distinguish all his work; he read his
lines aloud, several times, for the town. In ringing prose, he pointed out
that the colonies were useful to the Crown only to the extent that they
prospered. (Bernard himself evoked the killing of the goose that lay the
golden eggs.) Already they paid taxes, sending considerable funds across
an ocean while eking out only a modest subsistence themselves. Further
heightening apprehension, Massachusetts knew that a Stamp Act too was
under discussion. Adams probed the logic behind both pieces of legislation: "For if our trade may be taxed," he asked, "why not our lands?" And
why not the produce of those lands, "and in short everything we possess
or make use of?"

The response was as artful as it was vigorous. Only some New
Englanders participated in the molasses trade. Especially outside Boston,
most owned land. And Adams went further: Were taxes levied upon the
colonies without representation, did that not reduce them from "the character of free subjects to the miserable state of tributary slaves?" The colonies claimed their rights as British citizens not only by charter but by birth,
a statement the meeting would modulate. But what amounted to the first
public salvo against imperial authority fell to Adams. So did an equally
dangerous suggestion. Adams asked that the other colonies endorse the
Massachusetts appeal, so that "by the united applications of all who are
aggrieved, all may happily obtain redress." By mid-June a committee began
to sound out other American legislatures.

Nothing Adams included in his first public paper diverged from sentiments he had long expressed. And his opinions aligned with those of Otis, with whom he had clearly conferred. In a much-read 1764 pamphlet, Otis contended that anyone who took property without consent deprived a subject of his liberty: "If a shilling in the pound may be taken from me against my will, why may not twenty shillings? And if so, why not my liberty or my life?" He threw in a reminder that the colonies had, until recently, been settled without the least expense to the mother country. They prodigiously enriched Great Britain. No manufactures from a European power other than Great Britain could be introduced to the colonies, "and no honest man desires they ever should." He affirmed the "undoubted power and lawful authority" of Parliament to legislate for America.

As uneasiness mounted around the new legislation, Adams emerged from the shadows, seeming, over the summer of 1764, to step out of some sort of comic-book phone booth. Otis may have launched him; the two were in close contact. Adams evidently turned out additional unsigned pieces for the House. He may have been propelled by British overreach, to which he would owe his career. There was a third possibility, too: if Elizabeth Wells and ambition did not arrive together, they arrived simultaneously. At twenty-eight, Elizabeth was fourteen years Adams's junior, the fifth daughter of a family friend who worshipped at the Old South Church. The match was advantageous on neither side: Elizabeth's father was the prominent distiller who, newly bankrupt, had sold off his sugar-boiling utensils and household goods. Adams himself continued only to muddle along; after 1764, he would devote less time than ever to making a living. His former mother-in-law attempted to ease the new couple's burdens by bestowing on them a wedding present in the form of a household slave. In a town where one in five families owned enslaved people, it was a traditional gift. Adams balked. "A slave cannot live in my house," he declared, insisting, "If she comes, she must be free." Emancipated, Surrey remained a fixture at the Adams address for nearly fifty years. In conjunction with a Rhode Island doctor, Adams began to formulate a campaign against slavery. In mid-1766, he joined a committee to introduce a bill prohibiting the importation of enslaved people, one of several efforts over the next decades to eliminate an "odious, abhorrent practice."

In a ceremony that joined the families of two parishioners and that provided a stepmother to his grandchildren, the Reverend Checkley married the couple on December 6. We have no image of the bride, whom Adams called Betsy. At a time when it was thought sufficient for a woman to know how to make a shirt and a pudding, Betsy Adams had studied the classics, reading widely in history and divinity. She enjoyed political discussions with the wives of her husband's colleagues. She could, remembered a relative, "converse upon any subject and give a solid and sensible opinion on most." Betsy would have reminded Adams of what resourcefulness looked like: when wartime provisions later made pens scarce, she improvised with a pair of scissors, dipping the points in ink. She begged her husband to forgive her penmanship. (It was exemplary.) Cannon blasts a few miles from her front door would not unsettle her. Inconveniences were trifling, she swore, especially when founding a mighty nation. Steady of mind, cool of temper, she was deeply principled, enough so to carry an immovable grudge. Her husband solicited her views and read aloud to her from his correspondents. He relied on her to convey messages to associates. Betsy was renowned for her housekeeping, which in Boston meant she was a champion of thrift. Adams's children became hers; there are hints of a miscarriage, but none of any additional pregnancies.

Having spent seven years on his own, Adams advocated enthusiastically, early in his second marriage, for the institution. "You will allow me to be a tolerably good judge," he wrote a relative poised between bachelorhood and wedlock, "having had experience of each in double turns." He confided that he had carried around a couplet in his head since his youth: "Sure is the knot religion ties / And love well-bounded never dies." In a giddy letter of the same season, Betsy dictating to her husband, who transcribed her words, the two asserted that one might expect one's greatest happiness in matrimony. She was easy, light-hearted company; Adams would tease about her sauciness in looking over his shoulder while he was writing—"a trick I cannot break her of," he revealed to his correspondent, in a letter that she previewed.

A year after their marriage, the two spent a summer weekend as houseguests of John and Abigail Adams. Abigail found the couple charming: "In them is to be seen the tenderest affection towards each other, without any fulsome fondness, and the greatest complaisance, delicacy, and good breeding that you can imagine, yet separate from any affectation." They reminded her of a Scottish love poem, in which mutual esteem meets mutual desire. Adams was always happiest, he would report later, from Philadelphia, with a letter from Betsy in his hand. After ten years of marriage, she wrote her husband: "Indeed my dear I am never more happy than when I am reading your letters or scribbling to you myself." As for what she saw in Adams, political obsessions and professional misfires aside, we have the word of a notorious tough grader. Betsy's new husband, wrote John Adams, was a man of "refined policy, steadfast integrity, exquisite humanity, genteel erudition, obliging, engaging manners, real as well as professed piety, and a universal good character." He attached only one caveat. His cousin attended too much to the public good and too little to himself and his family.

Already Adams had begun to scour Boston for young talent. It was not lost on him that John, an ingenious young lawyer, had waited impatiently for someone to suggest how he might make his name; or that dashing John Hancock had inherited a fortune. If a Harvard graduate delivered the finest commencement speech on the subject of liberty a man had ever heard, he could count on a visit from Samuel Adams. He endeavored to instill certain notions in the minds of every promising youth, warning against hostile, long-plotted designs. He pruned and polished young associates' prose. He urged protégés to center stage. He cultivated an affection for America or, as John saw it, produced ardent patriots. Within a few years, the worst thing a Crown official could say of a man was that he "was brought up at the feet of Samuel Adams."

Over the course of 1764 everything came together: the well-honed sense of vigilance, the hard-luck stories Adams collected in lieu of taxes, the resentment against overeager, overreaching officials, the attention he had garnered for his early, unsigned prose, the stray grievances and the chiseled logic. Time was about to accelerate, though first it stuttered to a halt. The initial weeks of married life were quiet ones, spent indoors amid a stalled cityscape. Boston Harbor froze at the end of the year, when temperatures hovered between four and nine degrees. The wind howled incessantly, the hardware clanging and chiming at the wharf. It felt, noted the papers, like Siberia. Then came the snows. New Year's Day delivered a blizzard. Walking remained treacherous for several blustery weeks, when Boston was effectively cut off from the world.

For anyone with time to read, it was the perfect season to pick up Thomas Hutchinson's first volume of New England history, in bookstores that December. From the 1620 settlement of Massachusetts Bay, Hutchinson had worked his way up to 1692. In an odd advertisement of a preface he apologized for the defects of the work. Colonial affairs would not interest the larger world; from his provincial perch he wrote for his countrymen alone. Doubtless they would find many of his pages irrelevant, but it would be a shame if New England's early years passed into oblivion. The colonists had brought to Great Britain a wealth and power that exceeded all expectation. They had left their native country, Hutchinson wrote, at a time when he had little cause to believe his words loaded, "with the strongest assurances that they and their posterity should enjoy the privileges of free natural born English subjects." He hoped they would continue to contribute to the greatness of the mother country. He trusted—a quid pro quo nestled softly between the lines—that American liberties would never be abused.

THE PASSAGE OF the Sugar Act, James Otis noted in 1764, "has set people a thinking, in six months, more than they had done in their whole lives before." Currents of discontent wafted through New England. The words "Whig" and "Tory," never before bandied about in America, were dusted off, the latter as a term of reproach for officers of the Crown. The "common people" styled themselves Whigs, noted Hutchinson, acknowledging a low rumble in the distance, as did another Bostonian who devoted his leisure hours to the historical record. Whatever began to disturb the thin New England air impressed itself as well that winter upon an obsessive hardware store owner who normally dealt in padlocks and copper kettles. In January, thirty-five-year-old Harbottle Dorr began to preserve a run of Boston newspapers, often in multiple copies, convinced—without any particular evidence—that he was reading the first draft of something. It would be a shame if it passed into oblivion. Dorr had plenty of material; Boston produced one-fifth of all colonial papers. In their margins Dorr decoded pseudonyms and clarified allusions, laughing and jeering, identifying heroes and excoriating villains. He too tended to his volumes when he could, in his case at his Union Street shop, annotating, indexing, and—in a sprawling, spiraling crazy-quilt—cross-referencing. Dorr's instincts were sound. As John Adams would announce at its end: "The year 1765 has been the most remarkable year of my life."

Preceded by months of rumors, word of the Stamp Act arrived in Boston at the end of May. Parliament passed it to raise much-needed revenue but also to make a point; obstreperous hints had been poorly received in London. When taxation had been discussed previously, the colonies had been spared on account of "their infancy and inability." This time the bill passed handily, sailing through the House of Lords without dissent. On March 22, 1765, the king signed into law an act requiring an embossed coat of arms on the upper left-hand corner of any document you could name. You could not print a colonial newspaper, write a will, obtain a liquor license, or buy so much as a calendar without a stamp. As of November 1, 1765, a Harvard diploma would cost two pounds, a pack of playing cards a shilling. Political appointees were to distribute the stamps and collect the tax. Warnings that the colonies felt hemmed in on all sides fell on deaf ears in London, where no one seemed to care that a bolt of wool could not be transported from one colony to the next, or that a colonial printer could not produce a Bible, when it could practically seem that an American horse needed to be sent to Great Britain to be shod.

Boston had weeks to accustom itself to the news. It waited to learn only when the Act might take effect, on what terms, and what provisions would be in force before the province fumbled on the revenue side, as even Hutchinson assumed it would. The initial reaction was muted. Adams would write of the Stamp Act only later in the year; the spring of 1765 found him still attempting to extract blood from stones. He placed an advertisement in a May newspaper warning that delinquents should remit their taxes immediately or expect to meet with prosecution, given the manifold strains on the town.

A bit of behind-the-scenes jockeying took place when Andrew Oliver, the senior of Adams's tax guarantors and a well-liked Council member, applied for the lucrative post of stamp collector. In response, a campaign was launched to block his reelection to the Council. Hutchinson braced for further displeasure, having done his best to temper a petition against the Stamp Act. While he disapproved of the legislation, he knew it would fall to him, as chief justice, to enforce it. In an unsent letter of June 4 he sounded nervous. He hoped his critics would remain quiet. The next day he collected himself. "The Act," he declared, "will execute itself." It left no room for evasion. Quibbling over a few corrections, he preferred to field questions about the first volume of his history. When time permitted he continued guardedly with his account. He had reached the years when he had to worry about causing offense.

Mid-July brought word of a blaze of indignation in the Virginia House of Burgesses. Virginia alone, it asserted, enjoyed the right to tax Virginians. Massachusetts blushed at its own moderation. A number of "factious and insolent" pieces appeared in the papers, though not everyone was on the same page. Even Otis believed the Virginia resolves treasonable and said as much, amid a crowd on a Boston street. New York lobbed several volleys against the Stamp Act as well. Days later the Massachusetts papers erupted, a shocked Bernard noted, "with libels of the most atrocious kind." The town grew more combustible as the summer wore on. Hutchinson began to worry about keeping the peace when the Act went into effect. He did not relish the task before him.

A week later he discovered how far disaffection had progressed. On Wednesday, August 14, Boston woke to a chilling sight. On the south side of town, at the corner of Essex and Orange Streets, stood a 120-year-old elm, planted by settlers soon after the colony's founding. From a branch of the massive tree hung an effigy of Andrew Oliver. While there were no playhouses in Boston, its residents knew a thing or two about street theater; the figure swung just above the main road into town, where by daybreak a gaping crowd had assembled. The "stuffed and dressed image," as Hutchinson described it, bore the initials "AO" on its right arm. Its left arm announced: "What greater glory can New England see / Than stamp men hanging from a tree." A breeze animated the dangling figure, which sported a surprisingly fine pair of pants. Around midday one of the labels blew off. His face disguised by a handkerchief, a bystander climbed a ladder to reattach it. As he made his ascent some in the crowd below noted that he wore silk stockings and an equally expensive pair of trousers.

Word spread quickly; effigies did not regularly hang in Boston. This one seemed a brazen threat. Great numbers from every neighborhood ventured over for a glimpse. To some, the effigy served as educational exercise: a procession of several hundred schoolboys were led out, flags waving, to take in the sight. Neighbors offered to remove the ghoulish figure but were dissuaded. Bernard was displeased when most of his Council shrugged off the stunt as "boyish sport." He disagreed, directing Hutchinson to enlist the sheriff. Would he and his officers cut the horrid thing down and cart it away? Sheriff Greenleaf returned before long. His officers could not dismantle the effigy without danger to their lives.

Again Bernard appealed to his Council, which again preferred he ignore the affront. Attempts to intervene would only aggravate the matter. A long altercation followed over a question that was to shape the next years: How to discourage insubordination when authority had no effective means to do so—and risked reinforcing it? Meanwhile most of Boston trekked to the south side of town to investigate. Benjamin Hallowell, a prosperous ship captain who had lent Adams money and whose debt the Adams brothers had proved unable to repay, ran into Samuel there that Wednesday. A customs comptroller, Hallowell had reason to find the sight disconcerting. He found Adams peering up into the branches of the stately tree, a five-minute walk from his front door. What did he make of this? asked Hallowell, himself a man of strong opinions. "He said he did not know, he could not tell. He wanted to inquire," Hallowell remembered Adams having answered. The phrasing may have crumbled in the transmission. The vagueness rings true.

At dusk the dummy was cut down, covered with a sheet, and paraded solemnly past Bernard's home and the Town House, to a small building Oliver had recently erected. It was understood to be a stamp office. Without recourse to axes or hammers, it was, in five minutes, reported the papers, exploded "into atoms." Word spread that Oliver's house was the next stop. Hurrying to his in-laws', Hutchinson sent the family running. In the street, the mob decapitated the effigy. Tossing the head into Oliver's yard, they fed the rest of the figure to a bonfire. They then launched a hail of stones at Oliver's windows and shutters. Soon the crowd was indoors, amid fine carpets and damask curtains, disappointed to find Hutchinson rather than Oliver, for whom a party set out in search.

Bernard—having by now fled to the fort in Boston Harbor with his wife and youngest children—believed Oliver would be murdered if found. The governor requested that a drummer beat an alarm to summon the militia. The militia colonel informed him that every regimental drummer in Boston was already in the street. At around 11:00 p.m., Hutchinson returned to Oliver's house to attempt himself to disperse the crowd. He found china smashed and furniture destroyed. Surely, he implored, the crowd had spent their rage. A volley of stones and bricks met his plea. With minor bruises, he escaped through a back room. For much of the rest of Boston the evening ended with a late-night bonfire, to which lengths of Oliver's fence, his coach door, and its cushions were sacrificed.

The following evening Bernard set down his account of the disturbances from the safety of Castle William. Facing the town, he wrote by candlelight. He could see a bonfire in the distance, "by which I understand that the mob is up, and probably doing mischief." (He was mistaken.) His Council offered little assistance. Bernard settled for issuing a reward for the arrest of the perpetrators and a proclamation for the preservation of the peace. That afternoon several gentlemen called on a sobered Andrew Oliver with some advice: Unless he were to resign his commission, "his house would be immediately destroyed and his life in continual danger." To the satisfaction of his callers, Oliver agreed.

Around 9:00 p.m., a mob of several hundred descended on Hutchinson's mansion, where they knocked furiously. To bolted doors they shouted that they wanted only the lieutenant governor's word that he had never written Great Britain in support of the Stamp Act. Windows began to shatter. From the back room in which he had secreted himself, Hutchinson heard a question: Should they begin with the coach house or the stables? Neighbors stepped in, swearing that Hutchinson was not at home. One—an elderly tradesman, active in town meetings—waded into the crowd. How had the lieutenant governor done them the least wrong? A leader replied that Hutchinson was understood to have encouraged the Stamp Act, "as an early method of gulling the people of their liberty and property." After an hour, the neighbor managed to head off the crowd. Hutchinson's relief was immense. He suspected that if he had been obliged to answer he would have enraged his callers on some other count.

In the wake of a riot more violent than Massachusetts had seen for at least a generation—the daytime crowd numbered around 3,000—several things became clear. In the first place, Bernard realized, it would not be possible to enforce the Stamp Act. Word circulated that any man who offered to sell the official paper would be killed. Bernard railed against the rabble, but men of consequence fleshed out its ranks. He counted at least fifty "gentlemen actors" among the ruffians. An even larger contingent of respectable men lurked, he sensed, "behind the curtain." The effigy had come by his excellent wardrobe honestly. And irate though the people of Boston were, they seemed to direct little of their fury at their governor.

At dusk on August 26 a new bonfire burned. Under a bright moon, a mob formed. The air filled with cries of "liberty and property." The home of an Admiralty Court official was soon ransacked, its papers carried away, after which Hallowell, who had met Adams under the effigy, received a visit. The Admiralty papers burned before his door. The mob then threatened Hallowell, relieving his home—newly built and among Boston's most elegant—of its clothes and valuables, afterward raiding its wine cellar and continuing the short distance to Hutchinson's. Word reached the lieutenant governor just as he sat down to dinner with his family. A man's house was not reliably his castle; Hutchinson fled with his children. Minutes later the doors splintered open and a horde poured in, tromping with axes from the cellars to the third floor. They sliced through wainscoting. They ripped down curtains and dismantled walls. They hacked beds to pieces. Before dawn and under the eyes of several thousand spectators, they gutted the household, ultimately dismantling even its cupola, as the sun rose.

In the eight-hour siege, looters carried off family pictures, jewelry, silver, clocks, andirons, multiple sets of china, Hutchinson's black silk Council gown, his telescope and microscope, and the servants' apparel. Feathers floated from windows. Clothing turned up across Boston. The papers Hutchinson had collected for decades were strewn through streets, history trampled by history. They included his commission as lieutenant governor, which surfaced later, its stamp excised. One of the most beautiful homes in Massachusetts was reduced to bare walls, its carpets, curtains, furniture, garden, and trees destroyed. Hutchinson made an affecting appearance in court the next morning, the sole man on the bench without judicial robes. He had only the clothes on his back; he had borrowed a coat. He looked stricken. With God as his witness, with tears in his eyes, he swore that he had never directly or indirectly, in New England or Old England, assisted, promoted, or encouraged the Stamp Act. A year earlier he had also discouraged a petition against it, however. He had watered down the House's response. Parliament may have overstepped, but a law was a law. Rights, to his mind, paled beside obligations.

From miles around crowds flocked to survey the damage in north Boston. They roundly condemned the vandalism. They also remained passionate in their opposition to an act of Parliament, something foreign to Hutchinson, who prudently weighed his words and tactfully hedged his bets, who worshipped reason and carved out excuses for authority. He knew himself well. "My temper," he noted, "does not incline to enthusiasm." That was of little assistance in a season when, in the previous day's shirt, he was left to denounce wicked men who spread false reports and destroyed the peace and order of a community.

WHERE WAS SAMUEL Adams in all this? There is no indication that he ever warmed his hands at a bonfire or escorted an effigy through the Town House, hurling insults at those inside. Even Hutchinson never placed him there. But nor was there reason to believe that Adams needed, as he told Hallowell, to make inquiries. Few Bostonians would have been better informed. From his *Independent Advertiser* days he knew about effective protest. He was on intimate terms with many of the disguised gentlemen. Through his contacts in the streets, he would have learned something of the effigy arrangements. He downplayed the events of August 14; it was unlikely that the crowd had anything more than an effigy-hanging in mind to start. At the same time, he liked to believe that the people of England—finding their rights invaded and discovering themselves frustrated by legal redress—would have responded in the same fashion. As for the "truly mobbish" event of two weeks later, the largest town meeting he had ever attended had condemned it the next morning. All Boston recoiled from that tragic scene.

Adams may not have resisted the temptation to view the wreckage at Hutchinson's address, where he noted that little remained but the walls. More than ten thousand made the pilgrimage by summer's end; it was impossible to avert one's eyes from what Hutchinson deemed "the most barbarous outrage that ever was committed in America." Certainly Adams spent some of that time in smoky back rooms, especially in the counting room above a distillery in Hanover Square, amid painters, printers, brass workers, and jewelers. Well provisioned with punch, biscuits, and cheese, a closed society plotted their next moves. In 1765 some subsection of those tradesmen began to call themselves the Sons of Liberty, as did groups in other colonies. Adams seems to have been intimate with but did not figure among the Loyal Nine, an association to which a printer friend belonged, and which had likely arranged for the Oliver effigy. The right club—"the nurseries of statesmen, lawyers, physicians," as John Adams later termed them—mattered as much as did the right pew or the right business address. A Boston man could belong to so many societies and associations that he was rarely at home for dinner.

Samuel Adams wound up more often at his desk, which was where John found him when he paid a mid-September call. Samuel wrangled with a new assignment. The town had charged him to draft instructions to their House representatives, normally issued in the spring. Events demanded urgent guidance, however. He explained that he hesitated in his attempt to pin Boston's astonishment to the page. As John remembered it, Samuel confided that he "felt an ambition, which was very apt to mislead a man, that of doing something extraordinary and he wanted to consult a friend who might suggest some thoughts to his mind." What he submitted was a sane reminder of the pillars of the British Constitution. The most essential right of a British subject was to be represented in the body that taxed him. The Stamp Act—which ignored the crushing debt under which Massachusetts labored, having defended the king's dominions—was onerous. It was precedent-setting. And it was wrong. Adams exhorted the Massachusetts representatives to vindicate "the inherent, inalienable rights of the people of this province." A congress of several colonies was to be held early in October, which Otis was to attend. It was hoped that those men might prepare a petition to the king. Overall Adams's was a tame document. He neither exempted the colonies from parliamentary authority nor denied Parliament's right to tax. Parsed paragraph by paragraph at a time when wealthy men quietly shuttled families and valuables out of town, it was unanimously adopted by the House and published in the *Gazette*, two days after stamped paper arrived in Boston.

Adams's September instructions were the last he was to draft from the town to the House. Boston held a special election just over a week later, to replace a deceased representative. After a prayer led by Adams's former father-in-law, the town proceeded to a vote. On the morning of

September 25, it elected Adams to the empty seat. He was sworn in on the second floor of the Town House in time to hear Bernard's address to the House and Council. The governor weighed his words carefully. He had passed no judgment on the Stamp Act and did not intend to. But while the measure might be inexpedient, it could not be ignored. If the colony denied Parliament's authority to pass the act, did they not also deny its authority to repeal it? Was relief not more likely if they behaved respectfully? Bernard stressed the "general outlawry" that would result were resistance to continue. Customs houses and courts would close. Credit would evaporate, fraud run rampant. People would go hungry. It was a strong speech that—after a plea for damages to be paid to Thomas Hutchinson—trailed off faintly.

Bernard also took it upon himself to disband the House until nine days before the Stamp Act was to take effect. At the very least, he felt he could prevent the assembly from "adopting the follies of the people and confirming their obstinacy." Surely tempers would cool before November 1. He applied to the House for guidance regarding the bales of stamped paper. He was astounded to hear that the shipment was "none of their business"; the Massachusetts representatives hoped His Excellency could excuse them, but they could neither advise nor assist. Bernard sent the paper to Castle William. It was clear it would be destroyed if brought to town.

When the legislature reconvened late in the month, Bernard met with a fiery response to his speech, a response entrusted to Adams. The House would have communicated its sentiments earlier, he informed the governor, had it not been so unceremoniously adjourned. It was a shame he had not denounced the Stamp Act. He was meant to be their "head and father"! Why had he not advocated for the colony? And what was all this talk about "general outlawry"? Surely Bernard did not believe the House had encouraged "the late disturbances"? It was unkind of him to cast aspersions on a province "whose unshaken loyalty and indissoluble attachment" to the king had never been called into question and never would be. Adams directed Bernard's attention to how quickly the people had suppressed the disorder, inserting a subtle dig about the governor having made himself scarce in its midst. Bernard should stop hyperventilating. He only aggravated matters when he suggested they were "on the brink of a precipice."

Parliament, continued Adams, had exceeded its bounds. Inherent, inestimable, inalienable American rights had been invaded. Both the king and Parliament had previously acknowledged that the colonies legislated for themselves. Massachusetts counted on Parliament to repeal the regrettable Act. In the meantime, the House hoped the governor would understand that they could not lift a finger to execute it. As for the destruction of certain homes, the House regretted the losses of those who had suffered in the disturbances. But the popular pulse beat high. No compensation would be forthcoming. Why should a crime committed by a few devolve on a whole community?

Adams had been busier still. Bernard had every reason to conclude, as he did that week, that in five short years his office had become "more troublesome and disagreeable than I could possibly have expected." The reconvened House moved to appoint a committee to issue a set of resolves. They had no sooner met than Adams pulled the document—"ready cut and dried," Bernard exclaimed—from his pocket. A sort of miniature Magna Carta, it consisted of a fourteen-point statement of Massachusetts rights. No man could take another's property without consent. It was unreasonable for American subjects to pay charges to a far-off government in which they were not represented.

Bernard received the document with bitterness. A more attentive reader, Hutchinson noticed that Adams had parted ways with Otis, in New York at the congress assembled to address the Stamp Act emergency. Otis believed that parliamentary representation would remedy American concerns. Adams believed such representation impracticable. Separated by an ocean, thousands of miles, and any number of misconceptions, Americans, Adams explained, "can no more be judged of by any member of Parliament than if they lived in the moon." Hutchinson noticed something else, too. Nowhere in Adams's document could Hutchinson find an acknowledgment of Parliament's supremacy, a supremacy Otis always affirmed. If the colony denied its authority to tax, why could they not altogether deny its authority? Adams may have been emboldened by rumors from abroad: the papers reported that week that London coffee-house wagers were 100 guineas to ten that the Stamp Act would be repealed when Parliament met in November.

The polish of the resolves surprised neither governor nor lieutenant governor. "I know the mint they come out of," grumbled Bernard, describing Adams, in a London dispatch, as "a considerable writer in the *Boston Gazette*." The document aligned perfectly with his beliefs, soon to prove those of the Massachusetts House. Colleagues testified that Adams served henceforth as its soul, director, and conscience. They applauded his single-minded focus. Bernard winced at the House's brusque tone, so different from any that had been used with him before. Admired in the other colonies, Adams's resolves were read in Great Britain as "the ravings of a parcel of wild enthusiasts."

Meanwhile defiance and dread pooled all around. How to proceed on November 1? Hutchinson could not imagine how the colony would survive without law or trade, especially over the harshest months of the year. What would become of the sailors, or the families who depended on the fisheries? Did Massachusetts really intend to drift into "general outlawry"? It did. The Stamp Act had upended government, but it had also drawn colonists together. Up and down the American coast, effigies hanged and were fed to bonfires. Some received mock trials or burials. Others were beaten with cudgels or shot through with pistols. There were Stamp Act monsters, twelve-foot behemoths with illuminated heads. Also up and down the coast, stamp agents resigned in terror. There would be some coordination among the efforts, which resorted to the same language, the same iconography, and the same crowd-pleasing tactics. The colonies seemed to incite one another, as reports ricocheted from one to the next. Adams spoke for merchants, lawyers, shopkeepers, craftsmen, and printers when—describing the consternation from one end of the American continent to the other—he observed: "Nothing could have given greater disgust than the Stamp Act."

Consensus regarding the Stamp Act was steadfast and universal— more so, it has been suggested, than it has been on any American issue before or since. What remained unclear was the form resistance should take. How to mark the indignity of the day without inciting violence? What laws applied? Perhaps, Adams ventured in a pseudonymous newspaper piece, mediation might, with courts closed, replace litigation. It would be interesting to see who paid his debts without the weight of the law bearing down on him. (Those who glimpsed Adams behind the pseudonym must have howled.) The public had never clamored so loudly for resistance, and with "such a thundering, all-piercing voice." If you asked anyone what he intended to do after November 1, you met, noted an incredulous Hutchinson, with shrugs. The House sullenly refused to so much as address the question.

Hutchinson's plight remained the talk of the town. All denounced it. No one lifted a finger to alleviate it. A month after the riot, he appeared still in borrowed clothes. His mansion sat empty, desolate, and ruined. He fired off appeal after appeal, concerned that events had swallowed his misfortune, that his case had grown stale. It was unpopular; those who expressed sympathy trusted he would destroy their letters. (He did not.) The same day that Bernard complained of Adams having pulled pre-prepared resolves from his pocket, Hutchinson compiled a massive, eleven-page inventory of his losses, down to the large japanned living room mirror, the ninety dinner plates in the closet, his daughter's scarlet riding hood, and the coachman's striped waistcoat. He wrote for redress to everyone he could think of, at home and abroad. On October 25 he wrote King George. He worried that people had begun to treat him as if he had been the casualty of a fire or earthquake rather than of a lawless rabble. Already the elm on Boston's south side boasted a copper plate, identifying it as the "Tree of Liberty."

Hutchinson knew of the ill will that had piled up against him. In unguarded moments he spoke of the years of accumulated resentments. He dated the animus from a currency crisis of the 1740s. Political agitators had "artfully improved" on old grievances. He dared not commit his candid thoughts to paper. "We are in such a state," he lamented, "that it is not safe to write, scarcely to think." To breathe a syllable in favor of the Stamp Act was to invite looters to your door. If this was liberty, he bristled, from his country estate, he wondered what constituted tyranny.

Adams meanwhile labored to pry apart the events of August 14, when Oliver was hanged in effigy, and August 26, when Hutchinson's house was pillaged. He repackaged vandalism as idealism, extracting principled pronouncements from street theater. He minimized the violence of both evenings: The people had meant only to sacrifice a straw figure. The small stamp office and Oliver's mansion regrettably "fell in their way." Damage to the second had been modest. Oliver had nonetheless resigned his office, to universal satisfaction. Adams denounced the plunder of August 26, in which the town had had no hand. In the midst of the unrest the governor had fled to the Castle. From his behavior one could infer, noted Adams, that the mob had risen up spontaneously. Had Bernard expected trouble, surely "he would have thought it his duty to have been present."

The reassurances did nothing to flush Bernard from his refuge. He ventured out only for meetings. Three days before the Stamp Act was to take effect he appealed to his Council for assistance. He had long understood that a "grand jubilee" was planned for November 1, a gross affront to the Crown. He braced for full-out street warfare, an insurrection of poor against rich, utter anarchy, and—given the obligatory end to port traffic—famine in Boston. He was all the more skittish given the date for Stamp Act execution, which coincided with November 5. The colonists had restyled Guy Fawkes Day as Pope's Day; boys and girls took over the streets that afternoon, demanding money from door to door and shattering the windows of holdouts. In Boston, North and South End mechanics and apprentices traditionally waged a street battle after nightfall, when—in a display of anti-Catholic fervor—carved images of the pope were wheeled around town; popish tyranny represented the flip side of English liberty. The revel had come to involve broken heads and bloody noses. In 1764 the leader of the North End gang had emerged so badly bludgeoned that he remained unconscious for several days. A five-year-old had been crushed under carriage wheels. Bernard's Council unanimously agreed that no crowd could be allowed to assemble on either November date. They ordered a military watch for the week.

Two days later, the Boston militia commander called on Bernard. He would need to revoke the prohibition; it was impossible to so much as summon a drummer. Bernard fretted that all government would cease on November 1, though wondered it had truly survived August 14. His bags were packed. The best idea, he wrote London nervously, would be for him to sail home. He was powerless, useless, defenseless, at the mercy of the people, a prisoner at large, allowed to pose as governor in the Council room "provided I don't attempt it anywhere else." He worried about blows to the head. Adams and others swore that nothing would reconcile the colonies to the Stamp Act. It had wholly and abruptly overturned a government. Only to a trusted relative, late in the fall, did Bernard feel he could hazard a few frank queries. Had Parliament truly not anticipated opposition to the bold, unbounded Act? Had this really been the season to introduce so great a novelty to America? The colonies could not afford taxes. The people were, Bernard reported, "actually mad, no man in bedlam more so."

ON THE BRINK OF A PRECIPICE

I could never plan a thing and get it to come out the way
I planned it. It came out some other way—some way
I had not counted upon.

— MARK TWAIN

NOVEMBER 1, 1765, dawned blurry and gray. A thick fog coiled itself around Boston, the weather seeming to commiserate with a sullen people on an "ill-dreaded, never-to-be-forgotten" Friday. Bells tolled mournfully. Shops remained shuttered. In the harbor, ships lowered their flags to half-mast, as they did along the entire American coast. Despite Bernard's efforts to discourage protest, word spread that the great elm now known variously as the Tree of Liberty and the Liberty Tree blossomed with effigies. The figures this time represented George Grenville and a New Hampshire–born Member of Parliament understood to have proposed the Stamp Act. Each bore damning labels on his chest. Under the elm, a sullen crowd milled about until midafternoon. Thousands followed as the effigies were cut down and carted across Boston to the Town House, where the House and Council were in session.

Bernard's eyes bulged as the procession approached. At its head was a tiny, red-haired shoemaker named Ebenezer Mackintosh, newly fitted with a magnificent blue and red uniform. A gold crescent glinted at his neck. Over one arm Mackintosh sported a rattan cane. In his hand he held a speaking trumpet, with which he broadcast orders to his troops—mob members, in Bernard's view, masquerading as sergeants and corporals. Mackintosh had led the crowd that attacked Oliver's house. He had been instrumental in the riot that destroyed Hutchinson's, for which Sheriff Greenleaf had arrested him. Threats of reprisals followed. Without consulting Hutchinson, Greenleaf released him.

Mackintosh now led a procession of several thousand with stately precision. A retinue of horse followed. Bernard understood that—risible though it sounded—the peace of the town had been entrusted to a rascally, twenty-eight-year-old shoemaker. This was what happened when government landed in the hands of masons and carpenters! Insult clambered atop injury: Mackintosh marched arm in arm with a Council member, who complimented him on the troops as they extended sour regards to the Town House. The procession continued around Boston and outside its gates, to the gallows, where the effigies were suspended a second time. Cut down and thrown to the crowd, they were torn to pieces, limbs flying through the air. The newspapers stressed the calm that followed. How misplaced were the fears of those who anticipated violence! The quiet proved that the terrors of August 26 in no way reflected Boston sentiments. They amounted rather to "the lawless ravages of some foreign villains, who took advantage of the over-heated temper of a very few people of this place." Hutchinson that week filed no fewer than five appeals for compensation.

The disingenuousness extended across the front page of the November 4 *Gazette*, to which Adams had contributed the lead article. Under a pseudonym, he lauded Prime Minister George Grenville, the great statesman and patriot. Adams extolled Parliament, "the wisest and most august body on earth." "He understood the best of Kings" stood ready to hear colonial appeals. Adams then strung up a set of villains, the "canting, cringing, smiling, hypocritical" Massachusetts men who attempted to wheedle Americans out of rights and privileges. The blame lay on those unrelenting, untrustworthy administrators. He had no need to name names. He hinted at a larger plot to ruin America by degree and took additional aim at Bernard, suggesting that he had not only poisoned the waters but contemplated subduing the country by force. (Regiments were posted elsewhere in North America under Thomas Gage, chief military officer in North America. The corps offered for Boston was, Bernard regretted, large enough to provoke but too small to protect. And while he angled for them, he hesitated, for fear of retribution, to formally request them.) It was a first attempt at a favorite Adams phrasing: Great Britain endeavored to subdue America by artifice, even while she would have preferred arms.

Some viewed the Stamp Act as a Pandora's Box. Adams deemed it a blessing in disguise. It had awakened millions to the fragility of their rights and privileges. It had exposed those "tools and sycophants" whose treachery might otherwise have gone undetected. It had united the colonies. They now had the king's ear. No one should so much as handle a stamp, Adams advised, in a newspaper that was—like papers all over the continent—published without one. Nor should anyone resort to violence. Redemption, Adams promised, was in sight. In the meantime, "Let everyone study to be quiet, and do his own business, as far as the circumstances of things will allow." His essay figured in a bundle of seditious writings that Bernard submitted to the London Ministry.

Adams pressed his arguments further over the next weeks, when Massachusetts, along with the other colonies, labored to make itself heard in London. He knew what he was up against. Bernard and Hutchinson wrote Stamp Act resistance down to the insolence of a few Boston "political scribblers" who "spit their venom" against the king and Parliament. Adams did his high-minded best to counter those allegations. Parliament had the good of the colonies in mind. At so great a remove it stood to reason that it might misconstrue colonial interests, however. Bernard that week regretted, before the House, that he could not impose unsolicited opinions on his superiors. Was that not his job, demanded Adams? America needed friends who would not be "silent upon maxims of prudence, through fear of giving offense."

Reports of a behind-the-scenes truce between the gangs who traditionally squared off on November 5 in no way reassured Bernard, who grudgingly revoked his order against the pageantry. He feared the groups had reconciled for purposes that had nothing to do with destroying a rival band's pope. There was reason to believe Adams instrumental in the diplomacy: two days earlier he had arranged for Mackintosh to be served a warrant for back taxes. Adams instructed the sheriff to collect the money or imprison the cobbler. He had pressed no other delinquent claim in the previous months. He then dropped the demand. Hardly tractable, Mackintosh seemed thenceforth willing to follow orders from the Sons or their founding members, the Loyal Nine.

At noon on November 5, carriages hauling effigies of the pope and the devil converged outside the Town House, where Bernard met with his Council. Again he was treated to the sight of miniature Mackintosh in his resplendent blue and red, the cane dangling raffishly from the wrist. Around Mackintosh music swelled; the figures seemed to dance on the wheeled stages. Several stuffed stamp men dangled among them. To Bernard's horror, no one in the chamber dared emit a syllable of disapproval. In full view the two bands sealed their union, the shipwright who headed the North End gang marching south while Mackintosh and his band proceeded north. Followed by a crowd, the parade continued around town before alighting at the Liberty Tree for refreshments. At the end of the afternoon the celebrants warmed themselves around a bonfire, to which the effigies were fed. By dark the streets were deserted. No one could remember a quieter November 5.

Days earlier, donations had been solicited door to door for a dinner to commemorate the peace. So great was the sum raised that an elaborate celebration took place, dubbed the "Union Feast" and billed as a tribute to Mackintosh for having delivered an orderly Pope's Day. Every merchant of note was invited. Most attended. John Hancock, who appears to have underwritten part of the banquet, served as master of ceremonies. The former rivals toasted each other on an evening that left Bernard sputtering anew. Alliances between the masses and the merchants made little sense to him; here was an expertly choreographed truce between two warring bands of thousands of men at a time when he could not persuade the Boston militia to heed their own captain. Under his nose and despite his efforts, the mob was establishing "a formal democracy," words that sent chills up a royal governor's spine. Boston seemed to intend to operate independently of the king. The newspapers brimmed with invective. One spoke and moved warily. Members of the House who disapproved of Adams's letter to their London agent could not summon the courage to oppose it.

On December 9, the *Gazette* would report that the merchants of the town had met the previous Tuesday and agreed neither to order goods from Great Britain nor to purchase those already imported until repeal of the Stamp Act. Several hundred had already signed their names to the boycott, which followed New York's and Philadelphia's. Hutchinson scoffed. He could not imagine Americans clothed in rough homespun. He knew better than anyone that there were virtually no nails, paper, or paint manufactured in the colonies. There were no mirrors or silver in America either; he had dispatched his eldest son to London with a list of items from the vandalized home to be replaced.

Nor was the street theater over. As the Pope's Day celebration wound its way under the windows of the Town House, fifty-nine-year-old Andrew Oliver shuddered. The dangling effigy bore the inscription: "The devil take him who takes his commission." Oliver had never formally resigned. It seemed he had not emphatically enough distanced himself from the office. An amiable man, far from the most intrepid of souls, already familiar with incensed mobs, Oliver did his best to disappear. Hutchinson chided him. His brother-in-law was overreacting! The inscription did not necessarily refer to him. Oliver squirmed all the same. It was terrifying to have one's home pillaged and garden flattened, mortifying to have one's likeness strung up and fed to a fire. He had not himself suggested that Great Britain levy the tax.

On December 16 a *Gazette* publisher called on Oliver, a letter in hand. Did he intend to accept his commission? The publisher—it was Benjamin Edes, an Adams intimate—warned Oliver of the danger of silence. Edes was holding the presses. Taking the paper, Oliver penned a short statement on its back. As he prepared for bed late that evening he received a note. His statement was insufficient; the people of Boston demanded a public resignation the next day at noon. He could expect the greatest cordiality. Were he to fail to appear he could expect to meet with the displeasure of the Sons of Liberty. Oliver woke to learn that a hundred posters, pasted throughout Boston, advertised his resignation under the Liberty Tree. Effigies were being stuffed. He drafted a statement, delivered to a group of town leaders, a group that included Adams. They assured him it would satisfy. Could he avoid further humiliation, Oliver asked—a cold rain came down that day in a pitiless deluge—and offer his resignation from the Town House? He could not. Oliver arranged to make the miserable walk in the company of trusted friends but found himself instead trudging through the mud, over nearly half a mile, with Ebenezer Mackintosh at his elbow. Before a crowd of two thousand, positioned under the limb from which he had hung in effigy, he swore that he had done nothing to facilitate the distribution of stamps. Under no circumstances would he enforce the repellent Act. To cheers all around he was sent on his way. (Among the crowd, the newspaper-obsessed Harbottle Dorr found the sight deeply gratifying.) Hours earlier, an ocean away, Parliament met to discuss repeal but opted instead to adjourn for the year.

The torrents continued the next day when, in a town meeting, Adams was appointed to chair a committee to petition Governor Bernard. The distributor of stamps had resigned. No stamps could be procured. In the meantime business and justice stood at a standstill. Surely courts of law could reopen? The logic left Hutchinson muttering. The same individuals who had bullied a Crown officer into resigning now asked what legal reason could possibly exist to prevent courts from proceeding without stamps. The customs house did not wait for an official response. After some squabbling, it reopened for business that day.

That evening the Loyal Nine enjoyed "a very genteel supper," to which they invited Adams. He joined the *Gazette* editors, Benjamin Edes and John Gill, as well as several artisans and shop owners. The organizers of public demonstrations, the Nine were on intimate terms with the House. With toasts all around, the group celebrated their cunning in the Oliver affair. They were satisfied not only with their excellent work—they had composed the letter, printed the ads, and posted them as Boston slept—but with the profound secrecy surrounding it. They trusted no outsiders and permitted no copies of papers. They were particularly pleased that all credit for the matter fell to Mackintosh.

The group had a specific question for another guest, Samuel's gifted cousin, John. How to interpret the constitutional questions at stake, and who should do so? Surely the judges themselves were not the proper parties to decide whether their courts opened or not. John thrilled to the assignment. It seemed to him the first time anyone had posed such a question since the time of William the Conqueror—or the time of King Lear. In his deliberations he paraphrased the query of his cousin's Harvard thesis: With courts closed, was the colony not adrift, cast from the king's protection? And if the colony was cast from the king's protection, did it owe him allegiance? John felt he would have staked his life on the answer. Most courts would reopen by year's end. Hutchinson refused to comply. Threatened with violence, he handed his probate office to his younger brother, for safekeeping.

It was the next December day—rain pelting his windows—that John Adams concluded that 1765 had been the most remarkable of his life. The Stamp Act had electrified a continent. The people were "more attentive to their liberties, more inquisitive about them, and more determined to defend them, than they were ever before." The stamps sat in unpacked bales. Protests had been heroic, passionate, erudite, and creative. A young Newport woman refused to marry until the odious legislation was repealed. Other female patriots refused to do their part to populate the colonies, which should serve British manufacturers right. From Canada to Pensacola, families shuddered at the Act, even if they but dimly understood it. A landowner in Massachusetts who sent his servant to the barn on a dark evening discovered the servant refused to budge: he was afraid, he explained, of the Stamp Act. (Hutchinson, who told the story, doubted the landowner any better informed.) Posterity, John swore, would applaud the spirited resistance. Meanwhile Crown officers trembled, emptying homes in town and retreating to country estates.

Early the following week John ventured into Boston to confer with Otis. He could find no trace of him until he called on Samuel. His cousin took him in hand, leading John to a smoky garret; Samuel knew precisely where everyone was. He introduced John to the weekly meeting of the Monday Night Club, which John took to be the inner circle of inner circles. The welcome was warm; it would be some time before he realized what conscription looked like. These were the amiable men who determined how and whether things appeared in the papers. They were responsible for the secret communications and imperceptible influences. "Politicians all," they were intimate with and deeply fond of one another; John enjoyed their heady analyses of governors and merchants, elected officials and demagogues. He praised Thomas Cushing, the son of Adams's former employer, for his constancy. Cushing was, John inferred, "famed for secrecy and his talent at procuring intelligence." Otis alternately blazed and raged. No one impressed thirty-year-old John as much as his cousin, however. Samuel, he noted, opted "always for softness, and delicacy, and prudence where they will do, but is staunch and stiff and strict and rigid and inflexible in the cause." Of them all he had, in John's wide-eyed view, "the most thorough understanding of liberty, and her resources, in the temper and character of the people, though not in the law and Constitution, as well as the most habitual, radical love of it, of any of them—as well as the most correct, genteel, and artful pen." John detected on the faces of each man a certain melancholy.

Certainly Betsy and their children saw little of Adams over the last weeks of 1765, when he worked overtime, if only partly in view, invisible at times even to his keen-eyed colleagues. He spent the early winter coordinating efforts and making introductions, connecting men whose interests aligned or could be coaxed to. You might well meet the captain of the North End gang at his dinner table. Adams's compliments could be found joined to a summons—marked "Destroy after reading"—from the Loyal Nine. He was in and out of many houses, though doubtless no longer that of his onetime creditor, Andrew Oliver. Two or three gentlemen of fortune stood behind the rival gangs. Adams stood on good terms with all. He knew who had supplied Mackintosh's finery; he may have recruited him. He calmed, cajoled, and conscripted. He left John pondering "secret, invisible connections and communications." Several days later, Samuel explained to his cousin that he had great ambitions for him. Methodically and furtively, as if plotting an intricate heist, he built a team, so that he commanded, John later understood, "the learning, the oratory, the talents, the diamonds of the first water that his country afforded without anybody's knowing or suspected." Unrest may have delivered Adams to the House, but he had not himself delivered the unrest. His charge for the next years would rather be to tamp down disorder, to impart patience, and to see to it that no additional houses fell haplessly in the mob's way.

At the end of 1765 — as the colony wondered whether the New Year promised ruin or salvation, as Bernard wondered whether he would wind up under the Liberty Tree, as Hutchinson wondered whether he should flee (he kept all in order to leave at a moment's notice) — Adams seemed everywhere and nowhere. On December 25 John Adams pulled Shakespeare's *Henry VIII* from the shelf. He had in mind a scene from Act I in which the king is reminded that a tax formulated by his advisors will cost him his subjects' loyalty. Henry VIII countermands the edict; delivering his people from venal courtiers and a crushing duty, he sidesteps a revolt. Days later, John opened his *Boston Gazette* to discover that someone had published the very scene. Its contributor had appended a note. Was Henry VIII's act of mercy not particularly relevant at the present time — even if the sixteenth-century sovereign failed to hold a candle to their beloved monarch? The coincidence left John marveling anew at hidden machinery and mysterious influences. He recognized neither the jovial tone, the easy erudition, nor the pseudonym of his cousin Samuel.

ALTHOUGH PARLIAMENT HAD passed an act that it had reason to suspect might appear unreasonable and swiftly discovered it had passed an act that appeared unenforceable, it did not address the issue of its mutinous colonies until January 1766. For the most part it ignored colonial disorder. Without an ounce of corroboration, the people of Massachusetts anticipated news of repeal; word that Grenville had been replaced as prime minister heightened expectations. Hutchinson felt less sanguine, though admitted that nonimportation—which he had dismissed as mere puffery—had begun to exact a toll. The slump in business weighed more heavily in London than did colonial rights; were the Stamp Act to be repealed, his correspondents agreed, it would be for European rather than American reasons. Meanwhile Hutchinson braced for the convulsions with which the colony would greet disappointment. He waited impatiently and in vain for the mails. The strain took a particular toll on Bernard. Was relief nowhere in sight? He had not understood that his was a post he was to maintain, he wrote sullenly, "'til I was knocked on the head."

Adams expected news by mid-April. In the meantime, on behalf of the Boston Sons, he reached out to Providence, Rhode Island. What did their Sons think of an intercolonial union of writers "to prevent the cunning and artifice of some designing men who perhaps may attempt some other method to enforce their schemes"? New York hoped to establish such a body, connecting South Carolina with New Hampshire. Together they might defend the liberty of the press, essential in foiling attempts to oppress. Adams began as well to modify the terms of the debate, raising questions, grumbled Hutchinson, that no one would have dared raise two years earlier. Over the March 15 weekend, the heaviest storm of the winter blew through Boston, leaving unfordable drifts on all sides. In the study off his second-floor bedroom, Adams turned from the gusting winds to his desk; Monday's *Gazette* carried a piece that laid out the colonial position in airtight terms. Of their own volition, America's settlers had chosen the king of England as their sovereign. Had they not, the Crown would enjoy as much authority over them as over "the inhabitants of the moon." Their compact was, however, with their sovereign alone. The colonists were in no way accountable to the people of Great Britain. Precisely as was done at home, the Americans passed legislation with the consent of their representatives. Adams urged the point to the logical extreme. As the two governments functioned identically, would it not make as much sense for the colonists to tax Great Britain as the other way around?

Only at the end of that March week did Massachusetts hear well-founded hints that Grenville's successor, Lord Rockingham, advocated repeal. A few stirring speeches aside, the question met with stiff opposition in the House of Commons. Rockingham was to contend with a problem that Adams and his friends had only begun to grasp: Great Britain knew painfully little about her colonies and seemed to care even less. Transactions at Court—and the adventures of assorted mistresses—preoccupied the king's ministers more than did disturbances in far-off America. In London there was little understanding of what precisely existed on the other side of the Atlantic, nor, before 1768, so much as a department dedicated to its administration. Grenville had long considered his revenue act. When finally it came time to formulate it, no one could be found to draft the legislation as no one sufficiently understood American judicial procedures. Colonial administration was little more professional. American dispatches had accumulated for years unopened in a secretary of state's closet.

The colonists knew that imperial ignorance shaded into condescension. In their far-off world they were understood to be primitives, partially civilized, like the Scots or Irish. It was unclear if they spoke English. Some Britons wondered after the color of their skin. While the colonists understood they occupied what their ancestors had termed "the outside of the world," they would have appreciated it all the same if the mother country could locate them on a map. Some in London seemed confused as to whether Philadelphia lay in the West or the East Indies; Great Britain's American holdings were thought to consist of islands, New England and Virginia chief among them. The problem went deeper than the occasional blunders of what Otis deemed "stupefied secretaries of state." Five generations earlier, Great Britain had been delighted to divest itself of a troublesome band of dissidents. Those dissidents had planted a British flag on far-off territory. The relationship remained muddled. The Massachusetts charter made no mention of Parliament. Only at difficult junctures—in the midst of an impressment riot, for example—did anyone squint to try to ascertain how exactly the colonies fit into an empire. Under the circumstances was it really surprising, asked Bernard, that the ideas on one side of the water and on the other were so different? He wrote all of America's political ills down to that lack of definition. To reconcile the mother country and her North American possessions would be an arduous and prolonged task, even, he suspected, were the Stamp Act removed from the equation.

While Boston was convinced of vindication at the end of March, the town knew nothing official for weeks. News of Stamp Act repeal arrived only on the morning of May 16. From one end of town to the other bells tolled, ships showed their colors, guns roared. Weeks earlier, confident of redemption, the Sons had advertised the form celebration was to take. After sermons of thanksgiving, the day was to be given over to "innocent diversion and amusement," four words Bernard read as "mobbing." Just after 1:00 a.m. that morning bells began to peal, beginning with the steeple nearest the Liberty Tree. Music sounded throughout town an hour later; the sun rose to banners hanging from steeples and over doorways, as to a Liberty Tree festooned in bright streamers. Swelled by strolling musicians, the streets were soon impassable. At noon cannon boomed at the Castle, a salute the ships in the harbor returned. "Benevolence, gratitude, and content seemed," reported the papers, "the companions of all." Joy smiled on every face, including some unexpected ones. A Boston woman began her day by taking up a collection for those in debtors' prison, empty by the end of the afternoon.

Bonfires dotted the town that evening, when all who could afford to were asked to illuminate their homes; Boston appeared ablaze. And the Sons outdid themselves. On the Common they erected an illuminated obelisk, decorated with portraits of various royals and patriots. It was a mild evening; giddy with relief, everyone—including Bernard and his Council—gravitated to the Common. Those who lived at the center of Boston opened their homes. On the lawn before Hancock's illuminated mansion stood a 126-gallon cask of Madeira, freely offered to revelers. Inside, Hancock wined and dined "the genteel part of the town." He too had erected a stage. At dusk, rockets flew from both addresses, as over the next hours Boston enjoyed the most dazzling display of fireworks yet seen in New England. At 11:00 p.m. a massive wheel atop the obelisk discharged hundreds of explosives into the air, the signal to retire, accomplished in an orderly fashion. No one was to think the Bostonians mobbish. The following evening, the Sons supplemented the lamps on the Liberty Tree, fitting the old elm with as many lanterns as its majestic limbs could bear. Neighboring homes glowed with colorful, life-sized transparences of the king and queen, as well as of those who were understood to have advocated in Parliament for the colonies. Words, newspaper contributors agreed, could hardly do justice to the spectacle, duplicated throughout the jubilant colonies.

The colonists had been advised to meet repeal with gratitude. It was time to salvage their reputations and acknowledge the forbearance of the mother country. A thank-you note, the Massachusetts agents in London added, would be welcome. No one was more eloquent than a Bostonian; the province could set a fine example for her sister colonies. Nor should they conduct themselves as if in triumph. It was best not to appear, as Adams put it, "haughty and disrespectful." Gloating was less the problem than wording: Grenville had put up a bitter fight, declaring the colonies in "open rebellion." The king himself opposed repeal, to which no one cared to attach his name. Who was to say American demands would stop here? And how to uphold both the right and Parliament's honor while repudiating the legislation? The solution came in the form of a new act. It circumvented the word "taxation" but included a clause affirming the Crown's power to legislate for the colonies "in all cases whatsoever." Denials of that power were deemed "utterly null and void." Repeal was certain only once the Declaratory Act was in place, and then only after late nights of acrimonious debate.

The new legislation briefly stopped the Sons in their tracks. No one cared to spoil a hard-won, long-anticipated celebration, however. Hutchinson swept the Act—a mere formality, so vague as to seem innocuous—under the carpet. Otis did the same. Adams stumbled over the Declaratory Act. Parliament had had a chance to bury her misstep in oblivion. While repealing one arbitrary, oppressive, and unconstitutional act, it had insisted on the right to do so again, a thousand times over, whenever it pleased. For the sake of harmony, he fell in with the festivities. But the spirit in which repeal was extended stuck in his craw, as did the ominous legislation itself. The colonists were, he would note, "not so void of understanding as to overlook" its meaning. On behalf of the House of Representatives, Adams that spring drafted a reply to the people of Plymouth, who thanked Boston for her exertions against the Stamp Act. To a tribute to the rising greatness of America he attached a reminder. Some men looked upon the colonies with envy. Those individuals, history would reveal, wickedly conspired to deceive the mother country "into measures to enslave us."

Law for fewer than five months and never enforced, the Stamp Act galvanized America's lawyers. It united her merchants, the town and the country, the squabbling, disparate colonies. From the Caucus Club it created the Sons of Liberty, of which many American towns boasted branches by 1766. It introduced Samuel Adams to the stage in Massachusetts, as it would Patrick Henry in Virginia. It plumped up the papers, the power of which it deliriously affirmed. "The press hath never done greater service since its first invention," declared a Rhode Island printer who, with many others, found himself suddenly in the opinion rather than the news business. The press emerged the real heroes, with Boston's writers leading the colonial pack, Adams chief among them. And while the Stamp Act put him on the map for one set of uncollected taxes, it cast another by the wayside.

Adams embraced the misbegotten legislation with the Puritan relish for adversity; what had been calculated to oppress had invigorated. It had emboldened a people until recently thought mere primitives. They were not so simpleminded after all! With only a bit of unfortunate breakage, they had made their voices heard. Assessing the months of turmoil, a rueful Thomas Hutchinson observed: "Power, once acquired, is seldom voluntarily parted with." Gazing east, Adams elaborated. "Power is intoxicating," he wrote, "and those who are possessed of it too often grow vain and insolent."

BOSTON HAD AN additional opportunity to express itself that May. For several months already, Otis and Adams had conducted what may qualify as the first province-wide political campaign in American history, publishing a blacklist of thirty-two men identified as "the governor's tools." Many had been in office for decades. Friends of the Stamp Act, they should be replaced in the spring elections. In the exhilaration around repeal the "liberty party," as Hutchinson dubbed them, scored a resounding triumph; nineteen of the blacklisted thirty-two lost their seats. His popularity soaring, Adams returned to the House with more votes than anyone else. That May he also tapped twenty-nine-year-old John Hancock, who had failed in an earlier bid for the House. John Rowe, a gregarious, well-established merchant, had been in the running. Gesturing toward Hancock's stately home from the Common one day, Adams remarked to a companion that perhaps another John might prove more useful. The honor, Adams calculated, would please the young merchant. His fortune would please the party. Hancock became a representative that spring.

At the end of May 1766, Otis was elected Speaker of the House and Adams its clerk. The position left him to care for the assembly's papers, a responsibility that yielded interesting results. As clerk, Adams could determine what was published, what appeared with a strategic delay, what was read aloud, and what disappeared into a coat pocket. He drafted resolutions and petitions, on one occasion taking it upon himself—despite his oath to administer the office "faithfully and impartially"—to substitute a more radical paper for the one on which the House had agreed. By force of personality and by virtue of his position, he wielded an outsized influence over his fellow representatives. The post also provided him with a salary of just under 100 pounds. It took the edge off poverty.

A free-for-all erupted when the House submitted its choices for Bernard's Council. They failed to include his closest associates, men who now appeared as complotters against American liberty. The governor's power to reject House candidates had largely fallen into disuse, tending, as it had in the 1740s, to create ill will. Bernard now availed himself of it, vetoing six of the House's choices, Otis among them. It was distressing enough that the election installed two vicious enemies in strategic roles in his administration. He had no intention of including his greatest adversary among his advisors. The upset—it could be a curse to know more Massachusetts history than any man alive—reminded Hutchinson of nothing so much as the Land Bank year. That debacle, too, he may have recalled, had introduced a Samuel Adams to the House.

With the sweep of the popular party, Otis and Adams effected a miniature political revolution. The breach between governor and Council was never to heal. Hutchinson was voted out of office for the first time since 1742. There was some sympathy for a man who had lost a house for the sole crime of having served the colony, an injustice best articulated by the lieutenant governor himself: "No one has suffered so much in public service," he sighed, a claim that, in eighteenth-century New England, was inarguably true. As Bernard saw it, his government was "totally unhinged." Indeed it was in the hands of a radical new regime; the Massachusetts voters had sent the entire Hutchinson–Oliver clan packing. Writing on behalf of the House, Adams launched a little spitball. Released from the vexations of politics, those worthy personages would now have more time for leisurely study of the law.

Bernard greeted the new administration with what many heard as "a most nitreous, sulphurous speech." He passed quickly from the joy of repeal to the abuse his lieutenant had suffered. The House had deprived the government of its ablest servants, scolded Bernard, demanding an improvement of the general temper. The speech left even close associates cringing. It called for a vigorous response and found one: Given the universal joy over repeal, Bernard might, Adams chided, have glossed over popular discontent and private resentments. The governor seemed inclined to assign those sentiments to the House. It entertained no acrimony. It was unrepentant for having prevented certain gentlemen from serving their country. "At such a time," Adams explained, casting some aspersions of his own, "for true patriots to be silent is dangerous." Bernard maligned the province in intimating that it as a whole had besieged the home of their lieutenant governor. "Under cover of the night," Adams explained, "a few villains may do much mischief." The people had discountenanced the rabble-rousers. A change in administration should not be confused with an attack on government. The king and Parliament had every right to expect that repeal would produce harmony and tranquility. Why was the governor standing between Massachusetts and cheerful obedience?

Two days later Adams returned to run additional circles around the royal governor. As for Bernard's slew of vetoes, the House would not be intimidated. They had evaluated each Council candidate according to his merits. They had deliberated fairly. Adams veered from the curt to the disingenuous: If his Excellency had had strong feelings about who sat on his Council, he should have communicated his wishes. The House were not mind-readers after all! "Even the most abject slaves are not to be blamed for disobeying their master's will and pleasure when it is wholly unknown to them," he protested.

Few questions raised temperatures as effectively as the question of restitution for riot victims; Hutchinson's volley of petitions could not be ignored. London ordered Bernard to recommend compensation, a recommendation he turned into a requisition, a change not lost on the House. Was the governor trying, bellowed Adams, to dictate to them? He took a minute to lecture the Massachusetts governor on the difference between a right and the propriety of exercising it, a lesson Stamp Act rancor might already have driven home. Bernard suggested the colony attempt to redeem itself. Adams corrected him. The governor's touching concerns for Massachusetts were misplaced. Its reputation was intact. The governor's "high resentment and sharp language" left however, much to be desired. Might he in future confine the high-handedness to his proclamations?

Adams's was a superb piece of sophistry, as he was surely well aware. The "unprovoked asperity of expression" of which he accused Bernard was his as well. What did the clerk of the House actually have in mind? Entranced by liberty, forty-three-year-old Adams reared from any abridgement. He labored to dispatch a crew of entrenched, obdurate administrators. An upper house composed of the governor's cronies served no one. Plural office-holding offended. He spoke from long-held conviction when he railed in June against the "dangerous union of legislative and executive power in the same persons." It made for a tight oligarchy, of which Hutchinson, with his bouquet of titles, was the poster child. Adams spoke frankly of unseating Bernard. He did not know if his replacement would be any more congenial. "Why then won't you be quiet with him?" he was asked. Bernard had lost the people's confidence, Adams replied. He preferred to keep the governor off-balance, affrighted of his constituents. Mostly he aimed to set back the clock, to return to the laws as they had been established before anyone had taken it upon himself to contemplate reform.

Adams wanted a governor sympathetic to colonial concerns—our authorities malign us was to become his battle cry—a wish that ran counter to Hutchinson's one desire. The lieutenant governor hoped to be compensated for the gutted mansion. (The sacking was all people could talk about, reported John Adams. For his part, he wished Hutchinson a natural, early death.) Bernard wanted only the sunny, straightforward administration he had expected on his arrival. To his mind that necessitated restructuring the Massachusetts government. Over and over he suggested reforms of its "rotten Constitution." At the very least the Crown should itself appoint the Massachusetts Council. The resentment wore him down. He began to inquire about other postings. Might the Carolinas, or Jamaica, or Barbados be available—or really any address other than Boston? Some posts were more lucrative than others. He did not care to consider one that might appear a demotion. Jamaica, he feared, would not be kind to his complexion. Nova Scotia might at another time have seemed a banishment. It looked attractive in 1766.

What Adams and Otis dreamed of on one side, and Bernard and Hutchinson on the other, mattered less in 1766 than what they could be said to want. All went out of their way to mangle the others' meaning, glimpsing, or pretending to glimpse, something more sinister in the wings. Over and over Bernard found his words twisted beyond recognition, scrambled from "what they know I meant to what they know I did not mean." Nearly since its founding, New England had dreaded a rapacious coven of alien officials. Those oppressors now seemed to hover on the horizon. The colonies misconstrued every imperial act as an attempt to oppress. The Crown misconstrued each objection as a stride toward independence. A dangerous dance, familiar to every adolescent, had begun: hints of refractory behavior produced assertions of authority, which produced refractory behavior. In accounts of Parliament's repeal deliberations, Adams heard over and over that the colonies were in open rebellion. No idea, he protested, could be further from the truth! The colonies were proud subjects, as they intended to remain. He could not stress enough how distant were any thoughts of separation, a figment of Thomas Hutchinson's imagination. The problem, as Adams saw it, was misrepresentation without corroboration. As did many, he sensed a conspiracy.

Hutchinson too believed in a designing, wicked cabal. To his mind it began now, when Adams and Otis stirred stray embers of political discontent into a full-blown plot. From the minute he entered the House, asserted Hutchinson, Adams had separation in mind. Adams professed that aim "without reserve, in private discourse, to be independency; and from time to time he made advances towards it in public, as far as would serve the great purpose of attaining to it." Hutchinson more likely jumped the gun. For all his diligence and fair-mindedness, for his deep dive into the law and his encyclopedic grasp of colonial history, he little understood Adams. Nor was he keen on abstract principles. They unsettled institutions. The intrepid neighbor who had fended off the first mob swarming toward Hutchinson's door had spoken exactly when he said that the lieutenant governor was a friend to the country, though "not always so much in favor of liberty as some others."

The finger-pointing extended in all directions. Bernard took to hinting broadly, skittishly, loudly, to London, and to Gage, that British regulars would not be unwelcome. He was hardly requesting them. But he would not turn them away were they to be offered. He could do little more than close his eyes and hope that—after some miracle of transatlantic mind-reading—they might materialize. Gage tried to make it easy for him, sending a letter with which he could requisition troops. Bernard shuddered. A chief of the faction had boasted "that if any person was known to apply for troops to come here, he would certainly be put to death." Meanwhile the leaders of the 1765 riots walked the Boston streets with impunity. No one could be found to testify against them. No officer dared apprehend nor any attorney general prosecute them.

Which meant that, to London, Bernard appeared vaguely incompetent. To explain how his administration had faded to a mere shadow, he sensationalized events. A crisis, even if manufactured, made him look better. Adams was not wrong to complain that Crown officers misrepresented the colonies;

to take Bernard at his word was to believe Massachusetts in revolt.* He could be histrionic, invoking comparisons to the Salem witch trials. He thought the same psychology at work. Even those who did not subscribe to what Otis and Adams purveyed pretended that they did, to avoid trouble. When, Bernard wondered, would the people wake from their frenzied delusion? (He consoled himself that he was at least acting more wisely than had the governor who tangled with witchcraft in 1692.) Nor did anyone care to listen when Bernard offered some clear-eyed assessments. The colonies and the mother country had radically divergent ideas of their relationship. In Britain, the American governments were understood to exist by pleasure of Parliament. In America, they claimed to be perfect states.

On one subject all parties could agree. There had been a rapid and wholesale evolution in thinking. The popular leaders had had so much success that the people enjoyed convictions, pretensions, and expectations "which," Bernard regretted, "had never entered into their heads a year or two ago." It was impossible to reason with someone convinced that an act of Parliament made of him a slave. The end of 1766 found Bernard too wishing the entire Stamp Act chapter relegated to oblivion. Repeal should have spelled the end of the matter, the imperial misstep fading with the fireworks. That it turned instead into a beginning would be largely the work of Adams. He assisted in separating Bernard from his Council. He assumed firm control of the House. Withholding, repackaging, and disseminating information, he transformed its clerkship into a bully pulpit. Prior to the 1760s, no one had really given much thought to the constitution of colonial government. Adams sounded its foundations. And he polished his art—refining abstract ideas to crystalline logic— until, as Hutchinson glumly acknowledged, he arrived "at great perfection." Adams soon took over entirely from Otis in making Bernard's life miserable. "That more pernicious devil," as one informer dubbed him, he turned repeal less into an opening act than an overture.

---

* He may have suspected how he was viewed by Crown officers elsewhere in North America. "A governor of spirit and dignity" would, they believed, have Boston tightly under control.

PERHAPS I AM CAPTIOUS

Politics, as a practice, whatever its professions, has always been
the systematic organization of hatreds.

— HENRY ADAMS

THE RAPTURE of repeal echoed throughout the colonies; New England resounded with hundreds of sermons of thanksgiving. Adams spent the winter celebrating in his own fashion. He did not urge his horse out to admire a wild goose on a spit, cranberries simmering in a skillet, at a friend's house. After a mishap, he avoided riding. He indulged in no Masonic rites. Unlike many of his close associates, Adams never belonged to a Boston lodge. Delighted to emerge from what he termed "the late times of universal distress, despair, and a course of great confusion," he hesitated to relax his guard. He did not see that there was call to be thankful for the retraction of an unconstitutional act. While others ventured out to hunt turtles, or to catch bass with spears, Adams fretted. He seemed to define himself by resistance. Two artillery companies washed up late in the fall, driven into Boston Harbor by poor weather. Who, wondered Adams, was responsible for their support? Massachusetts would surely provision the unfortunate men. But why was this their obligation? Did it not amount to taxation in another form? Troops were unnecessary and dangerous. The questions were the more pertinent as New England shuddered still at rumors of British regulars. Had they been at his disposal, Bernard would easily have enforced the Stamp Act.

Some also continued to sully the Massachusetts reputation. "There is a set of men in America who are continually transmitting to the Mother Country odious and false accounts of the colonies," Adams wrote their London agent, for the House. The clandestine reports seemed more suited to the administration of a Nero or Caligula. Then there was the Declaratory Act, to Adams's mind a sort of lurking serpent which, "concealed and not noticed by the unwary passenger, darts its fatal venom." The Act acknowledged American revenue only in passing. But its offhandedness confirmed Adams in his belief that a next attempt at taxation would simply be more furtive. When the imagination ran wild, Adams warned, it fixed on false dangers, trotted out to justify unnecessary shows of authority. "Perhaps I am captious," he conceded, aware that he might be conjuring a few specters of his own.

Those concerns he dispatched to a Charleston, South Carolina, merchant he had never met. The previous fall, Christopher Gadsden had attended the Stamp Act Congress with Otis, much impressed by the erudite, inquisitive straight-talker, soon to be known as "the Sam Adams of the South." During what many took to be an era of renewed tranquility, Adams reached out to Gadsden for a reason. Only by their mutual efforts had the colonies defeated an objectionable act. Only in their mutual efforts would they deter future encroachments. "I wish there was a union and a correspondence kept up among the merchants throughout the continent," Adams wrote, eager to assemble a different kind of coalition, venturing for the first time beyond New England.

Boston's opposition movement was loose-limbed and organic. One group shaded into another; there was neither a single mastermind nor an obvious chain of command. Power shifted hands, migrating among social tiers. At a given moment Mackintosh might lead the parade, or Adams and Otis, or a band of merchants. Benjamin Edes, the *Gazette* publisher, belonged to the Loyal Nine, who used his office as their mail drop. Edes did not belong to the Long Room Club, which met over his shop, and to which Joseph Warren, Otis, Adams, and Paul Revere belonged. Otis was not a member of the Sons; Edes was a member of neither the Monday Night Club nor the North End Club. Adams frequented all three.

Nonimportation—the most effective tool in demolishing the Stamp Act—had been quietly coordinated between the small businessmen of the Loyal Nine and Boston's principal merchants. No one sat at the radicals' red-hot center for the simple reason that there was none. The circles overlapped. At a minimum, Adams could be found along the perimeter of each.

When the Sons of Liberty called on John Adams for assistance, they attached a postscript to their summons. His cousin sent his regards—and strongly desired John's participation. Samuel Adams left a great deal of himself in smoky back rooms, but it is clear that he knew precisely which back room to frequent; that conversations there seldom proceeded without him; and that he connected men whose thinking, by the time they left the room, converged as well. He seemed to exert an uncanny influence on men's minds. He knew when to alarm, when to soothe, flatter, intimidate. Choking on their admiration, his enemies termed this his "black art."* A born committee man, he thrived on collaboration. The common cause exhilarated him. Hutchinson never accused Adams of having directed a mob or precipitated a riot. At the same time, whenever intimidation was hinted at, whenever persuasion seemed in order, Adams, or his after-image, could generally be glimpsed nearby.

Soon after his election, Adams arranged for the House to construct a gallery. It went up in a matter of days. For the first time, the people of Massachusetts could observe their representatives in action. As Adams saw it, for the first time the representatives could look up at their equals. The gallery suggested that the government served its constituents rather than the other way around. The people could make their voices heard, as they did, in less than elevated terms. Bernard blanched: Was the State House now a theater? He was especially irritated when he realized that Adams packed the gallery, issuing invitations to a hand-picked group,

---

* Adams worked an additional kind of magic, to the despair of one customs official. A Boston mob—furious enough to "threaten destruction to the globe"—could be summoned from nowhere "in the twinkling of an eye." Boston's leaders could just as instantaneously produce dead calm, lending the impression, for months on end, that Boston was "the best regulated town in the world."

privy to information that was kept from the governor, often for weeks at a time. With spectators came an escalation in language. Those on the floor played to the audience, speaking, or speechifying, to the visitors. The rabble, as Bernard saw them, could now listen to Otis rant, for nearly two hours, against the mighty men who formulated colonial law. He dismissed the House of Commons as a "parcel of button-makers, pin-makers, horse jockeys, gamesters, pensioners, pimps, and whore masters." Adams also began publishing House proceedings, buttressing Bernard's charge that some seemed, by every available means, intent on carrying government "nearer and nearer to the common people." What struck one side as suffrage appeared as insolence to the other.

Bernard's superiors in London failed to hear the greater part of what he conveyed—statements like "I am the worst paid of the royal governors" may not have helped—but regularly he pointed out something that should have given pause. As early as November 1765, "good men and bad men" had unaccountably banded together. A swarm of people huddled behind a few brazen desperados. Since when did property-holders instigate riots? The derision seeped out everywhere. Bernard moaned about "the low and ignorant men who had crept into the House." His Council consisted of "creatures of the people." Bernard and Hutchinson mocked Adams and his breed as "a junto of patriotic grandees." They surely noticed that Adams was the sole member of most committees who could not so much as append an "Esquire"—the honorific reserved for minor colonial officials—to his name.

Otis and Adams knew of the contemptuous terms in which they were described to London. They complained bitterly of the misrepresentation. In the midst of the Stamp Act crisis the Massachusetts House hired its own agent in London. Over Bernard's objections, to counter reports submitted by Crown officers, the House voted in 1766 to make his position permanent. For his part, Hutchinson felt effectively muzzled. He was baldly informed that he might write whatever he liked in his history but had no business criticizing the Massachusetts legislature in his letters. He took pains to restrain himself that fall, when the most contentious issue before the House remained compensation for riot victims.

Hutchinson topped the list, estimating his loss at a colossal 2,218 pounds. Though they vowed to punish the perpetrators and reimburse the victims, the House stalled for months.

Bernard found the delay infuriating, a singular display of impudence after "the greatest instance of tenderness and leniency towards complaining and offending subjects which history can give." The House explained their inaction any number of ways—they needed to canvass their constituents; applications had been submitted improperly; it was unclear if Boston alone should shoulder the burden—but the truth was very simple. Grateful though they were for the reestablishment of their privileges, the Massachusetts representatives were reluctant to fulfill directives from London. They had even less interest in gratifying Thomas Hutchinson, whose house some seemed more inclined to destroy all over again. He discharged some of his anxiety by applying himself to the second volume of his history. The years leading up to 1750 proved soothing.

From the age of twenty-six, Hutchinson had, as Adams put it, "enjoyed every honor and favor in the power of his native country to confer upon him." By 1766 the lieutenant governor held so many offices it was a mercy that he wrote of himself, in his history, in the third person; the narrative would be incomprehensible otherwise. No one had ever stockpiled so many positions nor, Adams correctly suspected, would anyone ever again. They struck him as incompatible. How could one man serve in two branches of government? It was unwise to combine the impartial administration of justice with "the meanders and windings" of politics. Hutchinson had not only reserved for himself four of the most important provincial offices, but had seen to it that the rest were distributed to family members. At different junctures both John and Samuel Adams compiled lists. Together they nearly filled a page. Hutchinson was related even to the clerk whom Adams had replaced in the House.* The sensitivity to

---

* Massachusetts men commonly handed offices on to sons, as Adams knew well. Hutchinson himself condemned the practice, tending as it did "to make all offices

tyranny abroad was all the greater given what appeared to be the stranglehold at home.

To Otis, the lieutenant governor was "Thomas Graspall," dictator general, as indeed he might have been had he been dishonest as well as quietly ambitious. He likely had his eye on the Massachusetts governorship, which he had every reason to expect. No one was better qualified. John Adams obsessed often about Hutchinson, who unfailingly sided with the Crown, but in 1766 John seethed especially at the adoration showered on the lieutenant governor. Hutchinson had been styled "the greatest and best man in the world," a living paragon, on par with Alexander the Great or Julius Caesar. The people had raised him and his family "to almost all the honors and profits, to the exclusion of much better men."

On that subject even moderate people had agreed for some time. In the years between the Land Bank and the Stamp Act, Hutchinson had managed to antagonize both debtors and smugglers, which, as has been noted, accounted for a majority of Massachusetts men. Two decades of grudges came hurtling back at him. That he was rich and easily envied, a non-lawyer who played at the law, was bad enough. Something else tugged at the Adams men. Was, asked John, this "amazing ascendency of one family foundation sufficient on which to erect a tyranny?" Did that clan not seem to be colluding against provincial interests? Adams and Otis aired the qualms widely; it took relatively little effort to turn Hutchinson's into the face of despotism. It was whispered that he had encouraged the Stamp Act in his correspondence with London, that more men stood to profit from the Act than was revealed, that it had practically been written in his home. Colonial rights were all well and good. But revenge on a much-reviled, much-envied figure of authority was also enticing. It served as the bouillon cube in the roiling water. There seemed no end to the spite against Hutchinson when, late in 1766, his enemies prepared for an election six months away. Even people he respected that

---

hereditary." Nevertheless, he saw no objections to the mingling of legislative and judicial responsibilities, a practice that dated to the earliest days of the province.

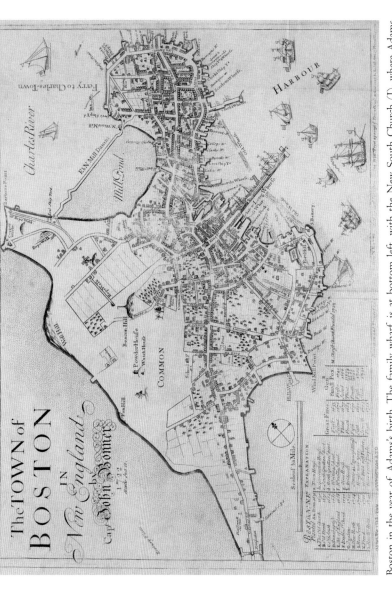

Boston in the year of Adams's birth. The family wharf is at bottom left, with the New South Church (I), where Adams worshipped, a short walk up Summer Street. The Town House (a) is located at the upper right, at the top of King Street, the continuation of Long Wharf. For some time still it would be possible to tend a potato patch in central Boston.

An eighteenth-century Parisian printshop, a more genteel address than was Edes & Gill's, where Adams spent his Sunday evenings. Reams of paper line the room, its rafters tented with drying pages. Printing was a grimy, laborious, accident-heavy business, and to one visitor a curious one: here were the *Boston Gazette* editors and their friends, "cooking up paragraphs, articles, occurrences, etc.—working the political engine!"

Governor Francis Bernard, short and heavyset, but a figure of much distinction. An amateur draftsman, steeped in Shakespeare and partial to Handel, Bernard had little taste or aptitude for intrigue. Though he had hoped to wind up in New York or Philadelphia, he affably looked forward, on his 1760 Boston arrival, to "a quiet and easy administration."

Thirty-year-old Thomas Hutchinson on a trip abroad, just after the Land Bank fiasco. The embroidered waistcoat hints at his close correspondence with his London tailor, to whom Hutchinson deferred — "a yellow metal button or blue mohair button, as you think most genteel" — given Boston's distance from high fashion.

Hutchinson's North End mansion, built by his grandfather, sacked in 1765 by the mob. "Such ruins were never seen in America," the lieutenant governor reported, after one of the finest homes in the province was reduced to a sorry shell. Thousands witnessed the vandalism. No one raised a hand to stop it.

The Town House as it would have appeared at the end of Adams's life. Hutchinson calmed a furious, late-night crowd from its balcony on March 5, 1770. Six years later, in a very different mood, Bostonians gathered under the balcony for the first Massachusetts reading of the Declaration of Independence.

John Adams as painted by John Singleton Copley shortly after the signing of the Treaty of Paris in 1783. John met with a hero's welcome in France, where he was understood to be Samuel. "It being settled that he was not the famous Adams," John wrote of himself, he became "a man of no consequence—a cipher."

Abigail Adams in 1766, shortly after her marriage to John. She found the Samuel Adamses charming, tender with and highly respectful of each other, yet unpretentious in their mutual devotion.

Mercy Otis Warren, sister of James Otis and wife of James Warren, the author of plays, poems, parodies, and an early history of the Revolution. From her front-row seat, she believed posterity as much indebted "to the talent and exertions of Mr. Adams as to those of anyone in the United States." The respect was mutual. In July 1772, Adams hoped her husband might be so good as to tell Mercy "that I have all that regard and affection for her which a man, especially a married man, can in conscience have for the wife of another."

Otis at thirty, already a brilliant lawyer, not yet Adams's mentor. He would succumb to mental illness, wandering and rambling, a friend observed, "like a ship without a helm." Adams thereafter eclipsed him, offering excuses around town for "the man I love most heartily."

John Hancock at twenty-eight, a year before Adams facilitated his election to the Massachusetts House. The gold-edged, velvet frockcoat hints at their troubled future; Hancock's "pomp and parade" struck Adams as inconsistent with republican principles. Hancock spent a fortune buying adulation, a largesse that extended to Adams. As friends pointed out, were it not for Hancock, he would have landed in debtors' prison.

Joseph Warren at about the same time, six years out of Harvard, already Boston's most popular doctor. For the next decade he worked hand in glove with Adams, who considered him his closest confidant. Having sent Paul Revere racing to warn Adams and Hancock of arrest in April 1775, Warren would be dead two months later. His arm rests on a set of anatomical drawings.

Samuel Adams posed early in the 1770s for Copley, who depicted him in the spirit of his confrontation with Governor Hutchinson after the Boston Massacre. With his right hand Adams grips the town instructions. With his left he points to the Massachusetts charter. Copley's palette is subdued; the surfaces plain; the lighting dramatic; the canvas all urgent personality. If the staged pose does not, the columns behind Adams remind us that this is a history painting: the rule of law can stand in need of vigorous defense. Widely, often awkwardly, copied, the portrait seems to have been as much an instrument of propaganda as was its subject.

General Gage sat for Copley in the fall of 1768 while arranging Boston quarters for his troops. He rests a hand as lightly on his baton as Adams tightly grips his scroll; the general seems the milder man, though there was, as contemporaries remarked, a striking resemblance between the two, born within a few years of each other. Gage serenely directs our attention to regiments drilling in the distance.

Paul Revere's first political cartoon. At the edge of a precipice, a Stamp Act dragon attempts to make off with the Magna Carta. Sword drawn, Boston advances to slay the monster, Rhode Island and New York, Virginia and New Hampshire following behind. The Liberty Tree bears the date on which Andrew Oliver's effigy swung from its branches. As he did elsewhere, Revere adapted a previous artist's work, adding figures and subtracting others but preserving the allegorical elements, down to the aerial spray of bullets.

A wildly popular London cartoon, in circulation within hours of Stamp Act repeal. "Mr. George Stamp," bends over the coffin of his favorite child, "Miss America Stamp, who was born in 1765 and died hard in 1766." One of the flag-carriers is Solicitor General Wedderburn, soon to thunder that Adams's prose had introduced Americans to "a hundred rights of which they never had heard before, and a hundred grievances which they never before had felt."

With his magic lantern, Father Time narrates a 1783 version of the American Revolution. The conflagration, he explains, can be written down to "the little hot spitfire teapot that has done all the mischief." The four continents appear in his audience; America — represented by a Native American — takes a seat atop bales of stamped paper. A French rooster blows on the fire as British forces flee before the rebel army, Native Americans leading the charge.

winter asserted, in discussions around reparations, that he was a man of unconstitutional principles. Here he came up against Adams, who, Hutchinson wrote, had "a talent of artfully and fallaciously insinuating into the minds of his readers a prejudice against the characters of all whom he attacked beyond any other man I ever knew."

Late in the year the House voted finally to reimburse riot victims and to indemnify the rioters. Hutchinson found the second provision distasteful but breathed a sigh of relief. He would be compensated in full. It was closure of a kind, though much remained still to be done to restore tranquility. On January 28, 1767, Hutchinson rode to the Town House in the governor's coach for the opening of the Massachusetts legislature. Bernard had requested his company. He was nervous about his speech. As he had since 1749, Hutchinson took a seat among the members for the address. Behind them hung magnificent, larger-than-life portraits of Charles II and James II, along with more primitive likenesses of earlier Massachusetts governors. Hutchinson remained at Bernard's side when the representatives withdrew afterward to their chamber. Although he had lost his seat that spring for the first time in eighteen years, he assumed that, as lieutenant governor, he held an ex officio position on Bernard's Council. Others felt differently. Adams would suggest that "only a warm imagination or an excessive love of power" could justify Hutchinson's presence. It was "a manifest impropriety." Even if silent, he influenced deliberations. Since when, Bernard shot back, did the House dictate to the Council? Indeed they spoke more combatively than they had before Adams's arrival. They seemed intent on depriving the governor of his lieutenant's assistance. Bernard was blunt. He had no intention of invading the rights of the people. But nor did he intend to suffer intrusions on Crown prerogative.

Both sides scurried to the history books, hurling chapter and verse of New England precedent at each other. Adams insisted that nothing in the Massachusetts charter countenanced Hutchinson's presence. He held no seat in either chamber. What was he doing in the room? He dispatched his opponent to the penalty box: it was all the more astonishing that the lieutenant governor sabotaged the Massachusetts charter when he had so recently thanked the House for the generous reimbursement of his losses. Hutchinson had attested to "the fresh obligations he felt himself under to support the rights, liberties, and privileges of his countrymen." For tranquility's sake and to spare himself further abuse, he stepped aside. He would attend no further sessions. He could do nothing right. The House condemned him for dereliction of duty.

Privately Hutchinson complained of the House's intemperate humor. "In short it looks as if they were desirous of making all the world their enemies and if they ruin the country some of the chief of the faction who are in a state of bankruptcy or insolvency will be at worst as well off as they are now," he wrote, stabbing at Adams. He attempted to ignore the influence of two or three wicked men, but the bruising took a toll. The study of New England history proved a meager palliative; just after the 1767 celebrations of the anniversary of repeal, his nerves gave out. Hutchinson ascribed the breakdown to the "long continued ill-usage received from my countrymen," to the humiliation at home and the stony neglect from abroad. Flattened, he retreated to his country estate in Milton, where he hoped, after thirty years, to cure himself of the habit of public service.

Bernard wrote the collapse down to the unrelenting attacks, noting in May that Hutchinson had "lately been ill to a degree alarming to himself." Andrew Oliver's health also suffered after the riots. "I am the only heart of oak among them," Bernard boasted to London, sounding irked with his lieutenant governor, out of commission for part of April and all of May. The bluster went only so far; the House attempted to reduce Bernard to a cipher, in which effort he assisted. He did his best to make himself inoffensive, using as few words as possible, straining his speeches of substance. (That of January 28, 1767, was four lines long.) The people were "barefaced" in their impudence. The abuse was constant. He had some idea of the opposition's endgame. In one of Bernard's friends Adams confided: "I really believe that when we part with this governor we shall not get so good a one again." Why then the torrent of abuse? inquired the friend. Bernard had lost the trust of the people, Adams explained, "and it is not to be recovered." The exchange found its way back to Bernard, as Adams surely intended.

Bernard sounded alarms. These were not trivial "domestic squabbles" likely to subside on their own. They demanded urgent attention. Might someone exert some authority? It was no longer a question of reforming the Massachusetts government but of disciplining a set of ruffians intent on ruining the province. With a new election nearly upon them, Bernard still did not know whether London approved of his purge of the Council a year earlier.*

Was anyone listening? He relented in his applications for a transfer. Especially after remarks like Adams's, he had no interest in humoring, as he phrased it, a spoiled child. He eagerly awaited some kind of check on the heedless Massachusetts House. He met instead with hand-wringing over Stamp Act repeal—misgivings built steadily in London—and with what another frustrated official termed "inconsistency, inability, and concession." Over and over Bernard applied to Great Britain for stern measures, the nanny attempting to rouse the distracted, martini-mixing parents. Over and over he met with silence. In July 1767, Bernard's patron and relative, Lord Barrington, commiserated. London made little progress on the American front. Previous administrations had got everything wrong. But what was right, and who should attempt it? he asked. Barrington, the British secretary at war, was to have his answer soon enough.

ADAMS HAD FEW illusions of how he was viewed but got a taste that summer of how the previous decades would be remembered when Hutchinson published the second volume of his New England history. In 1767

---

* An April *Gazette* piece reminded voters that while representatives served for only one year, there was no end to the mischief they could wreak in that time. Voters should carefully consider the candidates. The artful would suggest a rich man best suited, as he seemed least vulnerable to corruption. Preferable was a man on intimate terms with poverty, "because his virtues will more surely keep him out of the reach of temptation than the riches of the other." Who better to defend against the encroachments of ambitious men and vindicate a people's injured honor? Harbottle Dorr easily caught the allusion to Adams, "who," Dorr scrawled on his edition of the paper, "has always proved himself a steady, wise patriot in the worst of times." Adams believed both wealth and poverty pointless qualifications for office. While the latter was less dangerous, neither should figure in the calculus.

Adams could read the first account of the Land Bank scandal. Hutchinson derided the "fraudulent undertaking." He maintained that even Bank directors had worried that the enterprise placed too much power in the hands of the people. The colony would have been a shambles had Great Britain not intervened. And he crisply noted that no one at that time had questioned parliamentary authority. Hutchinson dispatched a box of printed pages to London, directing them to be presented—stitched as they were in blue paper, or bound by a London printer should that seem more respectable—to sixteen colonial agents and British officials, a list that included George Grenville and Charles Townshend, the new chancellor of the exchequer.

The first half of the year had been a bruising one for Bernard, who spent it teasing apart popular politics and private revenge. He had expected the best treatment and received the worst. Again the friends of government, as he called them, fared poorly in the May elections. Again he lost his Council. He hoped to forward records of the House proceedings to Great Britain but found he could not: Adams had delayed their printing. Bernard's spirits consequently soared when in midsummer word arrived of new revenue acts. It was high time authority reasserted itself; the prospect, as he saw it, reassured "almost every person of fortune and fashion." There would be, Bernard breezily assured London, no more insurrections. He believed the opposition thunderstruck, which may at some addresses have been true. Adams was unsurprised. The news only validated some of the half-truths he had propagated.

Stamp Act repeal continued to sit poorly in Great Britain. Colonial ingratitude made matters worse. There had hardly been a word of thanks! Audacity seemed everywhere on the rise. Massachusetts had compensated riot victims reluctantly; New Jersey and New York had evaded additional Crown legislation. Picking up where Grenville had left off, Townshend devoted the first months of 1767 to a new set of revenue proposals. Having reviewed various options, he settled finally on an American import tax, to be levied on a host of items from oranges and olive oil to glass and paint. Townshend anticipated a revenue of some 40,000 pounds, equal to the cost of supporting American governors and justices, to whose salaries it would be applied. Some wondered how the duties differed from a stamp tax, but few London arms needed to be twisted. The point was as much political as financial. All agreed that parliamentary sovereignty should be reaffirmed. The Acts would moreover insulate colonial administration from the whims of independent-minded assemblies. They breezed through Parliament. The king granted his assent on June 26, 1767. The Townshend Acts reformed the customs service, establishing a five-man board of inspectors in America. For some reason, it was decided to settle those new officials in Boston. As Adams dryly noted, geography seemed to play little role in the posting, Boston being "very far from the centre of the colonies."

Customs commissioners were not the only visitors expected in Boston. Early in the fall, rumors circulated that a Halifax regiment was to land imminently. In the *Gazette*, Adams responded to that news with bluster. A body of troops might well be in readiness, he wrote, under the pseudonym "Determinatus," but America would defend her liberties at any cost. Between slavery and death, the choice was simple, and "the sooner the matter is brought to a crisis the better." He closed on a temperate note. Surely the rumors would prove unfounded. Parliament had too much sense and integrity to consider such a measure. Troops did not sail to Boston that week but—unbeknownst to Adams, the *Gazette* piece sailed east. At the end of August Bernard began forwarding the "weekly libels," labeled alphabetically. Within weeks he was up to "M."

On October 7, 1767, Adams and several House colleagues called on the governor at his Boston home. Given the new legislation winging their way, they requested that he convene the House. Bernard shrank from engaging with his visitors, whom he treated with "silent contempt." He had no interest in allowing the faction to enflame the province all over again and resolved to call the House together at the latest possible juncture, late in January. The official Acts arrived the next day, preceded by rumors that more onerous duties were to follow, with troops to enforce them. (Already Bernard had reached the letter "W.") Unable to secure a proper conversation with Bernard, without a legislative body in which to deliberate, Adams diverted to another approach. The Townshend and

Stamp Acts differed in one principal respect: the duties of the second could not be avoided. Those of the first could.

With friends he set about designing a boycott of various luxury products. In a town meeting late in the month, sixty Boston merchants agreed to suspend importation of various articles, from silk and snuff to clocks, watches, and cheese. An appeal went out as well to other Massachusetts towns. "Silent contempt" seemed however the order of the day; there was little appetite for most of the proposals. (One merchant signed and then changed his mind. Paul Revere agreed. John Hancock did not.) And Otis parted ways with his colleagues. He upheld the king's right to appoint customs officers in whatever number he pleased. He encouraged submission to the new duties, to which no other town or province seemed to object. Urbane, popular Thomas Cushing also indicated that his opposition ended here. Bernard reveled in the news; Adams and his crew had been squarely rebuffed. The governor retired his alphabetic barrage. "There is not," he reported, days before commissioners landed in Boston, "the least uneasiness and discontent at the late parliamentary regulations." He anticipated a quiet January session.

A shudder went through Boston when the ship carrying three commissioners docked on November 4, leaving them to disembark on Pope's Day, with streets at their rowdiest. It infuriated Bernard to no end that the town should be so much disordered by a few desperados—he pointed squarely at Adams—"whose own ruined or insignificant fortunes make the destruction of their country a matter of indifference to them." They had no respect for individuals of worth and property. The commissioners managed all the same to step eventlessly ashore, passing by a bonfire without affront. A mob planned for November 20, when the duties officially took effect, failed to materialize. The Liberty Tree sported no effigies. The opposition had splintered. Defections reduced them to their weekly libels. Massachusetts seemed calmer, crowed Bernard, than it had for some time.

The frustration must have been immense for Adams, who agreed that some were sowing seeds of discord but suggested that Great Britain had the wrong men in mind. If he had not often enough heard that winter that he had worn out his welcome with his incessant alarms, he could soon read as much. In early January, the *Boston Gazette* carried a vicious piece of doggerel titled "Simple Sammy." What a fuss Adams made with his nonsense and falsehoods! Why such folly and malice? "Is hunger the cause of your scribbling? / Do bailiffs knock rude at your cell?" asked its author. ("Be easy, poor Toad! while you're well," rounded out the refrain.) With his meddling Adams had exhausted the town. He should leave writing aside and devote himself to curing bacon. Smiles of satisfaction must have crept across Bernard's and Hutchinson's faces as they savored the eight stanzas.

Adams had heard it all before and would again, graphically and in rhyme; eighteenth-century New England was astonishingly rich in poets. The attack must nonetheless have surprised him, coming as it did in the *Gazette*. His critic was close at hand, launching missiles from his terrain. Adams issued no public reply. Generally he shrugged off affronts, advising friends to do the same. When John Hancock contemplated resigning from the House after a slight, Adams stiffened his spine: "You say you have been spoken ill of. What then? Can you think that while you are a good man that *all* will speak well of you?" He assured Hancock that if he knew the identity of his anonymous critic—as Adams likely did his of 1768—the insult would ripen into acclaim. There was no cause to lose heart "merely because one contemptible person, who perhaps was hired for the purpose, has blessed you with his *reviling*."

BERNARD HAD LONG assumed every seditious piece in the colonial papers originated in Boston. The spurious Rhode Island and New York datelines, he snorted, fooled no one. About the series of essays published in three Boston newspapers between the end of December 1767 and the end of February 1768, he felt differently. Names of various potential authors flew about but Bernard remained skeptical. No one in New England wrote so well. (The printers seemed to enjoy insisting that the pages came from New York.) "Letters from a Farmer in Pennsylvania" indeed originated in Philadelphia, if with a London-educated lawyer, who made one copy of his manuscript, mailed to Otis. When he looked for a defense of American rights, when he looked for "indefatigable zeal and undaunted courage," thirty-five-year-old John Dickinson looked, he explained, to Boston. Others might write with more élan, but no one published with more gusto. "She must, as she has hitherto done, first kindle the sacred flame," Dickinson wrote Otis, hoping Boston might work her Stamp Act magic again with the Townshend Acts.* For nine weeks his incandescent arguments lit up newspapers throughout the colonies; over the next years Adams would lean on them repeatedly, saluting Dickinson's dispassion and embroidering on his points. The Pennsylvanian presented the most serious challenge yet to imperial authority. Were he taken at face value, brooded Bernard, after reading his first installment, "the Parliament of Great Britain need not give themselves much more trouble to make laws for this country."

Again Massachusetts accepted a Southern torch and ran with it, if in a very different direction from the one Bernard or Hutchinson anticipated. As Adams explained in a voluminous missive to the London agent, surely if the evils and inconveniences of the Townshend Acts were plainly and courteously explained, London would deliver redress. The province continued to believe the king infallible and Parliament just. But it was nowhere written that the king could not be deceived or Parliament misinformed. Was there an actual difference between the Townshend and Stamp Acts? Did America really need rapacious customs officials, pensioners—the word rang like "parasites" to New England ears—who were both costly and dangerous? The House made a daring end run around Bernard, appealing directly, in letters either written by Adams or shaped by him, to five British statesmen. We are not undutiful, the House assured the Marquis of Rockingham. We are not disloyal, they assured William Pitt, First Earl of Chatham. We have not the slightest thought of independence, they assured the Earl of Shelburne. If they could be taxed without representation, they were free subjects in name only. They

---

* It was a dynamic that would continue for some time. As Dickinson put it later, "the cold regions of the North" served as an example to "the languid latitudes of the South."

demanded only a return to their earlier status, to the unalienable right to dispose of their own property.*

The letters left Bernard huffing. It was "irregular and unconstitutional" for the House to detour around him. If no one in Great Britain reprimanded the upstarts, they would usurp every power of government. They seemed intent on reducing Bernard to the nonentity he felt himself to be. His sufferings only increased; toward mid-January, Adams drafted another London dispatch. This one began with the words: "Most gracious sovereign." Speaking for the House, Adams begged leave to approach the throne. Before George III he laid the "humble supplications in behalf of your distressed subjects." The colony could be taxed only by elected representatives, yet it was "utterly impracticable" for the people of Massachusetts to be represented in Parliament. Adams had gone on to suggest that any taxes levied in England were therefore unconstitutional; the House toned him down, limiting its objections to the Townshend duties. Appealing to His Majesty's "wise and paternal care for your remotest of faithful subjects," Adams solicited relief. It was almost certainly at this time that his ten-year-old daughter came upon him reviewing his pages early one morning. Flush with pride, she exclaimed that her father's work would be touched by the royal hand. "It will, my dear," he shrugged, "more likely be spurned by the royal foot."

It might seem odd that their appeals bypassed the governor, Adams confessed to the London agent. "But it is my private opinion," he explained, "that there is a want of confidence between the governor and the House which will never be removed as long as this gentleman is in the chair." He did not feel it necessary to elaborate on any official communications as, he wrote cheekily, "I have the good fortune to have my own private sentiments so exactly expressed as to render it needless for me to say anything of them in this letter." Here he touched on a matter

---

* While they were vindicating themselves, they explained the Council fiasco, still a tender issue. Private resentments had played no role. Hutchinson, Adams clarified, had been exiled only after "calm reflection" upon the dangers of positing legislative, executive, and judicial powers in the same hands, "which in the opinion of the greatest writers, ought always to be kept separate."

that had begun to trouble Bernard. Otis and Adams controlled the House. They also controlled the *Boston Gazette*. The result was an echo chamber, as the authors of "the messages and remonstrances of the House and the writers of the libelous and seditious letters in the newspaper are generally the same."

Shortly after the House approved the petition to George III, Adams and Otis suggested it be circulated to the other colonies as well. Most of the House recoiled from the idea; Adams and Otis seemed on their way to suggesting defiance of all acts of Parliament. A fierce debate ensued. The proposal to share the document was defeated by a two-to-one margin, the surest sign yet, Bernard crowed, that the people of Massachusetts were returning to their senses. Hutchinson predicted there would be no further mischief. Days later, attempting further to right the ship, Bernard took it upon himself to chastise the House for their Council-gutting. He assumed a peremptory tone. Adams pounced. The following week the House revisited the question of circulating their petition to the king. On February 4, by a large majority, the Massachusetts representatives reversed course, instructing Adams to alert the other colonies. They also voted to strike the original, negative vote from the official record, where it would never appear. Adams had lobbied vigorously. He could only have been elated, though may not have guessed that he had initiated a proceeding that would set off a firestorm in London or, as Hutchinson saw it, one that "brought on consequences which much accelerated the complete revolt of the colonies."

As what would become known as the Circular Letter wound its way south, Hutchinson wrangled with a season of superlatives. He had never known the people more restless or the House more impertinent. The "professed patriots" had sent the governor one of the rudest messages he had ever seen. He had never known such irregularities as their London dispatches! He sounded the kind of panicked notes that Bernard generally emitted as he braced for disorder on par with that of the Stamp Act riots. In the midst of the various affronts, the *Gazette* published a scathing attack on Bernard, berating him for his "enmity to this province." He was a man "totally abandoned to wickedness." Leaping into action,

Hutchinson prepared a libel case against Edes and Gill. In March he impressed upon a grand jury that the piece bordered on high treason. They agreed, directing the attorney general to prepare an indictment by morning. When they reconvened, a majority had changed their minds. They could detect no trace of offense. The arguments offered that day in court could have issued directly, Bernard yelped, from Otis's mouth. It seemed that in the night Adams and Otis had tailed the jurymen, badgering them wherever they went.

"A True Patriot" applauded the integrity of the grand jurors in the March 14 *Gazette*. Directly underneath ran a piece by "Populus," converting the libel case into one of freedom of the press. Nothing so terrified tyrants. "Populus" added an appeal for patience. Political salvation was in the offing. Until that time, he counseled what the *Gazette* incessantly advocated: "No mobs, no confusions, no tumults." The advocate for calm was Adams. Hutchinson was never to know that "A True Patriot"—the author of "the most villainous piece of any which has yet appeared"—was Joseph Warren, the dashing young doctor who had nursed him, with near-daily visits, through his breakdown the previous year.

Adams was not without battles of his own that week. On the same March Monday that the Circular Letter appeared in the *Gazette*, he could be found reading a petition to the town. Smallpox and the Stamp Act had hindered his tax-collecting. From certain households he had received nothing for four years. Once more he pleaded for clemency. Not everyone inclined toward patience. With some difficulty, friends secured him an extension. The irony that Adams—who could not himself seem to collect taxes from his fellow Bostonians—devoted the bulk of his time to tutoring the town on that subject was not lost on the governor or lieutenant governor, who drew a direct line between the insolvency and the activism. Bernard wrote down Boston's troubles to three or four men "bankrupt in reputation as well as in fortune, and equally void of credit in character and in property." Their hold on the people of Massachusetts left Crown officers as mystified as did the rapid evolution in thinking. The very authority of Parliament now seemed in question, as initially only the right to tax had been. The House was under "the dictature of a few desperate men" who somehow held sway over men with fortunes a hundred times greater. Thomas Hutchinson did not believe it possible to be principled and poor any more than Samuel Adams seemed to believe it possible to be a patriot and rich.

Bernard took this "lowest kind of gentry" as seriously as he did their nonimportation ploy, to which Adams directed the energies he failed to summon for tax collection. It elicited little enthusiasm. Meant to take effect on June 1, 1768, the embargo had no chance of success without the participation of New York or Philadelphia merchants. They wavered. As for any proposed nonconsumption, Bernard was yet more disdainful. The very concept was ridiculous! All the wool in America would not suffice to produce two pair of stockings a year for each inhabitant. The colony could not manufacture nails at a viable price. Great Britain produced the bulk of American paper. The campaign was, Bernard swore, all bluster and swagger. Adams conceded that their efforts might seem to some inconsequential. But even if all did not adhere to the agreement— plenty of merchants had already submitted spring orders to London— many would. In May, rather overstating the case, he boasted of "a disposition among the people to furnish themselves with the American manufactures as never was known before."

As Bernard braced himself for insurrection, as he inquired again after a transfer and heard from an informer that his life was in danger, Adams published a folksy series of essays in the *Gazette*. The Philadelphia farmer had eloquently spoken of incursions against civil rights. But what, asked Adams, of religious rights? He launched into an attack on "Popery," one he fully anticipated would be "treated with sneer and ridicule" by artful men with designs on American liberty. There were multiple ways to subjugate a people: in three columns thick with innuendo, Adams rolled together Anglican authorities, "foreign superfluities," and the Stamp Act. In his own way he was campaigning. An election loomed. The attentive reader caught his point. On his copy, the newspaper-collecting Harbottle Dorr scrawled: "By Popery, means the representatives of some towns, who he supposed were the governor's tools."

It was an offensive that Bernard did not anticipate any more than he did another that spring, as the Circular Letter detonated in London. The mutinous spirit upended Harvard College, where undergraduates seized on a change in classroom regulations to stage a miniature revolt. It came to a head on April 2, when disguised students hurled bricks through windows. Most of the college joined the protest out of what one upperclassman termed "national sympathy." Emboldened by the Circular Letter, they reduced the faculty to Turkish despots. Lips pursed, Thomas Hutchinson allowed that "the spirit of liberty had spread where it was not intended." At one point, dissidents resolved to petition for transfers to Yale. The Harvard revolt ended with confessions, regrets, and, ultimately, amnesty for the "seditious."*

ADAMS'S POPULARITY TOOK a beating in the spring, when—tired of the browbeating and provocations, the thundering about boycotts—Boston returned him to the House by only a narrow margin. He stayed the course, "indefatigable," as Bernard had it, "in mischief." Hutchinson discovered as much days later, when he hoped to be restored to the Council. The first round of House voting put him in the lead but three votes shy of a majority. As a second ballot was to be administered, Adams interrupted. Had anyone noticed that the lieutenant governor was now a pensioner? Hutchinson had recently learned that he was to receive 200 pounds a year from the Townshend revenues. Otis then rose with the name of an alternate candidate; the subterfuge had been carefully choreographed. No man who valued his country should vote for the lieutenant governor! In a maneuver that seemed plucked from the Turkish tyranny, the two proceeded to fly about the House, Otis comporting himself, in Hutchinson's description, like "an enraged demon." Crestfallen, Hutchinson emerged from the second round of balloting with fewer votes than he had garnered in the first. His nerves held but he

---

* Nearly all involved remained at and graduated from Harvard, including a sophomore whose name appears nowhere in accounts of the campus unrest: Samuel Adams Jr. Like his father, he had matriculated at fourteen. Most of the protesters went on to become jurists and ministers.

permitted himself a dollop of self-pity. No lieutenant governor had suffered as had he. He saw no connection to his own plight when neighbors muttered about the British ship of fifty guns that had arrived in Boston Harbor a week before the election. Nor could he see past his disdain for the ignorant rascals who had assumed the reins of power, some of whom—the reference was clear—would be in prison were their creditors less merciful.

Though virtually the same age, Adams had long ceded to Otis, the Calvin, it would be said, to Otis's Luther. By the time Hutchinson offered his close-up of the duo in frenzied action—he produced nearly as many miserable accounts of the maneuver as he did of the destruction of his home—the pair had achieved equal prominence. To Bernard they were now "the two chief heads of the faction." Otis remained the most erudite lawyer in Massachusetts, as well as the legislator most given to verbal pyrotechnics. He blazed with an intensity that Hutchinson hoped signaled his imminent demise. Aware of the flights of frenzy, Otis permitted one person to call him to order; he entrusted Adams with the task of yanking him back, by the coattail, when he exceeded himself in the House. It was an imperfect science. For both the enraged demon moment and the bewildering reversals there was plenty of precedent. Otis's hesitation may have explained Boston's muted reaction to the Townshend Acts. He had initially opposed nonimportation. He then changed his mind, attaching retractions to repudiations. He denounced even his own brilliant 1764 pamphlet, the most powerful expression of colonial rights before Dickinson's. He fell into league with Hutchinson. He supported the Stamp Act. Among the pivots, the reversals, and the acrobatic about-faces, it was difficult to guess in what direction he headed. Having blocked Hutchinson from the Council—the lieutenant governor would never again be elected to public office in Massachusetts—Otis went on to make a speech affirming the absolute sovereignty of Parliament.

The vacillations left him open to attacks on all sides. He challenged George Grenville to a duel. He urged a second attack on Hutchinson's mansion. He raged that Great Britain should sink into the sea. (He exempted the king, fully aware that sinking George III constituted treason.) It was easier to assert that the Boston opposition was "scarce short of madness," as Bernard did that summer, when one of its members plainly seemed so. There may have been no better proof of Adams's patience or political agility than in the management of his mentor. Otis enjoyed rational days and irrational days, Whig days and Tory days. Silently Adams swabbed up the damage. By 1768 rivalry began to nip at the partnership. Their quarrels turned up even in the Adams-skewering doggerel. It was long known that Adams burnished Otis's prose and wrote over his signature; we can no more pry apart the men's words than we can determine who wrote *Citizen Kane*. For years, when Hutchinson groaned about "the principal demagogue" or "the grand incendiary," he meant Otis. After 1768 he meant Adams. The lieutenant governor grumbled that Adams had directed matters for some time, that he "covertly influenced more than Mr. Otis, though at the same time the public considered Mr. Otis as the chief." Henceforth there would be more cracks about desperate bankrupts and fewer about enraged demons.

When customs commissioners stepped ashore, they ascribed the leadership position to Adams, naming as his lieutenants Dr. Warren; Joseph Hawley, a brilliant lawyer from western Massachusetts, austere even by Adams standards and an uncommonly fine orator; James Bowdoin, a wealthy former intimate of Bernard's; and Samuel Cooper, the elegant, silver-tongued minister of the Brattle Street Church, devastatingly handsome and among the most appealing men in Boston. Adams was the opposition's undisputed head, "their political dictator." He came to exercise what Andrew Oliver described as "a secret influence" over the town, an influence that exceeded even that of his mentor. The ascension of Adams—"cool, abstemious, polished, and refined"—displeased Otis. In his lucid moments, Thomas Hutchinson noted, Otis discouraged designs of independence. Adams neither veered nor swerved. "It might be expected therefore that a perfect harmony could not subsist between them," Hutchinson observed, in pages he elected not to publish. Obdurate and ubiquitous, Adams coordinated the town meetings, the House, and the merchant committees. He cajoled grand jurors, finessed House votes, manipulated electoral slates, and massaged the word on the street. Bernard seemed to find himself face-to-face with him every time he turned around. Both Adams and Otis took their seats in the eleven-coach cavalcade that called on the governor in June 1768 to lodge objections against the new commissioners. Bernard received this delegation with exceptional civility. He passed around wine. He believed he had thoroughly charmed his callers. Otis assured him, Bernard crowed afterward, that he thought him a true friend to the province. Adams walked back the statement. If indeed Otis had said such a thing, no one else had heard it.

SHORTLY BEFORE NOON on June 21, 1768, Governor Bernard shared with the House instructions he had received a week earlier. He awaited a favorable moment; a wise man ran for cover, he mused, before tossing a bomb. His message was simple. George III commanded the Massachusetts representatives to renounce the Circular Letter. London instructed Bernard to dissolve the House if it refused to withdraw the document. His reward was a blistering tirade. For Otis it was an anti-government day; he shredded British authority for over two hours. His Majesty's ministers knew nothing of the business to which they were meant to tend. They never remained in office long enough to acquire the knowledge necessary to master it. (He was not wrong. Only that January had colonial affairs been consolidated into an American office and delegated to Lord Hillsborough, who had relayed the order to rescind the Circular Letter.) Nor, ranted Otis, did the British seem to understand the rights of Englishmen. There was not an individual among them capable of writing a petition so pure, so elegant, or so vigorous as that which Massachusetts had submitted to their sovereign.

Bernard requested an immediate answer. The House kept him waiting for nine days. Any misgivings about how to proceed were erased by letters that arrived over the course of the week. Virginia and Maryland applauded the nine-paragraph composition that London had deemed "extraordinary and unconstitutional." The solidarity—three additional colonies soon weighed in—left Adams beaming. It was, he and Reverend Cooper agreed, letters of support in hand, the most glorious day they ever saw! On June 29 Bernard finally got his answer. That morning the members of the House cleared the gallery, locked themselves in the chamber, and instructed the doorkeeper to bar visitors. By an overwhelming majority, they voted 92 to 17 not to rescind.* Hutchinson was aghast. These people did not seem to understand that they were dealing with the king! For his part Adams deemed the order "an impudent mandate." He hoped to create a common sympathy among the colonies, an effort that seemed to be paying dividends. Nothing had united America more than the Circular Letter—unless one counted Great Britain's demand for its retraction.

The House entrusted its response to him. Objections to taxing rather than regulating trade did not originate, Adams stressed, with a few desperate men. They were universal. "The most respectable for fortune, rank, and station, as well as probity and understanding" balked at the overreach. Surely it was not a crime to harmonize views among sister colonies? The Massachusetts House engaged in no coercion. They merely helped their fellow Americans to compose their minds at a time when some attempted to stand in the way of "calm, deliberate, rational, and constitutional measures from being pursued." Nothing pained the colonists so much as the displeasure of their sovereign. They meant no affront. They had been grossly misrepresented, though it was difficult to understand how House business, "constantly done in the open view of the world, could thus be colored." To his explanation Adams appended a bit of trademark table-turning. It should by now be abundantly clear who precisely were the "desperate faction, which is continually destroying the public tranquility."

Twice read aloud, clearly and carefully, the letter was accepted without emendation. A second letter was prepared as well, all or in part an Adams production. In a very different tone, the House responded to

---

* Over the months that followed, the number "92" was deemed auspicious and the number "17" shunned throughout the colonies. The House saw to it that the names of the "rescinders" were widely published. Their infamy followed them around for years.

Bernard's "direct and peremptory requisition." How could so innocent a measure have been cast in so odious a light? They questioned his reporting. They threw the law at their barrister of a governor: The Circular Letter was now historical fact. How could one rescind something that had already happened? Their petition had quieted a restless people. Quiet they would have remained, had they not learned that their application for redress had never reached their sovereign. The governor seemed to exhibit little of the paternal care he so often professed. From a firm sense of duty to God, king, and country, the House had voted their consciences. They hoped and prayed that in future His Excellency might subscribe to the same principles.

The same afternoon the House appointed a committee to request Bernard's recall. Adams sat at its head. They were both grandstanding and playacting. At the first meeting, Adams pulled a petition from his pocket; Bernard had cause to denounce Adams for walking about with fully drafted resolves at all times. It is easier to anticipate events when you are behind them; Adams also assigned parts to the different actors in advance. The committee could not have known how perfectly their work dovetailed with that of their beleaguered governor. With increasing urgency, Bernard harped on his three-year Calvary. He now dreamed even of New Jersey. To prevent consideration of Adams's petition, he dissolved the House. It would not meet again until after the May 1769 election.

The vote to uphold the Circular Letter represented an Adams triumph. It also entailed some delicate management. The House kept their response from Bernard, left to read it, along with everyone else, in the newspapers. In the Town House representatives' room, Adams and Otis engaged in a tussle over publication. Otis asked what Adams intended to do with his document. "To give it to the printer to publish next Monday," Adams replied. Otis challenged him. Was it proper for it to appear in the papers before Lord Hillsborough received the original? "You know it was designed for the people and not for the Minister," Adams reminded Otis, who accused him — the rivalry at a boil — of being overly fond of his own prose. Surely Adams should wait to publish the document at the proper time. "I am Clerk of the House, and I will make that use of the papers which I please," Adams parried. The dispute evidently delayed publication for a week, or so Bernard understood; the piece claimed the front page of the *Gazette* only on July 18, 1768. Dutifully Bernard submitted it to London, noting that the papers bristled with "a variety of sedition and calumny." He found them equally remarkable for what they did not contain. On a mid-July Friday, the Sons had directed a mob to assemble at the home of the inspector general of customs, John Williams, following a demand that he either relinquish his post or leave town. A crowd attempted to break into his courtyard. Williams held them off with a gun. Bernard searched in vain for an account of that riot. The Sons of Liberty had forbidden any mention.

One could not predict what the Sons would do next but one could expect the worst from each escapade, concluded Bernard. Adams seemed to anticipate precisely what government would attempt next. He too braced for the worst. Over a long, hot summer, Bernard feeling more and more desperate, Adams more and more in his element, the two battled over vocabulary. In June, customs officials impounded a ninety-ton John Hancock sloop, as much to silence a critic as to chasten a notorious smuggler. A crowd tossed rocks at the sailors who attempted the seizure. The crowd later assaulted two commissioners, tearing at their clothes; broke windows of their homes; and, having dragged it a half mile through the streets, burned the barge of another in triumph. The commissioners—or "swarms of bloodsucking customs house officers," as some had it—fled for safety to the warship in the harbor, later to the Castle. God knows where the fury would have ended, Bernard fumed, had more rum been on hand! Adams weighed in: The June incident indeed constituted a riot. But it was neither a great nor sustained one. Resentment naturally ran high after an unlawful seizure. The price was but a few panes of glass. And he defended his friend. Hancock had nothing to do with the incident. "Animated by his known regard to peace and good order," he had personally dispersed the crowd.

Early in July, some fifty Sons of Liberty trekked to Roxbury to pay a late-day call on a commissioner. He was not at home. They settled for trampling his garden and orchard and leveling his fences. Bernard supposed the incident would be reduced to "a frolic of a few boys to eat some cherries," as indeed it was.* The Sons advertised afterward in the papers: They had had no knowledge of this excursion! They could hardly assume responsibility for every indiscretion committed in their name. Nor could any of them rival Adams's disingenuousness. The morning after the barge-burning, papers had appeared on the Liberty Tree inviting the Sons to help clear the land of the vermin who had come to devour America. Bernard begged his Council to avenge the insult. What could the governor possibly have in mind? asked Adams. Why did he assume that "vermin" meant his Excellency or the commissioners? America's enemies did everything they could to paint her in unflattering colors.

Over and over Adams reduced a vandalized garden to a boys' frolic, a household raid to a few broken panes of glass. What Bernard termed "a great number of people of all kinds, sexes, and ages" became, in Adams's hands, "a few disorderly persons, mostly boys." He stopped at nothing, including the truth. He believed he was up against a governor who made it his business to turn every disturbance into a riot, every riot into an insurrection. (As Council member Bowdoin put it, Bernard "has a peculiar knack at making mountains of mole hills, and idle chitchat, treason.") The wife of a customs commissioner ushered her terrified children out a back door to safety when a large group of boys took to hooting and hollering one evening around her home. Adams had no intention of indulging the gender card. Legitimate fears were one thing. But everyone, he observed, was a politician now. "Whether this lady, whom Governor Bernard has *politely* ushered into the view of the public, *really* thought herself in danger or not, it is incumbent on him to show that there were just grounds for her apprehensions," he wrote. The papers filled weekly with Adams's fables, reported Hutchinson, which no one dared contradict.

---

* There were indeed a disproportionate number of boys in 1760s Boston, where half the population consisted of children, and where "boys" were men under the age of twenty-one. A merchant later railed that all violence would be written down to the work of boys, Blacks, or nobody at all.

Secretly he began to compile names, so as to have an answer on hand when asked whom to prosecute for treason.

All were cordial with one another when they met. And it was still just possible to continue on warm terms with someone with whom one were, as John Adams put it, "in antipodes in politics." But positions had begun to solidify, consciences to assert themselves. At his cousin's urging, John moved that year from Braintree to Boston. Lucrative government positions were dangled before him, each promising "a first step in the ladder of royal favor and promotion." He declined them all, despite repeated entreaties of a close friend. Given the direction in which politics seemed to be tending, John hesitated to put himself "in a situation in which my duty and my inclination would be so much at variance." He was not alone. Early in a damp August, nearly two hundred Boston merchants, invigorated by Otis and Adams, entered finally into a nonimportation agreement. They would buy nothing further from Great Britain until the repeal of the Townshend Acts. If Parliament chose to overlook this, they would overlook any insult to the Crown, huffed Hutchinson. There were laws against such offenses.

The laws on the books hardly mattered, as Bernard could not seem to enforce them. Late in the summer he unsuccessfully attempted to prosecute a virulent libel against Hutchinson. He made as little progress with the June 10 attacks on the customs officers. Though several hundred people had been on hand as the barge burned, no witness could be found. Solid evidence evaporated into thin air. Otis's diatribe against rescinding had been "the most violent, insolent, abusive, treasonable declamation that perhaps was ever delivered," yet none of the several hundred people who heard it could summon up a line. Bernard's Council were unrecognizable. They feared the people more than the king. And to govern without a Council, he discovered, was "to make bricks without straw." He believed troops would be necessary to return America to reason. Here he continued to wrangle with a catch-22. He could not request military assistance without a vote of his Council, to which he had hesitated to submit a request, and which by 1768 refused even to entertain the question. Why, wondered Bernard, were regulars quartered in New Jersey and Pennsylvania, where the people were perfectly obedient? At the same time he shivered at the thought that anyone might suspect he had proposed the idea.

In late June a committee confronted him. Had he requested troops? In good conscience Bernard could say he had not, if only because General Gage ignored his increasingly strident hints. It was difficult to say who dreaded the possibility of their arrival most: Bernard, who intended to make himself scarce by early September, having secured a leave; Hutchinson, who hinted that he would have nothing to do with them if they arrived; or Adams, alert as ever to slumbering serpents, who warned that daily hints of troops only further oppressed an irritated people. He did all in his power to counter Bernard's "slanderous chit-chat," enlisting — again as "Determinatus," in the August 8, 1768, *Gazette*—every scrap he could. To murmur, even to whisper, evidently now constituted a riotous spirit! It was difficult to account for commissioners who seemed afraid of their own shadows. He was no friend to riots or unlawful assemblies. But so long as a people retained "any sense of honor, liberty, and virtue," they were within their rights "to complain, and to complain ALOUD." The alternative was to "become poor deluded miserable ductile dupes," the victims of tyranny.

Three weeks later, a special messenger called on Bernard with a confidential letter from General Gage, in New York. He took mercy on the distraught governor. Their conversation should be treated, Gage warned, with the strictest secrecy. He begged for a speedy reply. Would Bernard let him know immediately whether he would like one regiment or two?

IT IS DANGEROUS TO BE SILENT

I agree with you that "it is difficult to say at what
moment the revolution began."
—JOHN ADAMS TO THOMAS JEFFERSON, 1818

ADAMS LABORED to expel an unloved governor, a prospect he long savored. He did not expect to meet with His Majesty's troops. For Bernard they could not arrive quickly enough. He thought them years late already. Rumors soon spread that—in addition to the New York regiments—two additional regiments sailed toward Boston from Ireland, dispatched after reports of the March and June disturbances.* Which left Bernard with the problem of how to break the disquieting news. He shuddered at the terrors that unannounced troopships would unleash in a short-tempered town; his informers urged him to flee the minute redcoats materialized. "And no wonder," Adams would observe, "that the man who had long been representing a whole country as rebels, and had been one of the principal instruments in bringing such a curse upon it, should at that juncture be under some apprehensions of danger."

Bernard devised what struck him as a clever solution. He would slip a hint of the news into private conversation. It was guaranteed to fly around Boston in minutes, as it did, delivering Adams and several other

---

* Bernard had been flustered when asked to decide the question of numbers. When he found that Gage's aide knew nothing of the more egregious incidents, he elaborated. Two regiments then made abundant sense.

representatives to Bernard's door. They had a simple question: Did he indeed expect troops? Bernard prided himself on his answer. He had heard private hints but as of that Monday no official notification.* Pressed, he allowed—"with a duplicity for which he has a peculiar talent," bristled Adams, who found the governor all "artful ambiguity"—that the town need not absolutely count on troops. The House stood dissolved; the delegation urged Bernard to reconvene it. He explained that he could not proceed without His Majesty's command. On this occasion he passed around no wine. He could afford to be offhanded. He was packing for a new post, soon revealed to be Virginia.

Boston met Bernard's shocking half-announcement with a shocking exercise of its own. In a town meeting on September 12, Otis, Adams, and Warren delivered a string of speeches. Each fit neatly into the next, "as if they were acting a play," clucked Bernard, who suspected a rehearsal. Cries went up for resisting the invaders by force. American liberties had been destroyed; liberty was as precious as life; and, argued one hothead, "if a man attempts to take my life, I have a right to take his." He was silenced. At the same time, several chests of old muskets were dredged up from the Faneuil Hall basement, their contents heaped in the middle of the floor. Was a war with France, someone asked, not likely? Should the weapons be distributed before they fell into the wrong hands? There were suppressed smiles all around. Under the circumstances, the selectmen voted that every Boston householder supply himself with "a well fixed firelock, musket, accouterments and ammunition." No French war loomed; to a great extent the colony's troubles could be written down to the fact that a long one had ended. The "flimsy veil," as Bernard put it, fluttered back and forth over the next weeks. Adams scoffed at the governor's intimations. Boston had long meant to convey those chests of arms across town. The transfer simply happened to have taken place that Monday.

The display of rusty firearms paled beside what followed. The selectmen—"tools of the faction," to Bernard—took it upon themselves to call a convention of Massachusetts towns. A French war was again

---

* In truth he had received confirmation ten days earlier.

advertised: over a rain-drenched week, representatives of ninety-six communities assembled in Boston for what was essentially a reconstituted House of Representatives. Bernard knew he must break up the convention—it was a historical first; no such assumption of royal authority had ever occurred on British soil—but quaked at the prospect. His predicament was all the more disagreeable as relief stood close at hand. He had fixed a day for his departure and booked a cabin. Screwing up his courage, he ordered the assembly to disband. Anyone who persisted would "repent of his rashness." The representatives of ninety-six Massachusetts towns ignored him.

Word leaked out that the convention had elected Adams its clerk and Cushing its chairman, inauspicious news to Bernard, who managed to pry little else from a room in which he assumed insurrection was being plotted. Otis arrived late, with a mysterious three-day delay, after which the Faneuil Hall doors were locked tight. Not everyone inside was of the same mind or even certain why he was in Boston in the first place. You could choose your grievance, from unconstitutional taxation to petitions that had failed to reach the king to the dissolved House to rumors of troops. In the press, Adams explained that the convention gathered—at a "dreadfully precarious" moment—to settle on "the most effectual measures for promoting the peace and good order" of the province.

Several parties emerged. The first preferred to do nothing. Another aimed to maintain quiet until troops arrived. Adams took a more aggressive position, though did not join those who vowed to drown in their own blood before allowing a redcoat to set foot in Boston. The French war was likely of his straight-faced invention; it was the kind of ruse he enjoyed. He soon discovered he was out of step with the rest of the province, which inclined toward moderation.* An army of officials and commissioners was one thing, Adams argued. But an actual army? He made little headway. Again tame, Otis silenced him when he attempted to

---

* The town of Hatfield pointed out that if war with France loomed, the province should only welcome British troops. They saw the convention as a Boston scheme to involve the rest of the colony in their quarrel. The town would be wiser to attempt a little humility and remorse.

speak ardently. In five days Adams instead learned a great deal about how imperial issues played out in the Massachusetts countryside, lessons that would not go to waste. Evidently it was in the course of these deliberations that he informed Hannah, then twelve and following her father's work closely, that he paid little attention to his popularity. "I will stand alone. I will oppose tyranny at the threshold, though the fabric of liberty fall and I perish in its ruins."

The delegates submitted a modest letter to Bernard, who refused to accept it. Adams tended to damage control, but the convention by no measure qualified as a triumph. Hutchinson thought its proponents had only made themselves ridiculous. Already there was rejoicing in some quarters: As the delegates assembled, a puerile song issued from a window at the Castle. It was attributed to the commissioners, removed to the harbor for their safety. The tune lampooned the foolish talk of liberty; the rascals and numbskulls so enamored of mobbing would flee at the first sight of redcoats. "While we quite transported and happy shall be," continued the verse, "From mobs, knaves and villains, protected and free." The convention sent shock waves around London, where word circulated that it had urged arms on all inhabitants. Stocks plunged with the November news of "the revolt of New England."

If the convention had not already planned to disband, the flotilla of transport ships that sailed into Boston Harbor on the morning of September 28 forced the issue. In light of the convention, having been led to expect resistance, the fleet arranged itself as if to fire on the town. Gage ordered an immediate landing. Samuel Hood, the commanding admiral, watched the Massachusetts representatives rush off, as one Tory chortled, "like a herd of scalded hogs." (Hood drew an equally unflattering picture of the royal governor, forced by events to relinquish dreams of Virginia. Bernard made for an abject sight, staring out longingly at the ship he had expected to deliver him from Boston the minute troops arrived.)* Newspapers that week predicted that all disputes would end

---

* In Commodore Hood's opinion, the sooner the weak-willed governor was gone from America, the better.

here, as Samuel Adams could not "bear the smell of gunpowder, and faints away at a drawn sword or bayonet."

He could not have missed the display of fireworks that exploded over the fleet the evening after their arrival, or the choruses of "Yankee Doodle Dandy" that floated into town from the harbor. We do not know where he was on Saturday morning, October 1, when—a mile from his front door—redcoats disembarked on Long Wharf. The streets bustled with traffic as Sheriff Greenleaf frantically commandeered Boston's carts to assist the new arrivals, their wives and children, with luggage. To stunned silence, nearly a thousand men and a train of artillery marched, bayonets fixed, flags flying, accompanied by fifes and drums and in a magnificent parade—flashes of crimson and gleams of snowy white against the muted greens and deep reddish browns of New England—up King Street, toward the Common. Awestruck families crowded every window. One woman watching the pageantry from her doorway caught the eye of a townsman who had sworn to oppose the landing with his life. He chided her; she should avert her gaze, as did he. "You are a very pretty fellow!" she snapped back. "You said that you would fight up to your knees in blood to destroy them, and you are now afraid to *look* at them!"

Boston went uncharacteristically quiet, a miracle for which Hutchinson and Adams accounted differently. Hutchinson believed the people petrified. Few had believed troops would truly land; armed guards before the Town House made an impression. Adams credited the September convention. It had sagely recommended peace and quiet out of loyalty to their sovereign. It had subdued those who advocated armed resistance. There was no sign of the insurrection that troops had come to crush. (In fairness, Bernard had been clear. He wanted troops not to suppress a tumult, but to rescue his government from the hands of a trained mob.) Commodore Hood smiled at the reception. Preconceptions melted away as Bostonians grasped that the troops were neither "cannibals nor street robbers." Abashed faction chiefs—Hancock and Otis, anyway—paid him calls.

Adams meanwhile did his utmost to make Boston appear dignified and Bernard ridiculous. Who would be so dim-witted as to think Boston would oppose the landing of the king's troops! The governor subsisted on ludicrousness. They should not be held accountable for what he gleaned from his spies, remunerated more richly the more sensational the information. "Some men," Adams would scoff, "are very apt to believe that which they *wish* were true." At the same time, what an insult for a free people to find themselves surrounded by fourteen men-of-war and invaded by one soldier for every three adult males. Was that not "a new and intolerable grievance"? Adams wondered, two days after redcoats paraded down the wharf. He paid no call on Commodore Hood, setting immediately to work. One person beat him to it. Troops had been in town for five days when a vandal took a knife to the portrait of Francis Bernard in Harvard Hall, excising a neat piece of canvas from the chest. In a note he explained that he had performed an act of mercy. Heartless, the governor would find it easier to review his loathsome administration.

Crown officers felt that fall that they had not slept as well in years. Not everyone was so lucky; it soon emerged that there were limits to Boston hospitality. Adams and his confederates conjured with the riddles of where Bernard should lodge the soldiers and who should provide their support. To his consternation, Hood discovered that the Massachusetts governor had arranged neither in advance. He billeted five hundred men at the Castle. The remainder settled temporarily at Faneuil Hall and in the Town House, where Bernard made every inch apart from the Council chamber available to them. Soldiers slept even in the file room where Adams and Otis had tussled. One regiment pitched tents on Boston Common, where they marched and countermarched. It became necessary to remind an artillery captain that there was no need for fifes and drums in the evening.

The law was inconveniently plain: the town had no obligation to lodge troops were barracks available, as they were, at the Castle. The stone fort was, however, three miles from town, which rather defeated the purpose of an order-restoring mission. Nor would it accommodate four regiments. Bernard had wrangled with the matter as the convention

sat; the idea, some soon grasped, was to make the Quartering Act impracticable, then denounce the authorities for having failed to observe it. To
the other colonies went word that the Council had voted the Castle sufficient for the troops, adding that four regiments sent "in consequence of
some children hollering on the 18th of March last, must be owing to the
most unkind and injurious representation." Rumors flew about that the
province was to be disarmed, martial law imposed, individuals seized
and sent abroad.

October devolved into a maddening scramble. Bernard appealed in
vain to the selectmen, the justices, and his Council. He groused that his
Council, like the House, did everything with an eye toward the press.
(The Council seemed actively to undermine the governor they were
meant to assist, the first defection of the kind.) In mid-October, General
Gage traveled from New York to review the inexplicably vexed landing.
Though received cordially, he met with the same stonewalling as did the
frustrated Massachusetts governor. Gage attended Council meetings,
where on October 17 a bare majority finally voted to clear the Manufactory House, a massive brick building in the center of town. Provincial
property, it could comfortably house at least one regiment.

The Council's was not the first discussion of the Long Acre Street
(today Tremont Street) address. Upon his arrival Colonel Dalrymple,
commander of the land forces, had sent a lieutenant to inspect the structure, which he ordered cleared in two hours. Its overseer refused. The
Sons of Liberty knew the largely abandoned two-story building made for
an ideal barracks; weeks earlier they had packed it with residents. By the
time Sheriff Greenleaf and his posse arrived to evict them on October 17,
doors and windows were barred and bolted. For a second time the overseer
refused to surrender the establishment. Hutchinson at his side, Greenleaf
insisted the inhabitants decamp. From cracked-open windows came the
response: The best lawyer in Massachusetts—it was Otis—had advised
them not to budge.

On a third visit, around noon the following day, Greenleaf managed
to slip his fingers under the sash of a cellar window. At the expense of a
bit of glass, feet first, he forced his way into the building, a deputy

tumbling behind. A scuffle ensued inside; all the unpleasant tasks seemed to fall to sixty-five-year-old Greenleaf, presumably less than spry. After a bit of swordplay, the residents took the burly sheriff hostage, locking him in the basement. A party of soldiers headed to the rescue, trailed by a crowd. Heated words flew back and forth. Greenleaf emerged unscathed but the building remained secure, "filled," as Bernard put it, "with the outcast of the workhouse and the scum of town." The sheriff settled for establishing a cordon around the building. If they could not evict its inhabitants, the authorities would starve them out. The next day children could be seen at the windows, crying for bread, as the baker was turned away. Provisions soon sailed over the soldiers' heads, into open windows, from the street. Bernard threw up his hands in defeat.

Ultimately Gage lodged his men in converted warehouses and commercial buildings, rented with difficulty and at Crown expense. They were deeply inconvenienced, as well as precisely where Adams preferred them: morally in the wrong. It would not be long before he made of the Manufactory House travesty "the first open and avowed effort of military tyranny," a violent attack upon citizens in the security of their own home — and a pointless one at that.

"No man can pretend to say that peace and good order of the community is so secure with soldiers quartered in the body of a city as without them," Adams wrote in the October 17 *Gazette*, prefacing the piece with the Latin for "Resist at the outset." Military and civil governments made for miserable companions, especially in Boston, where it was difficult to reconcile two populations, one sullen, the other boisterous. The differences went well beyond the incessant drilling and infernal "spirit-stirring drum and the ear-piercing fife" that woke John Adams and his household every morning. From the start British commanders faced a desertion problem; forty men immediately melted away. Boston was appalled by an early-morning display one late October Sunday: to the measured beat of drums, the entire soldiery assembled on the Common, where the chaplain of the Fourteenth Regiment administered the sacrament to a private dressed in white from head to toe. He was then shot for desertion. To drive the lesson home, his regiment was marched in solemn step past the corpse, blood pooling on the ground. Boston had witnessed nothing of the kind over the course of the previous war. Several townswomen had evidently lobbied the night before for a pardon, to no avail.*

Those details, Adams swiftly realized, were too valuable to remain in Massachusetts. Some could also be burnished. No sooner had the convention disbanded than he and several associates founded a news service. Unlike the *Independent Advertiser* of two decades earlier, this one made no nod to objectivity. Nor, given its mission, was the *Journal of Occurrences* ever to meet a slow news day. Instead, it made it its business over the next tense months to share with the rest of America the bitter consequences of stationing an army "on pretense of preserving order in a town that was as orderly before their arrival as any one large town in the whole extent of His Majesty's dominions." There was plenty of material. On their first full day in Boston, around noon, at a popular tavern, a British captain accosted John Rowe, the moderate merchant. The captain had expected Rowe to have hanged already, "for damn you," he informed him, "you deserve it." Surely, guffawed Rowe, the captain spoke in jest? No, replied the captain, he spoke in earnest. He went on to offer several variations on his hope that Rowe hang before his eyes.

Composed in secret, the newspaper pieces made for a brand of pure propaganda new to America. The genius of the enterprise was to dispatch them for publication to New York, where they might appear on Thursday, then to Philadelphia, where they appeared on Saturday, returning only later to Massachusetts, their origins obscured. As far south as Georgia one could read of the Manufactory House children sobbing for bread and water. The cross-pollination meant that one heard in Virginia that effigies of Governor Bernard and Sheriff Greenleaf had hung in New York for their Massachusetts misdeeds. Ben Franklin's son,

---

* To his surprise, Adams would manage—after a soldier's wife threw herself on his mercy, begging him to intercede—to spare another man from a barbarous whipping. In retrospect, Hannah Adams suspected the pardon a prelude to an attempt to buy off her father.

the royal governor, read of the abuses in New Jersey. By transmitting the accounts south, the *Journal*'s authors saw to it that colonists everywhere commiserated with Boston. Her abridged liberties threatened them all. And the *Journal* could accomplish what the September convention had not. In its pages Boston sounded martyred rather than mobbish.

With what amounted to a syndicated news service—at least eleven American papers carried the *Journal*'s reports—Adams and his confederates realized a second advantage. By the time the dubious tale of the worthy old man who discovered a soldier in bed with his favorite granddaughter boomeranged back to Boston, it arrived as news, displacing memory. An incident might land on the front page of the *Boston Evening Post* six to eight weeks after it had happened, or mostly happened, too late for anyone to recall whether the blood-curdling details were or ever had been remotely accurate. The paper was wildly popular, as lurid tales of girls pummeled after having rejected beastly advances will be. Nine-tenths of its content was fiction, "either absolutely false or grossly misrepresented," fumed Hutchinson, having imbibed a season of the finest tabloid journalism on American shores. Every insignificant detail found its way into the publication, he railed, which was to say that the *Journal* burst with muskets in faces and bayonets in chests, with slaves suborned, with near riots and attempted rapes, with tales of marauding soldiers and abused women, nightly scuffles and daily insults, robberies, complaints, and wishful thinking. Every redcoat seemed to have alerted every man, woman, and child in Boston that he intended to blow their brains out. For their part, the people of Boston appeared docile, if you failed to count cutting down the frame of the guardhouse the night before the structure was meant to be raised. Late on a Friday night Dr. Warren was challenged by an off-duty officer, who seized him by the collar. Warren knocked the officer to the ground.

Bernard was further dismayed to see that "Adams and his assistants" counted among their ranks a strategically placed confederate. In addition to the assaults on constables, to the boys dragged into court for having knocked down a sentry box with a football, everything said or done by the Council somehow also ended up—"perverted, misrepresented, and falsified"—in the paper. Bernard suspected that it landed there courtesy of James Bowdoin, who had assumed leadership of the Council and who rivalled Hancock when it came to civic largesse. Bernard confronted Bowdoin about the leaks, challenging him to name a government that worked effectively when its deliberations were advertised by "tavern politicians" and "newspaper libellers." He reminded Bowdoin that the Council had sworn an oath of secrecy. Curtly Bowdoin informed Bernard that they interpreted that oath to mean that they were to keep secret only those matters that required secrecy.

Were the devil himself contributing to the *Journal*—as, seethed Bernard, he seemed to be—he could not have assembled "a greater collection of impudent, virulent, and seditious lies, perversions of truth, and misrepresentations." To counter them all constituted a Herculean labor. (It was yet more frustrating, noted the ranking lieutenant colonel in Boston, as the administration was without recourse. To prosecute only served the *Journal*'s purpose.) The intent was plainly to raise a continent-wide clamor; the ricocheting reports were meant to draw the other colonies into the Massachusetts orbit. Hutchinson preferred the colonies remain as unconnected as possible. Left to themselves, he wagered, they would wind up at war with one another. In December he reported that Boston had managed to revive the spirits of New York and Pennsylvania, their ardor long cooled. At the same time, Bernard consoled himself that the troops behaved admirably despite the "heap of falsehood" in the *Journal*. They endured insults and frivolous indictments. The town was quiet. "This being the truth," he fumed, "how wicked and abandoned must be the author of the *Journal*?"

Amid the "heap of falsehood" nestled plenty of truth. No New Englander could have improved that winter on the *Journal*'s description: "One of the first commercial towns in America has now several regiments of soldiers quartered in the midst of it, and even the Merchants' Exchange is picquetted and made the spot where the Main Guard is placed and paraded, and their cannon mounted; so that instead of our merchants and trading people transacting their business, we see it filled with redcoats, and have our ears dinned with music of the drum and fife." Adams seemed to feel that if Bernard had exaggerated every disturbance that had preceded the arrival of troops, he would magnify every one that followed. Guards daily threatened to blow women's brains out, to clap the town watch in irons, to burn Boston to the ground. An ensign who took to a married woman attempted—having nearly broken down her front door—to court "that angel in the window" from the street. Her husband responded with a loaded pistol. The country butcher insulted by troops as he rode through town in his cart reported, hat in hand, to Colonel Dalrymple, on the abuse he had endured. "You are a damned scoundrel," Dalrymple informed him. "You was saucy, they served you right, and I don't care if they knock you down again."*

Winter did nothing to cool tempers. Nor did cheap New England rum, which left the soldiers in raptures. Desertions continued, despite the October example. Six or eight men could evaporate in a night. Nearly fifty disappeared between December and January. Bostonians enticed the regulars, who needed little enticing, a subject on which Adams merrily expanded. They envied the Americans' good fortune. They liked the country! (He was correct. British army life was brutal. And a fair number of Massachusetts redcoats had also been in prison months earlier.) The loss of men might alone suggest, Adams chortled, "that Boston is a very unsuitable place for quartering soldiers." The desertions introduced another irritant: posted at the town gates, sentries reminded Bostonians that they now inhabited a garrison town. Civilians did not appreciate being ordered to identify themselves. Nor did they appreciate being detained in the late-evening cold. Nothing could have driven the insult of occupation home more forcefully than troops billeted in the courtroom, a semi-sacred address.

There was plenty of cause for outrage without Adams having to

---

* Everyone read the *Journal* entries, though not everyone managed to penetrate Adams's disguise. James Murray, a Scottish-born merchant, rented his sugar distillery to the troops. Two weeks afterward, Bernard rewarded him by naming him a justice of the peace. The appointment, according to the *Journal*, enraged the town. Murray exploded. Would its author care to unmask himself, so that Murray might call him a villain and scoundrel to his face? He obliquely addressed Adams, whom he suspected had, under different names, written most of the defamatory pieces of the previous seven years, and whom he advised to reform his ways.

concoct what Hutchinson deemed "pretended facts" and "false reports." All the same he improved on each. He reheated old grudges. Into the *Journal* he ladled all the unresolved business of the previous three years, tossing in Georgia's and South Carolina's endorsements of the Circular Letter. He heightened flavors, inventing "the siege of the Manufactory House," an account that allowed him incidental revenge on Sheriff Greenleaf. He dusted indecencies with insults. Daily military parades were one thing. But cards and shuttlecock on a Sunday? Was it his imagination, or did the soldiers seem more frequently to saw wood on the Sabbath? Sunday horse-racing, theft, prostitution, and profanity were new to Boston. Here was a full-scale assault on New England probity, sobriety, and chastity.

As 1769 wore on, the *Journal*'s marauding redcoats made way for industrious women. Abused and assaulted, they were already the heroes of Adams's pages. They soon outdid one another with spinning parties. For each woman attacked—the misconduct seemed to pick up as spring approached, when an old washerwoman, alone at home reading the Bible, wound up thrown to the floor and nearly raped, her bundle of linen stolen—a Daughter of Liberty emerged to advertise American industry. There was a reason for Adams's preoccupation. In March 1769, Philadelphia finally joined Boston's seven-month-old nonimportation agreement; all three major American ports closed to British imports. A tax upon paint had sent all of America, the *Journal* claimed, "to explore their hills and mountains," scavenging for red and yellow pigments. Adams editorialized freely, which might have been what Hutchinson had in mind when resentfully he tipped his hat: with "great art, and little truth," the *Journal* succeeded wildly in inflaming the people. Five months after its encounter with the vandal, the Bernard portrait returned to Harvard College. Its painter, John Singleton Copley, had restored the canvas. The new heart looked impeccable, observed Adams, "though upon a near and accurate inspection, it will be found no other than a false one." He hoped the portrait would remain on display. The governor remained a scourge. But in awakening a continent, Adams acknowledged, he had "laid the foundation of American greatness."

At the end of January 1769 appeared another entirely accurate item. With some regularity, faction leaders heard that they were to be arrested on treason charges. Already their names had been submitted to London. Bernard proceeded to collect evidence, by secret, inquisitorial means, charged the *Journal*, "which is repugnant to law, reason, and common equity." Evidence might consist of little more than the expressions of two men glimpsed in public conversation. The malefactors were to be deported quietly, so as not to incite a revolt. Into what times they had fallen! It was like the end of the Roman Republic, "when street conversation (however innocent) was taken up by vagabond pimps, employed and paid for their pains, and carried to their superiors, who from thence formed the measures of the administration!" London had indeed considered and shied away from treason charges in the past, finally dusting off an obsolete statute for the occasion. Dating from the time of Henry VIII, it was the only one that could reasonably justify deporting a suspect to Great Britain for offenses committed in America.* In 1768 it was decided that—if Bernard could supply precise details rather than his usual dark hints—the leading incendiaries could be tried. Who precisely had called the Massachusetts Convention? Who had opposed the order to rescind? Most Crown officers expected Adams to be apprehended imminently, an assumption that added to his prestige and that disturbed him not at all.†

The suggestion to pursue charges arrived on January 16, 1769. Within the week, Hutchinson closeted himself with a spirited sixty-three-year-old Boston innkeeper who had served for decades in the Royal Navy. Under oath, Richard Silvester swore that late one morning after the June barge-burning he had happened upon Adams in the street, haranguing a group of men, on the south side of town. If any of the bystanders was known to Silvester, he could not supply his name. Of Adams he had a vivid recollection. Trembling, in great agitation, Adams exhorted: "If you

---

* The indignity of being transported "beyond seas" for prosecution would be immortalized in a 1776 document.

† Closely monitoring those deliberations, a French statesman noted early in 1769: "An attempt to seize the defenders of American liberties would precipitate a revolution."

are men, behave like men. Let us take up arms immediately and be free, and seize all the King's officers!" Thirty thousand men from the countryside, Adams swore, would join them. Though Silvester overheard only scraps of the conversation—he sensed he was unwelcome—he swore that Adams had repeated the lines in Silvester's home, in the presence of his wife, as recently as two or three days before troops had disembarked. He had heard Adams advocate for armed insurrection no fewer than four times. "We will take up arms and spend our last drop of blood before the King and Parliament shall impose on us," Adams had allegedly blustered.

Had he really urged armed resistance on a Boston street corner before at least one unsympathetic listener? Silvester shared other remarks that sound distinctly like Adams. He had, Silvester swore, equated taxation with slavery. He denounced the customs officials, governor, and lieutenant governor for having requested troops. Adams had plainly used terms at the convention that discomfited others. He had gleefully participated in the farce of the firearms. Silvester named the right names: while he gave pride of place to Adams, he informed as well on two of his close associates, one of whom, quailing before Silvester's hints, began to spy for Hutchinson. Silvester had Adams saying precisely what Hutchinson expected to hear. Troops had after all braced for armed resistance. The same soldiers now asked themselves what they were doing, without specific orders, in a well-ordered town. Even Hutchinson would report that regulars occupied Boston only to keep the people in a state of awe. It diminished by the day.

On the other hand, Silvester attributed the same sentiments, in nearly identical words, to different men at different times. According to him, all three had said: "The King has no right to send troops to invade us. I look upon them as foreign enemies." (An associate alone got credit for: "The King is a fool and a rascal, and ought to have his head cut off.") There was plenty of loose talk around Boston, where any number of people had sworn they would fight up to their knees in blood before permitting a redcoat to land. As Silvester indicated, Adams was someone who directed men, who looked to him for direction. He confidently unpacked—and advertised—ideas. Adams also knew that spies lurked everywhere. For years he had warned of those who ferreted out information to convey to their superiors. Even at his most scathing, he rarely approached the intemperance Silvester described. He wrote still of the king as "the greatest personage on earth." (Silvester had Adams saying they had no need of a king.) He knew what constituted treason, from which he maintained a respectful distance. It makes sense that he allowed himself more latitude among friends than he did on the page. But the alleged recklessness aligns neither with the cool logic of his prose nor with his prudent, disciplined thinking. No one understood better than Adams that for Massachusetts to take up arms without the support of her sister colonies was folly. He focused on tamping down violence, on proving that troops had arrived in Boston to quell a fictional opposition.

One other piece of evidence undermines Silvester's report. Bernard and Hutchinson had long lobbied for arrests of the *Gazette*'s "seditious libellers." If examples could be made of a few offenders — "the most wicked fellows among us of any upon the globe," as Hutchinson had it that December — order could be handily restored. He could not have been happy to see that the *Journal* reported on efforts to make treason arrests four days after he had deposed Silvester. Were there no secrets in Boston? He was plainly displeased weeks later to read that, despite its best efforts, the administration could locate no firm evidence of treason. The hesitation to arrest only emboldened the "liberty men." Unafraid, they could not be tempted to inform on one another. Hutchinson would preserve their ridicule in his history, frustration crammed uncomfortably between the lines. But neither in lines he published nor lines he excised did he mention Silvester's assertions, which he would have had every incentive to repeat, if he lent them any credence.*

Adams's fevered call to arms was probably every bit as accurate as the *Journal* account of the woman dragged by her hair or the imminent French invasion. How far evolved was he in his thinking, as strains of

---

* There is one other clue, if an unusual and undated one. Adams and his friends often conferred in a tavern. From the daughter of the establishment came a report that — while everyone else insisted still on moderation — Adams raised his voice for independence. She had heard him distinctly, she revealed much later, having secreted herself in a closet.

martial music interrupted his Sunday worship? The received wisdom is that he set his heart on American independence in 1768, an infinitely larger leap at the time than it appears in retrospect. Some—including Otis's astute, history-writing sister, Mercy Otis Warren—dated the Revolution from the hostile parade up King Street. Peter Oliver too asserted that independence "was settled in Boston in 1768, by Adams and his junto." Bernard believed that the die had been cast a year earlier. Others located the dividing line at the Townshend Acts. Modern scholars have followed Mercy Otis Warren's (and Silvester's) lead, asserting that Adams embraced the idea now. While he came to it early, it is impossible to say when he went from sensing he was at the end of something to recognizing he stood at a beginning. A great deal was indeed preconcerted, as Bernard griped. But for all the prophesying, Adams dealt as much in tactics as in strategy. He neither propelled himself into the future nor lunged toward a radical break with the past. He seems to have steered in the direction of Great Britain's skid, then kept going.

Before King George in 1774, Thomas Hutchinson would identify Adams as the first to embrace American independence. Certainly he lamented that the mother country proved so careless with colonial affections. He knew well that a rupture was possible, different from advocating for one. He balked at invented tales of insurrection as he did at the word "independency." He warned of self-fulfilling prophecies. He appears to have moved gradually from redress to revolt, making an art in between of resistance, enlisting men, women, and children, co-opting institutions, deploying boycotts and false reports, shaming and stigmatizing. The relentless cannonade in the newspapers was not the kind of shelling for which British troops had prepared. Adams resorted to a few tried and true techniques as well. His household included a formidable dog, a highly intelligent Newfoundland named Queue. Adams trained him to bite any redcoat that crossed his path. Queue bore the battle scars on his shaggy pelt.

ENLISTING AN ARMY of alter egos, Adams took the quarrel to paper. In the feather bed on Purchase Street, the world hushed all around, Betsy fell asleep to "the incessant motion of the pen in the next room." She could just make out her husband in the glow of candlelight surrounding his desk. A friend who regularly passed the household after midnight looked to the light in the second-floor window. No matter the hour, he assured himself that "Samuel Adams was hard at work writing against the Tories." Adams scratched out paragraph after paragraph, losing track of time until he heard the watchman outside. In swift, unedited bursts, the pages flew from his pen. One is left with the impression of a sleepless man, flooding the zone. Words came easily to Adams, who could churn a small grievance into an unpardonable insult before others had arrived at the end of a sentence. He was most at ease on paper. Here he and his moment embraced. It was a golden age for the printed word; with six Boston papers, New England dominated the news. Adams did not think in terms of pamphlets, looking instead to the *Gazette*, published every Monday. Instinctively he grasped what Tocqueville was to articulate several generations later and would remain true for many more: when you mean to rally a group of people to a common cause, your best friend is the newspaper, "the only way of being able to place the same thought at the same moment into a thousand minds."

It helped that the *Gazette* was the most widely read paper in and out of Boston; at least eleven other publications reprinted its pieces. As committed to ordinary citizens understanding their rights as to delivering up hair-raising accounts from an occupied town, Adams had no rival as a contributor. Tireless, he employed an assortment of pseudonyms, most with distinct agendas. As Candidus he launched ad hominem attacks on customs officials, newly returned to town. As Vindex he icily thanked them for having invited troops. A military force might elsewhere separate men from their senses, but it would "never awe a sensible American tamely to surrender his liberty." Adams was Populus when defending freedom of the press; TZ when disputing taxation with a writer in another paper; Shippen when inveighing against British bad faith. It was just as likely, Shippen pointed out, that loyal subjects of the king "intended to bring on an insurrection" as it was that a military force "secretly intended to introduce a general massacre." Critics reported the continent to be on the eve of rebellion. Vindex challenged anyone to prove it. Boston had demonstrated only "unspotted loyalty to their sovereign." In myriad ways and in any number of guises, Adams asked the same question: Are we — or is someone else — in charge of our destiny?

Through 1769 he adopted a new pseudonym at a regular rate of about one a month, molting, between February and May, from "EA" to "Urbanus" to "A Layman" to "A Bostonian" to "A Tory." He was not above a bit of expert character assassination, conducted, for reasons lost to us, as "Alfred." He was "EA" when — five months after the arrival of troops — he offered a little Blackstone-citing history lesson. Not only did English subjects enjoy the right to petition their king for redress, they enjoyed the right to possess and employ arms for self-defense. What cynic had transformed a basic constitutional right into *"a secret intention* to oppose the landing of the King's troops"? He was "A Bostonian" when defending the town against the unfounded claim that it was without government. As "A Tory," he offered an acerbic note of congratulations to Bernard on his being named a baronet, an honor partly bestowed to bolster Bernard's stature in America. The news arrived a month after the town petitioned for his removal, an effort that proved unnecessary. Two days before Adams took his swipe at the newly minted Baronet of Nettleham, Bernard read the happy news: rerouted from Virginia, he was to return to London.

Pseudonyms were the style of the day, Boston's version of a masked ball. They skewed classical. If you read only the essays in the papers you might reasonably conclude that ancient Romans peopled eighteenth-century New England.* The pseudonyms conferred a seal of intellectual approval; it was difficult to argue with Cato, Cicero, and Sallust. Adams did not overthink his, resorting neither to the waggishness of Benjamin Franklin nor the faux-rustic cadences of John Adams. He left it to someone else to sign himself "Locke." He never attempted a female disguise.

---

* No one has attempted a complete census, but one scholar counted 121 classical pseudonyms between 1770 and 1773 in the *Gazette* alone. The practice was the same throughout the colonies. At different junctures, George Washington identified with Cato the Younger, Fabius, and Cincinnatus, three names for which Adams never reached.

He rarely engaged in the petty tugs-of-war that left "Whole Truth" one-upping "Plain Truth." At times he opted not to sign a piece at all. (The 1769 essay that inquired whether guards would soon turn up before church doors, to prevent mobbing when services let out, was anonymous.) He seemed most naturally to inhabit Vindex and Candidus, the two longest-lived alter egos, one a Roman governor who rebelled against Nero, the other a second-century Roman general. On at least one occasion, Vindex wrote about Samuel Adams in the third person. Adams recruited Candidus to warn that "It is dangerous to be silent." In 1770 he would add "A Chatterer," "Valerius Poplicolo," "An American," "A Son of Liberty," and "Cotton Mather" to the repertoire. He was not above recycling, especially when it came to noting that a few well-placed men in America seemed intent on "having their own prophecies fulfilled, their misrepresentations successful, and their malevolence gratified." Vindex and Shippen borrowed most liberally from the *Journal of Occurrences*. In the last weeks of 1768, Adams published at least eight pieces over three different signatures. There would be no fewer than thirty pseudonyms in all.

The impersonations allowed him to stretch the truth in various directions. Without fear of reprisal, he could audition ideas and venture out on limbs. He could provoke, contradict, and disavow. The masquerade suggested too that discontent was general. Adams spoke not only for the community but as one. He seemed single-handedly to populate the "union of writers" he had proposed after the Stamp Act. He appeared on the same day under different names in different papers; in 1773 he quite literally ran the gamut from "A" to "Z." The *Massachusetts Spy* might print a "Letter from the Country" by an author who — though "situated at a great distance" — was eager to register his solidarity with Boston. Its author, in town, was Samuel Adams. He joined an infectious optimism with vivid descriptions of the evils at hand, issuing regular reminders of virtue and anthems to liberty. There were dissonant chords and mini-fugues. A one-man multitude, he could be silken, glowering, stabbing, melodramatic.

Adams had plenty of company in the pages of the *Gazette*, which printed nearly as much political material as the *Virginia Gazette* and the *New York Journal* combined. It found an eager audience. To Hutchinson's dismay, seven-eighths of Boston read nothing but that "infamous paper." It set the temper of the town. Andrew Oliver cursed its influence; if a reader did not share the convictions of the odious publication before he picked it up, he was a convert afterward. Adams spent his Sunday evenings setting type with the *Gazette* printers, an arduous labor conducted amid noxious fumes and below rafters tented with wet pages. Newspapering was far from a gentleman's profession. It could take an eye-straining day and most of a night — and copious quantities of beer — to produce four sheets. Poorly printed and expensive though they were, the papers were read aloud and passed enthusiastically from hand to hand, by men and women. You might head out to your neighbor's after dark to borrow his copy, or pick one up at the tavern.

How easily did Boston penetrate Adams's army of identities? Some were open secrets. "Discerning readers," Bernard informed London, "pretend to distinguish the different styles of several writers, and do it with great exactness." The newspaper-collecting Harbottle Dorr kept an eye out for Adams, among his heroes. Hutchinson dispatched a clutch of essays to London, noting that they were "generally supposed" to be the work of Adams. John was far from alone in failing to recognize his camouflaged cousin; Hutchinson did not initially recognize Vindex. The pseudonyms tormented him. Were Adams and his friends only required to sign their pieces, their arguments would be blown to bits! Adams routinely got credit for essays he did not write; plenty of other Bostonians railed against the insidious designs to deprive the colonies of "freedom and property and all that is worth living for on earth." (That piece was signed "Fervidus.") The prodigious output did not seem possible. A spring 1770 parody eviscerated each of the most vocal Whigs in turn. Adams merited a paragraph for his sins. Determinatus, idol of the vulgar, merited a second. Bernard felt he could identify Adams's voice, singular for "barefaced chicanery and falsity." He got to know it better than he liked. With his closet of disguises, Adams seemed to lurk around every corner.

Along with the chicanery came a great deal of creativity. Adams meant not only to unseat Bernard. He repeatedly promised—inaccurately—that the king would replace a governor whom Massachusetts disliked. He meant to rouse a people to their rights; to fold as many as he could into the political process; to forge a common cause; to elevate stout virtue over superficial luxury. Across the board he deployed the command of detail he had failed to summon for bookkeeping and tax-collecting. As Hutchinson tartly observed: "Mr. Adams's attention to the cause in which he was engaged would not suffer him to neglect even small circumstances which could be made subservient to it."

He ambushed language itself, demoting some institutions and promoting others. He knew that to alter thinking one must alter meaning. He renamed the Town House the "State House." The "province laws" became the "laws of the land," the "debates of the Assembly" the "parliamentary debates." He slipped a flippant "both countries" into one petition. Hutchinson found he had no choice but to adopt the neologisms or face fresh abuse. He would object when a 1773 set of House bills appeared in English rather than Latin, demanding they be resubmitted. What was so extraordinary, the House challenged Hutchinson, about plain English? Urging words like "inalienable" and "unconstitutional" into circulation, Adams turned others on their heads. By the late 1760s, a "patriot" was an individual loyal not to the British Empire, but to American rights. And a new entity emerged, which Adams largely juggled into being and for which he regularly spoke. "The body of the people" included even those who had insufficient property to vote at a town meeting. It was an entity to which, complained Hutchinson, "anything with the appearance of a man is admitted without scrutiny." You could call those assemblies whatever you like, he sniffed, but they more resembled a mob than a government. He dismissed them as general meetings of "Tom, Dick, and Harry."

Along with the vocabulary Adams exploited the imagery. If Crown officers took to changing the dinner hour in Boston, if an official took to stepping out in a suit of extravagant crimson velvet—the color alone offended the eye; the tailoring would have sustained whole families, reduced to poverty by British taxation—Adams saw to it that the *Journal* advertised the indignities. He organized celebrations of the first Stamp

Act riot, planting August 14 on the calendar to foster a defense of American rights, or, as some viewed it, to immortalize an act of civil disobedience. The 1769 jubilee was especially elaborate. Invitations went to every out-of-towner in Boston, as well as to Crown officers. (They declined.) The summer morning began with fourteen toasts, after which some 350 Sons of Liberty made their rutted way south to Dorchester, where they feasted on barbecued pig at long tables in an open field. Streamers fluttering, a sailcloth awning over their heads, they passed a lively afternoon, punctuated by cannon fire and lubricated by a second series of toasts.

Nowhere could the colonial mood be better read than in those tributes, drawn up the day before. The morning began with a salute to the king and queen, followed by a toast to "America and her brave Sons of Liberty." As Adams stressed to James Warren—an ardent, keen-eyed Plymouth patriot and Otis's brother-in-law—even trifling details mattered when it came to the public interest. The revelers toasted the daughters of Liberty; they toasted members of Parliament (though never Parliament itself); they toasted the liberty of the press, the perpetual union of Great Britain and her colonies, and American manufacturing. The forty-fifth and final toast sent a message to the Ministry that had ordered arrests: a cheer went up for hanging those who actually deserved it. An afternoon rainstorm failed to curtail the festivities, as a table malfunction would fail to ruin a subsequent one, though it left half the revelers drenched in gravy, punch, sauce, and marrow in their laps.

In 1769 a series of impersonations, performed by a comedian in the group, followed the feast, after which the assembly joined in song. Toward five o'clock, the carriages were brought round and—in a procession that extended nearly a mile and a half, Hancock leading the way, Adams just behind—the company clattered to Boston for a tour of the town. Despite the fourteen toasts in the morning and forty-five in the afternoon, the Sons remained, in every account, stone-cold sober. John Adams saw no sign of intoxication, though he did notice how much the affair kept resistance alive. Otis and Adams were canny, he felt, in promoting such festivities: "For they tinge the minds of the people, they impregnate them with the sentiments of liberty. They render the people fond of their leaders in the cause, and averse and bitter against all opposers." Conducted with perfect decorum, the anniversary was meant to have as little as possible to do with the day it commemorated.

On August 1, 1769, Francis Bernard quietly boarded the ship that was to carry him to London. There was no formal farewell. He left from Castle William precisely nine years after he had arrived with high hopes for what had seemed an agreeable posting. No sooner was he under sail than cannon boomed. Bells tolled. Flags rippled from housetops and from vessels in the harbor. They fluttered in one direction, then the other; the shifting wind left Bernard stalled several miles from shore, with a prime view of the revelry. As the departing governor rode at anchor in the harbor, Adams helped to hiss him offstage. "Whatever may be his first reception at home," wrote Adams, "impartial history will hang him up as a warning to his successors." All America rejoiced at the departure. Adams seemed to have proved his point; it indeed appeared that the king would recall a governor who displeased the people. The June petition he had drafted requesting that the king spare the colonies from Bernard's return sailed on the same ship.

LEFT TO CONTEND with the wreckage, Hutchinson brooded. He had never known a time when Crown officers stood more in need of advice. Absurd ideas circulated throughout America, especially in Massachusetts. He bemoaned "the artful performances of one or two designing men." At any other time they would have been irrelevant. Somehow they held the colony in their deluded thrall. With the *Journal* they proved themselves remarkably effective, extending their influence well beyond Massachusetts. (It was the *Journal's* doing that at Bernard's departure his effigy burned in New York.) By stressing individuals, Hutchinson inadvertently obscured the view; the Ministry came to conclude that the contest was one between all of England and three obstreperous Massachusetts men.* Fictitious quarrels, fretted Hutchinson, too easily invited real ones. "I tremble," he wrote on September 1, 1769, "for my country."

---

* In London, Franklin pointed out that the contest more properly matched three British ministers against all of America.

It was one thing to leave Crown officials cowering behind doors, another, Adams knew, to impress the sanctity of colonial rights upon an assembly three thousand miles away. Economic resistance had defeated the Stamp Act. Nonimportation seemed the effective answer to the Townshend duties. Adams went on an industry-promoting tear, describing communities that boasted more looms than homes. He extolled colonial wool and flax. Rhode Islanders, he claimed, had resolved to vote only for candidates in American-made apparel. A man was now more admired, he contended—on no evidence whatever—when he appeared in home-made garments than in "the most gaudy attire" of Great Britain. (In close touch with his tailor, Hutchinson contrived to parse the differences between yellow metal buttons and blue mohair ones.) The colonies manufactured glass, pipe, and oil. Soon they would manage without British paper. He could not get enough of the hyperactive New England spinners; as if from a sports stadium, he announced the tallies of skeins and the inconceivable speed with which the "true daughters of liberty and industry" worked. The full-day marathons included nine-year-olds and wealthy octogenarians. Women seemed intent on recovering American rights, which was more, wrote Adams, than their fathers and husbands had managed. They held the fate of the British Empire in their dexterous hands.

He protested too much. Support for nonimportation faltered toward summer's end, as word flew about that some duties would be eliminated. Adams insisted the boycott continue until all were lifted; the right itself must be repealed. As nonconsumption was as powerful as nonimportation, another initiative took off. Subscriptions were carried from door to door, so that each Bostonian might pledge to reject goods from those merchants who flouted nonimportation. That effort succeeded. Ten days after Bernard sailed, the number of nonsubscribers had shrunk from twenty-five merchants to seven. Among the holdouts were Hutchinson's two sons, Bernard's son, and a brash Scottish printer named John Mein. Hutchinson railed against the initiative, quibbling with the very definition of "merchant." It had come to include "every master of a sloop and broker, shopkeeper, or huckster," who now set policy for the most eminent traders. His sons were left to conduct business stealthily, at reduced prices, like smugglers. Again the lieutenant governor thought back to the Land Bank. Was this not a similar encroachment on royal author-ity? Could it be suppressed by the same statute? A treason conviction might not be possible, but there was a perfectly good law on the books for those who infringed on Crown authority. The penalty was capital pun-ishment.

At the end of August Adams weighed in as Populus, blasting those who attacked the agreement. He singled out John Mein in particular. A feisty character, Mein had arrived five years earlier in Massachusetts, where he opened a bookshop. It thrived. Soon he began to publish a newspaper, the most handsome in the colony if of a very different flavor from the *Gazette*. He could be belligerent; a September *Gazette* contribu-tor deemed him a "conceited, empty noodle of a most profound block-head." Mein applied to Edes and Gill for the name of their author. Edes replied that a fellow printer should know better than to make such a demand. The Scot responded by picking up a club and delivering two blows to John Gill's head. Bostonians who resembled Mein were after-ward pummeled in a dark alley. Mein took to carrying two pistols about town. And he made it his mission to point out that many who had signed the nonimportation agreement continued—under the table and despite solemn pledges—to import. He had no need to editorialize, opting simply to publish customs ledgers. The evidence was on his side, but Adams defended the honor of his fellow Bostonians. He had heard many tales from "this overzealous man." He issued an unveiled threat: "I would desire Mr. Mein to accept a word of caution, not to set himself in opposi-tion to an awakened, an enlightened, and a determined continent."

The following week, John Adams dined at the Otis household in com-pany that included Adams and John Gill. Tagging along afterward, he learned how his cousin spent his Sundays. At the *Gazette* office, together with several colleagues, Samuel Adams prepared the next day's paper, "cooking up paragraphs, articles, occurrences, etc.—working the politi-cal engine!" It functioned efficiently that autumn evening. Atop the first column of the September 4, 1769, edition appeared the names of the seven merchants who scorned nonimportation. Directly below, the *Gazette* reprinted Adams's petition to the king. For the House, he begged that the colony be relieved of Bernard, submitting a solemn catalogue of indictments, from abuses of power to injurious misrepresentations. A few words from Otis followed. He did not appreciate having been called a traitor and rebel in the commissioners' letters home. He took seriously his allegiance to the Crown. He demanded satisfaction of those "superlative blockheads." He named in particular John Robinson, who had sacrificed his cherry trees to "liquorish boys." (Robinson was also the wearer of the dazzling crimson velvet.) "I have a natural right," wrote Otis, "if I can get no other satisfaction, to break his head."

In the printshop, the smell of ink heavy in the air, John Adams noticed something else about the purring political engine. "The most talkative man alive," Otis clogged its gears. He could devote an entire evening to "bullying, bantering, reproaching, and ridiculing." Three-minute anecdotes consumed an hour, two stories an afternoon. The vitriol made its way into Monday's paper; some may have seeped out earlier in the weekend as well. Otis and Adams had called on the commissioners late Friday morning. Otis met with them again on Saturday. He requested meetings with each man, who, he suggested, should enlist a friend.

When he refused to acknowledge Otis's request, one official was informed that he was "a poltroon and a scoundrel." Another offered a faint apology. Early Tuesday evening Otis strolled into the British Coffee House, a Tory haunt. Robinson awaited him. Each demanded satisfaction of the other; an animated discussion devolved quickly into a furious dispute. Otis suggested they settle the matter elsewhere. As they turned to leave, Robinson attempted to take Otis by the nose, a serious insult. Missing his mark, Robinson struck him, possibly with a sword, more likely with a cane, on the forehead. Blood gushed forth. Sturdy Otis returned the blow, after which the room—thick with British officers and customs personnel—evidently exploded. Various officers moved in to attack Otis, who disarmed his opponent. Fists flew. Up went cries of "Kill him! Kill him!" Out came bludgeons and cutlasses. In the chaos the lights were extinguished. Sticks crashed over Otis's head. Robinson fled through a back door. Otis was carried off, bloodied and bruised.

Though nowhere on hand, Adams appears to have reported in the following week's paper on the brawl that left his closest colleague half-dead. By then it had acquired a different complexion. In Adams's version, Robinson instigated the fight after the commissioners had plotted to assassinate Otis. They had placed wagers on the contest. Adams introduced getaway vessels for the perpetrators. He quibbled with Robinson's claim that he had laid aside his sword; the doctors who tended Otis described wounds consistent with a sharp weapon. Either Robinson had not retired the sword or he had enlisted an accomplice. And what of the scabbard found on the floor afterward? Even for Adams, wholly comfortable at the intersection of allegation and surmise, this was a leap. (Otis's assistant never used the word "assassinate." Having attempted to intervene, he was ejected from the Coffee House with a broken wrist and blood streaming down his face.) Adams's version nonetheless prevailed. Most *Gazette* readers believed in a plot to murder Otis.[*] Hutchinson wrung his hands. There had been any number of witnesses. There might just as well have been a thousand. Were Otis to hang himself, the commissioners would be accused of his death!

Whatever he thought of a provocation that he so adroitly repackaged, Adams could not have been reassured by the state of Otis's health. The crack in the skull unsettled a fragile constitution. Garrulous before, Otis was insufferable after, mentally unmoored, adrift in a sea of words. He was a blight on the Monday Night Club, which he monopolized with a stew of "trash, obsceneness, profaneness, nonsense, and distraction." The stories that should have taken three minutes still took an hour but now Otis lost his way amid them, detouring for the indecent. Adams could only have turned away, as did others, with tears in their eyes. He handed out excuses and explanations. He insisted on respect; where possible, he smoothed the way. Though their opinions had differed, though

---

[*] The truth was probably closer to the account that "A Bye-Stander" supplied in Mein's paper, the *Boston Chronicle*. Otis bled copiously from Robinson's initial blow; the two thereafter entered into "a brisk manual exercise." No sword, cutlass, or other sharp weapon appeared. Nor did anyone threaten to kill Otis. He would pursue and win a case of assault and battery, though, as a point of honor, he declined the two-thousand-pound settlement.

Otis's views fluctuated wildly, though Otis savaged some of their closest associates, the two had collaborated intimately and traveled as a pair. Adams had finished Otis's sentences, no easy feat.

As if further proof were needed that newspapers constituted a blood sport, the enterprising John Mein continued his campaign with a late-October satire. On the front page of the October 26 *Boston Chronicle*, he dismissed Hancock as a fool and Cushing as an indolent nonentity, his hand deep in Hancock's pocket. Otis was a "muddlehead," Adams "the psalm-singer with the gifted face." Mein outed him as "Alfred" and revived the Land Bank affair. Those who blackened reputations should remember that skeletons rattled about in their closets, too. Mein was an unpopular character at many addresses; he had after all embarrassed most of the merchants who bobbed and weaved their way around nonimportation. Even Hutchinson found the "ludicrous names" distasteful and the publisher obnoxious.

Adams's threat proved prophetic that weekend. Mein and a colleague strolled up busy King Street just before sunset, late Saturday afternoon. From the rattling flow of traffic some twenty individuals closed in on Mein. Several were fashionably dressed; they carried spades, clubs, and canes. Mein cocked his pistol and began walking backward up the street, toward the main guardhouse, threatening to shoot the first person who laid a hand on him. As he reached the sentries, a shovel collided with his back, slashing his coat and bruising his shoulder. His colleague then fired his pistol. That, anyway, was Mein's version. In the popular retelling, he fired first. He survived the scrape but worried for his life, with reason; after he disappeared into the guardhouse his home was ransacked. "A deluded, unthinking rabble," as he described them, also took it upon themselves that evening to tar and feather a customs informer, carted through town.

An order went up for every house in the neighborhood to display lanterns in sympathy with the cause. Only Silvester, who had had such rich things to say about Adams, preferred to sit in darkness. (Several stones flew through his windows.) With minimal success, Mein spent the next days trying to attract Hutchinson's attention. The printer did not think he would survive a walk on a Boston street, a sentiment with which Hutchinson concurred. Meanwhile, having obtained a warrant, Adams set out, a sheriff and constable in tow, to arrest him. William Molineux, a wealthy hardware merchant, joined them. The four searched the guardhouse for over an hour but never located Mein, secreted deep in the garret, from which he later descended, making his way to the home of Colonel Dalrymple, in disguise. He escaped Boston weeks later on a British warship, little missed by anyone save, possibly, his bookstore patrons.

Hutchinson complained of gross abuse in the press but any number of Bostonians could have registered the same complaint. Even without Mein's contributions, Adams and his associates were ridiculed as "agonizing reptiles," an "execrable set of scrawling miserables," "small statesmen, who rave and drivel out their political frenzy and idiotism." Little was sacred in either camp. At one point someone in Adams's circle took an opponent to task not only for his spelling but for his punctuation, "splashed and splattered about in a very arbitrary manner."

Adams indulged in less name-calling. At least on the page, at least until 1770, he preferred astringent to scathing. His October piece as "Alfred" counts among the more acidic. He attacked those customs inspectors who—deprived of "the sweets of the Stamp Act"—hoped "to feast and fatten themselves" upon American spoils. He took savage aim at the Hutchinsons. Despite having been generously reimbursed his 1765 damages, the lieutenant governor refused still to defend colonial rights, leaving it to others to sacrifice for the good of the country.* Adams deemed such men public enemies. For the first time he mentioned independence not as an idea America should embrace but as one from which Great Britain should shrink. You can feel the temperature rising, the equanimity evaporating. "Good God!," Adams wrote that fall, two days before the town was to review nonimportation, "How much longer is it expected that the patience of this injured country shall hold out!"

---

* Adams raked Mein over the same coals. The Scot had flourished in Boston, where subscribers flocked to his paper. He could not have dreamed of greater success. "And what return has he made," asked Adams, "to the beneficent public?" The warm colonial welcome made the Gill assault especially indefensible.

Within a matter of days and in a very different tone, he offered a second retrospective of the 1760s. He did not normally go in for grandiosity; he did however mean to vindicate years of wrongs. In a document entitled *An Appeal to the World*—it was a favorite expression—Adams reviewed Bernard's overreactions and overstatements, the mishaps the governor upgraded to riots and insurrection, John Robinson's fruit trees, the Circular Letter, the September convention, the Manufactory House scuffle. Over thirty-four tightly argued pages, Adams attributed the invasion of a peaceful town by British regulars to a governor who insisted on believing a whole continent ripe for revolt. Bernard feared free speech and free assemblies. He could neither tell a straight story nor believe one. He was credulous, dangerous, ridiculous. Adams was passionate and laser-focused: Partial repeal of trade acts was immaterial. Higher principles were at stake. The 1769 *Appeal* is a masterpiece of lucidity if, at times, as true as was an Otis assassination attempt. Read aloud at the October 18 town meeting, it was unanimously accepted. The House ordered its publication. Given the length, it became a pamphlet. There had been a great deal to pack in.

Hutchinson had trouble getting his hands on a copy, held for distribution until after every London-bound vessel had sailed, presumably so that it would arrive in Great Britain before any gloss from him. When finally he obtained the pamphlet—the lieutenant governor was left to prevail upon a friend of a journeyman at the printer's—he was aghast. It was "shamefully evasive and fallacious." He suspected that Adams had had help from Bowdoin, which annoyed him even more. *An Appeal to the World* traveled abroad to individuals of influence, in the hope it might convert them. It was time to dissolve the customs board, repeal the revenue acts, and recall the troops. The Massachusetts agent in London saw to it that five hundred copies were printed and distributed to members of both Houses of Parliament, where it won admiration even from its detractors. Snorting, Bernard accepted congratulations on Adams's masterwork. He believed it would only do him honor.*

---

* He was right. When the charges were discussed four months later, they were found "groundless, vexatious, and scandalous." They closely prefigure a 1776 list of grievances.

Impatience seeped out all around the edges that winter. Adams campaigned to pressure Hutchinson to withdraw troops, useless in town, argued Adams, unless they were determined "to fire upon the multitude, and lay them dead upon the spot." No one felt safer for their presence. Their antics were ridiculous. Hutchinson claimed that Adams pushed the envelope at this time: when a radical motion came before a town meeting, he sailed into the discussion with the cry, "Independent we are, and independent we will be." The syntax is very much his, though some qualifier may have been lost en route to Hutchinson's front door.* More likely the timing was compressed. Hutchinson knew as well as anyone that certain ideas were to be kept out of sight; unthinkable for years, independence would be inexpressible for many more. No one spoke of it in 1769, when Adams was more intent on defending the Massachusetts charter from the battering of a family that seemed intent on its destruction. But the resentment built throughout occupied Boston, where not a day passed without incident and where Adams edged his way toward the combustible stage. Those who had been casting "pins and pebbles" against the colonies had managed brilliantly to alienate her affections. The arrogance was staggering. He trembled for his country. "Britain may fall sooner than she is aware," Adams warned, "while her colonies, who are struggling for liberty, may survive her fate and tell the story to their children's children."

---

* In Hutchinson's correspondence, Adams's battle cry also surfaces—unassociated with Adams—two years later. It was more in Hutchinson's best interest to report that he said as much than it was in Adams's best interest to issue it. He tended not to wave around sticks of dynamite.

AN EXASPERATED PEOPLE

*Is there not a sort of blood shed when the conscience
is wounded?*
— HENRY DAVID THOREAU

GREAT BRITAIN seemed intent on trifling away another winter, Adams contended late in 1769. She would pay handsomely, he predicted, for her inattention. He was pleased that even Boston's women and children had taken to laughing at the British troops. They had spared neither Mein his encounter with the shovel nor Otis the blow to the head nor an informer a coat of tar and feathers. Mostly they served as walking provocations. Bostonians, even well-dressed Bostonians, stalked red-coated sentries, blasting them with "all the abusive language they could invent." The vocabulary expanded to meet the task. The soldiers were "bloody-back thieving dogs," or "damned rascally scoundrel lobster sons of bitches." Returning to the barracks one winter evening, a group of soldiers met several fishermen, who insisted the redcoats confine themselves to the gutter "like other lobsters and scoundrels." Regulars were stalked, threatened, hissed at, knocked down, pelted with stones, mud, spittle, snowballs, and pieces of brick, dismissed by the magistrates to whom they took their complaints. The town made trophies of officers' swords and epaulets. And with two thousand soldiers, there were potential targets for every family in town. Barracks stood within blocks of Adams's front door.

Adams urged that the House insist on a removal of the troops when it reconvened that winter; Hutchinson vowed to defeat a vote that he knew he would be compelled to honor. Unwittingly, Adams assisted. Probably on account of his *Appeal to the World*, Hutchinson received word, at the eleventh hour, that he should delay the January 1770 reopening of the legislature until March. He feared an outcry but found that "the liberty heroes" seemed to have little to say for themselves. The exception was Adams. The House existed to redress grievances, inveighed Vindex. To prevent its meeting undermined its reason for being. The convention of the previous winter, he pointed out, had been called to fill this very void. He took a shot at Hutchinson's integrity. A worthy governor did not blindly follow orders. He followed his conscience.

For all the London foot-dragging—indeed there was no rush to address American affairs—Adams had his hands full that winter. By virtue of his position in the House, through unrelenting effort and the force of his personality, he could persuade a colleague to return a document to his pocket rather than read it aloud, where it might pique the interest of the acting governor. He remained however yoked to a partner whose wounds had healed but whose mental health deteriorated, leaving him marooned between fits of "frantic, impotent rage" and "sullen silent malice." Otis raved against his family. (His wife repudiated his politics.) He hurled rocks at Town House windows and fired guns from his own. He drank. He flew into frenzies of self-loathing, cursing the day he was born, keening that he had done his country irreparable harm. Forty-five-year-old Otis also remained, along with Cushing and Adams, as popular as ever. Adams proceeded tactfully, even when Otis pronounced himself finished with the cause.

His heart broke as he offered excuses around town for "the man I love most heartily." He hesitated to commit criticism of Otis to paper. He asked that even vague reproaches be destroyed upon reading. He begged for indulgence, given Otis's long service in the cause of liberty. Where possible, he folded him into committees. He shrugged off the biting criticism, the "banter and ridicule" with which his colleague greeted him. He made quick work of rumors of dissension. Having once followed behind, Adams sailed out in advance, troubleshooting.

There was volatility closer to home as well. Samuel Adams Jr. did not sail as serenely through Harvard College as had his father. As a freshman, he had participated in a 1766 student protest that began with a flying slice of bread and ended with half the undergraduates suspended. Since that time, young Samuel had been admonished for participating in "the affair of the lewd woman." He had left campus for a night without permission. He made a practice of stealing wood for his fire. As a senior, he was in 1770 demoted six places for having stolen ducks that were dressed, cooked, and served in his room. All evidence points to Adams having been a tolerant, trusting parent—"I am sure you will never condescend to be a companion of fools," was his idea of discipline—but the Harvard antics could only have proved an unwelcome distraction.

Most urgently, nonimportation efforts stalled. Hints of partial repeal had mollified New York and Philadelphia. Boston alone voted to extend its boycott beyond January 1770. Balking, several merchants began to sell goods immediately; the issue remained as raw as the presence of troops. Adams appeared on the second page of the January 8 *Gazette* as Vindex; as Determinatus, he claimed most of the front page as well. He reminded defectors of the social compact. Did they also enjoy the right to set fire to their homes, even if they might destroy the neighborhood in the process? "Where did you learn," he chastised, "that in a state or society you had a right to do as you please?" He singled out for special opprobrium several men who unblushingly resolved to violate an agreement to which they had sworn. Did these faithless individuals really mean to flout the laws of honor, honesty, humanity? The rights and liberties of future generations demanded their compliance. Every *Gazette* reader knew that two of those faithless souls were the sons of Thomas Hutchinson, who shared his address and directed a business in which he was a silent partner.

A committee formed a week later to call on the defectors. Well over a thousand people followed it to the Hutchinson mansion. Raising a window, the lieutenant governor inquired, needlessly, after their business. The committee announced it had come to negotiate with his sons. Might they discuss the matter inside? "By no means," Hutchinson shot back. The chair replied that he was sorry Hutchinson thought the visitors unworthy of admittance, to which the acting governor countered that they might understand his reluctance if they thought back five years. Amid the crowd he noticed several individuals who had sacked his home. The interview continued through the window, where Hutchinson, flanked by his sons, argued that the agreement was invalid. He decried the mass visit. "When I was attacked before, I was a private person. I am now the representative of the greatest Monarch upon earth, whose Majesty you affront in thus treating my person." The committee assured him it had business only with his sons and proceeded to call on the other Boston holdouts. At the advice of friends, Hutchinson relented the following morning. His sons entrusted the proceeds for tea they had sold, along with the key to their warehouse, to the committee.

No sooner had he done so than Hutchinson regretted his concession. It rankled more with time, especially as other merchants stood firm. The shame of having been outmaneuvered came to feel a greater blow, he found, the distress eating away at him, than had the ransacking of his house. Somehow political power had migrated to the wrong hands. A thousand carpenters, joiners, and carters gathered one day, twelve hundred the next. The law prohibited such assembly, as Hutchinson had reminded the callers at his window. Their visits from home to home, in vast number, demanding the return of goods, struck terror in their hosts. And their cursed meetings had no more right to regulate trade than to declare war on a foreign power.

On January 23, 1770, Hutchinson sent Sheriff Greenleaf to order the Faneuil Hall meeting to disband. Greenleaf begged not to be required to speak Hutchinson's words aloud. The moderator stepped in, conveying an appeal to "persons of character, reputation, and property" to detach themselves from the extralegal efforts of the rest. Respectable men should not consort with hoodlums. By unanimous vote, some fourteen hundred Bostonians, the minority of them merchants, dispatched Greenleaf to inform the acting governor that they were "determined to keep consciences void of offense towards God and towards man." The meeting went on to proscribe additional offenders, a list that included two women. Hutchinson was left to storm feebly against a new reign of terror. He dealt Adams a backhanded compliment: the acting governor felt he was up against writers who "have talents beyond any other persons on the globe at misrepresentation." The gatherings included justices of the peace, town representatives, and several "professed lawyers" — all men, Hutchinson sputtered, who should know better. He demoted "our political heroes" to "our madmen." At least one of them, he noted, was acquainted with and willing to employ every trick in the book.

Adams worked some of his magic that January on a diminutive Scot who refused to subscribe to nonimportation. Visits to his home had produced stalemates. Adams proposed to a large meeting that they call on the holdout at the end of the day. Rumors of the excursion, Adams knew, would reach him before any delegation did. The Scot soon enough rushed in, visibly agitated. Bowing in turn to the moderator and to Adams, he announced that he agreed completely to their terms. The miraculous conversion brought down the house. After a thunderous ovation Adams motioned to a seat at his side, indicating with a courtly bow that the merchant could henceforth count on his protection. Others fared less well in the meetings, where strong-arming reduced at least one prominent Bostonian to tears. On another occasion, Adams produced a list of importers to be declared enemies to the country. Though several had now agreed to sign, Adams proved pitiless. Their crime had been too great, their conversion too slow. "God perhaps might possibly forgive them," he announced, "but he and the rest of the people never could." The meeting backed him unanimously. Hutchinson compared the methods to that of the highwayman who, pointing a gun at his victim's head, politely demanded his purse.

The January 1770 assemblies introduced new terrors as well as a new cast. The meeting's refusal to disperse went to Hutchinson in the hand of John Hancock. Thomas Young, a thirty-eight-year-old physician of a more radical disposition than Adams and on closer terms with poverty, delivered vibrant harangues. William Cooper, the longtime town clerk and a *Journal* contributor, reliably turned up at Adams's side; Cooper was the elder brother of the smooth-spoken minister of the Brattle Street Church. Among the most theatrical of the Sons, William Molineux, the fifty-three-year-old hardware seller, came to assume Ebenezer Mackintosh's position. Molineux took to organizing weekly demonstrations of schoolboys before the shops of proscribed merchants, having wagered that civil authorities would not arrest children, happy to toss stones and raise a racket. The nonimportation meetings launched another effort: women all over town swore, at the end of January, to abstain from drinking tea, to "save this abused country from ruin and slavery."* By March, Adams crowed, the young women of Boston shunned the pernicious herb as vehemently as they embraced their spinning wheels.

Not every Boston merchant succumbed to intimidation. Delinquents found store windows shattered, their homes smeared with dung. They were chased from taverns, expelled from clubs, hooted in the streets. Poles with carved wooden heads were planted before their shops, an allusion to the heads of executed criminals displayed in Europe. Some—like a mild-mannered shopkeeper named Theophilus Lillie, who continued to display prohibited goods—found themselves threatened with bodily harm. On a Thursday in late February, a pole went up before Lillie's North End shop. Already he had spoken with the committee. And he had taken his case to the press. For the life of him, he could not understand why "people who contend so much for civil and religious liberty should be so ready to deprive others of their natural liberty." He probably further failed to redeem himself when he pointed out that there were multiple brands of tyranny.

The morning after the pole went up, a Lillie neighbor named Ebenezer Richardson seized the reins of a cart and attempted to plow through the sign. A crowd assembled. A minor customs official, short, broad-chested Richardson was an unsavory character. He was known to secret a hatchet under his cloak; he was a reputed informer and adulterer. Adams loathed him. With a volley of sticks and stones, the crowd drove Richardson the short distance to his home. He managed a few words with his wife before heckling boys pelted the house with rubbish. Mrs. Richardson lobbed it

---

* More than four hundred women had agreed to the boycott by mid-February, their daughters following behind. They made an exception only for illness. A cynic noted that invalidism seemed, suddenly, on the rise everywhere.

back. She met with a stone. Glass shattered and window frames splintered. Hutchinson tried to dispatch Greenleaf, who begged off. The stones flew faster. Richardson produced a musket, eliciting a hail of every object in sight. Resting his gun on a sill, he swore at the boys, who responded with bricks. Richardson opened fire. Two boys crumpled to the ground, one bleeding from the thigh and hand. Little Christopher Seider took eleven pellets of birdshot in the torso. He was carried off. Dr. Warren pried the slugs from the nineteen-year-old but could do little for Seider, who died that evening.

Brandishing his musket and a cutlass, Richardson resisted arrest. He was escorted to prison with difficulty; many in the street preferred more immediate justice. Adams devoted the next days to political theater. On February 26, a funeral procession assembled under a light snow at the Liberty Tree, outfitted in biblical quotations. Five hundred schoolboys marched in pairs before Seider's casket. Six pallbearers followed, chosen by Seider's parents, who had presumably not chosen the Latin inscriptions that decorated the casket. "Innocence itself is nowhere safe!" announced the first. Thousands walked behind it through snowy streets. Thirty coaches took up the rear of the half-mile-long procession, which brought the town to a standstill. Hutchinson deemed it America's largest funeral but did not attend, the papers having made clear that friends of liberty alone would be welcome. Adams and Betsy did, probably in separate groups. Seider was the son of poor German immigrants. "A grand funeral was, however, judged very proper for him," clucked Hutchinson. He knew well what Adams and his colleagues intended; the papers burst with tributes to "this little hero and first martyr to the noble cause." The *Gazette* devoted so much space to the Seider tragedy that they had no room for the week's scuffles with soldiers. Attacks continued against importers. Some hired armed guards. The rest slept with guns by their beds. Lillie fled his shop.

The incident left Adams with "a barbarous murder" to retail; he could now properly speak of an injured country.* He, or someone who sounds

---

* Although a March court convicted Richardson of murder, it did not sentence him. Hutchinson believed the case one of justifiable homicide and applied to London for a pardon. Adams would complain in November that justice had still not been served.

suspiciously like him, sketched the deathbed scene in the press. With stoic pride, eleven-year-old Seider had greeted his parents. With care, he thanked the doctors who tended him. With dignity, he thanked the clergy who prayed for him. Seider was said to have been returning from school when he happened on the battle under Richardson's window. No one remembered him stooping for a stone. Heroic literature was stuffed posthumously in his pocket. Had the Sons the power to resurrect the child, Hutchinson fumed, they would not have done so, "but would have chosen the grand funeral."

FOUR DAYS AFTER Adams's extravaganza, ill humor pooling all around, a midday brawl erupted steps from his door. Around a steaming tar kettle, ropewalk workers exchanged blows with grenadiers from the Twenty-ninth Regiment. The soldiers battled with cutlasses and clubs, the workers with long sticks used to twist lengths of hemp. They went four rounds. Though considerably outnumbered, the ropeworkers drove off the soldiers. Scuffles continued through the weekend, as cutlasses flashed and insults flew. By Sunday a cudgel had, too. A private wound up with a fractured arm and skull. Mutters of revenge made the rounds. One woman overheard a soldier say that he had been ordered to head out Monday only armed and in company. A minister and a tailor were each urged to stay home that evening. In a shop, a grenadier's wife crowed that before Tuesday the soldiers would wet their swords in New England blood.* The Hutchinson maid who spent her Sunday near the ropewalks heard there would be a fight the following evening. Ringing bells would signal a brawl rather than a fire, information she did not share with the acting governor. His Council did, warning that "it was apprehended that the smaller frays would be followed by one more general." Later in the

---

Richardson spent a miserable two years in prison before fleeing Boston. He wound up in Philadelphia, to which a warning went in the fall of 1773: Whoever found this "bird of darkness" should have him tarred and feathered.
* The Twenty-ninth were far from alone in spoiling for a fight. Should there be any disturbance, one soldier's wife warned, she would fold a stone in her handkerchief and bash in some Bostonian brains.

year Adams would insist that soldiers—gloating "that many who would
dine on Monday would not breakfast on Tuesday"—had promised blood
running in the streets.

Under a slim moon early on the evening of March 5, parties of soldiers
could be seen prowling the streets. According to Adams, to make himself
an authority on the next hours, they carried bludgeons, bayonets, and
cutlasses. The town's winding lanes crackled with tension as, amid drifts
of fresh snow, Boston came alive. Blows were exchanged in several neighborhoods. A crowd collected on King Street, near the customs house;
they hurled snowballs, oyster shells, and chunks of ice at a sentry, taunt-
ing him and creating a commotion. Earlier he had tangled with a few
boys, whom he attempted to strike with the end of his gun. Whistling
and shrieking, they returned with friends. The sentry cried out for assistance. Thomas Preston, the regimental captain, rushed to his side,
accompanied by eight men. They, and their bayonets, electrified the
crowd.

Preston ordered his soldiers to level their guns. The townspeople
surged toward the jagged semicircle, pressing closely upon the redcoats,
nearly impaling themselves. A hat would not fit between the soldiers and
the civilians, too close to hurl anything but words—as they did, from
every direction. Their backs to the brick customs house wall, the soldiers
found themselves surrounded on three sides by jeering Bostonians, push-
ing and shoving, the ground slippery underfoot. "God damn you, fire and
be damned, we know you dare not," they shouted, whistling at the "cow-
ardly rascals" and attempting to knock muskets free. Overhead, the bells
began to toll. Moonlight glinted on the weapons. A concerned citizen
maneuvered his way through the crowd. A hand on Preston's crimson-
coated shoulder, he asked if the soldiers' guns were loaded. They were.
Did the captain intend to fire upon the inhabitants? By no means, Preston
replied, as he must truly have believed. He stood directly in front of
his men.

No sooner had he spoken than a stick slashed through the air, sending
a grenadier sprawling across the ice. A shot rang out. Seconds or minutes
later came another crackle of musket fire. Cries of "To arms, to arms!"

filled the air. The town drums beat for a militia; bells rang frantically. Many scrambled home for guns. Some cowered behind frosted windows. Others rushed to King Street. Suddenly there was talk again of the newly oiled munitions at Faneuil Hall and of reinforcements from the countryside. The crowd swelled to over a thousand.

Before the situation deteriorated further, someone had the good sense to sprint the half mile to Hutchinson's house to alert the acting governor. The town was in an uproar. The sight of dead bodies and crimson snow had made it wild. There would soon be carnage everywhere. On the south side of town, the bells interrupted a meeting of the Monday Night Club. Its members snatched hats and coats and ran out to assist, they too evidently assumed, in quenching a fire: Bells rang in the night for only one reason. John Adams was among the club members who joined the throng streaming toward King Street. His cousin may have been as well. Only amid the pandemonium—the bells clanging furiously—did they understand why some had traded buckets for clubs and canes. Soldiers had fired upon civilians. The good citizen who had confronted Preston nursed a scorched sleeve. Blood had splattered the waistcoats of bystanders. It stained fingers. It gushed from a massive wound in a victim's head. At least one man gasped for breath on the ground. Another was lifeless.

In the street Hutchinson found himself amid sticks and cutlasses; he would not know until afterward about the club that had been lifted over his head, then quietly snatched away. He collided with a group rushing home for weapons, whom he persuaded to follow him instead. With difficulty he was conveyed through back alleys to King Street, where he attempted to shout his way through a conversation with Preston. Had the captain ordered his men to fire on civilians? Hutchinson crossly demanded. Preston replied with equal sharpness. The men had fired of their own accord, though in the commotion Hutchinson could not make out his words. Later there would be other difficulties in obtaining explanations; Hutchinson would say that there were so many disparate accounts of the evening that he could not possibly supply a true one with all the time in the world.

Swept up the stairs to the Town House balcony, he pleaded with the townspeople below. He promised a full and impartial inquiry. Nothing further could be done that evening. At length he prevailed on the crowd to retire; only a small huddle refused, their breaths misting the icy darkness. Hutchinson immediately began to depose witnesses. By 1:00 a.m. he had arranged for the regiments to return to their barracks. By 2:00 a.m. he had arrested Preston. The eight soldiers who had either fired or not fired joined him in prison. By 4:00 a.m. the town was quiet. Hutchinson knew early on there were two casualties; by dawn there would be another. Five men had been wounded, most of them apprentices and immigrants. A forty-seven-year-old Black sailor had been shot twice in the chest. Two bullets in his back, a teenaged ship's mate had died on the spot. By the time Adams got his hands on events, it had been their misfortune to have faced hooligans "with guns loaded and bayonets fixed, trembling with rage, and ready to fire upon a multitude in the street." The evening seemed drawn from the *Journal of Occurrences*, among the few points on which Hutchinson and the *Gazette* concurred.* An ocean away, hours before Preston's men fired, Parliament had begun its debate of a repeal of the Townshend duties.

Invisible on March 5, Adams was the center of attention the following morning, when Hutchinson convened his Council. He summoned as well the commanding officers of the Boston regiments; he wanted as many Crown officers in the room as possible. Boston was at a boil as, across town, doctors conducted autopsies and tended to the wounded. At the Town House, Hutchinson found the selectmen waiting for him on the doorstep. Would he, they inquired, kindly remove the troops at once? Inside, several Council members echoed the request. Next came a delegation of justices of the peace from neighboring towns; few in Suffolk county seemed to have managed a full night's sleep that Monday. Hutchinson answered the selectmen and justices as he answered his Council. He was without authority to order an evacuation.

---

* The *Gazette* account of March 12, reprinted throughout the colonies, included a little obituary for the *Journal of Occurrences*. In cataloguing the indignities Bostonians suffered at the hands of soldiers, the paper had performed a public service. Since it had ceased publication—it seemed to have accomplished the bulk of its mission with Bernard's departure—"our troubles from that quarter have been growing upon us."

From the selectmen Hutchinson learned that the town had also convened an emergency meeting. They appointed a committee, Adams at its head, to call on Hutchinson. As John Adams later drew the picture, his cousin stood late that morning before a sober, bewigged crew in scarlet cloaks and gold-laced hats. The commanding images of Charles II and James II peered over their shoulders from ornate gold frames. Hutchinson sat at the head of the Council table, Colonel Dalrymple at his side. Before them Adams delivered what John considered one of the most significant speeches of the age. The gist alone survives. It was a precarious moment. Nothing would restore the town to order, contended Adams, but the immediate removal of the troops. Hutchinson stood firm. Under no circumstances, he countered, as he had already three times that morning, would he order an evacuation. He regretted the events of the previous evening but had consulted with the officers of two regiments. They answered to their general, in New York. Hutchinson could not countermand him. In whispers, he conferred with Dalrymple and Andrew Oliver, their heads bent close together. Oliver felt that the town had artfully commandeered the situation. They had left his brother-in-law two choices: he could comply with their demand or he could leave the province. For his part, Colonel Dalrymple offered to withdraw the Twenty-ninth Regiment. Hutchinson disliked the idea but ultimately conceded. The regiment had made itself obnoxious. It could move to the Castle if that would appease the people. He assumed the matter closed.

Adams conveyed Hutchinson's reply to the town meeting, swelled by afternoon to between three and four thousand people. Packed into the pews of the Old South Church, they deemed the removal of a single regiment insufficient. Late that Tuesday Adams made his way across Boston for a second time to remind Hutchinson that, by the Massachusetts charter, the governor—and in his absence the acting governor—assumed command of all military and naval forces within his jurisdiction. Was there to be more carnage in Boston? he asked. The troops, Hutchinson repeated, had their commander and their orders. He could not interfere. Adams warned Hutchinson of the price of his intransigence: The Massachusetts towns would descend on Boston. Ten thousand men would expel the troops if Hutchinson did not. The night ahead "would be the most terrible that had ever been seen in America." Hutchinson reminded Adams of the definition of high treason.

With a vigorous dash of nineteenth-century color, John Adams painted the scene. His cousin was no orator. On great occasions, however, "when his deeper feelings were excited, he erected himself, or rather nature seemed to erect him, without the smallest symptom of affectation, into an upright dignity of figure and gesture, and gave a harmony to his voice, which made a strong impression on spectators and auditors, the more lasting for the purity, correctness, and nervous elegance of his style." The sixth of March, 1770, was one such occasion, though the style hardly mattered. Few seemed to share his aptitude or appetite for wearing down an opponent. And no Bostonian more expertly rattled Thomas Hutchinson; it was as if the previous three decades had prepared Samuel Adams for this afternoon. "With a self-recollection, a self-possession, a self-command, a presence of mind, that was admired by every man present," he rose. He stretched forth a trembling arm. The town had voted. No redcoat could consider himself safe in Boston. Nor could any inhabitant. "If you have power to remove one regiment," Adams enjoined Hutchinson, "you have power to remove both." Three thousand people awaited his decision. "They are become," added Adams, his voice sonorous, "very impatient. A thousand men are already arrived from the neighborhood, and the country is in general motion." It was nearly dusk. An immediate answer was expected. Any bloodshed would be on the hands of the acting governor, who should consider his life in danger.

The language was potent, stronger than Hutchinson cared to repeat or so much as recall.* It made for a spellbinding moment. Adams's ultimatum set every pulse in the room racing. Even Dalrymple reported that Adams made him quake; he seemed more impressed by him than by the lieutenant governor. All parties admired Adams's "discretion, his ingenuity, his sagacity, his self-command, his presence of mind, and his

---

* His accounts of the afternoon would consist of a snarl of long, tortured sentences. He lurches from justification to uncertainty and back again.

intrepidity." Adams focused only on Hutchinson, "weak as water," as unsteady as he had ever seen him. "I observed his knees to tremble," Adams later revealed. "I thought I saw his face grow pale (and I enjoyed the sight)." He had personal reason to savor the moment but deferred to something loftier. Adams thrilled to the display of "determined citizens peremptorily demanding the redress of grievances."*

An excruciating silence followed. Hutchinson could see no way forward without additional violence. While he seriously doubted that a mob could drive off six hundred well-trained regulars, he did not care to approach that Rubicon. He recanvassed the four Crown officers in the room. They remained of the same mind. Hutchinson alone resisted a concession. It would be difficult to explain to London. Agonizing, he looked to Dalrymple. He preferred an officer make the decision. The previous night had been the worst Hutchinson had known in fifty-nine years, including that on which his home had been pillaged. No one else in the room, he was reminded, believed he could deny the will of the people. Finally Hutchinson informed Adams that he would ask Dalrymple to remove both regiments to the Castle. Adams's admirers would deem the confrontation pivotal. Hutchinson emphasized its import as well, though for a different reason: Samuel Adams's triumph, he cringed, "gave greater assurances than ever that, by firmness, the great object, exemption from all exterior power, civil or military, would finally be obtained." In his many miserable accounts of the afternoon he rarely mentioned Adams by name, as if preferring not to put a face to his humiliation.

The streets were nearly dark when Adams returned to the Old South. A hush fell as John Hancock rose to announce his news. The room then erupted, echoing for some time with shouts and applause. The meeting also voted a night watch for the town until the troops had evacuated. Hutchinson could hardly do so; he did not want to appear to have raised

---

* Writing as "A" in a July *Gazette*, Adams would say of Hutchinson that it was only "with the utmost difficulty he was at length prevailed upon, by the unanimous advice of his legal Council, by the remonstrances of the people, and by the blood of his fellow citizens inhumanly spilt on the ground."

a militia to drive out British regulars. (Nor did he trust a militia that had helped to destroy his house.) The committee themselves volunteered to patrol. For the next two weeks, with muskets and cartridge boxes, John and Samuel Adams, along with Hancock, Molineux, Warren, and a host of others, walked the Boston streets until dawn. Hutchinson disapproved deeply, miserable that he had lost control of the military. He would say later that he had spent whole nights lying awake, fearful that he would be called to account for neglect of his duty to the king. These presumably counted among the worst such evenings.

John Adams deemed his cousin's showdown with Thomas Hutchinson worthy of Livy or Thucydides. It struck him as deserving of portraiture. The great painter John Singleton Copley caught some of its flavor when Adams sat for him later, over a long series of sessions. Copley depicted Adams with the intensity on display throughout the duel; it may explain why Adams is on his feet when so many of Copley's Boston subjects relax into their chairs.* Adams quite literally takes a stand, ramrod straight, militant in his bearing. He is a man fortified by, mobilized by words. With his left index finger he directs us to the Massachusetts charter. With his right hand he clenches the town instructions in a manner that suggests that ideas, too, deliver lethal blows. The result is a battle cry of a painting, much copied through the 1770s. Adams defends the charter like "Moses with his tablets, Luther with the Epistles," as one historian has put it. The picture hinted that an occasional check might intrude, but that—as Hutchinson feared—"the progress of liberty would recommence." Two classical columns, of a majesty to be found nowhere in Boston, loom behind Adams. A quarter smile plays on his lips. Among Copley subjects, he is, with the exception of Paul Revere, the least well-dressed. He takes his stand in a crumpled russet coat from which a plain white ruffle emerges at the wrist. He would be unfashionable even if his lapels did not appear to be taking flight.

Two weeks later troops still stomped about Boston. Adams prodded.

---

* Copley painted another Boston resident on his feet, also directing our attention with his index finger. It is the portrait closest in feel to that of Adams; the subject was General Gage, who sat for Copley while arranging quarters for the troops.

Dalrymple had sworn to evacuate them immediately. Forty-eight hours had been required to land the men. Why was it taking weeks to remove them? In the end, Molineux accompanied the redcoats to the wharf—"to protect them," it was explained, "from the indignation of the people." On March 27, 1770, Boston was at last free of all soldiers save for the nine behind prison bars. "Thus," groaned Andrew Oliver, "has an unarmed multitude in their own opinion gained a complete victory over two regiments of His Majesty's regular troops."

OVER THE NEXT harried weeks Adams focused not on how he would be portrayed but on how the events of March 5 would be; there is no better instance of him bracing for and improving upon events. A tragedy had relieved the town of troops. But how would the rest of the province, the other colonies, and the British Ministry react? There was much to do, in little time and for immeasurably high stakes. For starters, the evening of Monday, March 5, needed a name. Adams appears to have been the first to refer to the skirmish as a "horrid massacre," a name that stuck.* It was imperative as well to dredge from the murk a coherent narrative. Nothing about the twenty chaotic minutes had been clear, least of all to anyone in the thick of them. Soldiers had fired on and killed civilians. But had Preston—a cool-headed, popular officer with a reputation for benevolence—ever issued a command? Some distinctly heard him order his men to fire. Others swore he had not. (The concerned citizen who had accosted Preston distinctly heard the word "fire" but could not say who had spoken it. As Preston himself put it later: "In short, it was scarcely possible for the soldiers to know who said fire, or don't fire, or stop your firing." A dockworker in the crowd swore that the word "was in everybody's mouth.") Who had attacked whom? Had snowballs flown through the air, or had those been bricks, clubs, and sticks? Were thousands of people, or fifty, on hand? Witnesses reported that the first victim carried

---

* Hutchinson preferred "the unfortunate action of the troops." A despondent Captain Preston, writing from prison, went with "the late unhappy affair." In London it registered as "the unfortunate event of the Fifth of March."

a stick. Others saw him empty-handed. There was disagreement even on the position of the moon. A sentry had been assaulted. Minutes later, three or four men lay dead. What had happened? All agreed the snow was a foot deep, the evening bright. On all other counts it was cloaked in shadow, an obscurity that Adams rushed to illuminate.

By Wednesday a town committee was in place to collect depositions, sworn over long days before justices of the peace. Only one side submitted them. They would be attached to a hastily composed narrative of the evening, written either by Bowdoin with help from Adams or the other way around. The two produced an overview of the discontents that preceded March 5. Having arrived to collect duties, supercilious customs men had embroiled themselves in political schemes. They had excited tumults, exaggerated in order to summon troops. On their account—they were nearly accessories to murder—Boston now had an outsized funeral to plan. Late Thursday afternoon, the town's shops drew their shutters closed. Bells tolled for miles around as four cortèges made their halting way, from separate addresses, toward King Street. A train of mourners followed, pleating themselves into tight rows amid narrow streets. In the Tremont Street burial ground the bodies were lowered several steps into the town tomb. The crowd was estimated at ten thousand. Hutchinson described the mood differently a week later, when a fifth victim was laid to rest. "Every funeral," complained the lieutenant governor, "brings thousands of people together and inflames them against the troops." Two or three victims remained still in critical condition. He worried about the trials ahead.

Adams shared his concern, wresting the narrative from official hands. In the *Gazette*'s account of the evening, Preston commands his men to fire, with gruesome results. Crispus Attucks, the Black sailor, is killed instantly, "two balls entering his breast, one of them in special goring the right lobe of the lungs and a great part of the liver most horribly." (Others would report that Attucks, armed with two sticks he had fished from a woodpile, had led a roaring brigade.) Adams rinsed the evening of all crowd action and premeditation. At dawn on Tuesday blood coursed through King Street, from which it was tracked around the neighborhood. A week later, Edes and Gill published a Locke-heavy sermon delivered at the Second Church by the minister who had recently succeeded Adams's brother-in-law. In *Innocent Blood Crying to God from the Streets of Boston*, he discoursed on red-stained pavement and corpses wallowing in gore.

As depositions were taken, before memories had fully congealed, a Boston artist offered up something more powerful than any sermon or newspaper account. Henry Pelham, Copley's half brother, drew a crisp line of soldiers firing—in a concerted volley, amid clouds of billowing smoke—into a heap of unarmed civilians. The commanding officer urges his men on, from behind. Attucks appears nowhere in the picture, titled *The Fruits of Arbitrary Power, or the Bloody Massacre*. The body count is off, as is the number of soldiers, far from all walls. No one attempts to jostle muskets. Pelham drew liberally on his imagination, but his work, too, could be improved upon: he lent the engraving to Paul Revere, who produced his own version, hand-colored and on sale before the original.*

From Pelham Revere borrowed an outsized woman, wringing her hands amid the mayhem. Like Pelham, he upgraded wardrobes; his huddled bystanders look nothing like waterfront workers. Revere also replaced the psalm that accompanied the original with eighteen grisly lines. Boston's hallowed streets were now "besmeared with guiltless gore," courtesy of the barbarians who "grinning over their prey / approve the carnage and enjoy the day." He outfitted the soldiers in eye-popping scarlet. Their victims appear in muted blues and browns, save for the blood that spurts from their sides. Revere plumped up the moon, as if to better light the scene. He omitted many things—there is neither a snowball nor brickbat in sight—and added two details that hint at the long arm of Adams. Revere relabeled the customs house "Butcher's Hall." And into a second-floor window he inserted a musket, emitting puffs of smoke.

No part of Adams could have believed in what Revere depicted; all the action is on one side of the engraving, the misery on the other. Accuracy, however, was not the point. What mattered was to extract maximum

---

* Pelham believed he had shared the engraving with a man of honor. Livid, he accused Revere of having cheated him "as truly as if you had plundered me on the highway."

propaganda value from the frightful evening when—as Adams and the committee on which he sat soon alleged—the soldiers had engaged in "a settled plot to massacre the inhabitants." (No customs men nor calculated plot figured in the initial accounts.) Nor was Revere alone in implicating the commissioners. Several deponents swore that they saw guns fired from the customs house. One went so far as to fit John Robinson, Otis's Coffee House adversary, into the window. (It was difficult to say for certain, the witness explained, as the figure had knotted a handkerchief across his face.)

Within days Adams had bundled together the massacre, the murder of young Seider, and the "intended assassination" of Otis, all orchestrated by the commissioners; the troops were not the only interlopers he hoped to run out of town. Ninety-six depositions were collected, affixed to the narrative, and sent to London. *A Short Narrative of the Horrid Massacre in Boston* did not circulate in Massachusetts, where nine men awaited trial for murder, or so Adams and his colleagues claimed; they knew the essential skirmish was the one for the narrative. Adams could only have been taken aback when a parcel of military depositions slipped out of Boston Harbor on March 16, sailing to London on a man-of-war into which Robinson had secretly loaded his belongings in the dead of night. The depositions suggested not only that the Bostonians had instigated the affair, but that they had conspired to raid the customs house treasury. In a matter of days, the story had mutated at both ends.

In Great Britain, *A Short Narrative of the Horrid Massacre* would go up against *A Fair Account of the Late Unhappy Disturbance at Boston*, a pamphlet that, among other things, argued that to call the events of March 5 a "massacre" was "a very gross abuse of language." It painted the people—reckless after months of harassing troops—as the aggressors. One account seemed designed to enflame, suggesting that the violence had been premeditated, like the 1572 slaughter of Huguenots in France, or the 1641 slaughter of Protestants in Ireland. The other demoted the evening to a "ridiculous fray." The soldiers had "remained passive as long as the laws of self-preservation would admit." The town hurried copies of their narrative to nearly a hundred individuals of distinction in London, including the king's brother. Adams also dispatched *Innocent Blood* abroad, where some ranked the Second Church minister among fiction-loving fanatics.*

Mostly Adams tended to damage control, assuring Benjamin Franklin, newly elected as a Massachusetts agent in London, that the town's version derived from a fair and open inquiry. The other consisted of glaring falsehoods. Its authors should be ashamed. No man of "tolerable reputation" could have sworn that the people intended to plunder the king's chest! Adams had less cause for concern than he realized. In the battle over the story, overseas papers latched on to the more lurid account. In Great Britain, too, blood ran through Boston streets, where customs men had requested troops and where snowballs were met with muskets. It helped that the Twenty-ninth Regiment was notoriously ill-behaved. At their Halifax posting it had been necessary to read them the Mutiny Act.

Adams exerted himself as well to bring on the trials quickly, while emotions ran high and victims languished. With equal art Hutchinson labored to delay. He did not care to sacrifice the "unhappy persons" in prison to a murderous town. Others also preferred to avoid the case while tempers flared: One judge excused himself, citing an attack of nerves. Another twice attempted to resign. Adams sat on a committee that demanded Hutchinson appoint substitutes, to avoid a postponement. The acting governor settled instead on an early June trial date. That news sent Adams and a band of friends barging into Superior Court, a crowd trailing behind. Adams apologized for the abrupt visit but appealed, with visible emotion, to the robed justices. Was there not a moral obligation to try the cases immediately? Disinclined to offend the town, the justices agreed to an immediate trial. Soon afterward, one suffered a fall from his

---

* On April 30 you could also read in London of a very different prelude to the evening's events. A bludgeon-toting throng had gathered toward dusk at the Liberty Tree. By eight thirty they had made their way to Faneuil Hall, where they demolished market stalls. Planks in hands, they proceeded to the barracks, where they beat soldiers unlucky enough to find themselves outside; challenged others to come out and fight; attempted to pry open barrack doors; and threatened to murder the Customs House sentry. The account would be disputed the next day by a Massachusetts friend, who emphasized Hutchinson's order to remove the troops. If he meant to restrain them so as to prevent future disturbances, did he not tacitly admit that they had incited this one?

horse. His colleagues refused to proceed without him, effecting a post-ponement until August. Hutchinson detonated a fresh set of explosions when he attempted to move the venue. Preston's safety worried him, as it did the captain, who feared a lynch mob. Secretly Hutchinson arranged for the prison keys to wind up each evening in the hands of someone other than the prison keep.

Preston met with a different set of unwelcome callers: In July Adams led a delegation to pose a few questions about an account that had appeared over the captain's name in the London papers. Preston had denounced those he claimed were contorting history and poisoning the minds of potential jurors. He insinuated that the people intended to rob the customs house and murder the sentry. Surely an officer of Preston's integrity could not have produced such a statement—especially as he had contributed a markedly different note to the Boston papers, protested Adams. Was the London account his, or had others meddled with it? Preston admitted the pages did not conform to what he had written but would not elaborate. He was displeased by the visit. (He was also lying.) Publicly Adams pressed ahead, eager for Preston to clarify accusations which only "malice and guile could form against an innocent commu-nity." He challenged the prisoner to supply a single shred of proof.

Adams's ubiquity can be read in Hutchinson's misery: he felt belea-guered, out-foxed, alone. He anguished over Adams's morning-after ulti-matum. Had he conceded too readily? He was appalled to discover how many Bostonians had raced out armed on March 5. He had narrowly averted a full-scale insurrection; it had been a miracle that there had been so few casualties. The people struck him as raving, delusional, blood-thirsty. In mid-April, word of the Townshend repeal arrived, setting the town on fire all over again. Partial repeal, even Hutchinson conceded, was worse than none at all. Yet again Parliament neglected the issue at hand. The town bells clanged incessantly as Adams, Molineux, Young, and Hancock convened meeting after meeting.

Hutchinson second-guessed his way through the spring. He heard that no matter how cautiously he proceeded, the opposition intended to persecute him until they had worn him down. His hands were tied;

Adams seemed to have all the rope. Resolute and popular, he made new recruits. He manipulated the House. He dominated the press. He collaborated so closely with Bowdoin, in the Council, that Hutchinson knew that if he "met with opposition from the one, he had reason to expect like opposition from the other." It was at this point in his *History* that Hutchinson veered from events to introduce capsule biographies of the "so-called patriots."* Samuel Adams was unimpressive, "but the determined spirit which he showed in the cause of liberty" compensated for any number of flaws. It vastly exceeded that of anyone else in the province. Hutchinson deplored his bare-knuckle tactics but acknowledged his powers of persuasion: "He made more converts to his cause by calumniating governors, and other servants of the Crown, than by strength of reasoning." He could blacken a character more effectively than anyone Hutchinson had ever met. He wrote with consummate talent. Adams seemed to have resolved the eternal Harvard College thesis question about ends justifying means. Which, Hutchinson acidly supposed, quieted "the remorse he must have felt from robbing men of their characters, and injuring them more than if he had robbed them of their estates."

Boston struck the lieutenant governor as every bit as crazed as it had been in the days of witchcraft—or, he added, the Land Bank. A gentleman could no longer expect to meet with common civility. "The inferior people" met constantly, in assemblies twice as large as the number of legal voters. Nothing intimidated Adams, who persisted in implicating the customs commissioners in the massacre. Taking the hint, they again fled to the Castle. When they returned to Boston over the summer, they found their houses vandalized. In one case a purported messenger, calling at midnight, reached through a parlor window to pummel a commissioner. Word went around that the officials had staged the attacks, shattering their own windows and knocking themselves about in the

---

* John Adams—vain, and of overvaulting ambition—had nearly been bought off. He was as zealous as and more talented than his cousin, but lacked Samuel's stamina. Hancock was a piffle of a man, addicted to popular applause. Bowdoin displayed a dark genius for intrigue. Hutchinson's portraits align squarely with Mein's caricatures.

street. Meanwhile, the House officially endorsed Adams and Bowdoin's massacre narrative. Hutchinson could not convey to Bernard, still the titular Massachusetts governor, how Boston had changed. Even respectable men huffed now about resistance. The militia drilled constantly. Adams and his associates blustered that they would honor no act of Parliament of which the town disapproved. It was, wrote Hutchinson, high time the malefactors were shipped to London.

While Adams had little time for correspondence over the next weeks, Hutchinson entered into one of the most intensive letter-writing periods of his career. He did all he could to nudge the trials incrementally ahead. He moved the House to Cambridge to contain the infection. The further the legislature sat from tumultuous Boston the better. He could see that the aftershocks of the massacre would endure for some time. Ten months in Bernard's chair had impaired his health; early in the spring, without recourse to the word "resignation," which he struck from his draft, he quietly suggested that London replace him. He could not uphold a government under the weight of a people determined to trample its fundamental principles. The letter of resignation sailed around March 27, 1770. Somewhere on the high seas it crossed Lord Hillsborough's letter of mid-April, appointing Hutchinson the royal governor of Massachusetts.

Hutchinson missed the point when he again declared that men with little to lose could "wish for nothing more than some grand convulsion." But he was right that the "unfortunate action of the troops in firing upon the people" had proved a boon to the faction. It propelled them to the moral high ground. It left Adams in control, as firmly if not quite as serenely as Copley immortalized him. There would have been additional cause for jubilation in July, when the family came together for young Samuel Adams's commencement exercises. Resplendent in coarse black cloth of American manufacture, the 1770 graduates sported neither ruffles nor lace. After a Latin oration and a dialogue in Greek, the audience was entertained with a sample of Chaldean, the first demonstration of biblical Aramaic in America. Adams arranged for his son to study medicine; the eighteen-year-old would apprentice with the talented Joseph Warren while preparing for his master's degree. It may have been at this

Harvard commencement that a minister heard Samuel Adams announce, to a large group, that it was every man's obligation to destroy tyrants. The remark made its disconcerting way back to Hutchinson. It was certainly on a sultry day that summer that Adams ventured out in a carriage for a bit of fresh air with his cousin. He dined afterward with John and Abigail. In the course of the afternoon Samuel unabashedly confessed that—as far as he and his family were concerned—he never looked ahead, formulated a plan, or attempted in any way to provide for the future. Flabbergasted, John did not ask, or perhaps did not need to ask, if his cousin subscribed to a longer view when it came to the public good.

JOHN ADAMS AGREED in the spring to defend Preston and the soldiers, an assignment that earned him taunts and snickering in the street. It is unlikely he would have agreed to represent Preston without having consulted his cousin, unlikelier still as John's colleague on the case, Josiah Quincy Jr., did confer with Samuel before accepting the charge. Adams appears to have had a hand in selecting the lawyers for the prosecution as well. Delivering some eighty affidavits on March 9, Molineux alerted Robert Treat Paine that he was the selectmen's choice to represent the families of the deceased. Paine was the colleague who found his way to the law only after having failed at every other profession. He shone in company but distinguished himself more for his booming bass voice than for any courtroom genius. Paine would, Molineux assured him, have his chance to make a splash in trying the case against "the execrable villains."

Acquittal seemed highly unlikely. All were intent on a fair trial, however; it was essential to prove Massachusetts a province where the laws of England were faithfully upheld, where the most reviled interloper could expect fair-minded consideration. Samuel seemed at ease with his cousin as attorney for the defense: John would see to it that Boston secrets remained safe. Samuel could easily have slipped *A Short Narrative*, printed nearly overnight, into circulation. He did not. He took the high road, Adams-style. The account was withheld, he explained, so as to extend "the greatest humanity towards those men who spilt the blood of citizens, like water, upon the ground!" He knew full well those pages were meant for London consumption in the first place.

No faction leader was in the Queen Street courtroom as jurors were selected late in October. Nor did any seem to anticipate a packed jury. Adams was indignant to learn that the regimental baker was seated, along with one of Preston's close friends and at least one avowed Tory. They were joined by a juror who had sworn that "he would sit until doomsday" before he would vote to convict. Preference seemed to be given to out-of-towners. The sole question jurors were to resolve was whether Preston had issued an order to fire. Some witnesses swore he had but diverged on the details. No one could agree even on his uniform; many departed from the depositions they had offered in the *Short Narrative*. To Adams's dismay, the contingent of redcoats with loaded muskets carried no weight. A sentry had stood in danger. The people of Boston appeared the aggressors. All were instructed to forget Revere's absurd engraving.

Reasonable doubt crept into the room around noon on the third day. Hutchinson began to feel sanguine even before he took the stand, where he related his testy conversation with Preston. A unanimous vote would be needed to convict. Early on the morning of October 30, after six days of testimony—it was the longest trial yet held in Massachusetts—Preston was acquitted. The verdict surprised no one. Nor did it convince everyone of the captain's innocence. Hutchinson congratulated himself, crediting the outcome to the hard-won delay. It had "brought truth to light." Adams heard the details only later but hardly cared: The courtroom consensus was that Preston had a right, even a duty, to protect his besieged sentry. John Adams had argued that to have fired after an assault by "a riotous mob" shouting "Kill them! Kill them!" by no definition qualified as murder. His cousin assumed that the same logic would exonerate the soldiers, their trial set for November 20. Samuel Adams had every plan to attend.

He wrestled in the meantime with the implosion of the nonimportation agreement. New York had defected in July, Philadelphia in mid-October. The Sons continued to harass Boston importers who "preferred their own little private advantage to the welfare of America." (Lillie remained among the offenders.) When a letter from New York explaining its defection was read in a Faneuil Hall meeting, it was ordered torn to pieces and thrown to the winds. Boston merchants agreed to continue their boycott of dutied tea, but Adams had his work cut out for him. Publicly he maintained that he had never held high hopes for the effort. As a rule he tended to overpromise then stand back to admire, wide-eyed, the underwhelming results that exceeded his tepid expectations. The people of Boston remained attached to the idea, he insisted, even if its merchants did not. In truth, interest had faded. The colonies blamed one another for the economic pain and political defeats. They were at one another's throats, where Hutchinson preferred them.

It was no easier to seat an impartial jury for the soldiers than it had been for Preston. None of the twelve lived in Boston. Adams could hardly restrain himself: How could Roxbury or Milton men evaluate testimony when they were unfamiliar with the witnesses? This time he figured among the sixty or so spectators who heard a presiding judge, in sable and scarlet robes, declare the trial to be the most solemn ever held in America. The court was to determine whether eight of their fellow subjects lived or died. Adams concurred. "To see eight prisoners brought to the bar together, charged with the murder of five persons at one time, was certainly, as was then observed, affecting," he reported, but could not help himself: Yet more affecting had been the scene on March 5. He appears to have stood in the crowded second-floor room for each of the next eight days, taking rapid, disjointed notes and submitting them, less than constructively, to Paine, again arguing for the prosecution. Did it not make sense, implored Adams, to point out that the people acted from legitimate fears, given the soldiers' dastardly conduct? Had the Bostonians as much right to walk about armed as the soldiers, especially after dark? If eight men engaged in an unlawful act during which one of them killed, were they not all guilty? It was annoying, but as Adams was too well aware, all the legal firepower was on the other side.

Paine's task was easier in light of Preston's acquittal; if their captain had issued no command, his soldiers had fired without orders. That made them murderers. Some eighty-five witnesses took the stand, few of whom had seen the same thing. Revere's engraving may have worked its magic; some even testified that Preston had stood behind his men. The defense argued against the fanciful engraving and the ostentatious funerals, designed to "inspire a glow incompatible with sound, deliberative judgment." They had no need to address a premeditated British plot as none emerged. Nor did any unruly ropemaker. In his December 4 summation, John Adams wrote the affair down to "a motley rabble of saucy boys, Negroes and mulattos, Irish teagues and outlandish Jack Tars," relatives of the anonymous marauders who had demolished Hutchinson's home and of the unsavory crew who had instigated the Knowles Riot a generation earlier.* The jury could vote to acquit with clear consciences. He declined to portray Boston as riotous or to call witnesses who might. He was also realistic. "Every species of rubbish" had been thrown at the troops. Were they to behave like stoic philosophers? They had committed homicide, but there were, argued John, justifiable forms of homicide.

After a short deliberation, the jury returned with a verdict of not guilty for six of the men. Not every grenadier had fired; to convict all eight would have been to condemn an innocent. The two who could be proved to have fired and killed were convicted of manslaughter, for which they were branded on the right hand. (John's heart went out to them. "Noble, fine-looking men," they burst into tears as, with a hot iron, Greenleaf seared an "M" into their thumbs.) Having spent nine months in a filthy prison, the exonerated six walked out of the courtroom and passed virtually unnoticed, in broad daylight, to their barracks. "There certainly is a stock of virtue in the country," wrote a relieved Hutchinson later that day, "though sometimes overborn by the violent efforts of some as bad men perhaps as any upon the globe." His faith was restored. He displayed even a flicker of pride. His countrymen had made "pretty good distinctions for an American jury," having opted to free the guilty rather than convict an innocent. It should shame those who drew up the *Short*

---

* John Adams emphasized the dozen club-carrying sailors in the crowd. What could one expect, when there was such great antipathy between sailors and soldiers "that they fight as naturally when they meet as the elephant and rhinoceros"?

Narrative. Its authors struck him, over a soggy season, as more depressed than they had been in years.

It took only five days for one of those bad men to launch a separate trial, accessible to more than sixty spectators and supplying a verdict more in line with expectations of the spring. For the occasion Adams resurrected "Vindex," who had dilated earlier on the danger of stationing armies among civilians. While Adams would have preferred a conviction, a compassionate display of justice was useful too. He was fortunate in that the trials confirmed that no one truly knew what had happened on March 5. He saw his opportunity and ran with it, through the thicket of conflicting accounts, supplemented with courtroom papers. Under a pseudonym, he asked Paine to send over his closing argument, which the court reporter had been too exhausted to transcribe. Everyone had comported himself well in the courtroom, Adams acknowledged. But for the record, belligerent, bloodthirsty soldiers had fired without orders. They had struck citizens with bayonets. "If these are not instances of assault, I know not what an assault is," he declared. The soldiers had been in no danger from the civilians. They could have retreated, he argued, conveniently removing the brick wall behind them. Not for a minute did he buy "their lamb-like meekness and immaculate innocence."

Through December and well into January, in a series of ten essays, often on the *Gazette*'s front page, Adams saw to it that the evening of March 5 conformed to the engraving above Boston mantelpieces. He fixated on a soldier whom witnesses had seen the morning after the massacre, his bayonet coated in five inches of dried blood. Several had testified to his savagery. The law allowed for human passions, Adams conceded. It did not indulge malice and rancor. Shooting your victim was one thing, goring him afterward another.* The jurors, argued Adams, had been faulty. They were unfamiliar with the witnesses, not all of whom

---

* John had argued that one could not infer anything from a bloody bayonet. It might after all have fallen into a pool of blood in the street. In the *Gazette*, his cousin begged to differ. It was far more likely that "this very bayonet was stabbed into the head of poor Gray after he was shot" than that it had simply fallen into the blood that "ran plentifully in the street."

were credible. Several were less credible once Adams had finished with them. On his deathbed, one reported that Bostonians had pelted soldiers. Was it not odd that no one else had witnessed this? asked Adams. The victim assured his doctor that he forgave the redcoat who had shot him; the man had acted in self-defense. As deathbed speeches went, this was heartrending. According to his landlady, the deceased was an unsavory character, however. He was unlikely to have managed to attend properly to the questions asked of him, laboring as he was under a mortal wound. He had not made his declaration under oath. He was also, Adams added, a Roman Catholic.

Speaking "on behalf of those who cannot now speak for themselves," Adams colorfully resurrected several of the deceased; he had none of Hutchinson's difficulty portraying character. A student of navigation had been on the verge of his engagement. Another victim had blamelessly headed out to borrow Monday's newspaper. He carried no weapon. How could he have, when he crumpled to the ground with arms neatly folded across his chest? Attucks had been leaning on a stick when killed, hardly a threatening posture. As for the stick itself, Attucks had as much right to carry it given the various provocations as had a soldier to carry his musket. Had he killed the soldier he might have been strung up as both a murderer and traitor. Meanwhile, the soldier who had shot Attucks dead had been convicted only of manslaughter.* Though deposed, many material witnesses had inexplicably not been called. This was what happened when you held a trial nine months after the crime!

Adams posed several legitimate questions: Why were the soldiers not in their barracks at 8:00 p.m. in the first place? Who could say, in the darkness, whether soldiers or civilians brandished clubs? Preston testified that he ordered his men not to fire. Adams was no soldier and had no desire to become one. But he very much doubted that the words "Don't fire!"

---

* In the courtroom John Adams drew a radically different picture of Attucks, painting him as formidable in his bearing and largely responsible for the evening's carnage. Having "undertaken to be the hero of the night," he led a small army brandishing clubs up King Street. He assured the people they had nothing to fear from the soldiers. They would not dare to fire. "Kill them, Kill them, Knock them over!" he had urged. "And he tried," John alleged, "to knock their brains out."

figured among the commands of the British army. Surely there was a clearer formulation in the heat of battle? He could not stress often enough how ridiculous it was to say the soldiers had been at the mercy of the inhabitants when the reverse was true. It was as essential to prove that there had been no plot on the town's part—the deceased did not even know one another!—as to prove that there had been one on the other. A standing army in time of peace was as deep a violation of American rights as were duties on paper or tea. Adams posed the question generated by every confrontation between civilians and the military: Could the side with the guns truly claim they had fired in self-defense?

He was weeks into his campaign when he picked up a critic who challenged him, nearly week for week, in the *Boston Evening Post*. Philanthrop knew that Vindex was Samuel Adams. Adams may not have known he dueled with the attorney general, Jonathan Sewall. Even-keeled and intimately versed in the trial details, Sewall took Adams to task for trafficking in phantoms, tossing about loaded words, burying one side of the story. Adams seemed intent on proving that all in authority traitorously plotted the ruin of America. Did he really mean to suggest that, after four judges and twenty-four jurors had devoted weeks to the case, they were fools and he alone could discern the truth? An opponent did nothing to break his stride; Sewall only invigorated Adams. He did not mean to cast the jury, the judges, or the witnesses in an unflattering light.* He cared only for truth. He launched snowballs and oyster shells of his own, dwelling on wicked men who preferred to oppress rather than govern. Men entered into political associations for the sake of equality, the true end of government. The "multitude" of which Philanthrop despaired happened to consist of the very individuals whom government was meant to serve, the force "to whom even Kings and all in subordination to them are, strictly speaking, servants and not masters."

Hutchinson was appalled to see that Adams was relitigating the entire case, poisoning the minds of the people. He expected that Sewall would

---

* In truth he maligned all three, though he never once took a stab at the defense. It is difficult to imagine what conversations between the cousins must have been like over these months.

provide the ideal antidote: "It is really necessary that these wicked people should be answered in order to keep better people from being again perverted," he wrote an intimate. Sewall could not rise to Adams's polemical heights, however. And Hutchinson had more reason than ever to regret that most of Massachusetts read the *Boston Gazette*. By the time Sewall launched his last volley, Adams was looking ahead to commemorations of March 5. The massacre had now occupied him for nearly a year.

Bent on shaping history before it receded into the past, he continued in his effort to design a new calendar. At noon on March 5, 1771, the bells tolled for an hour in every Congregational steeple as they did again after dark, when thousands flocked to Paul Revere's North End home. Revere exhibited a brilliantly illuminated triptych. In one window glowed the stenciled ghost of young Seider, a finger in his gushing wound, his weeping friends at his side. In the next window, soldiers fired at innocents. Several victims lay on the ground amid puddles of blood. In the last window sat a robed figure of America, a cap of Liberty perched on her head, a grenadier pinned under her foot. She pointed to the murder in the second panel. Thomas Young delivered a solemn address that evening, summoning the ghosts of the massacre and "the imputations of treason and rebellion" with which the town had been unfairly charged. The dioramas were Revere's and the speech Young's but the stage management was all Adams's: Dr. Young spoke from the Manufactory House, where British soldiers had starved children. Adams hoped the indignation-rousing March 5 would be remembered forever. It would be celebrated annually until 1783, when it yielded to the Fourth of July, another invented occasion, but a national rather than a local holiday and a meeting of the minds rather than a crossing of swords.

All would be calm, Hutchinson complained early in 1771, were it not for several men surnamed Adams. He was mystified by the obstinacy of the younger one. John had exhibited much promise. From the older one Hutchinson expected nothing better. Samuel Adams had always meant trouble and always would. He might call himself Vindex but he more properly qualified, Hutchinson felt, as "Malignus" or "Invidus." The commemorations continued through April with a second oration, which denied the authority of Parliament. Hutchinson deemed it treason. Freely distributed afterward, the printed versions were devoured, noted John Adams, "by everybody that could read, and scarcely ever with dry eyes." His cousin made those speeches "the engine of bringing forward to public notice young gentlemen of promising genius." Any number of revolutionary careers began with a Massacre address. John applauded his cousin's lavish memorials. They worked.* No one would have agreed more vehemently than the lieutenant governor. As Vindex, Adams kept the word "massacre" alive. The public declamations, the evening illuminations, the hair-raising talk of murder and complot kept the minds of the people in constant ferment, Hutchinson sputtered, and after "the fairest and most deliberate trials which had ever been known, struck a damp upon the spirits of all who were hoping for peace and quietness."

---

* John Adams learned the lesson well. In 1776 he suggested that July 2—another date that fell off the American calendar—"ought to be solemnized with pomp and parade, with shows, games, sports, guns, bells, bonfires and illuminations from one end of this continent to the other from this time forward forever more." He believed the massacre orations invaluable, as he did the King Street battle itself. In retrospect it struck him as more significant than Lexington, Saratoga, or Yorktown.

I SHALL STAND ALONE

*No man lives without jostling and being jostled; in all ways he has
to elbow himself through the world, giving and receiving offense.*
— THOMAS CARLYLE

FOR ADAMS the next three years constituted a crusade against peace and
quiet, in which peace and quiet seemed — until the very last, when he
scored a masterstroke — to be winning. He was forty-eight. Across the
province attention had drifted, the mood lightened. As a Hutchinson
in-law put it, the faction were left to "gnash their teeth in sullen silence."
Many in London believed the colonial dispute resolved. Wretched men
would blather no further about imaginary rights. So calm was Boston that
when word of his appointment as royal governor reached Hutchinson
early in March, he did not hesitate to accept. The awkwardly timed,
abjectly worded resignation letter was buried at both ends.

Hutchinson was sworn in nine days after the 1771 Massacre oration.
Andrew Oliver stepped in as his lieutenant. In a departure from tradition and
in a move finessed by Adams, the House withheld its congratulations.
Hutchinson was more surprised by the Congregational ministers, who went
out of their way to avoid endorsing the new governor while enumerating
their multiple expectations of him. He settled for replying with equal chilli-
ness. British warships sat in the harbor. Preston had sailed safely home. The
madness had subsided. The faction were not so cunning as they liked to
believe. The quiet came as a greater blessing, Hutchinson swore, than might

any addition to his private fortune, an easier claim to make given his princely new salary of 2,000 pounds. Adams thought it extortionate.

That spring he discovered that he could expect as little from friends as from enemies. He threw himself into the running for Registrar of Deeds, a minor Boston post, but one worth ninety pounds a year. The salary would come in handy when young Samuel was starting out in the world; the medical student would have no opportunity to squander the sum his father had. Adams's 1771 opponent was the longtime registrar, a fashionable North End conservative with multiple homes and exquisite taste in Madeira. Someone raised the specter of Adams's tax delinquencies weeks before the vote; he lost the election in a landslide. Having lobbied for him, John Adams felt gutted by the process. The registrar and his friends crowed about their victory, John sniffed, "like dung-hill cocks." He fumed about ingratitude. Public service had earned him only a slap in the face. John bid a happy farewell to politics; by mid-April he had shipped his furniture to Braintree. He resolved to devote himself to the law and his farm. He would live off potatoes and seaweed for the rest of his life, a decision he swore, on April 20, he would not regret.

Late the next day he called at his cousin's. He found Samuel in the company of Otis, Dr. Warren, and Plymouth-based James Warren. Otis appeared lucid and sober, a resurrection that proved less than pleasant for his host; Otis resumed his political career as a Tory. The House sat unhappily in Cambridge, in the Harvard College chapel. At its opening session, Adams proposed that they desist from business until returned to their proper home. It was inefficient for them to work far from their files. They were cold without their Town House fire. They had no place for their committees; their presence disrupted the college. How did they know that the "next freak of a capricious Minister" would not remove them to some other address? Displacing the House, Adams argued, constituted an undue exercise of power.* The new governor pushed back. They had

---

* By the time the displacement became a complaint against the king rather than Hutchinson, the charge would be convening a legislature "at places unusual, uncomfortable, and distant from the depository of their public records, for the sole purpose of fatiguing them into compliance."

plenty of room. They should ignore geography and tend to business. Harvard students might learn something from attending their sessions.

Either out of envy or his newfound conservatism, Otis undermined Adams at this and every subsequent turn. In a fiery speech he denounced Adams's motion. The governor had a right to carry the House across the province if he saw fit. Shock waves rippled through the room. Disaffection had receded, leaving Adams bruised by the acquittal, battered by the collapse of nonimportation, stranded on an ideological island. He acknowledged the setbacks but believed, as he wrote James Warren, "they rather make one faithful than desperate." Steady resistance was a tall order. Too many mistook pusillanimity for prudence. Private business distracted from "the rugged path of virtue." He remained steadfast, convinced that the patriot no more abandoned his cause than did the soldier his post. He would stand alone. Some wondered how he held off the snarling derision. Adams was a man of sensibility; the blows, one acquaintance inferred, surely landed. Those who loved America, he remained confident, would never desert him. He was unflinching, but touched too on his secret weapon, one especially valuable in 1771: "The opinion of others," he assured his former father-in-law, "I very little regard."

He let the new governor stray little from his view, well aware that Hutchinson counted on indolence and inattention. He intended to supply neither. Instead he traded Vindex for Candidus, settling, in the *Gazette*, early in June 1771, on a strategy that had worked before. If he could not find an injustice at hand he would salvage an old one. He did not mean "to disturb the sweet repose" of his fellow citizens but did want to draw their attention to several matters. In his longest stretch under a single pseudonym he published eighteen pieces over the next six months. Boston rarely went more than two weeks without an Adams essay, even when he fell ill, as he did that autumn.

With frequent assists from Locke, Hume, Montesquieu, and Dickinson—"whose works I wish every American would read over again," Adams wrote—he set off on a rampage. He began reasonably enough. That must have been an addled soul who announced the faction dissolved, the people returned to their senses! They continued in their "manly opposition"—a synonym for "courageous," the adjective counted among his favorites—to intrusions on liberties. America's enemies did their utmost to lull her to sleep. The colonists must resist those enchanting lullabies. Vigilance was a moral obligation where despotism lurked. Naturally a tyrant labeled those who opposed him "incendiaries" and "desperadoes." One should not be put off by such epithets. His loyalties were to liberty and truth. If that constituted a faction to some, he was "content to be in *their* sense of the word a party man."

He could not let go of the Circular Letter and its happy effects. To the consternation of Crown officials on both sides of the ocean, it had united the colonies. He replayed the affront of the Stamp Act, the arrival of troops, the events of March and June 1768, the petitions ignored and events exaggerated, the "slanderous chit-chat" of Francis Bernard, soon enough "a pimp rather than a governor." Adams commended the Boston pamphlet, *An Appeal to the World*. He played up the cooperation and down the violence. "Our incendiaries," Hutchinson accurately observed, "have consumed all their fuel and are raking the ashes of old newspapers." The town was quiet, resistance confined to the pages of the *Gazette*. Politics fell away as business recovered from the interruptions and intimidations. The town was awash in imported merchandise, trading at robust prices. The only 1771 mob was the one that assembled to drive a band of prostitutes from town.

More and more shrilly, Adams eviscerated Hutchinson, whom he made a courtier, a puppet of Lord Hillsborough. The true American would never stoop before a man who trampled his liberties, Adams insisted, maintaining that no one on the continent toadied more spectacularly than the royal governor. Hutchinson was like a teenaged girl, "surrounded with dying lovers, praising her gay ribbons, the dimples in her cheeks or the tip of her ear!" How could a man born in America, on whom the country had bestowed every honor, so traduce her? Hutchinson freely handed out Massachusetts offices to family members. He appointed brothers, cousins, and in-laws to posts.* Adams began to say

---

* Adams did not know that Hutchinson attempted that spring to find a government post for Richard Silvester, who continued to inform on Adams. Silvester had fallen on hard times, which may have explained the tall tales: it was likely Silvester who at the

what he and his friends had long discussed privately: Rome had proved that native sons too could be tyrants! Even there he slashed away. Ultimately the Caesar analogy fell apart. The Roman tyrant, Adams thundered in the *Gazette* that fall, "had learning, courage, and great abilities."

Occasionally he interrupted himself to make a point under a different pseudonym. But more raspingly and with greater and greater urgency, he insisted that smooth, subtle tyranny was at the door, if not already in the house. By early 1772 he also arrived at a new point. If Parliament could not make a law consistent with an American charter, why should Americans submit to any law handed down by Parliament? As for what should be done, he had an idea. There was a reason the Circular Letter burned so bright in his mind. "I have often thought that in this time of common distress," mused Candidus, "it would be the wisdom of the colonists more frequently to correspond with, and to be more attentive to, the particular circumstances of each other."

The same week he wrote to Arthur Lee, the Virginia-born, London-based physician with whom he had corresponded over the previous months. Adams circled back to a thought he had articulated days earlier and half-forgotten. What if a society of respectable citizens met annually in each colony, to defend themselves against their common enemies — and to promote a better understanding with Great Britain? "This is a sudden thought and drops undigested from my pen," Adams confided. It would be arduous to organize representatives for such an ambitious undertaking. "Nothing, however, should be despaired of," he added.

Nine days later Hutchinson forwarded Candidus's most recent diatribe to London. In this case Adams's identity was no secret; Hutchinson recognized the work of "the chief incendiary in the House." He believed moreover that nothing appeared in the *Gazette* without the approval of Adams, who had a lock on the press. The faction was dying but dying hard. Their followers were carried away "with the sound of tyranny and liberty and other big words the force and meaning whereof they do not

---

end of 1770 (falsely) reported that Adams attempted to raise twenty thousand men to seize Castle William.

comprehend." Many had awoken from their delusion but failed to muster the courage to admit they had. Hutchinson believed that he, and reason, would prevail. One should, he concluded, never despair.

He had triumphed and knew as much; the change in the Massachusetts temper had come about more quickly than anyone could have expected. There were but a few flies in the ointment and one pest in particular. "The Devil himself is not capable of more malevolence," Hutchinson sighed. The popular leaders could still get away with murder. Were one of them to marry his mother no one would mind, he huffed, so long as he continued to bellow about American liberties. Adams alone seemed unwilling to abate in his virulence. He "would push the continent into a rebellion tomorrow if it was in his power," Hutchinson reported. He avoided engaging with him or his associates. The upper hand made it easier. Massachusetts was calmer than it had been for five years.

Given the quiet, he ventured a few suggestions. Was this not the time for some reforms? The colony begged for a flogging. All America would fall in line if London tamed the irascible Massachusetts House, silenced the town meetings, and investigated treason among the "pretenders to patriotism." Meanwhile, the provincial thirst for tea exceeded anything the mother country could imagine. Nearly all of it was imported illegally. Did it not make sense to lower the duty, so that East India tea might replace its smuggled Dutch counterpart? He attempted a few calculations. Boston and Charlestown alone consumed 340 pounds, or a chest, of tea daily. The countryside consumed yet more tea than Boston, where it was drunk morning and night, especially by women, enthusiastically by the poor. The Indians drank it twice daily. Hutchinson figured that thirst translated into a staggering 2,400 chests a year for the province as a whole. (He was in a position to know. The bulk of his income and his salary were drawn from tea duties or East India stock.)* By a modest count, Great Britain forfeited well over 75,000 pounds in revenue to smugglers.

He made a few symbolic adjustments to his new position, sending to

---

* Or, as John Adams put it, "Mr. Hutchinson never drank a cup of tea in his life without contemplating the connection between that tea and his promotion."

London for royal portraits to preside over public rooms. And he began to split his Sunday worship between the Anglicans and the Congregational-ists. The former seemed more consistent with his title, though he thought it best to keep a foot in each camp. (Interestingly, it was one of the few decisions for which Adams never skewered him.)* For the "loose absurd principles" that floated about town Hutchinson had a solution as well. There was an easy way to end denials of parliamentary sovereignty "by the Lilliputian assemblies of America." Behind the scenes, he took it upon himself to dismantle what remained of the faction. Some headaches took care of themselves. John Adams had withdrawn. Otis reverted to drink. Declared insane, he was carried off, bound hand and foot, and placed under a guardian's care. Sensible Thomas Cushing ceded to Hutchinson's ministrations. Benjamin Church, a silky, thirty-seven-year-old London-trained physician and *Journal of Occurrences* contributor, quietly became an informer.

Others required a little assistance. At the end of 1771 Hutchinson heard that Hancock had sworn off all connection with Adams. We do not know his reason. Hutchinson may have, but focused on exploiting the rift, reminding Hancock of the toll politics took on his private affairs. He recruited friends to fan the flames, an easy assignment; there was a rea-son why Hancock was caricatured as a man with a grin on his face, a dunce's cap on his head, and a bandage over his eyes. Many believed him putty in Adams's hands. Within weeks, Hutchinson boasted that the two faction leaders would never reconcile. Hancock had not seen Adams since November and had no desire ever to do so again. While he was at it, Hutchinson stirred up animosities between Franklin and Arthur Lee in London. Why was a man of Franklin's stature, he asked, associating with ruffians? He tossed bones in all directions, convinced that everyone had his price. Before Hancock he dangled a Council seat.

---

* The newspaper-collecting Harbottle Dorr railed against those who took "the sacra-ment according to the Church of England, to qualify them for their offices" — especially when the British Ministry had made clear that was unnecessary. Despite the show of devotion, Abigail Adams believed Hutchinson unversed in any religious feeling whatever.

Overall, Hutchinson basked in self-congratulation. There remained only an impotent faction purveying imaginary grievances. The rest of the province was as fond of government and of him as they had been for seven years. Soon there had not been such calm since 1760. They had heard the last of Adams's "mad measures." The people were sick and tired of their "misleaders." The faction was in disarray, the colonies estranged. Hutchinson preferred each remain a separate island and seemed on his way to getting his wish. "It must be something very extraordinary ever to reconcile them," he wrote in June 1772.

ADAMS'S TRAVAILS only increased. Under a pseudonym, the attorney general offered some advice in the papers to a certain public defaulter who should relent before it was too late. He had plunged "a whole state into disorder and confusion." Adams might well have a talent for troublemaking, Sewall wrote, but talent was no excuse. A cutthroat was no less criminal "because he uses a fine sharp razor rather than a ragged knife." Adams insisted that he was immune to abuse; the fortitude would come in handy. He was mocked as "the disinterested and truly patriotic dictator Mr. Adams." In April an intimate extended condolences to Elizabeth Adams. She was thirty-five. It is not impossible that she had lost a pregnancy. At a disconsolate moment Adams expounded on the balm of intimacy. What was life without it? "The tears of sincere friendship are refreshing like gentle showers after a scorching draught and always produce the harvest of solid comfort," he wrote, sounding little like a political dictator. At the end of a bitter winter—it had been too cold to allow a dog outside—came, early in March, a record-setting blizzard. Boston disappeared under a seven-foot blanket of snow just before the annual Massacre oration, when Dr. Warren dilated on the rise and fall of empires. He turned afterward to the mangled bodies and the groans of the dying, which he had observed as closely as anyone. To them he joined a full cohort of imaginary terrors: homes in flames, children barbarously beaten, and "virtuous wives" sacrificed to rampaging brutes.

The Hutchinson-seeded squabbling intensified to the point that John

Hancock launched a 1772 campaign to oust Adams from the House. In an April town meeting, Hancock proposed an inquiry into Boston finances, a move calculated to embarrass both Adams and Cushing, who managed the town lotteries. Adams had not been challenged since 1765; over the previous two years he had secured nearly every vote. The subterfuge seemed foolproof. Hutchinson was all relief. Without Adams, his troubles would be over. Hancock disparaged Adams across town, which left Adams paying calls to defend himself against comments falsely attributed to him. He elicited oaths from associates. He asked them to repeat purported statements before both men. He demanded precision. His honor was on the line. When asked about his former protégé, he suggested that Hancock acted not on his own but "was stirred up by others."

Hancock managed to detach nearly a third of Boston's voters from Adams, who received fewer votes than any other representative. In the hours after the election Lieutenant Governor Andrew Oliver rejoiced. His brother-in-law seemed well on his way to quashing the faction. "So long the idol of the populace," Adams was not invulnerable after all! Hancock did not accept the proffered Council seat but did accept a commission as captain of an eighty-man ceremonial guard. Busily he set about procuring gold-buttoned uniforms and musical instruments. Adams's dismal showing at the polls meanwhile set off alarm bells. Mutual friends rallied. There was too much at stake to permit the exploitation of petty differences; a year of hostility sufficed. There were stabs at reconciliation. Hutchinson was displeased but assumed that in all essential measures Hancock would forsake his former colleagues. He did, and he did not. He made a point of picking up Adams in his splendid coach so that the two might ride together to sessions of the House. Once there they rarely voted the same way. They proceeded to get on as well as two men nicknamed "John Puff" and "the psalm-singer" might.

The immediate issue in the spring of 1772 remained the House's return to Boston, where it had not met since nine months before British soldiers had fired on civilians. Hutchinson coached Hancock on how to resolve the impasse. Were the House to stress the inconvenience of their address rather than rant about violated rights, he would move them. He was himself eager for the transfer. Now that all was calm, he preferred the representatives closer at hand, where it was easier to launch charm offensives with periodic dinner invitations. Proffering language, steeling him against the "art and insidiousness of Adams," he prepared Hancock for the maneuver. Adams outwitted him all the same.

Hutchinson remained sanguine. He hoped to convert other members of the House, who would neutralize, he wrote Bernard, the "poison of that white-livered fellow that you used so much to detest." This he confided in what he termed "a chit-chat letter," one he never mailed. It may have seemed too small-minded for the former Massachusetts governor, but Hutchinson was generally circumspect when he wrote of Adams. He tempered phrases, trusting to allusions and crossing out clauses, at times expunging whole passages. Immoderate distaste sat poorly with a moderate man. And he knew what his letters were worth on the open market. What he thought of Adams in 1772 — "I doubt whether there is a greater incendiary in the King's dominions or a man of greater malignity of heart, or who less scruples any measures, ever so criminal, to accomplish his purposes; and I think I do him no injustice when I suppose he wishes the destruction of every friend to government in America" — would not make its way to Great Britain for some time.

By mid-June a compromise had been reached regarding the House but Hutchinson began to worry anew about the faction. That month he got another taste of Adams's "coarse, illiberal style" in a fresh lecture on charter rights. It would not be the last. In July arrived the news that the Crown, rather than the province, would in future pay the Massachusetts governor's salary. Immediately Hutchinson met with resistance over repairs to Province House, his official residence. The wind blew through it in winter. The Massachusetts assembly seemed determined, he reported, to allow it to crumble. Adams explained: As the House were no longer to pay their governor, his official residence was no longer their responsibility. The minute that changed, they would build him a palace.

He remained as flinty as ever. When word arrived that Hillsborough was to be replaced in London by Lord Dartmouth, a mild, notably pious man, Adams exempted himself from the jubilation. If a master were to be

A 1770 depiction of the death of eleven-year-old Christopher Seider, the first victim of Boston violence. He lies wounded to the right of Lillie's shop; Richardson disappears behind clouds of smoke. If the woman at center stage is meant to be Mrs. Seider, she assumes an unusual pose for a woman mourning a martyred son: she carries a pitchfork.

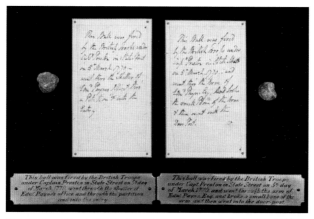

Two lead musket balls, fired at close range, purportedly by Preston's men at the Boston Massacre. They are said to have been retrieved from the doorway of Edward Payne, whose handsome home stood behind the King Street victims. One ball evidently traveled through Payne's arm and into a post. The other hit a shutter, of which it bears a wooden fragment.

Paul Revere's Boston Massacre engraving, copies of which hung throughout Boston over the spring and summer of 1770. Adapting a colleague's work, Revere added elements to make his account align more closely with Adams's version; it was essential to keep the people's minds focused, as Adams saw it, or in a state of agitation, as Thomas Hutchinson did. Revere labeled the customs house "Butcher's Hall" and inserted a musket into one of its windows. The sky is blue; the Bostonians well-dressed; there is not a patch of snow in sight. One side viciously lunges forward as the other, all innocence, recoils. A woman wrings her hands amid the huddle of Bostonians; though they regularly taunted soldiers, it was unlikely that any woman ventured out early that evening.

Americans throwing the Cargoes of the Tea Ships into the River, at Boston

A 1789 depiction of the Boston Tea Party, fanciful in most respects apart from the large crowd assembled at the wharf. The crew "disguised like Indians" have here become actual Native Americans. In broad daylight and under fanciful flags, their accomplices make off with a skiff piled with tea chests. One small canoe evidently did approach to claim jettisoned cargo that evening; several participants jumped down and capsized it, "in the twinkling of an eye."

Warships at anchor off Long Wharf, where soldiers from the Twenty-ninth and Fourteenth Regiments disembarked in October, 1768. In "a mighty and expensive parade"—it was the grandest anyone could remember—the regulars marched up the wharf and north along King Street to the Common. At least for the next months, Boston went quiet. The watercolor was prominently displayed around town; this version belonged to Thomas Hutchinson.

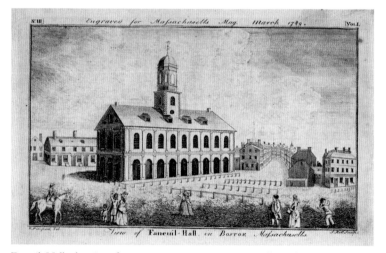

Faneuil Hall, the site of numerous town meetings as well as the extralegal 1768 Convention, held at a "dreadfully precarious" moment, just before the Long Wharf disembarkation. Market stalls occupied the ground floor; a vast, high-ceilinged assembly room stood above. With the 1775 British occupation, the hall became a theater.

A Daughter of Liberty, with musket, powder horn, and tricornered hat, from a Marblehead newspaper. The soldier had appeared in various earlier incarnations, when she seemed to prove—as the 1779 lines accompanying the woodcut had it—that "the world is now turned upside down."

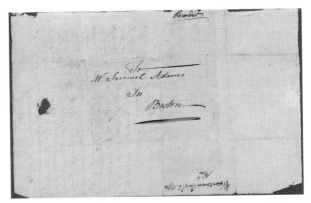

The envelope that carried Watertown's January 1774 response to Boston's committee of correspondence. The town believed Boston had done its utmost to protect East India Company tea, destroyed by customs officials and the governor, who refused all attempts to send it "back from whence it came."

Tall, reserved, immensely rich James Bowdoin, Adams's counterpart on the Governor's Council. No admirer of Governor Bernard, Bowdoin was said to be unable to so much as abide the mention of Hutchinson's name. The more florid writer, Bowdoin likely collaborated with Adams on the account of the Boston Massacre.

Thirty-three-year-old Paul Revere, in flowing, linen shirtsleeves and unbuttoned waistcoat, the rare artisan painted by Copley. The silversmith's hands are spotless; the table gleams. Revere nonetheless appears with his engraving tools and without a wig. He contemplates a half-finished teapot, already by 1768 a vexed symbol; he produced only one that year. Keen-eyed and quick-thinking, Revere did his best — even with a pistol clapped to his head, seven years later — to protect Adams and Hancock from capture in Lexington.

The parsonage to which Revere galloped on April 18, 1775, to warn Adams and Hancock of arrest. Outside the home, guards blocked his path: "The regulars are coming out!" Revere cried, with some irritation. The home was built by Hancock's grandfather; the engraving dates from 1868.

The Battle of Lexington. April 19th 1775. Plate 1.

1. Major Pitcairn at the head of the Regular Grenadiers.
2. The Party who first fired on the Provincials at Lexington.
3. Part of the Provincial Company of Lexington.
4. Regulars, firing on the road to Concord.
5. Col. Smith & M. Pitcairn ordering it.
6. The Meeting House.

The battle of Lexington, sketched days afterward from eyewitness accounts. The provincial militia figure in the foreground. On the left is the tavern to which Adams, Hancock, Clarke, and Revere had repaired the evening before to discuss a plan of action, and from which—early the next morning—Revere watched the redcoats approach. He was steps away when he heard the first shots. In his company Adams and Hancock fled by coach, hours before the engagement.

Samuel Adams as he stands today, clear-eyed and steadfast, before Faneuil Hall. The 1880 bronze is a replica of Anne Whitney's marble version that decorates the National Statuary Hall in the US Capitol. For the American centennial, an appeal went to every state for likenesses of its two most eminent citizens, with which to create a national pantheon. Samuel Adams seemed still at the time, in the words of one biographer, "without question the greatest person ever born in Massachusetts."

imposed upon him, he preferred the harsher one. He did not care to lose sight of the indignity. He reported that Tories wished a "confusion on me and my adherents" at the 1772 Harvard commencement, a toast he took as a compliment. He was undeviating and implacable. Were Moses to return with a divine commission, lamented Hutchinson, he would not manage to quiet Samuel Adams! On that front Adams's antipathy only grew. Of Hutchinson he wrote: "It has been his principle from a boy that mankind are to be governed by the discerning few—and it has ever since been his ambition to be the hero of the few." The governor possessed no true greatness, "and with all his art could never counterfeit it." He was a "public executioner of his country's rights."

Friends meanwhile worked overtime to effect a reconciliation. It helped that Hancock was "flattered by ideas of his own consequence," as a contemporary put it, Adams eager to dissolve personal slights for the greater good. Each had his partisans, though some publicly supported one and privately the other. Hutchinson watched helplessly as his ploy backfired. Every sort of attempt was made to heal the breach. It gradually closed, he observed, "and the wrath of friends, like that of lovers, issued in the renewal and strengthening of their affection and attachment until both of them had so far engaged in the cause, that all their personal, or private, interest lay in the success of it." Adams reassured Arthur Lee, who had heard in London of the defections, that Hancock had declined the Council seat. He had rejoined the opposition after "the imaginary conquest." Family lore suggests that it was to seal the peace in 1772 that Hancock arranged for Adams to sit for the Copley portrait, a picture Hancock displayed prominently in his Beacon Hill mansion.

AND THEN, AS if in reward for all the slights and censure, Adams finally got the assist he needed—from London. In August Massachusetts learned that its justices, too, would be paid directly by the Crown, from revenue duties. The news arrived, Adams announced, "like thunder in the ears." The provision planted the Massachusetts judiciary beyond the people's control, beholden to the Crown. It blurred the separation of powers. It was one thing for the governor to be a British pawn, supported by funds extorted from constituents, Adams erupted. Should those who handed down New England law be as well, in violation of the constitution—and at the expense of impartial justice? Seizing the moment, he prepared to pull a long-mused-about rabbit from his hat. Andrew Oliver shuddered at rumors: "I have heard that one of the demagogues has said that this will bring matters to a crisis." Over six weeks Adams canvassed the town, wrestling with intrigue on one side and apathy on the other. As an associate whispered: "We are brewing something that will make their heads reel."

Adams had a very specific sort of head-reeling in mind. For it he attempted to drum up enthusiasm in the October 5, 1772, *Gazette*. Three million people seemed barely able to make themselves heard. Meanwhile indignity followed upon indignity. Gently he slipped an idea into the drinking water. "Let us converse together upon this most interesting subject and open our minds freely to each other." American liberties should be the topic at every address. Some people seemed to be laboring under the influence of an opiate. "I wish," he wrote a new friend, "we could arouse the continent." He lobbied for a town meeting; behind locked doors, above the *Gazette* offices, he reviewed options with a newly sympathetic Otis. Could one confront a justice, in his courtroom, and ask if he intended to accept a Crown salary? Was it possible to appeal, citizen to citizen, to his sense of honor? Where was the line between impertinence and contempt of court? For the first time an objective observer might well conclude that—whether or not there was a conspiracy in Great Britain to oppress the colonies—there was indeed a conspiracy afoot in New England to resist Great Britain. From the town meeting Adams extracted only lukewarm measures. On its behalf, he twice dispatched deferential messages to Hutchinson. Might he confirm the news? Twice Hutchinson replied with lectures. The first, a friend observed, was insolent, the second stupid.

From Hutchinson's scorn Adams wrested a singular triumph, proposing something that struck most in 1772 as either treacherous or preposterous: a committee to state the rights of the colonies and broadcast them to the greater world. The countryside and Boston should work in tandem; once they were reconciled, Adams predicted, "a plan of opposition will be easily formed, and executed with spirit." The Massachusetts convention was still very much with him. "Where there is a spark of patriotic fire, we will enkindle it," he assured James Warren. He hoped to unite the colonies as ardently as Hutchinson wished them to remain discrete islands; an assault on the rights of one should be understood to be an assault on all. This, Adams explained later, was the true design of the entities he had in mind. They would enlighten and invigorate. They would divert the public from the inconsequential. They would serve "to circulate the most early intelligence of importance to our friends in the country, and to establish an union which is formidable to our adversaries."

Adams's newfangled committees would require many motions, much arm-twisting, and multiple hours. There was little appetite for them outside his closest circle and only lukewarm support within. Most Boston representatives and a number of prominent Sons edged away. He discounted the cold-shouldering; the meeting at which he summoned them into existence was small because their enemies had discouraged attendance. Men from the country stocked their cellars for the winter. Others believed there was no recourse but the most dire, from which they shrank. No more than three hundred people were at hand when, on November 2, intensifying his efforts after a series of votes and at the end of a full day of debate, just after 10:00 p.m., Adams nearly single-handedly willed the new entities into being.

He fitted his brainchild with the most inoffensive of names: A "committee of correspondence" sounded as flavorless as a "Son of Liberty" sounded irreproachable. His was, however, a daringly original institution, a news service, an alarm system, to some a proto-terrorist cell. There was a reason why Cushing sidled off and Hancock pleaded private business. Those who did not believe the venture amounted to treason worried that it would be rebuffed by the towns, defeating its purpose. Twenty-one men all the same assembled the next day, their first act a vote of secrecy.* One friend compared the innovation to the circulatory

---

* Adams was fortunate in that what Hutchinson termed Boston's middle class — merchants, sea captains, shopkeepers — cared deeply about judicial integrity.

system, though it would be some time before anyone realized that Adams had just wired a continent for rebellion. Only much later would the committees—Boston's met weekly, in longer and longer sessions—reveal themselves to be the "engines of a revolution," "furnaces of propaganda," "the germ of a government," "dangerous machines." The tracks on which an intellectual locomotive might run, the committees led directly to a gathering in Philadelphia. Looking back, a Loyalist would note that the colonies were "13 disunited bodies," unable to so much as assist one another, until the introduction of committees of correspondence.

Hutchinson scoffed. He noted that Adams had tamed Otis by placing him at the head of "the grand committee for stating their rights." How to take seriously an entity headed by someone who had just been released from his guardian's care—and was only on alternate days either sane or sober?* Among the rest of the crew figured men you would not care to meet in the dark, "as black-hearted fellows as any upon the globe." Hutchinson recognized a foolish scheme when he saw one. Adams and his colleagues were making themselves ridiculous.

By November 20 the Boston committee had produced a draft document. Adams, Otis, and Josiah Quincy Jr. co-wrote the first section, an affirmation of the natural rights of the colonists. Dr. Warren collaborated on the second, a catalogue of "infringements and violations" of those rights. Church wrote the third, an appeal to the other Massachusetts towns. No author injected the elegiac quality that the forty-seven-page document so nearly anticipated; it is a cool, straightforward performance. Government existed, wrote Adams and Otis, to protect natural rights. What liberty did the colonists enjoy if their property could be taken without their consent? They had as much power in Parliament as they did to choose the emperor of China. To the Massachusetts towns Church explained that Crown salaries for justices were both unconstitutional and the latest in a long series of abuses. Boston would welcome a free

---

* Earlier that week, a fishy-eyed Otis had taken it upon himself to lash John Adams with a few remarks about weather vanes. Why was John "moping about the streets" like an old man, dithering between Boston and Braintree? Had a year of public service already done him in?

discussion of their sentiments; surely the towns would not opt "to doze, or set supinely indifferent on the brink of destruction, while the iron hand of oppression is daily tearing the choicest fruit from the fair tree of liberty." Edes and Gill rushed out six hundred copies of the pamphlet, delivered by express riders to every Boston clergyman and Massachusetts town. A copy went even to a community of Indians. Its authors then sat back to wait. Hutchinson mailed a copy to London but felt the pages not worth their postage. The most subversive document yet, it did however present a strong case for its authors to be tried for treason.

Even close friends suspected that Adams had a heavy lift on his hands. Few towns leapt immediately on the committee-forming bandwagon. Some seemed actively to discourage their neighbors. Friends reassured Adams; he was attempting nothing less than raising the dead, which happened to require a miracle. By December 21, only Roxbury, Plymouth, Cambridge, and Marblehead had appointed committees. At least outwardly, Adams remained optimistic, gaily assuring his former brother-in-law, now in Rhode Island, that very little could separate him from his self-possession. He counted among his friends those who loved their country. He had no time for anyone else. William Checkley was not so far advanced as Adams in his political thinking. Were it not disagreeable, Adams would mail him a copy of a new pamphlet.

When John called on his cousin at the end of the year, he found him wholly engaged in public business but entirely at his ease, more genteel than ever. For someone who lived on close terms with poverty, he tended at home to every decorous detail. John did not peer too closely into the magic: Samuel was making do on ninety pounds a year at a time when a gentleman entertained well only on twice as much. (Much of the credit went to Betsy, to Surrey, and after about 1772 to a young servant boy whose education Adams oversaw. The couple relied as well on invisible benefactors. When the Adams barn disintegrated from neglect, friends took it upon themselves to build the family a new one.) John discovered that Samuel's house had been reglazed and painted, the rooms repapered and furnished. Even while devoting every minute to public service, he entertained in stylish simplicity. He hardly appeared among those

Hutchinson wrote off as men of "intemperate and furious dispositions, and of desperate fortunes."

Samuel spent the last weeks of the year neutralizing resistance to the committees and planning for the third anniversary of the Massacre. A colleague in tow, he called on John. Would he deliver the 1773 oration? He was everyone's first choice. Samuel did not need to state the obvious: there was no shrewder choice for the occasion than the lawyer who had secured the soldiers' acquittals. Taken aback, John declined. A tug-of-war ensued. John's health was feeble. He intended to avoid so much as thinking about politics. He longed for his country hut and forty acres. He was too old for declamations. In the flurry of excuses one can hear Samuel's insistence. Why again did his cousin hesitate? John wound his way around to the trial. He did not believe a March 5 oration incompatible with the jury's verdict. It was possible both for soldiers to be innocent and to have slaughtered innocents; he neither regretted his role nor believed the evening anything less than a massacre. But those subtleties would elude the public. He would be crucified. The taunts and reproaches with which he met already were bad enough, the "giggles and tittering of Tories" worse. His cousin pressed. John should consider the idea for a few days. John held his ground, among the few who could resist the will of Samuel Adams, who finally relented. There would be no hard feelings.

Adams met with more success in advising friends how to thwart attacks on the fledgling committees. To a Rhode Island correspondent he went further: Might their House consider reaching out to the other colonies? The effort would be more effective if championed by a colony with a better reputation. Shortly after the New Year, Hutchinson noted with consternation that several Massachusetts towns had followed Boston's wayward lead and seated committees. He held his fire for fear of bolstering the effort. By January he could bear the rain of falsehoods no longer. He was up against a "dangerous plot." What had seemed laughable in the fall was disquieting by winter.

On January 6, 1773, he unexpectedly convened the House for a long disquisition on the supremacy of Parliament. The frankness elicited gasps; sovereignty was a riddle around which all parties preferred still to dance. Scrapping all subtlety, Hutchinson argued that the question boiled down to the supreme authority of Parliament or the total independence of the colonies. There could be no doubts, questions, or middle ground. He knew he waded into hazardous territory but could no longer remain silent. With his speech he believed he had opened eyes— three-quarters of the Massachusetts representatives seemed unfamiliar with the constitution—and forced the faction into a corner. He was pleased with his performance. So was Adams, who thought Hutchinson's a wrecking ball of a lecture. His superiors, Adams beamed, would not thank him for the effort. The governor had awakened a people from their sound sleep.

The House knew that a great deal rode on its response to the governor; urgent appeals went to friends in Maryland and Pennsylvania for drafting assistance. Adams seems to have attempted an early version along with Joseph Hawley, the no-nonsense Northampton lawyer, John Adams's equal as a jurist and superior as a speaker. This time around Samuel had better luck recruiting his cousin. To John went a draft, neatly and elegantly composed, if long on what John termed "elementary principles of liberty, equality, and fraternity." Night after night, paragraph after paragraph, a small team waded through the document, as John replaced grandiose turns of phrase with prosaic points of law. (He worried that his cousin would be offended by his "garbling his infant.") Supreme authority rested not with Parliament but with God. Neither Parliament nor the king could limit natural rights.

In a break with precedent, the Council responded separately to the governor. It, too, denied parliamentary authority. Hutchinson grew flustered as opposition solidified around him. The constitution seemed to be ripped to pieces. He asked his Council if they might care to reconsider their position. They did not. In a replay of the Circular Letter, by forcing the issue a Crown officer only fueled opposition. Hutchinson squared off, he wrote Bernard, against "Bowdoin's genius in one house, and Hawley's and Adams's in the other." "What," he wondered, "will Parliament say to this?"

Impatiently he awaited their response; he could not get past the idea that to limit their authority in any way was to demolish it. "Adams brought above 80 towns to declare openly against the authority of Parliament," Hutchinson reported in February 1773, acknowledging that his speech had backfired. With "a great deal of low art and cunning," Adams had convinced Boston to enter into a "declaration of independency" from legislative authority. The province seemed to be belching forth committees. There was one consolation. Having invited Cushing to his house and softened him up with talk of repercussions, Hutchinson had winkled out of him the news that Adams intended to extend his appeal across the continent. Hutchinson believed he had nipped that effort in the bud.

On March 2 Adams berated Hutchinson all over again, reminding him that in the New England charter the king had acknowledged Massachusetts to stand outside his realm. Among the many books he threw at Hutchinson, it seems to have amused Adams to have tossed the governor's own. Even Hutchinson had written that parliamentary authority had not always been acknowledged in America. Just because they had suppressed the Land Bank—it was a rare, overt mention of the debacle— did not mean that the colony consented to Parliament's unilateral authority. Hutchinson had informed the House that such matters were "far above the reach of the bulk of mankind to comprehend." Surely, implored Adams, the governor did not mean to suggest that Americans were "of so little discernment, such children in understanding" as to imagine they were subjects of a legislature three thousand miles away, which knew nothing of their circumstances and which cared less?

By early March, one-third of Massachusetts towns had established committees of correspondence. Adams took evident pleasure in writing them, reaching, in his letters, for the high notes. As Hutchinson feared, he also began to look well beyond New England. Should they not "open every channel of communication"? Adams queried Arthur Lee's Virginia-based brother, Richard Henry, with whom he had begun to correspond. "The liberties of all are alike invaded by the same haughty power," Adams wrote. The conspirators oppressed each colony as suited their purposes. As things stood, Massachusetts got its news of South Carolina from England. Committees in every town would guarantee America's security. To the same end, he submitted the 1773 Massacre oration to Dickinson, the author of "Letters from a Farmer in Pennsylvania," in Philadelphia.* Might Dickinson publish some kind of rejoinder to Hutchinson's lecture? He apologized for the imposition, but surely—the argument sounded like one he had perfected—when it came to the public interest, one turned to "its ablest advocates." He left Hutchinson to complain privately that any punitive measures on which Parliament might settle would need now to be applied to every colony. Encouraged by Boston, Virginia appointed a committee. The infection had spread. In the spring election Adams received all but six votes, an astonishing recovery from the 1772 sabotage. Reassembling the coalition, he lauded Hancock. He defended Otis. He brushed aside all rumors of dissension, especially the accurate ones.

Teeth gritted, Hutchinson restored Adams to his earlier eminence. He was again "the restless incendiary," "the principal incendiary," or "the grand incendiary." Thomas Hutchinson had been in government a long time but never had he seen a legislature willing to vote unanimously as dictated by their leader or one in which a Council took direction from the House. He was neither pleased by the gentle reprimand he received for his January address nor reassured by the news that Parliament had little time for American questions, consumed as it was by the troubles of the East India Company.

EARLY IN THE winter, amid much secrecy, a bundle of letters from London arrived on Thomas Cushing's doorstep. They carried strict instructions. No copies were to be made, in whole or part. Under no circumstances were the letters to be published. They were to be shared only with several prominent men, then returned. Adams would have read them by March. He had dreamed of this very prize for years. Unhappily, he

---

* For the oration the church had been packed to the rafters with Bostonians of all ages. The speaker was Benjamin Church, who had squeezed through a window. John Adams could at least console himself that—for all of Church's Latin quotations and Shakespearean allusions—he would have delivered a more cogent address.

respected the embargo. "It is a pity when the most important intelligence is communicated with such restrictions, as that it serves rather to gratify the curiosity of a few than to promote the public good," he griped. Secrecy agreed with him. Wasted opportunities did not. Among the letters—purloined from a London desk and entrusted to Franklin, who dispatched them—were six of Hutchinson's from the late 1760s. If their contents could be disclosed, Adams believed, Massachusetts would be rid of its governor forever. Franklin claimed that had essentially been his intention: the letters would exonerate the king and Parliament, transferring blame for America's ordeals to those venal middle managers who had bartered away the country's liberties. Once the true villains were revealed, a bright, new chapter in Anglo-American relations would dawn. Adams needed no convincing. To his mind, Hutchinson had introduced all their present difficulties. America, and Great Britain, ought never to forgive him. Adams knew he never would.

While the documents could not be published, there was no ban on talking about them, leaving Adams free to proceed by innuendo and insinuation. Boston was soon aflutter. By May, whispers flew about that proof was on hand "of a conspiracy which had long been carrying on, for enslaving America." There was talk miles away that Hutchinson had urged the arrests of Otis and Adams, to be deported or decapitated. The documents, promised the newspapers, would "bring many dark things to light, gain many proselytes to the cause of freedom, make tyrannical rulers tremble." Having advertised the letters, Adams proceeded, after the spring election, like a seasoned showman. He announced to the House that he would soon share a momentous discovery. It would return the province to the happy state it had enjoyed in 1760. His news created a sensation, the suspense building hourly. Finally on the morning of June 2 he revealed to a full House that he had in hand a set of explosive letters, deeply prejudicial to Massachusetts. They were to be shared only under certain conditions. If his colleagues agreed, he might read them aloud. The gallery was cleared and the doors clapped shut, the representatives sworn to secrecy. Adams then proceeded to read Hutchinson's words.

We do not know with what expression he intoned the 1769 line "There must be an abridgement of what are called English liberties," but we know of the reaction. The House lost no time in voting that the letters subverted the constitution. They seemed to point to a settled plot; Adams's name appears atop the eighty-two yeas demanding Hutchinson's and Oliver's recall. By the end of the month he had crafted a petition to the king to remove both men, assuring his colleagues, without foundation, as he had earlier, that the king would not support a governor in whom the people had lost confidence. Repeatedly he harped on an additional point: the treachery was worse as the rapacious plotters were blood of their blood, born and educated in the colony they sacrificed to their own ambition. He left Hutchinson as exposed as had his plundered home. "The world," Hutchinson grumbled, "never had more bad men in it."

Given the extravagant claims, both an incensed public and Hutchinson's friends clamored to read the letters. Adams found himself in a quandary, obligated somehow to produce the documents without violating the terms of their loan. He enlisted Hancock; with good reason, Hutchinson took that summer to calling Adams a "master of the puppets." Matching sophistry with effrontery, Hancock in July informed the House that as he strolled one day across the Common, someone had slipped him a sheaf of papers. He supposed them copies of the purloined documents. He proposed a comparison. If Adams could confirm that the sets were identical, surely Hancock's pages could be published? As they originated from a different source, this would not constitute a breach of the agreement. From the gallery came peals of laughter. With this "childish tale," snorted Hutchinson, the House forged ahead.* A committee declared the copies genuine; Adams determined that the letters were effectively already in circulation. They would appear in four Massachusetts papers, afterward in nearly every American paper and in pamphlet form—but

---

* He could not have been entirely unsurprised. Years earlier, Bernard had trusted Adams with a public paper on the condition no copy be made. It appeared in the *Gazette* the next day. When Bernard charged Adams with having broken his promise, Adams assured him that no copies had been made. The paper had reprinted the original.

only after they had been sensationalized and summarized, and only after Massachusetts had read Adams's petition to the king. It argued that there had been a conspiracy of evil men who planned "to raise their own fortunes and advance themselves to posts of power, honor, and profit" at the expense of the province. They were responsible for all the animosity and moral corruption, the confusion and bloodshed. Might they be removed from their posts?

For Hutchinson it was a miserable summer. Gleefully Adams reported not only that the public had turned against him but that—a source of particular satisfaction—friends too kept their distance. The governor appeared flustered. Adams was only sorry not to be able to report him humbled as well. He continued publicly parsing the letters weekly into the fall, connecting dots, surfacing insinuations, discarding context, deconstructing whole phrases, all to prove that Hutchinson had as good as requested "a standing army into the country which gave him birth, for the protection of a few detestable men." He had gloried in the arrival of troops. He had helped the sheriff threaten the Manufactory House. Had he no decency?

Hutchinson could only marvel at his guile; it was not humanly possible to guard against such audacity. (Nor was it easy to wade through it. Hutchinson bogs down in outrage when writing of the episode.) Adams had turned half a dozen harmless letters into a great crime. Had the documents simply been published, no one would have noticed.* Adams was setting the colony ablaze with his "barbarous conspiracy." Hutchinson had written none of the letters in his capacity as governor. He had not been in office when troops arrived. As for the remark about the abridgement of liberties, all depended on what the meaning of "must" was: Hutchinson's line—"There must be an abridgement of what are called English liberties"—could read as an imperative or a prediction. (Hutchinson insisted he had meant the latter. He also argued he had said as much

---

* The stage management did not go unremarked abroad. When the matter became a *cause célèbre* in London, Solicitor General Alexander Wedderburn ranted that—while pretending to honor the injunction—one man had greatly amplified the fame of the letters.

publicly without anyone uttering a syllable of objection.) Was it unreasonable that he had been just a little bit angry at the destruction of his home? The House and Council insisted on a criminality to be found nowhere in the pages, which hardly mattered, moaned Hutchinson, as everyone preferred to listen to Adams rather than consult the documents. Adams moreover enlisted his brand-new committees of correspondence to spread the word. By July they sprouted everywhere. The faction would not dispose of him as easily as they had of Bernard, Hutchinson vowed, attempting, late in the summer, to calm himself. It was all huffing and puffing.

Indeed Adams took every liberty with the letters, cherry-picked, masterfully edited, then spliced together for maximum effect. Hutchinson returned the favor, insisting that Adams had already arrived at an address toward which he seemed to grope in 1773. In the fall, Hutchinson explained to Lord Dartmouth—taking care never, even at his most vitriolic, to mention Adams by name—that he was the first person to have openly, in a public assembly, advocated for total independence. "From a natural obstinacy of temper and from many years practice in politics [he] is perhaps as well qualified to excite the people to any extravagance in theory or practice as any person in America," Hutchinson reported, dating the conniving to 1764. Adams did precisely what he liked with the House, the Council, the town meetings. With "art and skill," he defeated every conciliatory measure. As an example, Hutchinson submitted the second of three essays Adams wrote that fall as "A." He made the governor out to be an "oily-tongued" monster, devoid of public spirit, having never met a man he believed his equal.* Hutchinson explained he would have bought off Adams with some public office—it was the time-honored method—but that Samuel Adams could no more easily be bribed than intimidated.

---

* A Tory writer would accuse Adams, too, of possessing "an oily tongue." While they differed on most everything else, the two sides exchanged interchangeable insults, each accusing the other of conspiracy, faction, demagoguery, delusion, and mad designs. Both insisted that quiet would be restored were only a few designing men eliminated. To Adams in 1769, Bernard had been "the greatest incendiary in North America."

For his part, Adams wished others might prove as incorruptible. The people would obtain relief only if they persevered. America must resist every ministerial blandishment, each of the "cakes and sugarplums." Ordinary citizens, acting in concert, were more powerful than they understood. Was it not time for a congress of some kind? The expense would be minimal, the advantages great. For good measure, he tossed Hutchinson's descriptions of him around for the public to savor. It always helped to remind readers of attacks on "a few ignorant leaders of the Boston town meetings." When he finished, Hutchinson's reputation lay in tatters. He would be compared to Nero and would burn in effigy in Philadelphia. There was plenty of precedent for editorial tampering, but never had an American annotator achieved such extravagant results with so shabby a remnant of truth. Adams set in motion a chain of events that would sink Hutchinson in America and Franklin in Great Britain, making of Franklin—who had never expected the letters to be made public and whom Adams still vaguely mistrusted—a revolutionary.*

In the battery upon peace and quiet, Adams quibbled with those who argued for patience. The Ministry, he contended, would never cede their outrageous point. They would coax and pacify, they would "do twenty other seemingly kind things," all in an attempt "to exercise the pretended right to tax us at their pleasure and appropriate our money to their own purposes." The colonies must band together. They must insist on their rights. Also, asked Adams on October 21, 1773, in a secret letter from the Boston committee of correspondence to the other committees, what was this new business with the East India Company? To placate the corporation, teetering on the edge of bankruptcy, the British Ministry was arranging to ship tea to America. Surely nothing good could come of that scheme. Adams suggested the colonies subvert it. He did not know that the ships had sailed already, four of them bound for Boston.

---

* Hutchinson obsessed for months about the letters and their origin. He never solved the mystery, among the many secrets Franklin took with him to the grave. Shredded publicly in London for his role in the affair, Franklin emphasized British hypocrisy. The Ministry had preferred to sacrifice him rather than their faithless Massachusetts appointees. Contradicting himself, he later admitted that the letters could only incite. His motives remain as cryptic as his source.

A REMARKABLE INSTANCE
OF ORDER AND JUSTICE
AMONG SAVAGES

We have too many high-sounding words, and too few actions
that correspond with them.
— ABIGAIL ADAMS, 1774

ADAMS WAS CORRECT about the cakes and sugarplums; the British Ministry indeed intended to force the colonies by any means possible to acknowledge the supremacy of Parliament. He was correct too about London's exasperation with Massachusetts Bay. It seemed to have passed through every adolescent phase, from impertinent to intractable to impossible. By the fall he learned that George III had deemed the petition on judicial salaries indecent. About a systematic design to reduce the colonies to slavery Adams was all the same mistaken. There was no plot against America.

What Adams and other colonial radicals misunderstood paled in comparison to the misapprehensions of the British Ministry, however. Before them came, in 1772, a simple if urgent problem. The East India Company, the second-largest firm in Great Britain, stood on the point of collapse. Chests of tea choked its warehouses. To unload that inventory, even at reduced prices, would rescue the company, undersell smugglers who blanketed the American market, dismantle an absurd Massachusetts boycott, and raise nearly a million pounds in revenue. It came as nearly an incidental blessing that with each affordable mouthful, the colonies would be acknowledging Parliament's right to tax. The Ministry could literally slip British sovereignty into the drinking water.

With little debate Parliament passed the Tea Act in the spring of 1773. It allowed the East India Company to export tea directly, without additional duty, and to appoint agents to sell that tea to retailers, eliminating the merchants in the middle. No one anticipated objections. Who could resist cheap tea? Adams erred in assuming that the British Ministry acted strategically when, for the most part, it acted expediently. But the British blunder was worse. After years of dispatches from Bernard and Hutchinson, the king's ministers believed the Americans motivated by dashed hopes and diluted fortunes when they acted on principle, if on principles that struck many as "extravagant absurdities." Few in Great Britain thought to use the words "tea" and "liberty" in the same sentence, when by 1773 the words were inextricable in America.

The sole item on which a Townshend duty remained, tea was already politically toxic. Little of it could have been brewed at Adams's address. He deemed it poison.* Even a politically indifferent merchant might refuse to serve it and forbid his children from drinking it elsewhere. John Adams fervently hoped the cup he raised to his lips at Hancock's house in the spring of 1771 was from Holland. (He did not ask.) One shied from the stuff, or professed to: there was nothing more ridiculous, huffed a Crown officer, than a circle of women at the tea table, pretending that the pale liquid they poured into their cups was coffee or chocolate. Of all the items Great Britain might choose to export, tea—that accursed, pernicious, baneful drug, that provocation and

---

* It was well known that the East India's merchandise was contaminated, reported the papers. Over time the tea bred a flea-like insect; it was packed by Chinese peasants with filthy feet; it was "infected with the plague"; it carried smallpox; it caused fevers, apoplexies, rheumatisms, palsies. Some resented the tall tales. In the December 23 *Massachusetts Spy*, "A Woman" suggested that those intent on political reform quit the "bugbears to scare children" and focus on the true dangers of importation.

pestilence — was the most controversial.* Of all colonial ports, Boston figured among the least congenial destinations. And of all the agents named to those lucrative posts, none could have been more offensive than the six appointed. Two were Hutchinson's sons, two his relatives, and two his close friends.

Philadelphia took the lead. Along with New York, it fully intended to prevent its tea from landing; it hoped Boston would join the common cause. On October 21, Adams and Warren weighed in. Parliament preferred to devote itself to the affairs of the East India Company rather than to the grievances of America. "They are much more intent upon increasing the power and influence of the Crown than securing the liberties of the subject," the two observed. Fortunately, an institution existed to address that very shortsightedness. This was, they explained, "the true design of the establishment of our committees of correspondence." There was no desire for a rupture, only to establish American liberty before the concept faded from view. Their letter went to towns in and out of the province with a request for secrecy, lest their "common enemies" sabotage plans. Over the next week a group from the North End met at the Green Dragon, a brick tavern blocks from the *Gazette* office that displayed above its door a hammered copper beast, tail curled, wings flaring. Its members, too, swore themselves to secrecy. They appointed a committee to demand that the tea agents report to the Liberty Tree to resign their posts and agree to return the tea.

Letters went out anonymously, lobbed into houses in the night. Violent knocking roused a Hutchinson son from bed at 2:00 a.m. on November 2; from the street came word that a messenger awaited with an urgent communication. Downstairs, Thomas Hutchinson Jr. discovered a summons wedged under his front door. Adams, Hancock, and a group of others nonetheless waited under the elm the following day in vain. That afternoon the agents gathered instead at the warehouse of Richard

---

* The rhetoric was as ardent elsewhere. "An Old Prophet" reminded the women of New York that every dish of tea henceforth drunk in America "may, in its consequences, tend to the spilling of an ocean of the best blood in the King's dominions."

Clarke, where a committee set out to fetch them. The second-largest Massachusetts importer of tea, Clarke was a Hutchinson in-law and a devout, straight-spined man, the kind of father who warned his children about loose, idle Boston youngsters. Politics little interested him. Trailed by a crowd, in the company of several associates, Molineux burst into Clarke's counting room. Would he pledge to reship the tea? "I shall have nothing to do with you," Clarke replied. By turns the other agents declined Molineux's request. He read aloud a paper drafted the evening before at the Green Dragon; the agents should consider themselves enemies of the country, an announcement that met with scorn. The callers departed, venting their resentment on Clarke's warehouse door, removed from its hinges and carted off. Glass shattered. An attempt to pry the agents—"Out with them!" "Get an ax!" the crowd bellowed—from the locked upper rooms failed. Adams, Warren, and Molineux were charged with securing resignations of the agents, who over the next days played cat-and-mouse with them, promising and failing to deliver answers, eluding them at their country homes, again in Boston.

For the next weeks it felt—with horns in the night and shards of menace in the air—like 1765 all over again. The logic was familiar. Without stamp masters, the Stamp Act could not be enforced. Without tea agents, nor could the Tea Act. There were a few critical differences, however. Adams found the East India consignees more odious even than stamp masters. Hutchinson swore not to repeat his predecessor's mistakes. The committee of correspondence reached out on November 6 to every Massachusetts town. And tempers had frayed substantially over eight years. Adams cultivated the discord, inserting an ominous paragraph into the *Gazette*. Soldiers from the Castle slipped quietly into town that week, armed, just before sunset. He claimed that they turned up in several neighborhoods, "brandishing their naked weapons and otherwise behaving in a most insolent manner." Writing for the committee of correspondence, Adams alerted the surrounding towns. Why were these men armed? Given the threats "to our common liberty," the committee dearly hoped that their neighbors might join them the following week at Faneuil Hall. It was the first use of the newly installed alarm system.

Hutchinson assured London that he would do all in his power to pre-serve the peace of the province and the interests of the East India Com-pany. At the same time, faintly rattled, he wrote his New York counterpart: "It's impossible in this town to judge of anything future." Adams burrowed into the murk of the next weeks differently, running himself ragged among the Green Dragon, the *Gazette* offices, and the agents' doorsteps. As early as November 9, he seemed to have hatched, or been complicit in hatching, a plan. While all of Boston awaited the agents' resignations and the arrival of "the cursed, noxious, infectious, dutiable herb," Adams penned a hasty note to Arthur Lee. If Lord Dartmouth had a proposal for the relief of a long-suffering people, he should reveal it. Otherwise, allowed Adams, another sort of resolution might be in the works. "One cannot foresee events," he confided, "but from all the observation I am able to make, my next letter will not be upon a trifling subject."

Eight days later a crowd surrounded Clarke's mansion, where a party was in full swing. It was interrupted by a rain of bricks and stones. From inside came a threat: "You rascals, be gone or I'll blow your brains out!" When the barrage continued, a Clarke son fired on the attackers, prompt-ing a two-hour siege on the family's windows. Still the Boston consignees held their ground, even after learning that the Philadelphia agents had resigned. Hutchinson applied for advice to his Council but found he could barely muster a quorum. Slowly it dawned on him that no other person in authority had any interest in safeguarding the property of the East India Company. The full-day assemblies and threats to Crown appointees exacted a familiar toll. "I am in a helpless state," he wrote pri-vately on November 21. The distemper only spread, courtesy of the com-mittee of correspondence, now firmly in charge.

Adams reprised his Stamp Act indignation that week in letters to every Massachusetts town. "When once they have found the way to rob us, their avarice will never be satisfied until our own manufactures, and even our land, purchased and cultivated by our hard-laboring ancestors, are taxed to support the vices and extravagances of wretches whose vile-ness ought to banish them from the society of men," he warned. The East India shipments threatened both America's physical and moral well-being. The *Dartmouth* arrived in Boston five days later, carrying 114 chests of tea.

ONCE A SHIP sailed past the Castle and into Boston Harbor, its owner had twenty days in which to unload and settle the duty on his cargo. The *Dartmouth*'s grace period was to expire at midnight on December 17, a date fixed on every Boston calendar. Were the duty not paid before the deadline, customs officials could impound and auction the goods. That regulation was as immutable as Boston logic now seemed: the minute the tea was landed, sold, and consumed, American liberties lay in ruins. The gravity of the situation was such that the committee met both before and after Sabbath worship on November 28. By dawn the town was plastered with notices: "That worst of plagues, the detested tea" had arrived. Tyranny stared them in the face. "Every friend to his country, to himself, and posterity"—the wording was pure Adams—was summoned to meet at 9:00 a.m., to join in resisting this new and most deleterious assault on American rights. As Hutchinson conferred that morning with his Council, crowds streamed, under tolling bells, to nearby Faneuil Hall. It proved too small. Business was delayed as thousands decamped to the Old South Church, Boston's largest structure and Adams's chilly address for the next days.

The meeting established early on that the tea must return to London without anyone disbursing a shilling of duty. Adams explained his position; as he could not trust the private virtue of his countrymen to refrain from consuming the tea, he preferred to trust to their public virtue in rejecting it. Few could have followed the hours of debate as closely as the ship's owner, twenty-three-year-old Francis Rotch, conspicuous in the pews and happy to remind the town of his predicament: He could not depart without a permit, which he could not obtain without payment of the duty. Were he to attempt to sail, the *Dartmouth* would be seized by His Majesty's navy. Already a warship commanded the channel. If by some miracle Rotch did manage to depart, his cargo would be impounded in London.

Adams rose with a solution. Shipowners applied for customs exemptions when their goods were lost or destroyed by storm. Was Rotch not buffeted by a howling political tempest? Several thousand Americans insisted he return his cargo. The vessel stood in great danger. The logic was rickety but Rotch agreed to submit an appeal. Adams hit some less gracious notes as well. The people had every intention of acting on their resolves. Rotch should do his best not to incense them further. Both he and the *Dartmouth*'s captain, James Hall, landed the tea at their peril.

Already predictions flew about that the tea would meet with fire or water; the meeting's leaders believed it imperative to protect the cargo from anyone who might attempt to burn it and afterward blame the town. At Adams's insistence, a watch was established; you could volunteer for it at Edes and Gill's office. For the next nights Adams, Hancock, Edes, and some twenty others patrolled the wharf.* Should anyone disturb them, they were to arrange for bells to ring throughout town. Six riders stood at the ready, poised to notify the countryside in case of emergency. Adams helpfully added that "for his part he had for some time kept and should keep his arms in order and by his bedside, as every good citizen ought, and if such notice should be given of an assault on the watch he should not hesitate, and he believed no one else would go out, without being prepared and determined what part to act." The watch was itself watched from a warship in the harbor. Admiral John Montagu sneered at the rabble parading the wharf, muskets and bayonets fixed, calling out "All is well" every half hour, like garrison sentries.

Despite his best efforts—the armed guards impugned his authority—Hutchinson could do nothing to dismiss the watch. Nor could he seem to interest his Council in breaking up the town meeting. On the 30th he dispatched Greenleaf on his sole authority with a decree. The meeting refused to hear it, at least until Adams stepped in; he recognized a dramatic opportunity when he saw one. Greenleaf directed the unlawful assembly to disband, an order that elicited loud hissing and booing

---

* A face-stinging assignment, it was not without its hazards. On a particularly black evening, one watchman tumbled off the wharf. It was low tide; he wound up drenched and muddy but uninjured.

and sent Adams into a twenty-minute tirade. A free people had every right to consult. Their safety stood in jeopardy. How did their proceedings differ from those of the House of Commons or the Massachusetts House of Representatives? (The answer was that those bodies were legal ones.) Adams shredded Hutchinson's proclamation point by point, as he had point by point vindicated the town of Boston in his *Appeal to the World*. By the time he got to the governor's assertion that he made his demand from obligation, bound as he was as "His Majesty's representative in this province," Adams allowed himself an attack on gaunt, six-foot, gray-haired Hutchinson. "He? He? Is he that shadow of a man, scarce able to support his withered carcass or his hoary head—is he a *representation of majesty*?" The remarks were met with shouts of approbation and wild applause. Greenleaf appears to have slunk off.

Adams tussled that afternoon with the town clerk, William Cooper. Whoever unloaded or sold the cargo, Adams announced, qualified as an enemy to the country. Cooper pointed out that whether Adams liked it or not, at least sixty worthy citizens imported tea every year. Should they all be stigmatized? After a warm debate Cooper exacted a concession; merchants who "inadvertently" imported British tea, Adams argued, could sleep soundly. He was clearly out in front, if more disciplined than some. John Rowe, part owner of one of the four ships, floated a half-humorous suggestion. Could tea, he ventured, not be made as well with salt water as with fresh? Similar suggestions for the "detested tea" had been called out and would continue to be called out from the gallery. The moderators ignored them.

Rowe's presence reassured Hutchinson. Surely private property was safe in the hands of the many merchants and reputable tradesmen in the Old South pews. The rabble, he assured Lord Dartmouth, were unlikely to enact any "mad resolves." He marveled at the odd, orderly coalition; those of different ranks had joined together and spoke with equal weight. His authority seemed at an end. Boston's representatives, selectmen, and clerk, as well as representatives from four or five other towns, were on hand; it was as if an entirely new regime had emerged from the shadows. All the malice and trouble struck Hutchinson as the work of a few, possibly even of one single man. He had his suspicions about the presiding genius. From the safety of his country home he listened carefully for wisps of defiance. At the conclusion of the November 30 meeting, Hancock vowed that "he would be willing to spend his fortune and life itself" in the worthy cause of American liberty. The boast flew around town. Hutchinson could find no one who would swear to having heard it.

By the time the second and third tea ships had tied up at Griffin's Wharf—the watch directed them to anchor alongside Rotch's *Dartmouth*—Hutchinson began to grasp that he had on his hands an infinitely more difficult assignment than he had suspected. He sealed the harbor. He took comfort in the presence of Montagu and his frigate. And he placed his hopes on the tea landing first in New York or Philadelphia, where more reasonable minds prevailed. Boston would have little choice afterward but to fall in line. A drizzle fell over the next weeks, unremittingly cold and sodden. Adams's advertisement appeared to have found a receptive audience. There was not a pistol for purchase anywhere in town.

Speculation ran rampant; it was as inconceivable to one side that the tea would land as it was to the other that it would return to Great Britain. Who would yield? Go-betweens, including the painter John Singleton Copley, Clarke's son-in-law, shuttled back and forth. In what must have been a difficult paragraph to write, Hutchinson explained to London that the committee of correspondence—operating in conjunction with those of five neighboring towns—had assumed direction of the matter. Those illegal entities had taken root in half of Massachusetts. He did not mention that they had essentially hijacked the House. Without additional snorts of disdain, he promoted the "disturbers of the peace" to the "usurpers of government." Meanwhile Rotch protested. He could not conceivably sail east. Already he was at odds with the tea agents, displeased that he had surrendered his ship to an armed guard, on the wharf every evening. He asked to be absolved of responsibility for his cargo. The agents refused. To the December 14 meeting Rotch confessed that he had agreed to register an appeal only because he was terrified. He would have consented to anything! If the people intended to destroy his cargo, it was only fair they reimburse him for the damages. He made every effort to sell the vessel at a discounted price. He found no takers. He would do all he could for his country but did not see why patriotism required him to plant himself first on the front lines. The meeting stood firm. By late afternoon Rotch had again agreed to request the necessary permits. This time he was dispatched with a spine-stiffening ten-man escort that included Adams. Were it to remain in Boston, Rotch's cargo would be impounded in two days, until which time the Old South meeting adjourned.

Many began to pick up the scent of violence; at some point that week an attempt was made — or so Hutchinson heard — to burn the ships. The watch foiled the plot. In an earlier meeting someone had argued that it was a pity they had not drowned the commissioners and that it was not too late to rid themselves of the governor, a diatribe that met with warm applause. Hearing that he would be assaulted if he landed his tea, Clarke growled that he would be torn limb from limb before he would betray the trust of the East India Company. He nonetheless fled to the Castle, along with the other agents. It was the third time members of the customs board had settled in behind the square stone walls in the harbor. From their uncomfortable refuge — given their number, they slept two to a drafty room — they followed events across the water closely. Again the Salem analogy emerged. Boston was unhinged. By 1773 America seemed to friends of the East India Company to evoke, more than any other, the words "deluded," "infatuated," "distempered," and "stark, staring mad."*

DODGING PUDDLES AND shrugging off a cold rain, thousands flocked to the Old South at 10:00 a.m. on December 16. In fourteen hours the tea would belong to the authorities. A great deal now depended on very little, or at least on one pesky formality. The meeting learned that day that

---

* The Salem analogy closely trailed the New Englanders. A 1780 Loyalist satire transformed Adams, Hancock, and their confederates into a group of wizards: "Sprung from the soil, where witches swarmed of yore / They come well-skilled in necromantic lore; / Intent on mischief, bustily they toil / The magic cauldron to prepare and boil."

both the customs and the naval boards had denied Rotch's request. A sole alternative remained. The meeting ordered Rotch to ready his ship for an immediate departure; to enter a protest with the customs office; and to set off over muddy roads, at top speed, to appeal to the one individual who could waive the rules.

Rotch was all mud-splattered deference when he landed, six miles south, on the governor's doorstep. He knew he was applying for an unprecedented exception. Hutchinson assumed the same posture with his drenched caller that he had when asked to clear Boston of troops. That decision still rankled; he seemed nearly to be compensating for it now. His position, he explained, was simple. He had sworn to uphold all acts of trade. Rotch would have a pass once he had cleared customs. Having received permission for a London leave, Hutchinson may have been particularly keen to avoid any appearance of again bowing to what he termed "a lawless and highly criminal assembly of men." He probed a little. What did his caller think the people intended? Rotch guessed they would force the ship toward the Castle, where it would be stopped by gunfire. They would then shrug that they had done all in their power to return the tea. Neither man envisioned an emergency.

Hutchinson ventured a suggestion: Might Rotch entrust his ship to Admiral Montagu until the crisis had passed? Rotch did not care for the Royal Navy to confiscate his goods. Nor did he feel that he, his captain, or his crew would again safely walk a Boston street after such a ploy. Hours earlier the lieutenant colonel at the Castle—exhausted from entertaining customs officials, tea agents, and their extended families— had weighed in. The Sons had done little but establish an armed guard and vent to New York and Philadelphia. They were now reduced to applying to Hutchinson for a special permit. He expected the tea to be towed his way at any minute, under Montagu's protection. With satisfaction he concluded: "They have run themselves aground."

The Milton interview was brief; Rotch rode north through a light drizzle before sunset. In his absence, Adams, Young, and Quincy delivered superfluous speeches and administered unnecessary votes. The use of tea was declared improper and pernicious, pernicious and improper. A committee formed to prevent it from turning up in other towns. Adams explained yet again why it was imperative that it not land. At about four o'clock the meeting began to disband. The people felt as if they had been "sitting upon thorns." They were kept in place a bit longer; there was concern about adjourning a spirited gathering on an unsatisfying note. In a bold tenor—he was the most impressive orator of his generation—twenty-nine-year-old Josiah Quincy argued that it was by now childish to look to half measures. We have some indication of how Adams spoke when he needed to fix his audience to their seats: the allegories came tumbling out. A friend remembered an Old South meeting at which Adams quietly rose, after a slate of violent harangues, to remind his fellow citizens of an old Greek philosopher. The sage lay asleep on the grass one day when roused by a sudden bite on his palm. Clenching his fist, he found a tiny field mouse in his fingers. As he examined it, the mouse bit him a second time, causing him to open his hand and release the captive. The moral of the story? "That there is no animal, however weak and contemptible, which cannot defend its own liberty, if it will only fight for it."

Rotch returned from his agonizing errand as the last light faded from the sky. He could not have been any more eager to face the Boston multitude than he had been to call on Hutchinson. Some six thousand people crammed into the Old South pews, at overflow capacity. Some were Whigs, others Tories. They had come from twenty-five miles around. Just before 6:00 p.m. a small commotion signaled Rotch's arrival. The candlelit meetinghouse met him with a deafening roar. What, he was asked, once the shouting and stomping had died down, had Governor Hutchinson replied? He would issue no pass. Would Rotch agree all the same to return the ship? A return would be ruinous, Rotch again regretted. Would he land the tea? Only, he replied, were he forced to comply with the law. At this juncture Adams stepped in. "They had now," he announced, "done all they could for the salvation of their country." He sent Rotch home to rest. The young man—he was half Adams's age—should feel at peace with himself. By a vote, the town declared itself satisfied with his efforts.

As Rotch was debriefed, a small section of the meeting began silently to detach itself from the west side of the room. Ten or fifteen minutes later war whoops and high-pitched whistles sounded in the street and on the meetinghouse porch. The cries elicited cheers from the galleries. To a neighbor it sounded as if devils had broken loose. The Old South began to empty into the mild night, to Adams, Hancock, and Young's dismay. They called for the assembly to remain; their business was unfinished. Several hundred people had left the room before Adams returned it to order. When finally he did, he moved that Dr. Young "make—or be desired to make—a speech." He was stalling, in the decorous, deep-seated Boston manner. For the next twenty minutes Young lectured on the detrimental effects of tea, on his certainty that his fellow countrymen could be trusted to refrain from its use, and on his confidence that every-one would stand in solidarity "in case any should be called to account for their proceedings." The last note alone was new, the others threadbare. Young met with an ovation, after which the meeting dispersed.

For once we know Adams's precise whereabouts. As the pews emp-tied, he remained behind in a huddle that included Warren, Young, and Hancock. He was about to miss two of the most consequential hours of American history, the non-trifling incident he had advertised five weeks earlier, and what he would soon term "as remarkable an event as has yet happened since the commencement of our struggle for American lib-erty." It was remarkable for many reasons, not least because—unlike the Massacre—this one produced barely a single eyewitness from a crowd of thousands. Had you managed to peer over the crush of bodies in the meetinghouse, you would have caught sight of the small band that caused the excitement. Soot-faced, fantastically attired, they proceeded with hatchets, clubs, and pistols to the harbor. Several stationed themselves on the wharf, where the watch this time melted quietly away. The remainder of the callers separated into three groups, led by a captain and boatswain. Communicating in an idiom of their own, they boarded the ships, beginning with the *Dartmouth*. On board they applied for keys to the holds and for candles. They sent the tidewaiters—the customs offi-cials on deck—ashore.

The sky had cleared; under a bright moon, the tidewaiters stood for the next two hours on the wharf, where the crowd formed a protective cordon around the costumed crew. Within minutes, they had opened the ship's hatches and descended to the hold. Some knotted ropes to the tea chests. Others hoisted them to the deck. To faux-Indian commands and whistled signals they slashed bindings and hacked open chests, heaving tea leaves and splintered wood into the harbor. They seemed to know some English; the captain of the last ship explained that his tea lay under several layers of merchandise. He was returned to his cabin with a promise that no harm would come to his other goods, removed and gently replaced. The sound of shattering wood carried as far as the Castle, where a customs official heard it give way to cheers. Only the contents of the chests failed to cooperate. The tea sank reluctantly. Mostly it collected in thick, furred clots around the hulls.

The men managed a backbreaking business with a precision that betrayed a familiarity with shipboard life. In about two hours, within firing distance of a brightly illuminated British warship, they emptied 342 chests of tea into Boston Harbor. The cool-headedness impressed everyone. As a Council member reported to Lord Dartmouth, "Perhaps never was more work of the like kind done in so little time, and with so little confusion." The meeting had successfully restrained those hotheads who wished that a few bodies floated in the harbor alongside the chests.* Tea carpeted the decks. There were harsh words only when someone attempted to salvage a few leaves; with the utmost decorum, the crew tidied up after themselves, sweeping the decks, confirming with mates that all was in proper order, replacing a damaged padlock. No one was hurt nor any other merchandise disturbed. When one of the visitors attempted to slip a few leaves into his pockets, he was tackled, driven up the wharf through a gauntlet of cuffs and kicks, and relieved of his contraband. The crew then marched off silently in tea-filled shoes. Behind them a blanket of calm descended upon Boston, still as on a Sabbath evening. It was, marveled Reverend Samuel Cooper, "a remarkable instance of order and justice among savages."

---

* Privately John Adams reflected that it would only take a few to "remove the causes of all our calamities." Hutchinson topped his list.

FEW BELIEVED, AS Adams, Young, and their confederates droned on, that Hutchinson would issue a pass. Only a small, carefully curated group knew beforehand what his refusal would mean. (That circle presumably overlapped with the committee of correspondence. Over the previous days it had made a point of ostentatiously recording that it transacted no business.) The crew had been vetted expertly and choreographed efficiently. A majority knew their way around a ship. They were not all Bostonians. Few could have been diminutive; a lead-lined tea chest weighed over 400 pounds. Someone—most likely Edes, who wound up with it later—kept a master list. We would not know their names until they were dead, by which time there were more conspirators than there could possibly have been in 1773.* They are most vivid to us in the sound effects: the war whoop, the crash of hatchets, the splash of planks, the thundering Friday morning silence.

We can account for only slivers of the hours that preceded the visit to the wharf. In the course of the afternoon a group had assembled in Edes's parlor, on what is today Court Street. They remained until dark; Edes's teenaged son refilled the porcelain punch bowl several times. With Rotch's return, some of them headed to a nearby blacksmith's shop, where they smeared their faces with soot. They wrapped blankets around their heads.† In red wool caps and a collection of motley coats, they looked like escapees from an impromptu costume party. The logistics were markedly less spontaneous. The crew worked, noted the papers, "as one man." One account has them comparing cargo manifests to the shattered chests, to be certain they had missed nothing, in the presence of seven thousand people.

As to who orchestrated the destruction of the tea, we remain nearly

---

* Adams would say later that the province was being punished for the work of some forty men, presumably the accurate number. He left no other clues.
† New England faces had long been blackened when it seemed necessary to dismantle a barn, rescue a deserting soldier, destroy a creditor's accounts—or terrorize a Tory, customs official, or Council member in the dark of night.

as much in the dark as was Thomas Hutchinson in 1773. Answers to questions about who the foot soldiers were resembled that provided by Ebenezer Mackintosh, who evidently boasted that "it was my chickens that did the job." No contemporary writer suggested, as historians have since, that Adams issued a preconcerted signal, that his remark that nothing more could be done had sent the conspirators flying.* Nor did anyone quote Adams advocating destruction. All accounts do agree that Adams was the prime mover, in and beyond the meetings.† As a sailor later testified under oath: "The questions proposed, or most of them, were taken down in writing by Mr. Cooper, and dictated by Samuel Adams, who appeared the most active in the business." For some time Hutchinson had acknowledged Adams to be "the chief manager on this side the water," the "director of the town of Boston." Informers later placed him on the wharf, in communication, by secret dialect, with the crew, but he did not need to be. All had been settled in advance. The very lack of fingerprints points to his unruffled, rigorous brand of stage management.‡ Responsibility was general and diffuse, the stunt designed so as neither to warrant troops nor facilitate a prosecution. A bit of destruction aside, all was conducted, as Adams described it, with "decency, unanimity, and spirit." The town had guarded the tea for weeks. "It cannot therefore be fairly said that the destruction of the property was in their contemplation," he asserted when, as promised, he finally shared his non-trifling news with Arthur Lee.

After what all acknowledged to have been "the stillest night" in an exceedingly long time, Adams did his best to seem as astonished as every other Bostonian that East India Company property had plunged into the harbor. While tea clumps stubbornly floated in the water—rowboats headed

---

* Rotch quoted the line when deposed in London. He did not deem it a signal.
† When a minister pleaded against any rash act, Adams replied he could hinder no one, but could promise that no tea would be destroyed that evening. The date was December 14—two days before the visit to the wharf.
‡ One heavy-handed hint of complicity survives. In a 1795 letter, an old friend reminded Adams that he had been at his side since the beginning of the American contest. "I was there," he wrote, "when you first beat the *bush* while others ran away with the *bird*." The coded reference may well apply to the events of December 16, 1773.

out to submerge them with oars and paddles—he dispatched Paul Revere with the sensational news to New York and Philadelphia. Despite foul weather, Revere made record-shattering time; news of the ill-fated tea would be rushed into print a week later. The people of Boston had made every effort to return the pernicious goods. As soon as it became clear that no pass would be forthcoming, Adams explained, "a number of people huzza'd in the street, and in a very little time every ounce of the teas on board of the Captains Hall, Bruce & Coffin was immersed in the Bay, without the least injury to private property." It is a sentence remarkable for its missing middle and that surely qualifies as the vaguest, most understated account of the evening ever written.* In 1773 you could say in a line what, two centuries later, would require a book. "The spirit of the people on this occasion surprised all who viewed the scene," Adams added, with a purr of satisfaction. He wrote in haste, eager to disseminate the earliest possible notice of "this interesting event." Tea ships were due imminently at three other American ports.

Adams this time made no attempt to fix a label to the evening, settling months afterward for "our opposition to the East India Act, as it is called." The idea was to emphasize principles over perpetrators. He was pleased that the news was not treated, as earlier protests had been, with "sneer and ridicule." He seemed equally happy that the resolves at the Old South—the same address, he noted, that had produced the demand for the removal of troops—had elicited "grave countenances." Within days a euphoric John Adams appealed to James Warren's talented wife, Mercy Otis Warren. Might she apply her poetical gifts to the "late frolic among the sea nymphs and goddesses"? He hoped she would include a certain protean mastermind. Coyly she replied that she should very much like to know whom he meant; several heroes answered to his description. She never elicited an answer, though did produce the twelve-stanza

---

* The sole competition is Hutchinson's sour one-liner of the same date: "Immediately thereupon numbers of the people cried out, 'A mob! A mob!,' left the house, repaired to the wharves, where three of the vessels lay aground having on board 340 chests of tea, and in two hours' time it was wholly destroyed." He too reverts to the passive voice.

"Squabble of the Sea Nymphs," in which she attributed the sterling deed to members of the Tuscarora tribe.

The stillest night yielded to the most exhilarating of days. It was as if the sun had come out after a dull, ominous season, as, obligingly, it did. Prospects seemed brighter all around. Having three years before argued in court that the law exists to "discourage and prevent riots, insurrection, turbulence, and tumults," John Adams exulted. "There is a dignity, a majesty, a sublimity, in this last effort of the patriots that I greatly admire," he cheered. Resistance should take a memorable form. This instance struck him both as magnificent and necessary. A principle—and ten years of labor—had been sustained. No damage had been done. It was difficult to feel sympathy for the East India Company or for the sly purveyors of sugarplums. "You cannot imagine the height of joy that sparkles in the eyes and animates the countenances as well as the hearts of all we meet on this occasion," Samuel Adams reported, equally aglow. He thrilled to the long faces of "disappointed, disconcerted Hutchinson and his tools." All congratulated one another on the happy event. With sunny composure, Boston proceeded with its business. No one would have guessed that some 10,000 pounds sterling—the contents of eight Hutchinsonian mansions—steeped in the harbor. Coffee prices rose.

The morning after also found Adams broadcasting breathlessly, via the committee of correspondence, to the Massachusetts towns. Untethered by punctuation, his words sail across the page. Every practical step had been taken, Adams explained, for returning the tea. There had been a commotion in the street, "and in a very little time" every ounce "was immersed in the Bay." The tea seemed to have taken the tumble of its own accord; in his version neither anyone in Indian dress, nor any actor at all, seemed to have played a part. While Peter Oliver wrote the escapade down to "Samuel Adams and his myrmidons," word circulated that a crew of Mohawks had done the deed. The *Gazette* noted that the perpetrators were "supposed to be the aboriginal natives from their complexion." Whether they were or not, with their hatchets, blankets, and "copper countenances" they appeared as such, reported one observer. They were variously men "painted and dressed as Indians" or "the Indians, as they were then called," or a disguised crew "assuming the name of Indians." A Dedham doctor believed the tea sunk by "persons called Narragansett Indians." The disguise slipped about; no one bothered to so much as differentiate among tribes, even while everyone was highly specific, and accurate, about the 342 chests. Admiral Montagu gamely winked and nodded along. Was it not surprising, he asked, that Indians operated a block and tackle as expertly as did his sailors?

An occasional awkward attempt was made to distinguish parties. The *Gazette* reported that when New York heard the news, they "highly extolled the Bostonians for what the Indians had done here." The closer to the event you stood the less you bothered with the charade. Adams opted for "a number of persons unknown and in disguise," or at least did until the wayward fourth ship turned up, having been blown off course, in Provincetown. Surely the Mashpee or Mattapoisett Indians would head off on snowshoes to see to its reception? (Clarke's men got there first.) The "Indians" camouflaged the committee of correspondence, transforming a riot into a raid. They buried vandalism in symbolism: to the colonial mind, the native American was an avatar of liberty. After a sustained war, no one needed a reminder that Indians were proud, fierce, and resolute. The iconography helped to needle the mother country with its own assumptions. Were Great Britain to treat the colonists as primitives, then the colonists would comport themselves as the primitives they were assumed to be.

Adams harped on the order and righteousness of the evening. "Even our enemies must acknowledge," he gleefully expounded, "that this people have acted upon pure and upright principles." His assertions aside, not everyone took delirious delight in the sacrifice of private property to public liberty. John Rowe thought the incident disastrous. Others pointed out that the vandalism merely bucked up Bostonian spirits, at great expense. From a friend's harborside home Admiral Montagu had watched the tea sail overboard. He expected calls for assistance but knew that he could have done little. The wharf was crowded. He could hardly have fired into a pack of innocents. (He counts among the rare spectators who left a report.) Montagu viewed the devastation the next morning in horror. What had got into these people? They paid, he cried, stomping off, no more attention to an act of Parliament than to an old newspaper.

Hutchinson was thunderstruck. John Adams watched the governor clatter past his window the next morning in his carriage, accompanied by Andrew Oliver. Council members flew across town. From all the activity John gathered that Hutchinson was busy preparing an inquiry. Hutchinson indeed knew it would fall to him to identify the culprits behind the "high-handed riot." He supposed he would need to promise rewards, which he also supposed would prove futile. Again he had difficulty assembling a quorum. This one took three attempts. (It could not have been lost on him that the committee of correspondence worked overtime while legitimate government was paralyzed.) He succeeded finally on December 21, when his Council defended the violence.

Hutchinson was indignant. High treason, he insisted, had been committed, a charge he downgraded to burglary. A week later he gloomily conceded; no justice of the peace, constable, or grand jury would assist with a prosecution. "I cannot find any persons who were at the meeting of the people willing to give any account in writing of the persons who were most active there nor of any of their transactions," he wrote Lord Dartmouth, sorely aware that somewhere between five and eight thousand people had assembled at the Old South. He consoled himself that the New York and Philadelphia teas would land safely. Bostonians would soon look like the hoodlums they were. (New York and Philadelphia ordered back their tea after hearing Boston's news. South Carolina's tea was unloaded but never sold.) It annoyed Hutchinson no end that the town carried on with impunity. In his discouragement he resolved to take his leave. Oliver could step in while he conferred with the London authorities.

The result was, Hutchinson chafed, all the fault of a sinister league. He could not say often enough how surprised everyone had been. Until the last minute no one had suspected a thing. Talking in angry circles he gnashed his teeth. It fell to him to explain to the directors of the East India Company how 342 chests of their property had landed—in view of a sixty-gun man-of-war, two frigates, and several smaller vessels—in

Boston Harbor. "Adams never was in greater glory," Hutchinson fumed. The more he wrote, the more Hutchinson began to suspect that the committee of correspondence had plotted their escapade from the beginning. They had held meetings "like a little Senate in Boston." They were never happier than when government opted for severity, which they could then exploit.*

In fairness, he was up against a masterpiece of actor-free drama. There was little interest in the identity of the perpetrators; no one dared to confide a name even to a diary. (When Hancock alerted his London agent to the event he could offer few particulars, "for indeed I am not acquainted with them myself so as to give a detail.") No one asked Samuel Adams, though there are hints someone meant to. On December 27, he intended to travel with a neighbor to a Plymouth celebration. For his safety, friends sternly forbade him from making the trip. He continued to exult over the unanimity: The Massachusetts countryside approved Boston's conduct. New York, Boston, and Philadelphia were all on the same page. "I think we have put our enemies in the wrong," he wrote, darting out from under the passive voice. But he knew well that a culprit, and a punishment, would need to be found. He knew his name would surface. Rumors circulated that he should expect arrest. Who, Admiral Montagu asked in its wake, was to pay for the little frolic? Montagu was certain of the prime movers if not of the actors themselves. Hancock, Adams, and several others had, he asserted, encouraged the "Indian caper." A 1774 Loyalist lampoon identified Adams as the Indian leader. "A sachem of vast elocution," his pronouncements filled the mouths of millions.

For his part, Adams knew precisely who the culprits were. Performing his expert table-turning trick, he pointed at the tea agents. Their employers had every right to demand indemnification; it was clear to whom they should apply. Boston had conscientiously protected the tea

---

* Judging from the secret pledge taken by fifteen members of the committee of correspondence on December 24, he was right. In a vow not to be entered into the record, they promised to vindicate one another should they be made "to suffer for any noble efforts they may have made to save their country, by defeating the operations of the British Parliament." Adams headed the list, which included Council members and merchants. It likely reveals the genius behind the evening of December 16.

for twenty days. They had labored day and night to return the cargo. Hutchinson had stonewalled. But for his intransigence, the East India tea would be safely sailing back to London. He should pay for its destruction.*

In early March 1774, a brigantine entered Boston Harbor with twenty-eight tea chests. They did not belong to the East India Company. While the town weighed its options, a crew in Indian disguise boarded the ship after nightfall. "With great regularity and dispatch," the committee reported, the visitors dropped the tea from Griffin's Wharf into the harbor. The owners of the cargo went quiet. Hutchinson suspected that even "if they could find out who were the immediate actors, they would not venture at present to bring any action in the law against them." They would only wind up like the tea agents, living as exiles at the Castle without hope of returning to Boston, their businesses ruined.†

LORD DARTMOUTH HAD instructed Hutchinson to eliminate the "unusual and unconstitutional" committees of correspondence. They displeased the king. From the towns and villages of Massachusetts Adams now heard, by way of those unusual and unconstitutional entities, a resounding chorus of support. They applauded the "vigilance, care and fortitude" of their Boston brethren who had, enthused the Newbury committee, saved them from destruction. Sandwich thanked Boston for having dispatched "that truly detestable herb." Colrain believed Boston had earned "the approbation and applause of every true-hearted, honest man." Had their enemies suspected how thoroughly the province understood its rights and privileges, gushed South Hadley, they would never have

---

* Many in London also took Hutchinson to task. Why had he not enlisted the military to protect the tea? Hutchinson defended himself in his *History*. He was criticized for not having granted the pass; he would have been equally criticized, he reasoned, for having granted it. At no point did he seem to consider the advice he had offered a close friend years earlier: "You must strive to be more of a willow and less of an oak."
† A Hutchinson son discovered as much in January when he ventured from the Castle to the home of his Plymouth in-laws. The visit sent the town bells ringing. A meeting assembled to warn the Elisha Hutchinsons out of town. It was already dark; they begged to spend the night. The family headed off the next morning at the direction of a large crowd and in a raging blizzard.

dreamed of attempting to violate them. Portsmouth declared itself roused at last from its lethargy. Some tongues pressed tightly into cheeks. The hamlet of Gorham professed itself so charmed by the Indian exploits that they were nearly inclined to forget wounds suffered at those ruthless hands.

If with the committees Adams and his associates had wired the colony, with the "mad action" of December 16 they threw the switch. Every town in Massachusetts had been "on tiptoe to come down" to express solidarity. In sentiment and vocabulary, the countryside sounded now like Boston. The talk was all manly resolves, abject slavery, subtle machinations. The imagery skewed biblical: Watertown evoked Mordecai, unwilling to sell its birthright for tea. North Yarmouth went with Esau. Ipswich believed London threatened the colonies with a curse "more deplorable than Egyptian darkness." (There was a reason why it was considered "sacred liberty." The people acted out of a fear that their religion, too, stood in danger. It hardly mattered that they were deceived, carped Hutchinson.) From a hundred villages came grandiloquent odes to life, liberty, and the pursuit of property, along with heartfelt thanks to "the metropolis." Nearly everyone mentioned slavery and taskmasters. No one mentioned shattered chests or native disguises. Lexington outpaced everyone else: three days before the Indian caper, with the blessing of Reverend Clarke, it fed every ounce of its tea to a communal bonfire. Charlestown followed suit at the end of the year. Boston disposed of a half-chest that had floated from Griffin's Wharf to Dorchester in the same way. The tea was both sunk and burned, like a witch.

Adams modulated the few dissonant notes. Concord thanked Boston for "every rational measure" the town had taken for the preservation of American liberties, insisting typographically on the adjective. It appeared in bold. Worcester pronounced itself "greatly alarmed" by the incident. Medfield applauded Boston's bravery in throwing off the chains that Great Britain had attempted to rivet upon a distressed people. At the same time, was it not absurd to bleat about liberty when the province bought and sold Africans, "taken from all that is dear to them in their native soil"? Nothing could be more repugnant to the ideals for which they contended. The Boston news had set bells ringing in New York; Philadelphia's committee congratulated the town. As far as South Carolina, many thanked Boston for having diffused the patriotic spirit. But from Paul Revere Adams knew that not everyone approved of New England extremism, qualms he did his best to smother. Some opposed East India tea only because — excluding American merchants from the tea trade — it established a monopoly.

Speculation began immediately as to how Great Britain would react to what Hutchinson termed "the boldest stroke which had yet been struck in America." The *Gazette* warned that those who spoke of assassinating "the most worthy patriots in this metropolis" should consider themselves marked men. John Adams failed to believe that the mother country would bother to act expeditiously; she seemed irresolute when it came to America. But he turned the question of redress over and over in his mind. Would London annul the charter, curtail American trade, send troops, order executions? Having quietly ventured home from the Castle, a customs collector posed a related question: Was this a declaration of war or an impotent act of sedition? He did not anticipate quiet.

Shrugging off the "frightful list of scarecrows and bugbears" that circulated about town, Samuel Adams reminded friends that he never allowed eventualities to disturb him. Evils revealed themselves soon enough. He preferred to stand at the ready. Ingenuously or not, he continued to profess surprise that anyone should have trouble distinguishing a lawless assault on property from a noble defense of liberties. (Many wrote about resisting tyranny. Adams alone wrote about a town "rationally destroying property after trying every method to preserve it, and when the men in power had rendered the destruction of that property the only means of securing the property.") The passions of a multitude would have their way. Restraints only galvanized. London might indeed send troops, Adams reasoned, but they would arrive regardless; there was a price to be paid whether the tea was drunk or drowned. It made more sense to suffer in the short term than to relinquish the principle. His compatriots had acted their consciences. They had placed the enemy squarely in the wrong. Heaven was on their side.

The Ministry saw things differently. The news from Boston delivered what Arthur Lee described as "an electrical shock." The king was incensed. The impertinence staggered. Those who went in for Rubicon-crossing had a field day. There was now no retreat; the colony must endure the consequences. In a curious twist, the first to do so would be Franklin. A month earlier he had found himself with no choice but to reveal that he had dispatched the stolen Hutchinson letters. On January 29, 1774, he came before the Privy Council for his reprimand. The news of the waterlogged tea had arrived days earlier. In a packed, overheated room, over a grueling hour, Alexander Wedderburn, the British solicitor general, stripped Franklin first of his dignity, afterward of his Crown positions. To roars and snickering, Wedderburn delivered the furious dressing-down that Adams, and Franklin's native town, more properly deserved. He made Franklin "the great abettor" of the Boston faction, who—with their committees of correspondence—had set the province in flame. They had produced their "great twelve-penny book," Wedderburn thundered, telling the Americans of "a hundred rights of which they never had heard before, and a hundred grievances which they never before had felt." It amounted to a ready-drawn declaration of revolt. He had heard that sixty or seventy towns had approved of these "extravagant absurdities"!* With the same moderation, the Bostonians had now destroyed the cargo of three British ships. There was some irony that Franklin should prove the first casualty. For several months more he counseled Boston to reimburse the East India Company. He remained intent on reconciliation. Adams—who had opposed Franklin's appointment as a London agent—would be some time in believing that he had America's best interests at heart.

At the king's request, Wedderburn and Edward Thurlow, the attorney general, set about investigating "the outrages" of December 16. Who was guilty, could they be arrested, with what should they be charged, and how were they to be prosecuted? Seizing public funds and mobilizing a guard

---

* From South Carolina, Christopher Gadsden congratulated Adams. "I almost envy you for the particular notice Mr. Wedderburn has been pleased to take of you in his defense of Thomas Hutchinson or more properly in his abuse of Dr. Franklin."

certainly qualified as grave offenses; on February 11, 1774, Wedderburn and Thurlow assured the king that the Boston violence constituted high treason. They agreed to prepare arrest warrants. Thurlow all the same requested airtight evidence before proceeding. Hot-tempered and foulmouthed, he was a ferocious debater. He did not lose arguments and did not intend to lose this one. Over the next days Dartmouth interrogated twelve individuals, newly arrived from Boston. Under oath they reconstructed events, beginning with the assault on Clarke's warehouse. Adams emerged as the most vocal party. Rotch swore that Adams, Hancock, Young, Molineux, and Warren were the prime movers, naming Adams first. Molineux had summoned Rotch to meet with the committee of correspondence, which Adams appeared to chair.

The Ministry compiled a chart of the principal actors and abettors. Though Adams's name figured prominently, no one could place him — or any other specific individual — at the wharf. Strictly questioned, even the tidewaiters could not name names.* Despite multiple interviews, the inquiry could establish no connection between the votes at the Old South and the destruction of the tea, or between the nebulous "body of the people" and any particular player. Sworn statements in hand, Thurlow reversed his decision. He would order no arrests. Prosecution would be technically impossible; the evidence was all hearsay. The king exploded: it had taken his attorney general and solicitor general two weeks to retract their own opinion! Boston and its renegades would need to be punished in some other way. The fury was great. "I cannot enough stress to you," Lee warned Adams in February, "how much they are out for blood." Boston should brace for a terrible revenge.

As Thurlow and Wedderburn combed through evidence, Adams spent little time attempting to read British minds. He took a few precautions, insisting on secrecy, at home and with friends. His daughter was cautioned not to share his whereabouts. He began to leave his signature

---

* The word on the London street was that solid intelligence planted Hancock and Adams behind the riot. Franklin could only douse the assertion in his trademark brand of ice-cold logic: If the perpetrators had thought it prudent to disguise themselves, would their leaders have been so careless as to have appeared as themselves?

off letters, which more often closed with the words "Your friend." He tended to a House anti-slavery petition submitted, after some discussion, by several Blacks, and that he may have helped to draft. Massachusetts had discussed abolition, and prohibiting the slave trade, since at least 1700. The bill against slave importation that Adams had helped to prepare in the 1760s had come to naught; he would return later to what he considered a repellent practice. With better success he held together the town committees. He promoted a plan for a colonial mail, independent of the royal post. The lack of easy exchanges with the South—a letter could take six months between Boston and Savannah, which communicated via London—hampered all resistance. "The colonies must unite to carry through such a project, and when the end is effected it will be a pretty grand acquisition," he wrote Warren.

In March Adams resurrected the booby-trapped issue of judicial salaries with which he had coaxed the committees of correspondence into being. All agreed American liberty trampled were judges beholden to London. Would the justices explicitly renounce Crown salaries? the committee now demanded. Hutchinson lamented that no one would have so much as entertained the question a decade earlier. In 1774, only one refused. Peter Oliver had no intention of being bullied by "Adams and all his factious hydra." If in his generosity the king offered him his salary, the chief justice would accept it. John Adams worried that Oliver would meet with tar and feathers for his obstinacy. It did not help that he was an especially steely, self-important character who gloried in the trappings of his office.

Adams maneuvered around Oliver's stonewalling with an assist from his cousin. From the recesses of history, John dredged up the concept of impeachment. Without precedent in America, it was evoked often enough in Great Britain. Was the American constitution, John asked, not a miniature of the British? It was a dangerous experiment but one worth a try. Deeming Oliver an enemy to the province, the House demanded his removal. Hutchinson refused, sending Samuel Adams to call on the Council. He began to address the governor, impeachment papers in hand. Bowdoin interrupted. Surely Adams had noticed that the governor was not in the room? His enormous chair sat empty. Simultaneously creating and charging through a loophole, Adams maintained that in Hutchinson's absence his power devolved to his Council. He proceeded to lay the twelve articles of impeachment before an empty chair, tantamount, he argued, to placing them before the governor himself. Hutchinson could do nothing but dissolve the House before they dredged up any further insults. He had had enough of Adams-designed technicalities. Word of Hutchinson's decision reached the assembly before the document did; the House locked its doors against it. In a final piece of business it requested the committee of correspondence write Franklin with a last-ditch attempt at redress. The House doors were then flung open.

Hutchinson had shared the news of his leave in the hope that it might appease the House. They seemed methodically to be dismantling acts of Parliament. Demoralized, he began to pack, scheduling a mid-March departure. Spirits sagged all around for Crown officers, but the political distress weighed especially on Andrew Oliver, less stalwart than Hutchinson, recently widowed, and a shadow of himself after five years of constant worry. Following a short illness, he died on March 3. So taut were Boston tempers that Peter Oliver, his younger brother, did not dare attend the funeral.* Hutchinson had looked with relief to Great Britain but felt he could not now absent himself. Without him, the Council would take charge. Unwilling to entrust the province to "the most malicious set of men that ever appeared at one time in any country," he canceled his trip. The previous three months, he declared on March 9, 1774, had been the worst since he had assumed office. "Such a mixture of improper, unnatural sentiment and reasoning, rude and indecent language, sophistical and fallacious twistings and evasions, oblique allusions and flirts, below the dignity of the Robin Hood or even a schoolboys' parliament you never met with before," he wrote. And that was without factoring in his financial losses — one-third of the tea in the harbor had been destined

---

* John Adams dismissed the loss. Andrew's death meant only that a different Oliver would succeed to the position; the same two families would "rule and overbear all things as usual." Peter Oliver was married to Hutchinson's eldest daughter.

for his sons, whose profits sank with the cargo—or the oration of four days earlier, on the anniversary of "what was still called the massacre."

For the honor Adams tapped John Hancock, whom he also introduced.* It was Hancock's first public address, delivered to the largest of Massacre audiences; John Rowe could not find a seat. Adams listened from the pulpit as Hancock described "vile assassins" and "drowsy justice." He decried a government that taxed without consent, dispatching fleets and armies to enforce its "mad pretensions." He took the opportunity to laud the importance of well-regulated militias. To the oration Hancock affixed a warning against the glare of luxury, a message for which he may not have been the obvious emissary but which even a tough critic found compelling. Any people who preferred "a wealthy villain" to "an honest upright man in poverty" deserved, Hancock lectured, to find itself oppressed. From there he glided to an overblown salute to patriots like Adams, impervious to temptation and unwavering in their commitment to their country. The tribute may have embarrassed but could not have surprised Adams, who had spent weeks closeted with Hancock.† The oration seemed as much a call to arms as a memorial; handsome and at ease on his feet, Hancock outdid himself on both counts. He hoped the shameful story of March 5 would "never be told without a tear" and it was not in 1774. A tender afterglow persisted for days. Even John Adams was bowled over; Hancock's delivery and composition exceeded all expectation. In the window displays that Monday appeared likenesses of Governor Hutchinson and Chief Justice Oliver. Decapitated, blood gushed from their necks.

Reports of Franklin's humiliation began to circulate in Boston weeks later, along with rumors of grave punishments. Finally a colony had

---

* Cynics suggested Adams drafted Hancock to bind him more tightly to the cause. While Hancock had moderated any number of meetings, he had steered clear of open pronouncements.

† No one pretended Hancock had written the address himself. It was likely the work of Reverend Cooper, in conjunction with Dr. Warren. Adams got extra credit here, too. Tories sniggered that Hancock's "hash of abusive treasonable stuff" was composed for him by Cooper and "the very honest Samuel Adams, Clerk, psalm-singer, purloiner, and curer of bacon."

succeeded in making itself a British priority. Warnings of troops were constant. By mid-April, when Adams dispatched Hancock's published oration to John Dickinson, the prospect of occupation was clearly before his eyes. The province was threatened anew with "that great evil," Adams explained to the faux Philadelphia farmer, the Ministry "being highly provoked at the conduct of the people here in destroying the East India Company's tea." He described the event as if it were one with which he was only dimly acquainted. It had all been Hutchinson's fault. Boston had suffered twice as much abuse as her sister colonies at every step in the struggle for freedom. Adams hoped she had not been twice as imprudent. They were, he wrote, going to need all the support the rest of America could afford her now.

The Ministry contemplated various punishments, attempting to settle on one that penalized Boston alone. For seven years the town had spewed commotions and insurrections. Every North American disturbance seemed to originate there. When it came to the tea, Boston had moreover incited New York. It had dispatched riders throughout the continent, in direct contravention of the law. It exhibited no remorse. Other towns in history had been disciplined, argued Lord North, for the misdeeds of a few. What authority did Great Britain have if it allowed the property of its subjects to be destroyed?* The punishment he had in mind was fair, appropriate, and effective. Four or five frigates alone could execute it. He considered several additional bills, of which Massachusetts would hear only months later. What became known as the Boston Port Act passed quickly at the end of March. As Franklin noted, America had never had so few friends in Great Britain. Violence had united all parties there against them.

On Election Day 1774, Adams learned what the "grave countenances" abroad had devised. General Gage would return to Boston as governor and commander in chief, a combination Adams found in itself objectionable. Gage carried orders to close the harbor until the town reimbursed

---

* Londoners for years blamed American unrest on the Stamp Act. By 1773, many — Thurlow and King George included — wrote it down to Stamp Act repeal. Enforcement in 1765 would have bred obedience later. The king ultimately attributed all his American misfortunes to "the fatal compliance of 1766."

the East India losses. He was to transfer the seat of government to Salem, fifteen miles north. Provisions, grain, and wood would need to be trucked overland, laboriously and at considerable expense, to Boston. As London had failed to connect names with overt acts of vandalism, Gage was also to conduct trials in America.* "The King," Lord Dartmouth reminded the new Massachusetts governor, considered "the punishment of these offenders as a very necessary and essential example to others of the ill consequences that must follow from such open and arbitrary usurpations as tend to the subversion of all government." A copy of the Port Act on his desk, Adams denounced its "flagrant injustice and barbarity." It was without precedent in English history. They had lost their senses in London. It would be a waste of time to attempt to reason with such people, just as it would be to comply tamely with the terms of their inhuman edict. "Our business," Adams concluded in May 1774, "is to find means to evade its malignant design."

---

* It turned out to be easier to decide to punish Boston than to codify the penalty. The port, it was discovered, could not be closed by royal edict; a statute would be necessary. Lord North handed Wedderburn and Thurlow a muddled piece of legislation, which together they recrafted. The solicitor general and attorney general were inveterate enemies. Thurlow cracked afterward that the Boston Port Act was the first time they had agreed on anything.

XII

THIS IMPORTANT GLORIOUS CRISIS

The hero is he who is immovably centered.
— RALPH WALDO EMERSON

As ADAMS saw it, Boston had been accused, tried, and convicted without
a hearing. No one had so much as alleged a crime.* "Outrages have been
committed within the town," he conceded. But was that reason to starve
an entire community? By the same logic the port of London should be
shut, as mobs often enough surrounded the king's palace. (The colonists
regularly pointed out that an American mob was better behaved than a
London one.) Before Gage had yet set foot in town, Adams assembled the
Boston committee of correspondence. With Revere went urgent letters
to New York and Philadelphia. Adams entreated the Philadelphians to
relay the message south. Boston was to be subjected, he wrote, to an act
contrary to natural justice and the laws of all civilized states. Warships
were to blockade her harbor. Her people were to perish from cold and
hunger. It was a warning, Adams noted, to any colony that might not
care to surrender its "sacred rights and liberties." London friends hinted
that New York and New Jersey were next. "The most favored can only
expect to be last devoured," he cautioned. One question alone mattered:
Did their sister colonies believe Massachusetts suffered for the common

---

* According to the *London Evening Post*, the charge was riot and trespass. And the
repayment was 30,000 pounds.

cause, an expression he slipped over and over into his rush of missives? If they did, would they suspend all trade with Great Britain? He begged for an answer by Revere's return.

At noon on a stormy May 17, General Gage and his retinue stepped ashore at Long Wharf. Hancock's nattily dressed cadets escorted them up King Street. The band played; the militia saluted the general as he passed. To acclamations, fifty-five-year-old Gage was officially proclaimed governor, a ceremony Adams likely missed. He was closeted that day in discussions of an intercolonial boycott. Was it not always in America's power, he again argued, "to distress the trade of Britain, and thereby bring her to her senses"? Preparations for Gage's welcome had consumed multiple hours; the new governor privately remarked that he would have preferred less ceremony and more submission.* A dissonant note sounded at the welcome dinner that evening when he proposed a toast to Hutchinson. Loud hissing filled Faneuil Hall.

Having spent two decades in the colonies, Gage knew them as well as any Briton. Already he believed Americans blackguards, Bostonians the greatest bullies of all. Gage was, however, an affable man, decent and patient, a gifted administrator if an undistinguished soldier. He expressed his regret for the unwelcome mission on which he had been dispatched. He was meant to return the colony to obedience. In addition to sealing the harbor, he was to apprehend and prosecute the leading rabble-rousers; that week the papers reported that Gage would return Adams and Hancock to Great Britain in chains. If New Englanders were so obsessed with justice, went the reasoning, it was time to offer them a taste of the stuff. The dignity of the Crown and the integrity of the law were on the line. Should they "kidnap and bring over as prisoners the leading patriots at Boston," warned the *Spy*, forty-eight hours after the King Street parade, "it is much feared it will cause an insurrection." All knew that additional troops, and additional legislation, followed.

Gage had assured the king that he could accomplish his errand with

---

* Adams had composed a pointed welcome. Robert Treat Paine sprinkled in some moderation and respect.

four regiments; a little strictness would go a long way. He quartered his men in tents on the Commons, anticipating a short stay. Surely "the thinking part" of the colony would opt for speedy amends. Indeed Gage was no sooner settled than a group of merchants proposed to reimburse the East India losses. Gage rejected the offer: The merchants had not destroyed the tea. When they recommended compensation in a town meeting, Adams and Cooper saw to it that the motion was quashed, all mention scrubbed from the record. At a late May meeting, Adams stationed friends at the doors to remind everyone, as he entered, that to reimburse the East India losses was to rivet the chains of slavery. Either the prospect or the warning terrified the naysayers into silence.

Both Gage and Adams were at the Town House on election morning, seven days before the port closure. Adams was unanimously elected clerk and Cushing speaker; Gage administered their oaths. Late that morning the town officials made the short walk in the company of the new governor and his Council, Hancock's cadets leading the ceremonial way, to the Old Brick Meeting House. For the election sermon, the minister took his subject from the book of Proverbs: "When the righteous are in authority, the people rejoice. But when the wicked beareth rule, the people mourn." Gage could only have sat awkwardly through the service. London expected a very great deal of him. His disposition and character were in his favor. The passions of the people were not. One British colonel worried that he would fail to meet with the respect he deserved. "Adams," reported the colonel, "rules absolutely in the Senate and in the streets." Again the poverty seemed to supply the motive: "A general ruin," sighed the colonel, "would make his circumstances comparatively better by being no worse than his neighbors."

From New York and Philadelphia the words "common cause" ricocheted quickly and comfortably back to Boston. The town would not suffer alone. Adams shared the responses widely, even while friends urged caution. Many still shrank from hotheaded New Englanders. To a Philadelphia correspondent Adams described his uneasy task: "It is hard," he acknowledged, "to restrain the resentment of some within the proper bounds, and to keep others who are more irresolute from sinking."

Forty-eight hours before the blockade was to begin, he maintained that Boston fear and shock would manifest only as calm defiance. "Nothing can ruin us," he warned—it would be his battle cry over the next year—"but our violence."

At noon on June 1, to the solemn tolling of bells, the city closed to all commerce. Many dressed as if in mourning. As Boston braced for ruin, Adams caught up with his brother-in-law, in Rhode Island, to assure him of the courage of their native town. Boston had no intention of bowing to an edict "barbarous beyond precedent under the most absolute monarchy." It would bear its martyrdom with dignity. He seemed already to be making room for June 1 alongside April 14 and March 5 on the calendar. "I verily believe the design was to seize some persons here and send them home," he noted, as if of someone else altogether. He sounds invigorated to live in an important age, one that would yield invaluable dividends. Great Britain seemed intent on "accelerating that independency of the colonies which she so much dreads." Privation was hardly the disagreeable companion some imagined. "I can live happily with her the remainder of my days, if I can thereby contribute to the redemption of my country," he wrote, as the bustling harbor went silent and the town wilted in anticipation of shortages of every kind. He seemed to wish a little patriotic austerity on everyone. It purified the mind. He had additional cause for high spirits: The man Adams believed a greater threat to American liberties than all others combined finally sailed for Great Britain that Wednesday. For six months Adams had been hoping to see the last of Thomas Hutchinson.*

Word of the Massachusetts Government Act and the Administration of Justice Act arrived the next day. As royal governors and Gage himself had long suggested, the Crown would henceforth appoint Council members. Town meetings other than elections were prohibited except by special permission of the governor, whose powers expanded. A fundamental revision of the Massachusetts administration, the Government Act would

---

* Hutchinson did not expect to be gone long. Gage was to restore order, after which Hutchinson would be reinstated, assuming that prospect remained agreeable to him. Or so went the thinking. Even the tea consignees seriously doubted he would return.

have prevented every aggravation Bernard and Hutchinson had faced over the previous years.* With the second piece of legislation—the 1774 acts would be known in Great Britain as the Coercive Acts, in America as the Intolerable Acts—the governor could arrange for criminals to be tried in another colony or in Great Britain. To Adams's mind, the first Act shredded the Massachusetts charter. The second protected the soldier who murdered the American who dared assert his rights. It was stern enough stuff to win additional converts. Before June 2, John Rowe had argued for East India Company compensation. He now reconsidered. "The people have done amiss and no sober man can vindicate their conduct, but the revenge of the ministry is too severe," he wrote.

Early that month the legislature assembled in Salem. Adams was not on hand at a subsequent session, as the Tories in the room gaily noted. "Where is your leader?" they needled his friends. Was he terrified of arrest? His colleagues had just enough time to fret before Adams materialized. He found a Tory sitting, in a gold-laced coat, surrounded by friends, in the clerk's chair. In what seat, Adams asked, did the secretary of the House intend to install the interlopers? "My company will not be pleasant to the gentlemen who occupy it. I trust they will remove to another part of the House," he instructed.

HE WAS AT his conspiratorial best that summer, when he could be glimpsed most distinctly in the stiffened spine, the beaten brow, the lingering thumbprint on the shoulder. In his March oration John Hancock had saluted the committees of correspondence. Reconfiguring the mission, Adams now reported that they were designed as "outguards to watch the designs of our enemies." He could be stern, challenging those who seemed tepid in their sentiments, who hesitated "to encounter and overcome difficulties" for liberty's sake, who deviated on a single

---

* For decades Massachusetts governors had stressed that Boston would be an orderly town under a different constitution. Bernard offered up various ideas for reform; he was instrumental in the 1774 discussions. Gage had himself long lobbied for increased Crown control.

detail. Did they, he demanded, stand firm? And he ventured a step further: Surely a general congress, composed of representatives from the colonial assemblies, was in order? It could not gather quickly enough for Adams, who headed the committee charged with crafting a response to the Port Act.

With him sat a wealthy, accomplished thirty-four-year-old Taunton lawyer named Daniel Leonard, once an ardent faction member, now—after Hutchinson's ministrations—a confirmed Tory. Sensible and handsome, fond of gold lace and gold brocade, Leonard insisted that Boston pay for the tea. In meeting after meeting Adams indulged him with a prodigious display of "smooth and placid observations." Theirs was a nettlesome affair. It required great delicacy. The people needed time to make up their minds. To hurry them would foster resistance. He sounded only conciliatory notes, leaving Leonard to conclude that Boston would opt for reimbursement. It was awfully hot, however, and they had put in a long day, Adams observed, as three grueling afternoons wound down. Was it not time to adjourn? A smaller, "self-created" committee then repaired to another room where, behind closed doors, over several evenings, it mulled a congress. "How should this plan (which was as yet a profound secret) be carried into execution?" asked Robert Treat Paine, John Adams's opponent at the Massacre trials. Paine had his answer soon enough. He was delegated to spirit Leonard off to Taunton, where court cases demanded his urgent attention. Paine assured his colleague the House would tackle no essential business before his return. The committee then settled on its congressional delegates, a slate that consisted of Bowdoin, Cushing, Paine, and the two Adamses.

In the House on June 17 Adams—speaking officially for the committee on which Leonard sat, but actually for the secret committee—proposed to some consternation that the colonies dispatch representatives to a general congress to be held in Philadelphia "or any other place that shall be judged most suitable." The committee recommended a special tax assessment to cover expenses. In mid-deliberation a Tory, claiming illness, slipped from the room, past a flustered doorkeeper. He hurried to inform Gage that the House was not debating conciliatory measures but was rather on the verge of organizing a congress. Gage dispatched the provincial secretary. He arrived to find the chamber door locked, the key secure in Adams's pocket. Gage had no choice but to dissolve the House, a proclamation the secretary read—he ended with "God save the King"—to the crowd in the stairwell.

There could be, fumed Gage, no worse Council or House. They were hellbent on resistance. They would not succeed. Dr. Warren hosted a high-spirited dinner that evening at his home, but Gage had cause for confidence. The Common was an armed camp; there was not room for a cow to graze. The only ships in the harbor were warships. The streets reverberated with drumbeats. (It was presumably this summer that Samuel Adams took John's seven-year-old son in hand to show John Quincy what tyranny looked like.) Fishermen who supplied Boston sent their catch by wagon thirty miles overland. Grain and wood prices soared. It was as expensive, grumbled one merchant, to ship from London. Massachusetts reeled from the additional Acts. And Adams overreached in a second June effort.

The committee of correspondence took it upon itself that summer to circulate a document called the Solemn League and Covenant. It pledged merchants to swear that they sold only goods imported prior to September. Every adult was to commit to buy no other merchandise and to break off relations with anyone who did until the port reopened. Copies surfaced quietly throughout the province, often introduced by ministers, some of whom went so far as to deny communion to congregants who refused to sign—or so a British officer reported. The document circulated for a month before it made its way to Boston, by which time whole towns had affixed their names, under the impression that they followed Boston's lead. In truth the idea had been for the countryside—which cared little for imports in the first place—to embolden Boston, where the Solemn League had originated, at the desk of Dr. Warren.

Gage plastered Boston with orders for the arrests of those who signed the "scandalous, traitorous, and seditious" document. Friends of government, too, leapt into action. They had had enough of the "infernal incendiaries" and their "black leader." Adams defended the agreement, insisting, as Candidus, that the countryside had prevailed upon the committee to disseminate the Solemn League. His was a preemptive strike; the Candidus essay appeared as a coalition of merchants resolved to eliminate the committee of correspondence once and for all. Adams presided over a debate that quickly grew raucous. More merchants assembled than had in years to demand the committee share all of its correspondence since the advent of the Port Bill. Selections were read aloud, along with the Solemn League; a motion was then made to abolish the subversive committee. Adams stepped out of the moderator's chair to defend his brainchild from the floor. Cushing replaced him, as Adams, Molineux, and Warren faced off against Boston's wealthiest men, particularly incensed by the Philadelphia and New York letters. It was ridiculous to think that any other colony should interest itself in the Port Act. It did not affect them! The town debated a motion "for censuring and annihilating" until dark. Adams reclaimed the moderator's chair the following morning, when the effort to abolish the committee faltered, an occasion for much hissing. "The better sort of people," reported Gage, had been outvoted "by a great majority of the lower class." Having nearly capsized the committee, the Solemn League sank under its own weight. The town commended the honest zeal of the committee of correspondence. They hoped it would persevere.

The Boston Port Act would succeed where the Solemn League failed; it proved more effective even than a postal service in uniting the colonies. By early July, a Philadelphia Crown officer lamented that the 1773 vandalism was entirely lost in the 1774 punishment; even those who disapproved of the first recoiled from the second. Adams gloated a little. With each effort to suppress the spirit of liberty, Great Britain managed only to promote it. At the same time, Boston's wharves were deserted, its warehouses empty, its streets hauntingly silent. Provisions disappeared from shelves and prices lurched upward. Overstuffed wagons lined the road from town, as those who could afford to packed up bedsteads and table linens, bacon and salt fish, and headed, in a general exodus, from Boston. One justice of the peace took to walking about with 200 lumpy pounds sterling of currency in his pocket, should he be banished at a moment's notice. He was among the lucky ones. Money was so scarce that, as one merchant swore, "you may as well ask a man for the teeth out of his head" as attempt to collect on a debt.

Lord North had gambled, Adams knew, on her sister colonies looking upon Boston's distress as "unconcerned spectators." He doubted they would passively watch as the "exuberant branches of democracy" were lopped off. And indeed donations rolled in: From Connecticut came flocks of sheep and eighty pounds of cheese; from Virginia wheat and corn; from South Carolina rice. New England settlements of every size sent potatoes, turnips, casks of olive oil, wood, shoes, and mooseskin breeches. From a New York distiller came brandy. Indians on Martha's Vineyard sent more than 200 pounds sterling. Contributions arrived from Canada and the Caribbean. Boston's papers energetically reported on the shipments, as if the town had sponsored a telethon. The philanthropy eased Boston's sufferings in small ways but did something greater still: it made of altruism an act of resistance. Each quintal of fish was to Adams a vote of solidarity and one for the "inextinguishable love of liberty." At the head of the emergency committee formed to distribute the largesse, he spent July writing thank-you notes. Soon the committee launched a sort of miniature WPA as well, assigning the unemployed work building wharves and digging wells, cleaning docks, and firing bricks.* Boston had always supported a fair number of poor, a demographic that now tripled. Who was vulnerable, and who was in dire straits? The committee devoted full afternoons to interviews. The misery was overwhelming.

The contributions, Boston's prudent conduct, and what Adams termed the "unexpected union of the colonies" frustrated the Ministry. Customs men marveled that four regiments, a company of artillery, and several men-of-war had failed to humble a town still stubbornly in the thrall of its "mad fanatics" and looking to a Philadelphia congress. In Salem, Gage nursed his dismay. While he did all in his power to secure an Adams

---

* Not everyone was happy with his assignment or his wages. Working for the troops paid better. And some donors objected to the allocation of funds. They had not intended with their largesse to repave Boston streets.

indictment, he could seem neither to charge nor remove him.* Reports of every sort reached Gage. Evidence kept its distance. In a secret communication, Dartmouth requested the letters that faction leaders read in the House. Gage could only disappoint. They took every precaution. Cushing made it his habit to deem letters private and file them in his pocket, from which they never reemerged. A mid-June attempt to bribe Adams came to naught.

From friends both at home and abroad, Adams heard that his enemies had grown rabid. In July an associate sent word: he had it on unimpeachable authority that Adams was to be arrested before any congress might assemble. Josiah Quincy was urged to steer clear of him. The reports occasioned no dismay. Adams was, noted a merchant, admired for his "*good* sense, *great* abilities, *amazing* fortitude, *noble* resolution, and *undaunted* courage." To the sister of a customs official, installed at the Castle, he seemed to govern absolutely, publishing endless falsehoods, making use of "various artifices to influence or terrify." A captain who felt sorry for Hancock— "a poor contemptible fool, led about by Adams" — choked on the impossible: "Would you believe it, that this immense continent, from New England to Georgia, is moved and directed by one man—a man of ordinary birth and desperate fortune?" The barracks master general marveled that the better sort squared off against Adams, "a poor man with very powerful wrangling abilities." He involved the other colonies in Boston's distress. In Great Britain, Lord Dartmouth was equally stupefied: How could anyone be gulled by such an absurdity as a committee of correspondence?

On a day when James Warren attempted yet again to impress upon

---

* His orders were to prosecute only if he could obtain a conviction. A botched prosecution would be counterproductive, "a triumph to the faction and disgraceful to government," as Dartmouth reminded Gage. There remained as well some queasiness about invoking a fifteenth-century statute to extradite Adams. The colonies had not existed in the time of Henry VIII, hardly a model of fair-mindedness. The accused would have no ability to challenge the jurymen, to avail themselves of counsel, or to call witnesses. Lord Dartmouth proposed a middle ground. Why not try the traitors in Nova Scotia? One official in the American department urged that someone conversant in Massachusetts law be dispatched before anyone attempted arrests.

Adams the dangers that lurked for him around Boston corners, Thomas Hutchinson, barely settled in London, was unexpectedly trundled off to St James's Palace. Lord Dartmouth escorted him to George III's private cabinet, where — after kissing His Majesty's hand — one of the most stylish men in New England apologized for his shabby attire. An emissary from another planet, he stood for the next two hours before the monarch he had done his utmost to serve. Royal robes aside, the king cut an impressive figure. He inquired as to how the new legislation had been received. Hutchinson could report only on Boston's distress. He had left too recently to guess what the other colonies would make of the acts. The king commiserated with Hutchinson on his purloined letters and ransacked home. Had personal malice played as great a role as party rage in those indignities? Hutchinson assured him it had not.

George III wondered after the cast of characters: Was Cushing the leading man of the opposition? He was Speaker of the House, Hutchinson reported, but — one did not like to correct one's sovereign — the greatest influence belonged to Samuel Adams. It was that July afternoon that Hutchinson spoke of Adams's "pretended zeal for liberty," adding that he "was the first that publicly asserted the independency of the colonies upon the Kingdom." The king peppered Hutchinson with questions, as much about the quality of the climate as about the texture of the ideas. He seemed at once to know a great deal about and to understand very little of America, a curious land where, as Hutchinson patiently explained, the clergy sided with their congregants against the government, and the people preferred bread made from rye or corn rather than wheat. ("That's very strange," said the king.)* London's leading authority on the colonial catastrophe over the next months, Hutchinson left the palace exhilarated. He spent his summer attempting to arrange East India Company repayment. The king emerged from the two-hour interview convinced,

---

* Hutchinson was impressed by the king's familiarity with American affairs but may have confused royal favor with royal wisdom. "The state of a king shuts him from the world, yet the business of a king requires him to know it thoroughly; wherefore the different parts, by unnaturally opposing and destroying each other, prove the whole character to be absurd and useless," Thomas Paine soon observed.

despite every hint to the contrary, that Massachusetts would soon submit.

"THE ULTIMATE WISH and desire of the *high* government party is to get Samuel Adams out of the way," a Boston merchant observed in August. Gage wanted nothing so ardently as to see Adams headed east, preferably in chains. August instead found him poised to travel south, his first excursion beyond the confines of Massachusetts. He was weeks shy of his fifty-second birthday. Vertical lines had etched themselves down the center of his forehead. His eyebrows, now bushier, pinched closer together. Hoping to spare him the sartorial embarrassment Hutchinson had felt before their king, kindhearted friends arranged for a sort of fairy-tale procession. Days before the Philadelphia departure, a knock interrupted dinner on Purchase Street. At the door stood an esteemed tailor. Might he take Mr. Adams's measure? The startled client complied, though neither Adams, Betsy, nor Hannah could pry from the tailor any clues as to who had enlisted him. The speculation continued at the table when the family was again interrupted, by Boston's best hatter. In short order an equally unforthcoming shoemaker appeared. A large trunk landed days later on the doorstep, containing "a complete suit of clothes, two pairs of shoes of the best style, a set of silver shoe-buckles, a set of gold knee-buckles, a set of gold sleeve-buttons, an elegant cocked hat, a gold-headed cane, a red cloak, and a number of minor articles of wearing apparel." In another contemporary version, a procession of nine benefactors came to call, presenting Adams in turn with a new wig, a new hat, the best silk hose, a fine suit, new shoes, and a query: Were his finances also in need of refurbishing? Adams conceded with a shrug that they were. The ninth caller bestowed a substantial purse. Adams announced himself afterward a man of fortune.

He needed no reminder of the grand scene that opened before him or of the significance of his mission. Friends weighed in all the same. "It is not easy to express how important your part is, and how much depends on your decision," Reverend Cooper stressed, writing under an assumed name. All eyes turned to Philadelphia; a continent was watching. Anticipation manifested differently in the cousins. John suffered an attack of nerves. He felt unequal to the task. It required "a more extensive knowledge of the realm, the colonies, and of commerce, as well as of law and policy" than he possessed. To shake off the dread, he took himself out for a walk. It was a lush season, the corn, rye, and grasses luxuriant at the edge of town. The stakes were inconceivably high, the options limited. He could not bear to consider submission. "We have not men fit for the times. We are deficient in genius, in education, in travel, in fortune—in everything," he brooded. About to take his place among "the wisest men upon the continent," he felt his provincialism profoundly.*

Thirteen years his elder, Samuel Adams too felt unequal to the task. He opted for humility. Mostly he harped on the miracle the Ministry had worked with the Port Act. Even those who condemned the vandalism clamored to help Boston.† London could not have devised a more effectual means to unite the colonies, he swore, bypassing his own contribution: with the committees of correspondence, he had installed the circuitry over which the fury coursed, in and beyond New England. The speed with which it built astounded the new Massachusetts governor, as it has historians ever since. Gage could not fathom how a group of farmers, in a tavern, warming themselves before a fire, might come to believe that their lands were to be taxed, their lives, religion, and liberty threatened. They were now, Adams assured South Carolina's Christopher Gadsden, whom he prepared to meet for the first time, "an inseparable band of brothers, each of whom resents an attack upon the rights of one as an attack upon the rights of all."

He passed multiple batons as he said his goodbyes. To Thomas Young went the task of opening his mail, to be collected at the *Gazette* office. With his neighbor and longtime collaborator Benjamin Church he left the committee of correspondence. It should, Adams instructed, meet

---

* By August 1776 he had revised his opinion. New Englanders were awkward, unworldly, vain. "In solid abilities and real virtues," John wrote Abigail, they also exceeded everyone else on the continent.

† George Washington and Thomas Jefferson counted among Port Act converts.

daily and report to him regularly. He conferred with Josiah Quincy, the brilliant young lawyer, about to sail secretly to London. Quincy was unofficially to argue America's case; Adams stressed the import of his mission. The day before the departure, Adams and Warren devised a means of circumventing Gage's ban on town meetings. Warren would preside over a provincial assembly, another extralegal body, charged in particular with military preparations. It would proceed from adjournment to adjournment, passed off as a single session.* Adams also discussed with Warren a set of resolves which should follow the delegation to Philadelphia. We know less of the domestic farewells, but emotions ran high; a sense of moment hung heavily over these hectic, prayer-heavy weeks. Adams entrusted his wife and daughter to the care of his son. He promised Betsy that he would write at every opportunity. Even if she shared John's trepidation about the adventure ahead she must have felt some relief as her husband trundled off, more dapper than ever she had seen him. For some weeks he would be beyond the reach of General Gage, left to sputter about the brazen insubordination of the demagogues who "chicane, elude, openly violate or passively resist the laws as opportunities serve."

Early on the morning of August 10, in full view of the regiments encamped on Boston Common, the Massachusetts delegates piled into an elegant coach before Cushing's front door. Two armed servants preceded them; four liveried Black slaves followed behind. A company escorted them to Watertown, where a large party awaited. Late in the afternoon, amid teary farewells, they slowly clattered south. The idea was to arrive early but also to gauge tempers and cement friendships along the way. In Hartford, dry and dusty, Adams met his longtime correspondent Silas Deane, who briefed the Massachusetts men on what they might expect from their New York counterparts. Their convictions, Deane warned, remained murky. Connecticut's were not. It stood solidly

---

* Gage had called for the selectmen in August 1774, to acquaint them with the acts. They were to apply to him for future town meetings. He was informed that this was unnecessary, as two sessions remained "alive by adjournment." Gage's face clouded. Were that the case, the town might keep the meetings alive for a decade.

with Massachusetts, ready to submit to any resolution of a congress that promised to be "the grandest and most important assembly ever held in America." Adams may have winced at some of the hyperbole of the next weeks — the rhetoric rose to meet the temperature — but would not have disagreed with Deane when he said that all depended on the Philadelphia resolves.

The delegates evoked tears and applause as they rode; if they had not yet grasped the extent of their celebrity, they did outside New Haven, where they met with a cavalcade of coaches. By the time the travelers approached town, every bell pealed. From doors and windows New Haven jockeyed for glimpses of the obstreperous, rock-ribbed Massachusetts men. Everyone vied to celebrate the conquering heroes, to share local news and marvels, to convey sympathy to persecuted Boston. The travelers met merchants and lawyers, the Connecticut delegates, and — at every stop — committees of correspondence. They learned whose son worked for the East India Company, who wished the Circular Letter had been yet more strident, who favored Gage while professing otherwise. They traded concerns about the weeks ahead. As a legislature without an executive, how could the congress enforce any laws? There were long afternoons of principles and priorities, tours of local attractions, and more names than they could hope to retain. "No governor of a province, nor general of an army, was ever treated with so much ceremony and assiduity as we have been throughout the whole colony of Connecticut," John Adams crowed, his cousin no doubt preferring the afternoons of politics to the garden tours.

Ten days after the Boston goodbyes the delegates rode into New York, escorted by a thousand armed men, a host of dignitaries, and a vast crowd. Music accompanied them. Bells announced them. With sentries outside their doors, they settled on what is today Pine Street. They walked across town, marveling at the gilded statue of King George on his high marble pedestal; the vast stone prison, college, and hospital; the regular streets and stately, painted-brick homes. In New York Boston's most celebrated ascetic came face-to-face with luxury; the furnishings, architecture, and table linens left a Massachusetts man reeling. New Englanders took breakfast seriously but a Bostonian went wide-eyed before the New York interpretation. The delegates sat down to silver coffee- and teapots, a splendid profusion of peaches and pears, plums and melons, toast and butter. For all the jouncing in the spring-less carriage over rugged roads, for all the clouds of fine dust and the suffocating heat, these would be the least abstemious, most leisurely weeks of Adams's life.

The invitations piled up; they could not accept them all. In New York they were delighted to read of Virginia's spirited resolves; the Southern colony had issued a bold July denial of parliamentary supremacy. Adams finally met John Holt, the ingenious printer who had propagated redcoat atrocities with the *Journal of Occurrences*. He shook hands with men he knew only by name and with others he needed to size up quickly. The weeks proved a blur later, when he found it difficult to sort out precisely who had said what. The delegates met their New Hampshire counterparts; joined forces with those from Connecticut; and received a call from four of the New Yorkers. They heard a great deal of General Gage, about to flush away a fine reputation in an office for which he was unfit. (Others believed Gage too honest to handle Bostonians, another way of stating the case.) Adams fielded a request for papers; already there was a sense that history was being made. They were exhorted to temper their language and avoid the vaguest whisper of independence, in or out of the room. It was a word that could transform a man into a leper.* There were heavy hints about the domineering "Goths and vandals" of New England; as the political climate grew cooler, the Massachusetts delegates could feel the suspicion lapping about them. Pennsylvania Quakers, they were reminded, would hesitate to collaborate with a colony that had persecuted their forebears. It was not always easy to get a word in edgewise. In

---

* In October 1774, Washington insisted that "no such thing is desired by any thinking man in all North America." John Jay would claim he never encountered the idea before 1775. Franklin swore that March: "I never had heard in any conversation, from any person, drunk or sober, the least expression of a wish for a separation, or hint that such a thing would be advantageous to America." John Adams insisted in 1776 that "Independency is a hobgoblin of so frightful mien that it would throw a delicate person into fits to look it in the face."

New York they largely listened, easier than attempting to keep up with people who talked fast, loudly, and all at once.

By August 27 they were in Princeton for a tour of the college. Over the course of a Sunday evening the delegates heard more about the cast they were to join, who were the plodders and who the drinkers, who were the leading lawyers and the best speakers. (Richard Henry Lee and Patrick Henry, they learned, were the Cicero and the Demosthenes of the age.) Two days later the New Englanders crossed the Delaware and rode down a wide, flat, well-tended road, past sweeping orchards and pastures, toward Philadelphia. Five miles from town they met a column of carriages. One carried several Pennsylvania delegates, including Thomas Mifflin, who had urged them to arrive in advance, and who hoped Adams would lodge with him. Dr. Benjamin Rush and his massive dome of a forehead settled himself among his new colleagues, briefing them as they rode.* The heat was oppressive. Before they had yet found their way to their lodgings, the new arrivals were whisked off, dusty and depleted, to the massive, redbrick City Tavern, recently and lavishly built, more a London address than a North American one. Up the steps they went to the vast, high-ceilinged second floor where, after some conversation, a curtain was pulled back to reveal an elegant dinner. Only later would Adams explore heterogeneous Philadelphia, the wealthiest city in America and now its publishing capital. Broad and regular, Philadelphia streets were well paved and well lighted. Its bustling harbor must have made a Massachusetts heart ache. Even the beer was better. They were among the first to arrive.

Another round of introductions now began. Adams met Gadsden, "the Sam Adams of the South." After a late night and a walk around town, he met Charles Thomson, "the Sam Adams of Philadelphia." Tall, ashen John Dickinson pulled up in a coach drawn by four exquisite

---

* In the Tory view, John Adams later submitted, they were "four poor pilgrims" huddled in a coach, desperate adventurers all. Cushing was harmless, John Adams and Paine of no particular talent. Samuel Adams "was a very artful designing man, but desperately poor and wholly dependent on his popularity with the lowest vulgar for his living."

horses. Spirits soared when the delegates learned of the Virginia colonel who had pronounced himself ready to march, with a thousand men, to Boston's relief. The social whirl continued, amid scalding heat, as they paid calls on the gentlemen who had called on them, some of whom cautioned against the Hutchinsonian types—the eminent Pennsylvania Assembly speaker Joseph Galloway was one—and as additional delegates filtered into town. By September 1 they had met twenty-five colleagues. It seemed they would be fifty-six in all, nearly half of them lawyers. Adams settled in at a Second Street home opposite the tavern. He heard flurries of opinions and raised glasses to countless exuberant toasts; already some Virginia men had begun to insist on a repeal of all revenue acts. The Massachusetts men felt everywhere killed with kindness. They came face-to-face with the exotic, discovering buckwheat pancakes and a thousand delicacies: turtles, floating islands, trifles, tarts, jellies, cheeses, curds, and creams—"everything," wrote John, "which could delight the eye or allure the taste."

On the morning of September 5, the delegates gathered at City Tavern and together walked the two blocks to Carpenter's Hall. Nearly everyone agreed that the tidy new building would suit their purposes. It was easier yet to settle on Virginia's Peyton Randolph as chairman—Adams found him to be a kindred spirit—and on Charles Thomson as secretary. Galloway could not shake the strong sense that both decisions had been settled in advance and behind the scenes, already understood to be Adams's coordinates. Like the New Yorkers, Galloway thought it unwise to oppose either measure. The Southerners and the New Englanders seemed to move in lockstep. At fifty-one, Adams was among the oldest delegates. Even the new finery could not disguise the fact that he counted among the least prosperous. An "Esquire" had only recently and erratically begun to attach itself to his name. Some were starstruck in his presence; the most conspicuous man in the room, he may also have been the least trusted. When later a colleague rose to Adams's defense he acknowledged those fears: "You may have been taught to believe, for what I know, that he eats little children, but I assure you he is a man of humanity and candor as well as integrity." Adams did not leave the overstaffed bag of political tricks in Boston but did stash the unwieldy ardor. He was all tact and performative mildness. At least to a meddling friend whom he knew to be in close touch with Great Britain, he continued to insist that the mother country had only to return them to their 1763 status and they would be happy.

In Philadelphia he found himself amid a group of men foreign to and often puzzled by one another, who spoke in dissimilar cadences and nearly hailed from different countries. They did not even divide a dollar into the same number of shillings.* His task was to make himself invisible, to sit back while Patrick Henry made an impassioned plea for a new form of government and the Continental Congress determined how to allot votes. Should Rhode Island carry disproportionate weight? Adams left the floor to Virginia, proud men from the most populous colony, one that shared New England's views but not its reputation for fire-breathing fanaticism. (John Adams would later claim that this was the reason Washington commanded the army, Jefferson wrote the Declaration, and Richard Henry Lee proposed it.) The idea was to fade into the background, to feel the pulses, sound the depths, and act through others. It became Adams's task to shake off the wild-eyed imputations that Galloway and others tried to fix to him. We know something of how he fared: he established himself as "the most cautious, artful, and reserved" of the New Englanders. They appeared "mere milksops" next to the Virginians, judicious beside the Rhode Islanders. The radicals all seemed to hail from the South. Gadsden declared himself ready to march to Boston with his musket.

It was easier to be circumspect given the palpable sympathy; only one colony's charter had been gutted, its commerce suspended, its principal business shuttered, its courts closed. Massachusetts alone lived with troops stationed among them. The Philadelphia prize, Adams well knew, was not independence but unity. It was crucial to arrive at mutual

---

* Jefferson later compiled a chart. Northerners were sober, industrious, designing, self-interested, and hypocrites in their religion; Southerners fiery, indolent, candid, generous, and free of religious convictions. One could calculate one's American latitude by the intensity of those attributes.

assistance, even if veined with mutual suspicion. So much of what he had accomplished over the previous years was predicated on the belief that ideas were contagious and that when men met, they changed their minds. Over punishing six-hour days—the delegates could manage little afterward but to eat and drink, then tumble home exhausted—he deferred to the sentiments of the whole, or claimed that he did, while maneuvering tirelessly behind the scenes.

The matter of voting settled, Cushing moved that Congress open their deliberations with a prayer. New York and South Carolina objected. Their ranks included Episcopalians and Quakers, Baptists and Presbyterians. How could they conceivably worship together? It was the larger question writ small: How to reconcile the diversity of convictions? On September 6, Adams rose for his first congressional speech. Personally he had no trouble with "a prayer from a gentleman of piety and virtue, who was at the same time a friend to his country." Though new to Philadelphia, Adams had heard that Episcopalian minister Jacob Duché fit the bill. Was there really so great a difference in their faiths? He knew he had a reputation to discard. He knew an Episcopalian would please his Virginia associates; he suspected it would also please the New Yorkers. The motion passed easily. An invitation went to Reverend Duché. At least one colleague that evening applauded Adams's "masterly stroke of policy."

Early the same afternoon a messenger rode into Philadelphia with a terrifying express. British ships had bombarded Boston. The soldiers and the town had exchanged fire. Six men lay dead. Resentment exploded into fury; there were shouts of war and cries of revenge. So great was the chaos that Congress adjourned until evening. Philadelphia's bells rang all day, as they would the next. The miserable Massachusetts delegation dreaded the arrival of every mail, terrified as much for their families as by what New England intemperance might mean for the common cause. Had the colony acted in self-defense, or had it overstepped? In a panic, John wrote Abigail that he hoped she would offer asylum to Betsy Adams and to Deborah Cushing. It was a torturous night.

A deeply receptive audience awaited Duché the next morning. He had chosen the thirty-fifth psalm; the plea for righteousness and the humiliation of enemies left tears glinting in every eye. A theatrical speaker at any time, Duché afterward launched into an affecting prayer for America, for Congress, for Massachusetts Bay, and for Boston in particular; it struck many as sublime, melting, the New England men could not help but note, even Quaker hearts. For another day Adams lived in excruciating suspense. Only on September 8 did he learn that the Boston bombardment was in fact a garbled version of Gage's September 1 dawn raid on Charlestown, where regulars startled the province by confiscating powder and field guns. Had the news not been contradicted, some feared that forty thousand men would have descended on Boston. As it was, thousands from the countryside lined the road to Cambridge, raised, it seemed, in a matter of minutes. Gage was pleased by the raid—he carried off the largest supply of provincial powder—but astounded by the reaction.

A week later, Paul Revere arrived in Philadelphia with the resolves for which Warren had arranged at the Suffolk County convention. They began in cheerful allegiance to the king and veered—by way of "gross infractions" and "a wicked administration"—to noncompliance with the Coercive Acts, strict economic sanctions, and an independent Massachusetts government and militia. The "numerous, brave, and hardy people" of Massachusetts Bay would act on the defensive so long as was reasonable but no longer, a provision Adams had stressed before his departure. It was understood that some individuals were to be seized for contending for American rights. Should such an outrage occur, every Crown officer could expect to be taken hostage. And should Massachusetts find it necessary, couriers would be dispatched from one committee of correspondence to the next, to summon the assistance of her sister colonies. Adams watched with delight as the document was read aloud to vigorous applause. Probably under the spell of the heart-stopping false alarm, surely thanks to some backroom ministrations, very much to the shock of the conservatives, Congress endorsed the nineteen resolves precisely as Warren had written them.* Paul Revere hurried a copy north for

---

* The only explanation for their folly, huffed a Massachusetts Tory, "was that they came into this vote immediately after drinking thirty-two bumpers of the best Madeira." By the time they had sobered up, Revere had already headed north.

publication. The Adams men rejoiced. America would support Massachusetts or perish with her. More conservative measures met with defeat over the next days, some of them erased from the record. Adams was pleased with his colleagues; Galloway had particular reason to curse him now. By October the congress had settled on a Continental Association, imposing the sanctions with which the Solemn League had fumbled. Every delegate signed on October 20.

Adams conveyed few details north, apologizing to correspondents for his vague letters. The congress worked in secret; much would need to remain opaque, as it remains to this day. Three choices essentially presented themselves to an assembly little interested in reimbursing the East India Company: a negotiation, a boycott, or a war. Adams knew the word on the street was that New England aimed not only at independence but at colonial domination, that—as he wrote Joseph Warren—"we are a hardy and brave people, we shall in time overrun them all." He made it his business to see that New England appear modest and judicious. He had achieved the great prize, one he cited in an October letter he drafted for Congress to Gage: Massachusetts, Adams warned the general, would be supported "by the united voice and efforts of all America." The American refusal to abide by the new acts was confined neither to a faction nor a town nor a single colony. He continued to nudge American enemies off the high road. While Congress sat deliberating the restoration of "a happy harmony between the colonies and the parent state," why was Gage building fortifications around Boston? With his unruly men, he was likely to create a rupture "which time would never eradicate." Judged too belligerent, Adams's draft was edited before it was dispatched.

Some afterward felt outmaneuvered by an inexhaustible force. As one Marylander put it, "Adams, with his crew, and the haughty sultans of the South," seem to have juggled the whole convention. Galloway marveled at the mastery. "It was this man who by his superior application managed at once the faction in Congress at Philadelphia, and the factions in New England," he later wrote. The no-sleeping, no-eating allegations date from this time. Indeed Adams appears to have played a magnificent double game. As he entreated Gage to desist from building fortifications, he was writing home to ensure that everyone was well armed and trained. Some suspected that he had choreographed the false alarm, a feat that seems beyond even Adams's powers. Congress adjourned on October 26, 1774, having agreed to reconvene in May if Great Britain failed to address their grievances. The Massachusetts delegates were back in Boston on November 9. John Adams did not think he would see Philadelphia again. From London, Josiah Quincy sent word that on receipt of the Suffolk Resolves, many considered Samuel Adams the foremost politician in the world. Quincy's contacts were evidently limited. On reading the document, Admiral Montagu erupted, "I doubt not but that I shall hear Mr. Samuel Adams is hanged or shot before many months are at an end. I hope so at least." Had the congress truly signed off on the Suffolk Resolves, Lord Dartmouth huffed, "they have declared war against us."

GAGE HAD FELT sanguine as the "so-called delegates" rattled off. His best sources assured him that the East India losses would be reimbursed. Every colony, he reassured London, had agreed to contribute to the debt. He believed as much for weeks. Otherwise he expected little from Philadelphia but another risible petition. He dismissed talk of defiance, astonished, like so many Crown officers, that Massachusetts farmers could be "vain enough to think they could be a match for Great Britain." Toward the end of September, having not yet learned of the Suffolk Resolves, he scratched his head. "It is," he observed, "somewhat surprising that so many in the other provinces interest themselves so much in the state of Massachusetts."

As he built and repaired fortifications, the town made its resistance felt at every turn.* A boatload of bricks sank at the pier. Straw spontaneously ignited. Carpenters, masons, and bakers vanished, as did a flock

---

* On their Boston return, the delegates agreed to meet regularly and to keep a watch on Gage. Assembling in the representatives' room of the Town House, they requested a fire. Gage ordered the custodian to extinguish the fire and lock the room. The custodian obeyed, after pointing out where he had left the key.

of two thousand sheep, as did brass cannon in the black of night.* Flum-moxed, Gage's men swore that devils had lent a hand. They had seen the cannon a half hour earlier. They were reduced to attempting to pry clues out of children. Sedition meanwhile gushed from the pulpit. (Galloway insisted that all but 12 of the 550 New England ministers inclined to rebel-lion.) The fall of 1774 was uncommonly warm; you could write at an open window through the end of October. Trees budded. Flowers reblos-somed. Still, the nights were uncomfortable under a thin canvas tent, especially as Boston proved unaccountably devoid of blankets.

The general expectation was that Gage would order arrests; friends of government persisted in the belief that a few desperados could account for all the madness. Into the tents on the Common some helpful soul lobbed a September proposal. Armed confrontation felt perilously near. The authors of America's miseries should prove its first victims. "Put [them] immediately to the sword, destroy their homes, and plunder their effects," advised the author, citing Adams first. Gage believed he had started down that road with a sailor named Samuel Dyer, caught enticing redcoats to desert. Under interrogation, Dyer revealed that Adams and Young had employed him to recruit shipwrights and carpenters in tav-erns, bribing them to swarm out at a moment's notice. Dyer swore that Adams had summoned him by letter to Young's home, where the two promised four pounds for every soldier suborned. He reported on a net-work of safe houses. He claimed he could reveal the secrets as well of the capsized tea. He knew many of those who had hacked apart East India chests. He would have figured among their ranks himself had he not fallen ill. Seized and fitted in chains, Dyer was shipped to Great Britain, where his testimony soon collapsed. Gage was thought foolish to have shipped him abroad.†

---

* Two three-pounders, spirited off during a 1775 roll call, were hidden first in a school-room and later at a blacksmith's. They served on the front lines before returning to Massachusetts, where in 1788 they were restored and christened the "Hancock" and the "Adams." The Adams later exploded.

† On his return, Dyer demanded satisfaction for the involuntary crossing. A pistol in each hand, he attempted to clap both to the heads of the two officers whom he believed responsible. He misfired, then availed himself of one officer's cutlass, with which he

Adams learned in mid-October of Dyer's deportation; he was appalled that yet another American right was being violated. (He did not seem to know Dyer.)* By then Gage was frustrated to the point of unease. The committees of correspondence had whipped an infection into an epidemic. No one, he lamented, could have guessed that the Port Act would have backfired as it had. He called in reinforcements. He could hardly defend Boston—much less conquer a province—with three thousand men. By November his number was twenty thousand. There were no further sneers about playacting, though there was plenty of it. Target practice on the Common was interrupted one fall day by chortling. What was so amusing? an officer challenged the jokester, who explained that an entire regiment had just missed a mark that he could hit ten times running. He proceeded to demonstrate. Before parting he assured the dumbfounded officers that his performance was nothing. He had a son at home who could toss an apple into the air and blast the seeds out as it fell.† The encounters in no way comforted the soldiers. Desertions ticked up.

National figures now, the Massachusetts contingent returned from "the grand American Congress" in high spirits. They arrived to tolling bells and to troopships lining the wharf. Domestic reunions slip more freely than do separations from the historical record, but this one must

---

slashed away at the colonel, nicking his neck and making a hash of his coat. (He had also fixed on the wrong men.) He wound up throwing the pistol at his victim and running off—directly into a meeting of the provincial congress, shouting that he had in hand one of the swords Lord North had sent to butcher them. He landed in jail, "a vagabond, and enthusiastically mad." Dyer afterward swore that British officers, Admiral Montagu included, had bribed him to make the accusations.

* Adams was unlikely to have provided any soldier with a suit of civilian clothes, lodging, four pounds, or three hundred acres of land, as Dyer testified. Even without his assistance, hundreds of regulars melted into the Massachusetts countryside however, where they were welcomed warmly. Some married local women. And some did not bother to so much as remove regimental jackets when they headed out to chop wood.

† There were other warning signs. "I can't help observing to you," reported a Boston minister, "that we have in this town a company of boys, from about 10 to 14 years of age, consisting of 40 or 50, who, in the opinion of the best judges, can go through the whole military exercise much more dexterously than a very great part of the regulars have been able to do since they have been here."

have been especially sweet: Adams had missed Betsy acutely. He found his family living in a distressed town, accustomed to alarms and musket shots. A sizeable fraction of its poor subsisted on charity. Colleagues had ably stepped in but found that replacing Samuel Adams made for a debilitating assignment. Efforts languished—and Boston grew more conciliatory—without him. The committee on donations daily parceled out contributions, the bulk of them addressed to Adams. Even in Philadelphia, bundles of relief money had been pressed into his hands. The committee supplied shoemakers with leather, spinners with wool, ropemakers with hemp. The work of acknowledging and distributing the contributions consumed the late-blooming master of detail. Thanks to New York flour, they would bear their trials "with becoming patience and fortitude." Supported by Virginia grain, they would continue to exert themselves "in support of our common rights." A form letter would have come in handy; instead Adams turned out countless variations on a theme. Tories alleged that the committee pocketed the funds entrusted to them, a charge easier to propagate given Adams's past. He issued a crisp rebuttal. The committee worked without remuneration. Their books were comprehensive, in order, and open daily "to the inspection of the whole world."

In his absence, he had been elected to the provincial congress that replaced the disbanded House. Not everyone had a stomach for discussions that revolved around arms and ammunition, cannon and mortars. Complaining of sudden illness, several representatives at one point begged to return home. Anyone who felt unwell should by all means leave, agreed Adams. They should also instruct their constituents to dispatch new delegates in their stead. Vanity won out over distemper. With pride, he reported to Lee on the Massachusetts newly minted minutemen. Every man between the ages of sixteen and sixty was armed or in training. The province had resolved not to prove the aggressors in any way. At the same time, Adams noted in January 1775, it appeared—with Gage's eleven regiments on one side, the inhabitants and other colonies on the other—"to be in a state of hostility." Great Britain seemed still not to grasp that "an attempt on one colony amounted to a quarrel with all."

In February he drafted appeals to Quebec and Montreal, inviting them to join the cause. Canada had long been an obsession; he and Warren had earlier dispatched secret agents. American rights were under assault, wrote Adams, with opposition to Great Britain dismissed as a bid for independence. And now fifty thousand people were to be punished for "what was done in all probability by only forty or fifty." Did the Canadians not endure similar injustices? He wrote with mutual safety at heart. To the Mohawks went a stilted appeal: were Great Britain to cut colonial throats, there would be no one to defend the native Americans from the same fate! "Be prepared with us to defend our liberties and lives," Adams pleaded, "for you, as well as we, are in danger." Adding an unrealistic flourish, he promised powder and guns of colonial manufacture.

He would have made his way around Boston—the town struck Betsy as "a den of thieves"—with care. Every Tory of note had fled to Boston, which had traded places with the countryside, now fully radicalized. On the street Adams could only have heard regularly that he deserved to hang. The officers behaved "like a parcel of children." After dinner one night they exposed themselves, front and back, at the doors and windows of a home, to full view of those in the street. They pointed pistols at children and robbed women. Two soldiers attempted to abduct Molineux's young son. They played "Yankee Doodle" over and over, on a Sunday, directly under meetinghouse windows. Gage ran himself ragged ensuring that no incident spark a crisis. Harassing and carousing, his men seemed to take their cues directly from the *Journal of Occurrences*.

By the time Adams learned that—in the eyes of King George—Massachusetts was not in a state of hostility but one of revolt, he was busy planning the 1775 Massacre oration. In itself it qualified as a provocation, he noted cheerfully, sounding like a fleet-footed cartoon character about to outwit a convoy of armored vehicles. How insulting that Boston should hold a town meeting in defiance of General Gage's orders! It was yet more affrontive, he beamed, that an address on the dangers of standing armies was to be delivered in the presence of one. Though the honor of delivering the oration had fallen to Dr. Warren once already, it was agreed that he should speak again. A fine actor with a mellifluous voice, he could be relied on for a commanding performance. There was an additional reason, Adams explained, hours before Warren mounted the pulpit: "It was thought best to have an experienced officer in the political field on this occasion, as we may possibly be attacked in our trenches." Would there be another massacre on the day set aside to commemorate the first? Adams braced himself, convinced that Gage's men would profit from the occasion "to beat up a breeze."

So much did apprehensions run high that tendrils of legend curled immediately around the morning. The Old South filled as soon as its doors opened and well before the scheduled event. Some who crowded the pews that warm spring day had heard that, were Warren to insult the king, an officer would launch an egg at him, the signal to draw swords and to eliminate the patriot leaders. Whether or not Adams knew of the egg, he took it upon himself to defuse the situation. Having by 1775 amended his maxim—"Put your enemy in the wrong, and keep him so is a wise maxim in politics, as well as in war," he wrote that month—he greeted some forty British officers as they arrived, settling them in the best seats in the house. He then installed himself on the Old South pulpit, draped in black. Hancock joined him. Before them the room was overcrowded, the aisles full. Additional officers spilled onto the pulpit stairs. In one account Warren made his entrance by a ladder, through a window. In another he did so in a flowing Roman toga, a rebuke to the fiery crimson sea before him.

In lines Adams must have read in advance, Warren delivered a powerful ode to justice and liberty. He provided a brief history of North America, a continent that Great Britain could claim with as much propriety as "the planet Jupiter." The Crown remembered it only when it began to flourish. Attempts to tax its prosperity then "spread a gloom over this western hemisphere." The overreach had produced a general inquiry into the rights of men. Warren denied any interest in independence. America was, however, unintimidated, prepared to wade through fields of blood if Great Britain failed to return to its senses. As there were no assaults on the dignity of the king, there was no cause for a flying egg.*

---

* The egg-carrier had evidently tripped on his way into the meetinghouse, crushing his missile and dislocating his knee. There may have been one other provocation: on the pulpit stairs sat an officer who conspicuously fondled a handful of musket balls

From the start, hissing, groans, throat-clearings, and rude laughter interrupted the address. One captain found himself attacked by a woman who threatened to wring his nose. An officer in regimental dress took exception to Warren's remarks with a cry of "Shame, shame!" Adams silenced the heckler, who challenged him to a duel. Adams waved him off.

As Warren finished, several things happened at once. Adams stepped forward to recruit a speaker for the 1776 address. It was not the usual procedure. He added a few insinuating remarks, referring to March 5 as "the bloody Massacre," words Warren had scrupulously avoided. Several officers cried out, their shouts echoed by soldiers and sailors in the room. Bouncing off the walls, "Oh fie, fie, fie!" became "Fire, fire!" At nearly the same moment drums and fifes sounded outside, where a regiment paused. Panic-stricken, the audience surged toward doors and windows. Adams left vindicated, convinced that—should a brawl have broken out—no British officer would have been spared. (Already he boasted that in street scuffles no Bostonian ever ceded the advantage.) It was, he insisted, time to "push for perfect political freedom." What indignities they suffered, he wrote the following week, omitting the March 5 provocation entirely, "rather than precipitate a crisis." To Richard Henry Lee he confided that he kept from the papers hints that Parliament considered renouncing the right to tax in exchange for an acknowledgment of supremacy. Half measures offended. "Let us take care," he warned, "lest America, in lieu of a thorn in her foot, should have a dagger in her heart."

Meanwhile wagons rumbled daily out of Boston, piling up at the edge of town, where soldiers rooted cartridges from candle boxes. Imaginations ran wild, primarily toward worst-case scenarios. On April 10, the *Gazette* published a letter from New York. Gage's men seemed intent on prompting Massachusetts to open hostilities. They should exercise extreme caution, the letter writer warned, "as all, under God, depends on your conduct at this time." Adams had by that Monday removed to the Lexington parsonage, riding daily to the provincial congress. It moved from town to town for security's sake. Betsy and Hannah too had

---

which—depending on the version—Warren either ignored or, without breaking his oratorical stride, covered in a white handkerchief, virtue muffling violence.

decamped; Betsy's mother, Samuel Adams Jr., and Surrey alone remained in Boston. Just before the provincial congress adjourned, Gage received the dispatch that Lord Dartmouth had posted in late January. It had suffered various mishaps in the transmission. Convinced still that all American unrest was the work of "a rude rabble, without plan, without concert, and without conduct," Dartmouth ordered Gage to imprison the malefactors. They had exhausted the king's patience. The time had come to take "a more active and determined part." Arrests might well trigger hostilities, but it was wiser to strike now, before opposition solidified.

A second copy of the order landed in Gage's hands on April 16. Within hours, in what he believed inviolate secrecy, he began to prepare the late-night expedition to Concord. Adams's letter to London of the same January week made better time. To Arthur Lee, Adams described the well-disciplined, well-supplied militia that drilled in every part of the province. They were called "minute men," he explained, as they could combine into a formidable army at short notice. They were determined, Adams wrote, "not to be the aggressors in an open quarrel with the troops; but animated with an unquenchable love of liberty, they will support their righteous claim to it, to the utmost extremity." He wished that the Ministry would cease listening to those who misrepresented America. He again pointed a finger at ambitious, avaricious Hutchinson. America would never forgive him, wrote Adams. Great Britain ought never either.

Lord Dartmouth in January explicitly ordered Gage to seize the opposition leaders. Gage in April ordered his lieutenant colonel to seize Concord munitions. His command was highly specific. The troops were to dismantle carriages, upend kegs of powder, burn tents, and scatter musket balls among ditches and ponds. He ordered no arrests. Some of his officers searched for Adams and Hancock that evening, as everyone from Paul Revere to the Lexington villagers feared they would. Gage knew their whereabouts, as he knew that the provincial congress was set to adjourn and the second Continental Congress to resume. Gage may have issued a verbal arrest order or dispatched a separate written one, now lost. Most likely, he exercised discretion with Dartmouth's command. A spring report had Gage hoping that the order to apprehend would be revoked. A manacled Samuel Adams, went the logic, would be fatal to the general and his troops. Gage had envisioned arrests on his June 1774 arrival. In July he suspected that he would need to tread lightly. Late in September he hesitated. By December he acknowledged that he had missed his moment. Were one leader arrested, ten would take his place. And Great Britain would appear the aggressor. He had no interest in detonating "an unnatural and unprovoked rebellion." A bold early-morning strike on Concord munitions seemed a fine compromise.

British soldiers did not, as any number of papers reported, search the parsonage for Adams and Hancock on April 19, 1775, slaughter the women and children, and leave the home in flames. After the unexpected engagement in Lexington, they did march the six miles to Concord, arriving around 9:00 a.m. They destroyed all the cannon, powder, and musket balls they could find. As Revere had warned, the country rose up to meet them, in increasing number. No sooner had the regulars marched out of Concord than—from behind what seemed every bush, wall, fence, hedge, and barn—they met with fire. Reinforcements joined the regulars in Lexington; the assault continued, with mounting ferocity, through the afternoon. You could chart its progress by the clouds of smoke that followed the rapid eighteen-mile retreat. By the time the exhausted redcoats returned to Charlestown, in darkness, a third of those who had set out soundlessly the evening before were dead or wounded.

Already there was sniping in London about the quality of Gage's dispatches, terse, vague, and—in the case of his April 1775 account—inexplicably undated. His report on the sortie makes no mention of the radical leaders. He may have preferred to avoid a subject on which he had failed to deliver; he also neglected to mention any fugitive cannon, another compelling reason for the march to Concord. In the meantime, Gage initiated the "unnatural rebellion" he had hoped to avoid—and without capturing the large cache of munitions of which he had heard, much of it carted off days earlier. Multiple officers stated afterward that the business of the expedition was "to seize a quantity of military stores, and the bodies of Messrs. Hancock and Adams." For different reasons, neither Gage nor Adams elucidated.

A Connecticut legislator crossed paths with the Bostonians as they hurried south amid the post-Lexington pandemonium. To his surprise, one of them "expressed himself much rejoiced that the battle had taken place." That was likely the same one who had deemed the morning of April 19 glorious, and who had brightly announced that Gage would effect a separation of the two countries were he to march troops out of Boston. Adams found himself back in Philadelphia on May 10. He rejoiced that Massachusetts had scrupulously honored the Suffolk Resolves. Only from necessity had the province resorted to violence. He never recovered the wardrobe he had assembled for the trip. Nor would he ever again sleep at his Purchase Street home, uninhabitable on his return.

THE NINETEENTH OF April transformed, wrote John Adams, "the instruments of warfare from the pen to the sword." His cousin distinguished little between the two. Even before the armed escort rescued him from Worcester, Samuel Adams had arranged for accounts of the Lexington encounter to travel, via four separate channels, to London. The Massacre experience had prepared him well. Dr. Warren stepped in with a circular on the "barbarous murders committed on our innocent brethren." Within days local justices had taken statements from one hundred eyewitnesses, including the Arlington woman who huddled in her bedroom with her eight-day-old child as her house was shot up and pillaged, her quilt, shoes, and negligee stolen. Any number of contributors took over from there. By the time they were done, redcoats had ravaged and plundered, murdering women and children and every living thing they came upon. Lexington would be, Adams insisted—Concord not yet in the picture—"famed in the history of this country." What he meant by "country" remained unclear. Would Congress approve or condemn the action? There were doubts and fears. All depended, he well knew, on New England proving the regulars had fired the first shot. He may himself have plumped up tales of British atrocities, which squared little with the truth and which—buzzing up and down the Eastern Seaboard—electrified readers.

The Massachusetts leaders simultaneously did all in their power to suppress alternate reports, stopping riders, breaking open the post, and confiscating envelopes. Gage cried that they published false, inflammatory accounts of the skirmish "and robbed the mails of all letters giving a different account of the affair from their own" even before he learned that the faction's report had beaten his official one to London by nearly two weeks. He had no doubt who had precipitated the crisis. The engagement, he stressed, could only have been preconcerted. No one could have raised so many men in so little time.

How much Adams subscribed to the published accounts can be read in how little he felt any need to elaborate on them. "I was with my friend Mr. Hancock near the scene of action at Lexington on the 19th of April," he informed a Maryland correspondent. Given the pieces in the press, Adams saw no reason to repeat the details "of that memorable battle." Some remained skeptical. Many in London too thought back to the Massacre. The faction's account of that clash had proved entirely fictitious, as this one surely would as well; it was as suspect as it was implausible. Adams had clearly written it, announced Hutchinson, advising Lord Dartmouth to ignore it. The king too dismissed the first accounts of April 19. It made no sense that well-drilled British forces had retreated before a pack of ragtag American farmers.

As Dartmouth waited to hear of arrests, Adams and Hancock rode to Philadelphia under militia escort. They traveled quickly but could not keep up with the news. Pennsylvania knew of the action by April 24, South Carolina by May 9. In an old military uniform, George Washington was preparing to ride to Philadelphia when he learned of the engagements. Adams cut a very different figure than he had nine months earlier. An artful incendiary then, he was a refugee now; for this trip south he had only the clothes in which he had hidden in the woods outside Lexington. Even he judged them indecent.* He and Hancock met with a triumphant welcome outside New York, when they arrived, fatigued and sun-scorched, on May 6. Miles from the city, a great cloud of

---

* It would be some time before he managed to visit a tailor. And it would be years before he submitted his accounting. He agonized over the expenses: Was the public really responsible for his attire?

dust coughed up an eight-hundred-man battalion followed by carriages, men on horseback, and thousands on foot. Musicians played. The whole city seemed to have turned out. There was danger of a stampede. Approaching with a harness, several well-wishers insisted on unhitching the horses from Hancock's carriage so as to convey the Massachusetts heroes into the city on their shoulders. This was likely the occasion — there were two attempts, miles apart — on which Adams intervened. "If you wish to be gratified with so humiliating a spectacle," he informed Hancock, "I will get out and walk, for I will not countenance an act by which my fellow-citizens shall degrade themselves into beasts." The rift between the two never entirely closed; the hurried trip under the searing sun may have been more uncomfortable than either delegate revealed.

Both fell into bed later than they would have liked after a flurry of conversations and, finally, a Fraunces Tavern dinner of fried oysters. Each wrote home the next day. Hancock described the hero's welcome. "In short, no person could possibly be more noticed than myself," he hummed. He sounds to have been traveling alone. (John Adams, Cushing, and Paine followed behind, the Connecticut delegates taking up the rear.) Carried away by the ecstatic reception — the New England men were "exalted to the skies" — he fails to ask after his fiancée, Dolly. Adams assured Betsy that New York had honored the travelers with a military escort. He omitted the roofs and doorways, stoops and windows crammed with admirers of all kinds, the tour of the town amid the roaring crowd. Two grenadiers in dashing blue and scarlet stood outside his door. He knew she was at her father's house in Cambridge. While he trusted her judgment, might she consider moving a little farther from Boston? He begged for news of Samuel Jr. and Surrey. He hoped Betsy would write as often as she could. She should not worry about him. He sounds robust, while Hancock — fifteen years his junior — wonders how he will manage with his swollen, sunburnt eyes. Escorted by six hundred armed men, the delegates made their way through New Jersey. Crowds lined the roads, delivering shouts and applause. To their relief they met with ardent approval. "The accounts of the battle," John Adams reported with relief, "are exaggerated in our favor."

The entourage swelled as they rode until—"rolling and gathering like a snow-ball"—they arrived on May 10 in Philadelphia. So thick was the air with acclamation that it terrified the horses. This time the delegates assembled in the two-story State House where, still stunned by the news, they initially seemed of one mind. Every heart bled for the people of Boston. John Adams believed it time to assume the offensive: The colonies should declare themselves free, sovereign, and independent states. There was, he contended, planting his Rubicon at Lexington and Concord, no other reasonable response. His cousin agreed. Whether he had come around to independence in 1768, as many claimed, or whether it had been his aim from the start, as Hutchinson believed, he ached for it now. It should instantly have been declared, he would say, on April 20, 1775. He also knew that—once the initial surge of sympathy subsided—the idea evoked terror in a great number of his colleagues. Sidestepping the word "independence," he opted instead for "this important glorious crisis."

In the deluge of the next weeks he bided his time, more visible outside the State House than within, trusting to the course of events, offering few pronouncements, reprising his astonishing act of restraint. It was an easier pose to sustain when every effort was underway to secure large quantities of gunpowder, when fifes and drums sounded hourly in the Philadelphia streets. He could not guess how Great Britain would react to Gage's defeat but braced himself for resentment, which he intended to churn into anger against the real villains, Hutchinson and the British Ministry. He found it easier to anticipate the next British move than the next American one; sixty men of different interests and sensibilities did not readily find themselves on the same page. At least their enemies now knew, he concluded, with a flash of pride, that Americans were not the "dastardly cowards" they made them out to be.

There were plenty of other names for the disaffected Americans who had stirred up so much mischief. "They are a most rude, depraved, and degenerate race, and it is a mortification to us that they speak English and can trace themselves from that stock," wrote a customs officer from blockaded Boston, a town populated by raging, deluded fanatics, with a "Jewish obstinacy of disposition." The contempt bled into humor. One wag inventoried the blacksmiths, sailmakers, and fishmongers who had arranged the congress. Dismissed as "the principal spring and manager of plots and conspiracies against the State," Adams again claimed pride of place. The deluded multitude would realize only after it was too late, lamented a Crown officer, that a scam had been visited upon them by a few "croakers of calamity." What could one expect from people with five newspapers at their disposal?

Others attempted finally to make sense of how a colony and a mother country had come to blows. Was this a case of the ungrateful child, or of Lady Macbeth? Jonathan Sewall, Adams's old sparring partner, shook his head in disbelief. Why would a people living in the finest climate under the mildest government, blessed with land and religious liberty, protected by the greatest power on earth, viciously defy a parent state that had "nursed their tender years"? He blamed "that ancient republican spirit" which the first settlers had planted and which had flourished in the New England soil. The root of the evil lay in Massachusetts, but a high-ranking officer was more specific still. The immediate cause for this tragic misunderstanding "originated in the disappointed ambition of one man, of great influence and no principle of public or private virtue." Adams had at his disposal a single weapon: the word "liberty."

AFTER APRIL 1775 there would be an uptick in assertions that the colonies had artfully plotted separation for years. By October, the king would write the American disturbance down to "a desperate conspiracy." Conciliation was unlikely, Hutchinson allowed, pointing a finger in the same direction as Sewall: "I believe it has been the determination of the man who has been the grand incendiary in Massachusetts Bay for seven years past to prevent or defeat such a proposal, every way in his power, intending nothing short of the present confusion from his first setting out as a politician." Occasionally an alternate theory flitted by. The *London Evening Post* published a 1775 letter from a Bostonian who observed: "There is no instance in history of the Mother Country knowing so little of her colonies as Great Britain does of America."

Gage, too, subscribed to the preconcerted-plot theory. Had the Port Act not furnished a pretext for revolt, something else would have.* With a fat packet of letters in hand from Thomas Cushing's abandoned home, Gage could report with authority that Franklin and the two Lees had incited matters. Again friends served Adams well: before soldiers took possession of his house, they paid a discreet visit and carted away two barrels of papers, "so that," one assured him, "those vultures have had nothing of yours to prey upon, which I know would have afforded hellish pleasures."

Gage harped on the delusion of the people and the duplicity of their leaders. "Mobs, or rather two or three worthless fellows at the head of the mobs" had led the way. As did Dalrymple, Gage believed that power should never descend into the hands of the benighted masses. (Dalrymple wrote the tart New England temperament down to the climate.) By June, notes of incredulity crept into the contempt. The Americans were "not the despicable rabble too many have supposed them to be," Gage allowed, explaining away the embarrassing April sortie. The brigadier general who arrived with Concord reinforcements marveled that the Americans had fearlessly crept within ten feet to fire at him. Gage may obliquely have addressed his decision to depart from his instructions when finally he reported, on June 12, that the most notorious traitors had fled Boston just before arrest orders arrived. The same day he declared martial law in Boston. He extended amnesty to anyone who laid down arms, exempting only Adams, Hancock, and anyone who aided or abetted them.†

Adams gloried in the distinction; he could not properly express his disdain for Gage or his proclamation. It worried him not at all over a nerve-wracking summer, when Congress managed only mincing steps forward. They had a constitution to write, a country to fortify, an army

---

* King George was of the same mind. The authors of the revolt had, he informed Parliament on October 26, 1775, "meant only to amuse, by vague expressions of attachment to the parent state, and the strongest protestations of loyalty to me, whilst they were preparing for a general revolt."
† He notably chose to do so when both men were far from Massachusetts. Four days later the provincial congress issued a counter-pardon, exempting only Gage and several Crown officers.

to train, a navy to found, an economy to regulate. In Betsy he confided that matters proceeded slowly but that he remained sanguine. That was before he heard the devastating news of the Battle of Bunker Hill. The British sustained twice as many casualties, but the June engagement claimed the life of thirty-five-year-old Joseph Warren, felled by a shot to the head. Adams's closest friend, Warren qualified over the stalled, post-Massacre years as very nearly his sole partner. Adams could name few causes so noble as the one that carried off the charismatic doctor, but the blow landed. It was the second such heartbreak. Shortly after the Philadelphia return, Adams had heard of young Josiah Quincy's death, on his London return, from tuberculosis.

His heart remained in Boston, where nearly half the town was missing, and where close associates sat in prison, the warden toasting them with a merry "Damnation to the rebels." (In the street outside, a saucy child countered with "Success to the Yankees!") Gage had sealed Boston as a hedge against attack. Adams was particularly anxious for Samuel Jr., on the list of residents Gage prohibited from leaving. Young Samuel tried and failed to escape under an assumed name. He had lost his mentor. He scrambled to find a place with a regiment. From Plymouth James Warren arranged a commission for him, only to discover that he had signed papers for a different physician with the same name. Adams refused to intervene, averse to patronage in any form. (The young surgeon ultimately wound up with a Connecticut regiment.) Gunfire could be heard daily, along with furious midnight cannonades. The reports were horrific. His Massachusetts colleagues looked to Adams for guidance. He felt helpless to assist. He hated imagining the terror Betsy must have felt so close to the thunder of war.

Provisions were scarce; the lucky Bostonian subsisted on a diet of salt pork alternating with salt beef. Thomas Hutchinson Jr. and his family of eighteen lived for a summer on bread and corn pudding. In August, to his horror, a selectman was "invited by two gentlemen to dine upon *rats*." Soldiers rummaged through deserted homes, butchering meat on mahogany tables. Adams learned over the next months that they had transformed the Old South into a riding school, having filled the meetinghouse with a thick carpet of dung. One pew served as a hog sty. An officers' bar was installed in a gallery. Other houses of worship became barracks or hospitals. "What punishment is due to General Gage for his perfidy!" Adams fumed. Regulars destroyed his mother-in-law's home. In August the 129-year-old Liberty Tree was felled, transformed into fourteen cords of firewood. It would have come as little consolation that—just after Samuel Adams Jr. finally made his escape—Gage began to rage against being cooped up in Boston. Impossible to defend and ill-situated for an offensive, it was worthless as a base of operations. "I wish," Gage exploded, "this cursed place was burned."

News seemed to Adams as scarce in Philadelphia as was firewood in Boston. Other colonies, he carped, knew more about what was happening at home than did the Massachusetts delegates. For no letters did he yearn as he did Betsy's. Her silence was a torture; he lived in a state of unremitting anxiety. (With a pluck and an indifference to possessions that served her well in her marriage, she later assured her husband that she could pick up and flee at a moment's notice.) He gulped down her letters, "cool water to a thirsty soul." Three in a week left him begging for more. He followed her movements closely, subsisting on glimpses provided by friends. He was unsurprised to hear of her "steadiness and calmness under trial." He knew her, he wrote, to be "possessed of much fortitude of mind." He must have smiled at the July report that thirty-five-year-old Betsy "looked as blooming as a girl." In July 1775, Abigail Adams rode the eleven miles to Dedham to spend the day with her "sister delegate." She found Betsy settled comfortably in a country cottage, "patience, perseverance, and fortitude for her companions."

Adams could not have been pleased when weeks of deliberation yielded, early in July 1775, yet another appeal to the king. Again the colonies attempted to reach over ministerial heads: Crown officers had engaged in deceptive practices and impolitic maneuvers. His Majesty's American subjects remained loyal. They hoped only for redress. Some expected the appeal that would become known as the Olive Branch Petition to deliver relief. The Adams men did not. By now Samuel's feelings were clear, as were New England's. The priorities were independence, confederation, and negotiations with foreign powers. It was this July that he complained it was his fate always to be in a hurry. They had yet to establish a government, organize a treasury, or arrest Loyalists.

By midsummer the New England Goths and Vandals seemed unable even to trust each other. Dubbing Adams "a certain eminent intriguer," one chastised him for the shoddy treatment of Hancock, who alone had saved him from prison. Robert Treat Paine blasted both Adamses, arrogant, conniving men who believed themselves of superior rectitude. Paine was sensitive to slights but may have had a point. The delegation was prone to epic quarrels. Even when not at odds, rumors circulated that they were. In June came a motion to elect a commander for the forces outside Boston, not yet a continental army. John and Samuel discussed the appointment early one morning in the course of a stroll. As John inventoried options, Samuel appeared flummoxed; he could see no path to unanimity. Did it not make sense, he asked, to appoint a New Englander to lead New England men? How to integrate the forces? It was John finally who rose in Congress to propose they agree on a general and to suggest, in fulsome terms, that only one man, by his character, skill, and experience, merited that appointment. He alone could unite the colonies. The speech sent George Washington darting from the room. It also mortified John Hancock, who—glowing through John's address—assumed the tribute intended for him. The outrage that spread across Hancock's face did not vanish when Samuel seconded the motion that Washington be named commander in chief, as he was that June. The maneuver would haunt Adams for at least a decade.

Over the winter the delegation learned that the eloquent, artful Benjamin Church—the Adams recruit who had written essays for the *Journal of Occurrences* and songs for the Sons of Liberty, and to whom Adams had entrusted the Boston committee of correspondence—turned out to have been as gifted at composing cipher as he was at lyrics. He had spied for the enemy for at least three years. Paul Revere had long harbored suspicions. Dr. Warren had never taken to him.* Church was the friend

---

* One medical apprentice wondered how it had happened that Church was out of funds one day, in possession of a large purse the next. The apprentice seems not to have shared his suspicions with his father, an Adams intimate. Church was likely on

who had asked, insinuatingly, why Adams's word always proved oracular. Privy to every secret, he had been lambasting the radicals behind their backs, Adams and Hancock most vociferously. Some would now conclude, Adams feared, that there was no such thing as public spirit. The best of men would appear suspect. The discovery left him meditating on morality. Church was notorious for his infidelity; though married, he had long lived with a mistress, about to be the mother of his child. "He who is void of virtuous attachments in private life is, or very soon will be, void of all regard to his country," Adams sighed, believing the two inseparable.* Shaken, not yet aware of how long Church had informed, he went on, trying, at uncharacteristic length, to work out his disappointment. In the absence of virtue a people would destroy themselves without the assistance of foreign invaders. "The public cannot," he concluded, "be too curious concerning the characters of public men."

Early in August 1775, an exhausted Congress took a month-long break. The delegation had been gone so long that they felt, at home, like aliens. Adams warned Betsy the stay would be short, though had yet to realize that he would spend the next six years commuting to Philadelphia. Either for his sake or hers he labored to reason out the sacrifice: "I have long ago learned to deny myself many of the sweetest gratifications in life for the sake of my country," he reminded her before setting out. It was the only kind of back-slapping in which he engaged, and even there he caught himself. "This I may venture to say to you," he wrote, "though it might be thought vanity in me to say it to others." In Cambridge he pressed a great deal into a few days. He visited Washington's headquarters, where the general labored to equip an army. He presumably saw Samuel Jr., still casting about for a regiment and decidedly unwell. Never robust, he had

---

Hutchinson's payroll well before his 1773 Massacre oration, which some speculated he had delivered with the governor's blessing, to embed him more firmly in the opposition.

* Adams may have had a point. Church's perfidy came to light when his mistress bungled a mail drop. Under duress, she wound up divulging every detail to General Washington. From prison, Church argued that he could not be guilty of treason as no civil government had existed at the time of his reports. He could hardly be guilty of spying, he added, as the information he supplied was of common knowledge.

been spitting blood. It did not help that he had been sleeping most nights on a plank. If there was hesitation in returning to Massachusetts as a proscribed traitor, his father did not reveal it. Adams effectively traded one congress for another, taking his place in Watertown as a provincial representative. The weeks proved so hectic that he neglected to discuss finances with Betsy, whom he left short on funds. Alone among congressional wives, she supported the family for some part of the next years with manual labor.

All awaited miracles; the delegates grasped at whatever distraction they could. In September, the Olive Branch Petition still in motion, John Adams reported "that two of the most unlikely things within the whole compass of possibility have really and actually happened." New England's most eligible bachelor had abruptly married Dolly Quincy, his fiancée of four years. A sprite of a woman, she returned with Hancock to Philadelphia. The second marvel was greater still. For years Samuel Adams had stubbornly refused to mount a horse. John needled him. Riding was salutary, the most efficient means of travel, as well as a social skill, essential to the statesman. Near Worcester, on Saturday, September 2, he finally prevailed. Two servants hoisted Samuel Adams onto his cousin's horse — "a very genteel and easy little creature" — and off he rode with aplomb, managing his mount with remarkable facility. Success came at a price; the next morning Adams found his chair a torture. John arranged for two yards of flannel, from which a Connecticut tailor fashioned an early American version of biking shorts. Adams found the three-hundred-mile ride restorative. He sounded invigorated on the Philadelphia return, as surely he was to learn that King George had declared the American colonies in rebellion. When the Olive Branch Petition reached London on September 1 it was treated with what Adams considered "insolent contempt." Lord Dartmouth refused to accept it.

ADAMS REMAINED CONFIDENT that the administration of George III — the same individuals who he believed had pitched the tea into Boston Harbor — would "produce the grandest revolution the world has ever yet seen." He also felt increasingly unconvinced that he was among those best qualified to assist with it. He would be hailed afterward as the most influential man at the first two congresses, but as 1775 drew to a close had little to show for his efforts. The issues piled up, as did the advice, the callers, the proposals, the offers of service, the prognostications, the back-biting, the unanswerable questions. It was unrelenting. Even well-meaning friends wrote, with a merciless lack of punctuation: "I hope to hear of you soon where is your fleet?" Riding lessons aside, he felt his age. He was old enough to be Jefferson's or John Jay's father. He requested a recall. "Men of moderate abilities, especially when weakened with age, are not fit to be employed in founding empires," he submitted.

No one else noticed him lagging. He could spend a whole evening debating whether America was in a state of war and if it was yet time to take the offensive, congenially matching a Georgia lawyer argument for argument. Colleagues thought him as vigorous as a man half his age. Discussions continued all day and well into the night, six days a week. When he was not debating or saltpeter-sampling or assessing fortifications, Adams was enjoying a pipe with the Virginia delegates or reviewing first principles with Philadelphia colleagues or fending off visitors. He wrote his personal letters to the chimes of midnight.

Mostly he stage-managed, endlessly convening men so as to assign the roles they were to play. He spoke seldom but commanded profound attention when he did, not because he declaimed with force, but because, explained Jefferson, he was "so rigorously logical, so clear in his views, abundant in good sense, and master always of his subject." He consoled himself that America could count for assistance on no one so much as Great Britain. Early in January, Philadelphia learned that a fleet had bombarded Norfolk, Virginia. The attack would help more, Adams maintained, than "a long train of reasoning" to confederate the colonies, the elusive object of the winter and one that seemed lost in the shuffle. When he mentioned it, whole delegations threatened to pick up and leave. Even his Massachusetts colleagues were of several minds. He had by now made himself clear; you can feel the mid-Atlantic delegates gravitating, in his presence, to the far side of the room. He could just barely mention "confederation." By 1775, the word on which he set his heart remained still "other matters."

His name tended to surface in the presence of audacity and did again in January 1776, when a Philadelphia pamphlet unsettled Congress. Adams mailed a copy to Betsy, who he hoped would pass it on to friends. Its author had shared it before publication with Adams, to whom many ascribed it.* Thomas Paine had only recently arrived in America but overvaulted Adams in his thinking and outclassed most other colonial writers in his lucidity. Venturing well beyond venal Crown officers and London overlords, Paine baldly asserted that there was "something very absurd in supposing a continent to be perpetually governed by an island." Where Adams had dealt in liberty and equality, Paine launched a full-out assault on monarchy and hereditary succession. He leapt far into the future rather than backward to the principles Adams hoped to reclaim. He challenged the warmest advocates for reconciliation to name a single advantage to a continued connection with Great Britain. Whether America had outgrown the relationship hardly mattered. The nineteenth of April had changed everything. The Rubicon was behind them.

Outside of Congress, *Common Sense* worked as an accelerant, meeting with a rapturous reception. And the pamphlet sent Samuel Adams back to his desk, where he resurrected at least three pseudonyms. As Sincerus, he argued that a return to 1763 would no longer suffice. Independence alone would resolve the contest now. The tone is caustic: It was time Great Britain left off attempting "the same wretched trick over again." Had Thomas Hutchinson really believed that a trifling force from Great Britain "would crush a little turbulent faction who disturbed their darling measures"? Beginning with the Medes and Persians, Adams trotted out examples to prove that insignificant nations historically overthrew great empires. In February the pieces ran in the *Philadelphia Evening Post*. Some were folded into an expanded edition of *Common Sense*, sold throughout the colonies.

---

* Extracts published in France were attributed to Adams, the "famed outlaw" and "one of the instigators of the Revolution." The pamphlet was both saltier and more radical than anything Adams ever composed.

Adams defended the idea of confederation where he could, but increasingly it seemed as if New England might well need to go its own way. With Franklin he discussed a union of the Northern colonies should no one else care to join them; Franklin promised that if Adams succeeded, he would throw in his lot with them. The frustration was great. Adams felt miserably wedged between Philadelphia languor and New England impatience. No Northern correspondent seemed to grasp what was taking so long. Why, Adams was asked, had *Common Sense* not worked the same effect on Congress that he had had on the people? There was plenty of mid-Atlantic resistance, much of it in the form of John Dickinson, who had so eloquently rallied the colonies against the Townshend Acts. Adams explained that the Philadelphia farmer daily urged accommodation on every man of influence, "the effect of which is a total stagnation of the power of resentment."

London had already determined to move troops to New York when Washington's fortifications of Dorchester Heights forced Gage's hand. In March 1776 came the news that Gage had abruptly evacuated Boston, leaving behind a heap of ruins.* It expanded as the winds refused to cooperate: With the departure stalled, the looting increased. By the time the regulars sailed, furniture floated in the harbor. There had not been enough room to embark the haul. From Philadelphia, the New England delegates begged for accounts of the evacuation but probably wished they had not. American troops reported streets overgrown with grass and littered with refuse. Everything of value had been stolen or smashed. Fences, steeples, and wharves had been destroyed. All the familiar landmarks — and the trees — were missing. Some hesitated to celebrate; Adams pronounced himself only delighted with "the removal of the barbarians." It was incumbent on Bostonians to rejoice at the departure of what he termed "the rebel army." He lobbied for fortifications for the defenseless town. As for independence, he found it absurd that some worried that a declaration might widen the breach. They had

---

* Reverend Andrew Eliot breathed a sigh of relief as they left: "We have been afraid to speak, to write, almost to think," a near-perfect paraphrase of Hutchinson's lament of a decade earlier.

already fought battles, raised armies, and blasted every act of trade to smithereens! Inveterate Tories, Adams observed in April 1776, as he would again, seemed to enjoy a more sophisticated grasp of politics than did moderate Whigs.

By April, he had begun to speak the word "independence" aloud. The South and the North were aligned. Only the five middle colonies hesitated. For the life of him, Adams could not explain how the question continued unresolved. He did his best to remain sanguine. "It requires time to bring honest men to think and determine alike even in important matters," he wrote Samuel Cooper, insisting that so long as he had done his best, he was not greatly chagrined when things did not go precisely his way. He knew he aimed at hearts rather than minds. He also felt he barked a little at the moon. He kept careful score, monitoring temperatures in each delegation. He worried about the prospect of peace commissioners, rumored to be heading west. British art, he warned once again, was more dangerous than British arms. His colleagues seemed intent on pursuing the conflict for a century. "The child independence is now struggling for birth," he reported in mid-month, as he began to sense congressional moderates losing their hold.

On May 8, 1776, the sound of heavy artillery could be heard for the first time in Philadelphia. "Thank God! The game's begun, no one can stop it now," legend has Adams exulting. "I wish that man was in heaven," one colleague groaned. "No, not in heaven, for I hope to get there some day myself," rejoined another. Days later, Adams could be heard answering a New York delegate who argued for patience and advocated compromise: "Our petitions have not been heard, yet answered with fleets and armies." The king had expelled them from his protection. Three committees formed: John Adams wound up on that for independence, Samuel on that for confederation. He urged Massachusetts forward even as he met with Philadelphia resistance: How were enlistments? Why were their presses so silent? What were the committees of correspondence doing? They had been designed to keep the people focused on the greater object, to divert them from "picking up pins."

By the end of May the pieces began to fall into place behind the scenes, where so much of the summer was orchestrated. It was agreed that Richard Henry Lee would introduce a resolution to dissolve all political connection with Great Britain on Friday, June 7. Adams played little role in the days of debate that followed but stepped in at a delicate moment with a long, last-ditch appeal to the wavering. It was the best speech a New England colleague had heard him deliver. On the eve of the vote, Adams sounded a private drum roll; a motion would be made the next day "and a question I hope decided, the most important that was ever agitated in America." Galloway would report to Parliament that the colonies split equally on the decision but that Adams had assiduously worked his art, to carry the vote by a one-vote majority. The acrimony was great. Some left Congress to avoid taking a stand. Others cast votes with doubt and regret.

In support of the late-June resolution, the delegates mutually pledged their lives, fortunes, and sacred honors, a sequence Adams surely would have reversed. We do not know in what order or in whose presence he finally put a pen to the Declaration of Independence; the silence of the congressional journals makes it impossible to say who was in the room at any given moment. The question could drive a painter, even an early nineteenth-century painter, to distraction. On a day that was not July 4 and that was likely in August, Adams placed his tidy, modest signature below that of a New Hampshire delegate and above that of John. The signature is at best a third the size of Hancock's, who seemed to have guessed that he would come down to us with, or as, a flourish.

Adams was afterward a little amazed, bathed in relief. He remained convinced that Canada would have joined the colonies had independence been declared when it should have been, in 1775. "But what does it avail to find fault with what is past," he consoled himself in mid-July. They should simply do better in future. Congress could now proceed to foreign alliances and a plan of confederation. He wreathed the decision in validations. They had proved eminently patient. Save for New York, they had all agreed. The Declaration of Independence—to Adams that summer still a "catalogue of crimes of the deepest dye"—more than justified long-suffering America "in the eyes of honest and good men." Already they had accomplished a revolution in thinking. He did satisfaction well, too well for some. Galloway claimed that Adams waited not a minute after the vote for independence had passed to announce that "he had labored upwards of twenty years to accomplish the measure." Others reported of Adams boasting, in the Declaration's wake, that he had for two decades inculcated republican ideals "among all the young gentlemen in and about Boston, and that he now saw the happy fruit of it." The number tended to increase with one's disaffection for him. On better authority, Benjamin Rush would say of Adams that independence had been "the first wish of his heart seven years before" the beginning of the war. Adams never resolved the math, or, for that matter, unlocked the puzzle of how a man averse to plans moved so tactically. There is no evidence whatever that he had independence in mind all along, as Hutchinson, Gage, Mein, and any number of others insisted.

By the end of July, the Massachusetts men keeled over with fatigue. John thought his cousin should have headed home six months earlier; he was hollowed out to the point of uselessness. Samuel took a two-month break from stifling Philadelphia in August. He had heard of the devastation that awaited him on Purchase Street but must have been taken aback all the same by the insults etched into the windowpanes, the caricatures on the walls. He found his garden trampled, the outbuildings flattened. The house had been stripped of all furnishings. Without the funds to repair the damage, the family removed to Dedham. Adams continued stoic. "We must," he reminded Betsy, "be content to suffer the loss of all things in this life rather than tamely surrender the public liberty."

Consensus had been elusive. Not everyone stood prepared for so momentous a change. But the Philadelphia delegates were now in accord. They could proceed in their struggle for liberty — "the best cause," Adams believed, "that virtuous men contend for." The people looked upon the Declaration as "promulgated from heaven." (In truth, scant attention was paid to it. Few located Rubicons in July 1776. The signers spoke little of the Declaration, and other than in Trumbull's canvas never assembled in the same room. The legend arrived later, nudging the Boston Massacre off the calendar, as a crop of statesmen elbowed Massachusetts provocateurs out of the picture.) Adams was ecstatic. A constellation of what he by summer could rightfully call "states" had reconciled disparate views to unite in a common cause. He did not bother either with an accounting of how long it had taken or of how exactly the object on which he had set his heart for some number of years had been achieved. There are numerous ways to improve upon events: he left the shattered glass, the howls in the night, the soaking tea and splintered doors, the roughing up and shaking down out of the picture. "Was there ever a revolution brought about, especially so important as this, without great internal tumults and violent convulsions!" he marveled.*

To the end he undersold. "The great event" had taken place sooner, he gushed, than he expected. The delay only proved the Americans the reasonable ones. It had been necessary, he acknowledged, loading his astonishing second act into a single sentence, "to remove old prejudices, to instruct the unenlightened, convince the doubting, and fortify the timid." But they had proceeded, one step after another, sensibly and systematically, parsing questions of immense magnitude from every angle, reconciling divergent temperaments, perspectives, and interests, "'til at length," he wrote, at the end of July 1776, "we are arrived to perfection."

---

* Tocqueville would assert within sixty years that the American Revolution "contracted no alliance with the turbulent passions of anarchy, but its course was marked, on the contrary, by a love of order and law."

THE BEST CAUSE THAT VIRTUOUS MEN CONTEND FOR

History's what people are trying to hide from you, not what they're trying to show you. You search for it in the same way you sift through landfill: for evidence of what people want to bury.

— HILARY MANTEL

"I AM APT to be displeased when I think our progress in war and in politics is slow," Adams griped a year later, as the idea of confederation — without which there could be no central government — met still with resistance. The minuscule matters crowded out the larger ones. His impatience wore him down, as did the staggering workload. During 1777 alone he sat on or headed the board of war, the medical committee, the committee for procuring cannon and the committee on foreign alliances. Regularly he wound up on committees to answer Washington's letters. He nodded to his limitations. "But I get out of my line when I touch upon commerce; it is a subject I never understood," he acknowledged. "I possess not the least degree of knowledge in military matters," he asserted, "and therefore hazard no opinion." "As I am not a judge in the matter, I am prudently silent and hear the opinion of those who are connoisseurs," he wrote of maritime affairs, which did not prevent his serving on the committee charged with founding an American navy. He managed only brief returns to Boston. "I wish for retirement and covet leisure as a miser does money," Adams conceded late in 1778. One admirer observed that had he devoted as many hours to raking oysters as he had spent, day and night, in the service of his country, "he would have been as rich as the most opulent speculator on the continent."

Late in 1776, the American army depleted, Washington despairing that "the game is pretty near up," Congress abruptly fled before advancing British troops to Baltimore. Colleagues described the town as a filthy backwater, a convent, the moon, "the damnedest hole in the world." Adams had not understood the panic—he was well accustomed to danger—but thrilled to the makeshift home.* Congress had never worked so efficiently. In September 1777, they fled again, landing ultimately in York, Pennsylvania. It was a dismal season. Spirits sagged all around. Adams reminded the assembly that America's eyes were upon them. Were they to wear long faces, long faces would become the fashion. Their cause was righteous. They should comport themselves as such. He could be dry-witted: word of the American victory at Saratoga traveled to Congress in October 1777 with a messenger who paused en route to visit his sweetheart. Congress voted a prayer to General Gates for the happy news. Adams proposed that the young suitor be voted a pair of spurs.

Increasingly, however, he parted ways with his colleagues, of different mindsets and priorities, focused more on the future than on his "ancient purity of principles and manners." Adams remained the soul of the New England delegation, but the talents that had served him so artfully for fifteen years proved, as a French envoy noted, "ill adapted to the conduct of affairs in an established government." The grievance-sharpening and loophole-locating were better suited to rebellion than statesmanship. The resolve ossified to rigidity. Even close friends found him uncompromising. It was difficult to account for men's peevishness, he shrugged after a tussle with Cushing, "and it is generally not worth one's while to attempt it."

In late October 1777, Adams predicted that confederation would be

---

* Imperturbable as ever, he scorned the Howes' offer of amnesty for those who laid down arms. Surely the Howes were not, Adams wrote in the *Gazette*, "such idiots as to expect your proclamation would meet with anything but contempt from the Independent States?"

decided in a matter of days, as indeed it was, although ratification would wait another three and a half years. His long service to his country had been the greatest honor of his life, but he pleaded for a respite. He hoped that Massachusetts might send in his stead a delegate with the "fortitude of mind sufficient to resist and despise" the stupefactions of flattery. Some seemed to guzzle bottomless cups of the stuff without a hint of queasiness. That morning John Hancock took leave of Congress, making a formal occasion of his departure. Hancock traveled with a troop of light horse that left the country people in awe. Several weeks later Adams ventured north himself. Tavern-keepers along the way complained; Hancock and his retinue had neglected to settle their bills. Their hosts pursued them with claims, much to the mirth of Tories, who chortled about King Hancock, the swindler. A crew of military and naval dignitaries turned out for the lavish ceremony that greeted Hancock in Boston, where cannon boomed on the hills, in the harbor, and on the Common. His bedraggled colleagues rode into town unnoticed later that week. The two journeys set the tone for the next decade, when resentments built. In Hancock's northbound mailbag he had carried a letter from Adams to Warren, railing against Hancock's unseemly thirst for accolades, tributes Adams believed dangerous. Congress had devoted a full afternoon to the question of Hancock's ceremonial send-off, the Massachusetts men voting with the minority, against their own colleague.

In Boston Hancock wasted no time in maligning the associate to whom he once vowed he would never again speak and to whom it now seemed he never would again. He nursed a rumor that Adams had participated in the Conway Cabal, a shadowy plot to oust Washington. Adams found himself severely censured in a town meeting for a conspiracy of which he knew little. Friends counted among the general's critics, but Adams did not. He had been away from Congress when the scheme was purportedly hatched. He assumed the truth would protect him—a curious refuge after decades in the misinformation business. "Mr. Hancock never thought me an enemy to General Washington," he reminded Betsy. He thought it best to leave Hancock to stew in his own iniquity. Privately he criticized his former protégé. He was heard to mention that he had himself put the feather in Hancock's cap. Each owed the other a debt uncomfortable to acknowledge.*

Friends warned that Bostonians seemed intent on sacrificing the original patriots "to the shrine of their idol." Adams consoled them as he had thin-skinned Hancock years earlier. It was the censure of fools and knaves all over again. "The history of mankind affords so many instances of men of exemplary virtue suffering abuse," he wrote, "that one would think it should cease to be thought a misfortune." Report after report reached him that former allies had joined the Hancock camp; men who had refused to take a political stand for years now worshipped him as if he were Thomas Hutchinson. If Hancock had not Hutchinson's abilities, Warren carped, he "certainly equals him in ambition and exceeds him in vanity." Were it reported that he had returned to Boston "to arrest the course of nature, or reverse the decrees of Providence," there were plenty who would choose to believe it.

Adams was delighted when France entered into an American alliance in 1778 but offended by the toasts Boston raised to celebrate the news. Why was the king of France lauded before Congress, the French army and navy before those of America? The military should not outweigh the civilian. He took pride in the fact that his detractors needed to resort to fictions to malign him. They might well angle for his recall; any number of men could serve better than he did, though none, he added, could serve more honestly. He insisted to all who would listen that though Hancock considered him his enemy, he did not consider Hancock his.†

Again well-meaning friends attempted to run interference. The breach only gratified America's enemies. A merchant who had plotted the fate of East India tea with Adams reminded him: Adams disapproved of those who let their passions get the better of them. Should he not

---

* Reminiscing at a post-Revolutionary dinner, a House representative turned to Hancock: "Ay, I remember we used to say that you found the money, and Sam Adams the brains." The conversation screeched to a halt. The speaker was reprimanded afterwards. There should be no harm, he protested, in stating the truth.
† He was not so oblivious as to keep score. Someone—very likely Hancock—had attempted to ruin him, Adams observed, seven times.

modulate his own? While he was at it, he might remember that America did not owe her independence exclusively to New England. On the second front Adams refused to budge. He had never said the country was obliged to New England for independence, only that New England's "principles and manners" accounted for its spirit. As for his disagreements with Hancock, could they, "either real or imaginary, be of any consequence to the world"? Indeed the two had quarreled. Their differences were unimportant. He did not dwell on them. He thought of Hancock only when his name happened to turn up in a Boston newspaper. And why should he apologize? He was the injured party! Nine days later he wrote again, supplementing his warnings about idolatry. He did not care to see the people in the thrall of an American demigod any more than in the thrall of a foreign one. He professed himself ready to forgive and forget. "No man," he swore on November 1, 1778, "has ever found me inexorable."

In truth "inexorable" described him perfectly over the next years, when the "serpentine cunning," the preternatural ability to reason men into measures for their own happiness, abandoned him. No longer the indomitable mastermind, he seemed to shrink back to the shapeless everyman. He stockpiled enemies. He tangled himself up in feuds that ripped Congress apart; he befriended unsavory characters; he offended America's advocates, including nearly every French envoy. The idealism got in the way. One emissary denounced Adams's "poorly reasoned attachment to the principles of democracy and to a speculative perfection of administration." Neither served a nation at war; they were unlikely to survive a peace. He was accused in New England of opposing any accommodation with Great Britain, in Philadelphia with facilitating one. He insisted on the annexing of Canada and the acquisition of Florida. He seemed to forget old friends. Why did New England not come to the rescue of South Carolina, demanded Gadsden, writing to the sound of gunfire, when Gadsden had supported New England since the clarion call of the Circular Letter? From Boston Adams heard there was no end to the calumny against him. The charges were groundless, he insisted, as the allegations piled up. He seemed to specialize in trouble and difficulty.* The third act was nearly as unsatisfying as Adams's first.

He spent much of the summer of 1780 in Boston, where he was instrumental in the wording and ratification of the state constitution. It was a document, he assured a visitor, that allowed for majority rule while checking the power of that majority. The idea was to harness the enlightened will of the people while blunting the "passions and whims to which they are too subject." Days after ratification, word arrived that Thomas Hutchinson had died in London of a stroke. The last years of exile had weighed painfully on the former governor, who continued to calibrate everything down to the weather in New England terms, and who puzzled to the last over his fall from grace.† He went to his grave convinced that, more than anyone, Adams had been responsible for the Revolution, a tribute Adams would no doubt have reversed. He never lost sight of the man who had so unwittingly shaped his thinking. Long after 1780, Adams raged against "the few haughty families" who were convinced they should govern and who assumed a populace would tamely submit. "This unravels," he sputtered to Richard Henry Lee, "the mystery of millions being enslaved by the few!"

August 1780 found Adams back in Philadelphia, brooding about the special fall election for Massachusetts governor. He was a believer in precedents; the state's first executive would determine much of the next years. A people derived their character from their leader. He wound up

---

* In 1783, Adams and Hancock both opposed the appointment of Benjamin Waterhouse as Harvard College's first professor of medicine. Waterhouse assumed Adams had his son in mind for the position. The problem seems to have been less nepotism than provincialism. As Waterhouse put it, "Mr. Adams's principal charges were that I had served my time with a Scotchman and a Tory, I had been in England, I was not a son of Harvard, and lastly I was a Quaker." Despite Adams's energetic canvassing and after much commotion, Waterhouse got the job.

† In a Boston newspaper Hutchinson read with a pang that his property had been put up for sale, though would never know that James and Mercy Otis Warren bought his country estate. "It has not always happened in like manner," a gratified Arthur Lee wrote the couple, "that the forfeited seats of the wicked have been filled with men of virtue." The Milton Street on which Hutchinson lived is today Adams Street. Reverend Cooper for some time enjoyed the furniture confiscated from the former governor's Boston mansion.

surprised and chagrined. An honest people, it seemed, were not "incapable of error." Betsy was aghast by the outcome, though when she shared her indignation, her husband reassured her. If the people remained vigilant, theirs might prove a fine choice. If not, they could correct their misstep. He hoped only that Hutchinson's successor would manage to discern his true friends through the plush fog of flattery.

John Hancock had showered the town with fire engines, libraries, church bells, streetlights, and free firewood. He had paid for the cloth that draped the pulpit at Warren's Massacre oration. He had sent young men through Yale. He had bailed out the fatherless and the widowed; he had spared the unfortunate debtor from jail. Having spent a fortune he got his money's worth. The common people, noted one minister, "have had his name so often dinged in their ears" that they would support him even while wholly ignorant of his character. A visitor to Boston dubbed him "the King of the Rabble." He embraced the role; a neighbor noted that "he lived and entertained like a prince." For his gubernatorial inauguration he appeared in a crimson velvet waistcoat with gold buttons. If Adams thought back to John Robinson, he made no mention. From Philadelphia he simply inveighed against "the intoxications of power." He had hoped never to see public servants who were motivated by anything but public welfare. If we elect unqualified men, he wrote Warren, "the administration of government will become a mere farce." Hancock would serve nine terms, Adams drifting further into irrelevance with each inauguration.

He remained an attentive correspondent, in part because he did not hesitate to scratch out a letter in Congress while a colleague spoke. He lit up the occasional newspaper. As "An American," he addressed the peace commissioners London dispatched in mid-1778. "I know it is very hard for you to part with what you have accustomed yourselves from your earliest infancy to call your colonies," he wrote, at his most scathing. The mother country had claimed the blood of innocents. Mutual affection was a thing of the past. "We freely forgive you, but it is not in nature that you should forgive us. You have injured us too much." He soon began to complain that writing had grown painful. The words wavered on the page. After Hancock's election he described himself as an old man. By the end of Hancock's administration, he qualified as a relic. He left Congress for the last time in April 1781. Word of Cornwallis's Yorktown surrender reached him in Boston, from which he never again departed, though the town felt increasingly foreign. Fewer and fewer remained with whom Adams could think aloud. Josiah Quincy, Joseph Warren, and William Molineux were gone. John Adams was in France, causing faces to fall when he turned out not to be his famous cousin. The 1783 Massacre oration would be the last. That spring James Otis died instantly when struck outside his home by a bolt of lightning. Samuel Cooper died at the end of the year. Adams never discovered that the charismatic Brattle Street minister had figured for years on the French payroll. For a princely sum, Cooper had undermined Adams's influence even among intimates, a sabotage at which the minister brilliantly succeeded.

Adams expected no recognition in his lifetime; he took little note when friends termed him "the man who had the greatest hand in the greatest revolution in the world." But he seemed truly to have believed he had seen the last of the crimson velvet suits. Well in advance of the 1783 peace treaty, he planted himself in the camp of liberty and knowledge, lobbing grenades into those of power and riches. He continued to applaud Old World simplicity when the new nation had moved on to postwar luxury. As if to prove his point, he and Betsy moved into a dilapidated house on the south side of Winter Street, a short walk but a far cry from genteel Purchase Street. Confiscated from its Loyalist owner, the modest two-story home had evidently once been yellow. It did not see a new coat of paint. The days of Boston clubs were over; there was less entertaining than there had been in the past. The household shrank, Adams's social life with it. Hannah decamped in 1781 when she married Betsy's much younger brother, a match that made Adams's brother-in-law his son-in-law. (Adams advised Thomas Wells that in marriage as in government, the light, liberal touch worked best.) The valedictory notes began here. "It is difficult for a man in years to persuade himself to believe a mortifying truth that the powers of his mind, whether they have been greater or less, are diminished," he told John. The crepe of nostalgia hung limply about. He missed the old circle, the congenial fireside chats, the sweet communion, or what struck others as the ceaseless machinations.

As early as 1775, a British officer had predicted that Adams owed his position to discord and would "sink into insignificance and beggary the moment it ceases." The first French ambassador to the United States was of a similar conviction. Adams seemed intent on creating obstacles, fearing his importance would evaporate with the peace. Nothing invigorated him like dissent. Having devoted fifteen years to the idea of popular sovereignty, Adams was horrified by the Society of the Cincinnati, over which Washington had agreed to preside. It was to bestow honors on descendants of military officers. Adams held that ostentatious shows of superiority had no place in a republic. (Dissension over the idea was widespread. John Adams, John Jay, and Ben Franklin sided with Adams.) Were hard-won liberties really to be sacrificed to another entrenched elite? The Cincinnati converted him overnight from visionary to scold. He reared from cults of personality; it was as essential to be on guard against the best of men as the worst. He admitted to only one brand of nobility. It could be found among individuals of all ranks and conditions; the "well-born" was the man or woman who perfected his or her mind. He issued ode after ode to free universal education, more essential even than laws to a republic. He promoted girls' schooling, which he considered vital. Already by 1790, when Adams posed for the Trumbull painting in which he would barely figure, over a third of Boston students were female. An uneducated people, he insisted, more often than anyone could have cared to hear, would not long remain a sovereign one.

By 1785 he could rage against extravagance only with a quivering hand. A few paragraphs exhausted him. He was sixty-three, convinced that—as he expressed it in Latin—"times change, and we change with them." Of few Bostonians was the adage less true. He made so many enemies in his implacable commitment to antiquated-seeming ideas that he wound up signing letters: "I am, my dear Sir, notwithstanding I have been otherwise represented in party papers, your old and unvaried friend." He seemed to crumple if he failed to head into the win⌐

argued stridently against a return of the Loyalists, men who had crowed that they "would travel fifty miles to blow out the brains of Samuel Adams and John Hancock." They had aided and comforted the enemy. They would undermine the new republic. The intransigence cost him additional friends. When in 1786 farmers in western Massachusetts rose in armed protest against taxes, ultimately exchanging fire with a state army, they could not count on the support of the man who had instigated years of popular uprisings. Adams drew an inviolable line between upending an arbitrary administration imposed from abroad and upending an administration freely and fairly elected at home. The second promised legal redress. Extralegal assemblies had served their purpose. The ringleaders of what became known as Shays' Rebellion were taken into custody. Adams believed that they should hang. The public tended to leniency. Hancock pardoned the prisoners.

Along with other disturbances, Shays' Rebellion pointed up the need for a more robust government than the Articles of Confederation allowed. Hammered out in Philadelphia, the Constitution went to Massachusetts at the end of 1787. Adams was among those elected to ratify it, though many doubted he would. He who had done more than anyone to knit together the colonies before the Revolution could not get his mind around centralized authority in its wake. As Adams wrote Richard Henry Lee that December, "I confess, as I enter the building I stumble at the threshold. I meet with a national government instead of a federal union of sovereign states." He believed the document incomplete without a Bill of Rights, one that included freedom of the press, the right to bear arms, and a clause ending the slave trade. The addendum nearly scuttled the effort on which the Constitution's proponents had labored for weeks. In the name of compromise, Adams withdrew it. Legend has it that Paul Revere ultimately prevailed upon him to support the Constitution with the news that a great body of tradesmen had come together at the Green Dragon. How many had they been? asked Adams. "More," replied Revere, "than the Green Dragon could hold." The rest were outside.

The Massachusetts Convention opened on January 9, 1788. Just over a week later, thirty-seven-year-old Samuel Adams Jr., debilitated by four grueling years of army service, died of tuberculosis. No hint of the loss survives in Adams's papers apart from his trembling notation in the family Bible, the last he would make. Samuel Adams Jr. willed his army pension to his father; overnight Adams found himself extremely well-off. There was some irony that he received in late middle age the inheritance that—had the Land Bank not intervened—he might have received at twenty-four. After a break for the funeral, the convention resumed, Adams largely silent throughout. By an agonizingly close vote, Massachusetts in February ratified the Constitution of the United States. The maneuvering restored the partnership with Hancock and seems to have reengaged Adams, who allowed friends to propose him in a special winter election for the US House of Representatives. A hail of abuse rained down from every direction. He was indeed a venerable patriot, but was he a firm Federalist? He had vilified General Washington! He lost in a landslide, defeated even in Boston.

In December 1789, an anonymous letter was lobbed over his garden wall. Its author warned Adams that he was under close surveillance and in grave danger. A faction had agreed the night before to silence him. If his correspondent were a true friend, Adams wrote in reply, why had he not come in person to warn him of the plot—or to divulge the names of the conspirators? As for the surveillance: "So in despotic governments are the motions of the subjects watched." He shrugged off what he deemed feeble efforts at intimidation, not because of any great courage on his part but because "we have never been a country of assassins." Americans were too moral and well educated to resort to such iniquities. He could not promise to restrain himself in his criticisms. "If a free inquiry into the measures of the administration of government is a crime," he warned, sounding no different than he had in addressing a royal governor, then he was likely a criminal.

In the spring of 1789, Hancock and Adams were together elected governor and lieutenant governor of Massachusetts. Something of a monument, Adams would prove the first port of call when French visitors and Venezuelan revolutionaries touched down in storied Boston. Admirers wrote of children they had named for him. As he had several times already, John urged his cousin to collect and publish his four decades' worth of writing. At the very least, might he provide a list? Both the Old World and the New World would find them of enormous interest. John advised against leaving the heroics to others; Samuel should preserve his place in history. More than any other founder he believed he answered to a single judge alone. He produced no advertisements for himself, watching passively as history warped into myth. He lived long enough to see how he would be depicted in the history books, a dispiriting exercise at best.* In an early copy of William Gordon's 1788 account of the Revolution, Adams was wounded to discover himself embroiled in the Conway Cabal. He read about details of which, in the course of actual events, he had never heard.

"Whose heart is not affected at seeing that venerable patriot Samuel Adams traduced in so many instances by Dr. Gordon?" gulped Benjamin Rush. The old patriots, Rush regretted, were forgotten, as invisible as if they had already departed this world. The distortions left him questioning the ancients. "What trash may we not suppose has been handed down to us from antiquity?" he wondered. Had Caesar and Livy extracted their accounts from the barbers of Rome? Like John Adams, Rush believed that the real Revolution had been waged long before Lexington and Concord. It had taken place in American hearts and minds, where one tactical genius in particular had worked miracles, unanimity congealing around him. Late in 1789 George Washington visited Boston. Hancock made himself unavailable, stuck on the question of which illustrious patriot should call first on the other. The dodge left Washington touring the town flanked by the Adams cousins. "Behold three men," John overheard in the jubilant crowd, "who can make a Revolution when they please." There, declared another, "are the three genuine pivots of the Revolution." It was an occasion for the portraitists, John exulted, affixing halos

---

* Paul Revere was asked in the 1790s to set down his memories of the evening of April 18, 1775. A modest man, he offered them up reluctantly. The ride lent itself to poetry as early as 1795, in stanzas Adams would have read, although Longfellow immortalized Revere only in 1860.

to the tall Virginian and his two squat escorts. He then checked himself: "But H[ancock]'s creatures will cast a damper on that."*

Hancock died four years later, an old man of fifty-six. Adams presided over the immense and lavish funeral, or at least accompanied the casket until his strength gave out. Staggering, he was escorted home. He ascended to the governorship in October 1793. Given what he termed "his old nervous disorder" he could no longer compose his own letters. The tremor flared for weeks on end, leaving his head and hand shaking violently, halting his speech. In his inaugural address he harped, as he had done since his undergraduate days, on Lockean ideals. Liberty and equality having been affirmed by the Declaration, they formed, he announced, the creed of the United States. Federalists were left plotting how to unseat a man who "has waded through a sea of political troubles and grown old in labors for the good of his country." They dismissed him as "that pure unspotted lump of patriotism." He had been intrepid and unwavering, in the vanguard at the most perilous times. His character and conduct were irreproachable. As the writer who signed himself "An independent farmer and one of the minutemen of 1775" pointed out before the 1794 election, Adams had risked the loss of his property, family, and life. His name would be venerated forever. The slanders continued all the same. Even the slipshod tax-collecting returned to haunt Adams. His ghost continued to fight it out with Hancock's in the press. Malicious doggerel circulated.

---

* No one spent more time afterward apportioning credit than John Adams, who early on fumed that Washington and Franklin would see all the glory, and that the history of the Revolution would "be one continued lie from one end to the other." In 1806 he railed against Washington, on whose altar every other patriot would be sacrificed. John Hancock, John Jay, Samuel Adams, and a host of others had been more essential. John engaged in a particular tug-of-war with the South. Jefferson had been nowhere on the scene when James Otis launched his crusade against British overreach. Otis had electrified 1761 Boston "more than Patrick Henry ever did in the whole course of his life." By 1817 Adams had settled on Hancock, Otis, and Samuel Adams as the founding triumvirate, "the most disinterested sufferers and firmest pillars of the whole Revolution." The essential characters, they had animated all the rest; they deserved the statues and the obelisks. On one count alone he had no words: "I shall not attempt even to draw the outlines of the biography of Mr. Samuel Adams. Who can attempt it?"

It was said that he had opposed Washington and the Constitution, that he cozied up too closely to revolutionary France.

From a residual loyalty and the conviction that he could do little harm he would be reelected three times. Many, including John Adams, regretted his parochialism. Samuel had been born a rebel; John hoped he would not die one. In 1796, even the town of Adams, Massachusetts—named for him during the Revolution—did not favor him with its votes. He doddered a little and knew as much. The best that could be said of him was said by Abigail Adams: "I respect his virtues, though I pity his weakness." She vowed to stand by her old friend. John was less forgiving, exhausted by the guile and single-mindedness, by Samuel's deep distrust of federalism. "He always had a contracted mind—though a subtle and a bold one," John carped. All his thoughts, friends agreed, were his own. Early in 1797, as Adams stepped down from a speech in the legislature, his legs gave out from under him. He fell backward, caught by quick-thinking colleagues before he reached the floor. Later that month he retired. No one was sorry to see him go. He could do nothing right. He had begun to use the carriage lent to him when elected, which left even James Warren raging. Here was Samuel Adams, "who used to boast that he could live on a turnip!"

He settled into obscurity on Winter Street, amid a small circle of intimates, surrounded by Hannah and her three children and assisted by Surrey. He had outlived himself; the son of John Singleton Copley, who had immortalized Adams at the height of his career, described him as "superannuated, unpopular, and fast decaying." John Adams recoiled from the undignified sight. He wrote later that he hoped not to overstay his earthly welcome as had his cousin, "a grief and distress to his family, a weeping helpless object of compassion for years." In his reveries, Samuel took pleasure in imagining that he had been useful to his country. From his spacious downstairs sitting room, amid his books and his portraits of eminent patriots—Washington claimed pride of place—he returned over and over to the unexpected triumph of the fledgling colonies.

After a short illness, he died early on the morning of October 2, 1803, age eighty-one, his family at his side. Bells tolled for a half hour. Bernard, Hutchinson, Gage, Bowdoin, Cushing, Gill, Sheriff Greenleaf, the newspaper-annotating Harbottle Dorr, and even George Washington were gone. So too were many of those farmers who had warmed themselves before the fire, among the first to prove that—as a Danvers minuteman put it, channeling Adams—"We always had been free, and we meant to be free always." Ruined, Edes would survive Adams for a few more months, Betsy for five years. Revere lived until 1818.

With a military escort, the funeral procession set out from Winter Street late on the afternoon of October 6. A train of thousands followed. Stores were shuttered and salutes fired but it was a muted affair. Adams had anticipated, often by years, nearly every point in the Declaration of Independence. He was hailed as the first to contemplate a separation from Great Britain. He had nearly proved a martyr to the cause. The funeral bells tolled only briefly, however. The Massachusetts governor made himself scarce. There was a bit of a game of hot potato as to who might best remember Adams. Some speeches rang hollow. "Called upon by the occasion to say something he could not say less," the *Independent Chronicle* reported of Adams's eulogist. Nine US senators opposed wearing the traditional crepe on their arms.

Eulogized in the Boston papers as "the Father of the American Revolution," singled out as the prime mover in private diaries, Samuel Adams was promptly forgotten. As one friend put it, "No man contributed more towards our revolution, and no man left behind him less." Adams supplied little to illuminate his convictions, his communications, or his "peculiar genius." He had helped to erect the intellectual architecture of a republic but had neither gift for nor interest in its political design. It is difficult to account for how, in his last decades, he lost his impeccable popular touch, easier to explain how he faded from view, as the revolutionary must after the revolution. He set more store in ideas than institutions; he encouraged an allegiance to principles over individuals. "The truly virtuous man and real patriot is satisfied with the approbation of the wise and discerning; he rejoices in the contemplation of the purity of his intentions, and waits in humble hope for the plaudit of his final judge," wrote the man who would be remembered as a firebrand and a scold.

He was laid to rest in the Granary Burying Ground alongside his first wife, in the company of Otis, Molineux, Treat Paine, the Massacre victims, various Tea Party participants, and at a distance from Hancock. The wrong kind of hero for the republic's early years, he would be resurrected with the centennial of the Stamp Act, by which time his remaining papers had suffered nearly as many indignities as their author. There would be no biography until 1865, no statue until the centennial of the Revolution. Overall, Boston preferred to minimize the messy street protests, to rinse the history of provocations and agitations. The destruction of East India property surfaced only a half-century afterward, repackaged as a costumed caper. The Fourth of July consumed all his holidays, shifting the focus of the Revolution while erasing Otis and Adams, their essays and innovations, the ragtag, rough-and-tumble tactics. Much of that history was not memorable until three generations later, when—as one historian has put it—the rebellion was reinserted into the Revolution, sanitized and without Adams.

The result was an odd afterlife. His cousin's services and sacrifices and sufferings were beyond compare, John Adams reckoned in 1819, though "a systematic course has been pursued for thirty years to run him down." Only one hero seemed to matter. By 1823, if remembered at all, Samuel Adams was the "great man [who] cleared the way for Washington." We dust him off at unsettled times, as the vicious demagogue rather than the decorous man of ideas, the street brawler rather than the cheerful champion of self-restraint, an old-fashioned Puritan rather than our earliest politician. He was an aristocrat of that other kind, inexhaustibly clearheaded and single-minded. In 1876 Congress installed a statue of him. Boston afterward commissioned its twin, in bronze. It stands before Faneuil Hall. "A statesman, incorruptible and fearless," reads the epitaph, a line true in two of its three points, for Adams a fitting ratio.

The most revealing tribute came from Virginia. When in 1800 Thomas Jefferson resumed a correspondence with Adams, the two had not seen each other for years, since, as Jefferson had it, "the anxious days we then passed in struggling for the cause of mankind." The storm was over. They were, each congratulated the other, in port. "Your principles have been tested in the crucible of time and have come out pure,"

Jefferson assured his colleague, thirty-two years after Adams had ventured to suggest that we fight more ardently for our liberty than for all else. He felt more affection for Adams than for any other patriot.

At the end of the year, after the ugliest of elections, Jefferson defeated John Adams to become the third president of the United States. For the first time in American history one political party prepared to hand power to another. In his inaugural address Jefferson aimed at reconciliation. It was time to banish intolerance and come together "with one heart and one mind." America remained, he argued, "the world's best hope." Its government was the "only one where every man, at the call of the law, would fly to the standard of the law, and would meet invasions of the public order as his own personal concern." Differences of opinion should not be construed as differences of principle. No one would have guessed that Samuel Adams, the old Machiavelli of chaos, stood behind those honeyed notes, but there he was: though delivered to the people of the United States, Jefferson addressed his remarks directly to his venerable colleague. The new president had done his best, he confided, to channel him. Adams should read the address as a private letter. "Is this exactly in the spirit of the patriarch of liberty, Samuel Adams?" Jefferson had asked himself, again and again. "Is it as he would express it? Will he approve of it?" He reached for the essence of republicanism, toward a pure expression of the founding ideals. He hoped he might also solicit the counsel of the man he considered the earliest, most active, and most persevering of the Revolution.

Adams brushed off the compliments. Indeed they had survived a mighty storm. It would be some time before prejudice receded and men returned to their senses. He too looked forward to a restoration of harmony, to the triumphs of truth and virtue. As for Jefferson's request for guidance, he demurred. Old men deluded themselves when they dredged up lessons from a past they only dimly remembered. He could volunteer no advice. Samuel Adams offered his blessing.

ACKNOWLEDGMENTS

No one could respond more promptly or generously to an eighteenth-century emergency than John W. Tyler, who also supplied three essential volumes of the *Correspondence of Thomas Hutchinson* in typescript. Colin Nicolson provided an early glimpse of volume six of the *Papers of Francis Bernard* and fielded his own battery of pesky questions; I nearly feel I should apologize that my subject so roughly handled each of theirs. I owe an equally outsized debt to someone with whom I have longed to discuss these pages and never could: Catherine S. Menand devoted years to an Adams biography that she largely assembled but never published. I have benefitted greatly from her years in the archives. My thanks to Louis Menand and to Connie Margowsky for having shared their mother's research and manuscript pages; Megan Marshall kindly connected the dots among us. "Imperfection attends all human affairs," Samuel Adams conceded; it especially attends the writing of books. For essential clarifications and invaluable corrections, I am grateful to John L. Bell, Joseph J. Ellis, James Green, David D. Hall, Jack Rakove, Nathaniel Sheidley, Robert Shimp, Richard Snow, Richard S. Trask, and Michael Zuckerman.

For archival assistance and permission to quote from archival materials, I am delighted finally to have occasion to thank: Rakashi Chand, Anna Clutterbuck-Cook, Peter Drummey, Elaine Heavey, Nancy Heywood, and Dan Hinchen at the Massachusetts Historical Society; William P. Kelly, Melanie Locay, and Shannon Keller at the New York Public Library; Tal Nadan, Kyle Triplett, Cara Dellatte, and John Cordovez in the Brooke Russell Astor Reading Room for Rare Books and Manuscripts at the New York Public Library; D. Brenton Simons, Lindsay Fulton, Tim Salls, and Sally Benny at the New England Historic Genealogical Society; Karen Li Miller and Karlyn Marcantonio at the Connecticut Historical Society; Dan Boudreau and Kimberly Toney at the American Antiquarian Society; Ben Cunliffe at the Staffordshire Record Office, Staffordshire, England; Emma Sarconi, Special Collections, Princeton University Library; Philip Palmer at the Morgan Library;

Leah Rosovsky, John Buchtel, and Will Evans at the Boston Athenaeum; Olga Tsapina at the Huntington Library; Joe DiLullo at the American Philosophical Society; Cary Hutto at the Historical Society of Pennsylvania; Hannah Griffith at The National Archives (UK), Kew; Annie Pinder at the Parliamentary Archives search room; Terese M. Austin and Jayne Ptolemy at the William L. Clements Library, University of Michigan; Heather Oswald at the Baker Library Special Collections, Harvard Business School; Micah Hoggatt and the entire staff at the Houghton Library, Harvard University; David Leonard, Beth Prindle, and Sean Casey at the Boston Public Library; Carolyn Waters and her colleagues at the New York Society Library.

For research assistance, literary assistance, tech assistance, fact-checking, caffeine, and interventions of all kinds: Wendy Belzberg, Lis Bensley, Michael Borum, Janelle Brenner, Karen Crane, William Dalrymple, Alejandra Dechet, Benita Eisler, Anne Eisenberg, Constance C. Ellis, Ellen Feldman, Alicia Googins, Laurie Griffith, Jodi Kantor, Mitch Katz, Souad Kriska, Josephine de La Bruyère, Emily de La Bruyère, Max de La Bruyère, Sophie Louise McNulty, Patricia O'Toole, Stephen Reibel, Robin Rue, David A. Smith, Rebecca Sonkin, Mikayla Thompson, Andrea Versenyi, Olivia Weeks, Charles Chauncey Wells, and Strauss Zelnick. Elinor Lipman, friend and first reader nonpareil, improved on every one of these pages. Tom Puchniak chased down images; Sara Georgini, series editor of the Papers of John Adams, produced elusive documents; Tom Wright supplied Latin translations; Erica E. Hirshler at the Museum of Fine Arts, Boston, brilliantly parsed Copley's Adams portrait; Jim Koch walked me through bar calls. Were it not for Nick Bunker's indispensable guide to the British archives I would still be searching for a sandwich in Richmond upon Thames. For additional help with images: Valerie Paley at the New-York Historical Society; Hannah Elder at the Massachusetts Historical Society; Deirdre Donoghue, Margaret Glover, and Jessica Cline at the New York Public Library; Marta Crilly at the Boston City Archives; and Brianne Barrett at the American Antiquarian Society.

Eric Simonoff is a prince among agents and an especially patient one. It is a privilege to work again with the matchless team at Little, Brown, especially with Michael Pietsch and Bruce Nichols, who read indulgently and edited mercilessly. My thanks to Terry Adams, Bryan Christian, Mike Fleming, Liz Garriga, Lauren Hesse, Anna de la Rosa, Craig Nelson, Michael Noon, and the absurdly talented, wonder-working Mario Pulice. Authorial acknowledgments fall into two categories: gratitude to those who were unfailingly present, and gratitude to those who excused the author's absence, often for years on end. For the all-occasion, renewable get-out-of-life card, as for so much else, I am indebted to the remarkable Marc de La Bruyère.

ENDNOTES

Adams stood at, behind, or in the vicinity of several of the most written-about days in American history. So as not to bury him or the reader bibliographically, letters archived at Founders Online appear with dates alone, Boston Town Records by volume. Principal players other than James or Joseph Warren are reduced to their initials. For clarity's sake I have slightly modernized punctuation and, occasionally, spelling. Volumes that I have pulled regularly from the shelf appear in the selected bibliography; they are cited below by author's name and abbreviated title. Archives and principal primary sources are abbreviated as follows:

BL   British Library
Clements   William L. Clements Library, Michigan
CHS   Connecticut Historical Society
Houghton   Houghton Library, Harvard University
Kew   National Archives (UK)
MHS   Massachusetts Historical Society
NEHGS   New England Historical Genealogical Society
NYPL   New York Public Library
PARL   Parliamentary Archives (UK)

JA   John Adams, *The Adams Papers,* Massachusetts Historical Society
Andrews   "Letters of John Andrews," *Proceedings of the Massachusetts Historical Society,* July 1866, 314–412.
BEP   *Boston Evening Post*
BG   *Boston Gazette*
BTR   Boston Town Records, 1729–1777 (Boston: Rockwell and Churchill, 1887), vols. 12–18.
CTH   John W. Tyler, ed., *The Correspondence of Thomas Hutchinson* (Boston: Colonial Society of Massachusetts, 2014–2021), 3 vols., vols. 4 and 5 in typescript.
Force   Peter Force, ed., *American Archives*
TH HIST   Thomas Hutchinson, *The History of the Province of Massachusetts Bay* (London: John Murray, 1828).

HH   Neil Longley York, ed., *Henry Hulton and the American Revolution* (Boston: Colonial Society of Massachusetts, 2010).

JHR   *Journals of the House of Representatives of Massachusetts* (Boston: Massachusetts Historical Society, 1919–1990), 65 vols.

J of O Armand Francis Lucier, ed., *Journal of Occurrences: Patriot Propaganda on the British Occupation of Boston* (Westminster, MD: Heritage Books, 2009).

PFB   Colin Nicolson, ed., *The Papers of Francis Bernard: Governor of Colonial Massachusetts, 1760–1769* (Boston: Colonial Society of Massachusetts, 2007–2015), 5 vols., vol. 6 in page proofs.

PO   Douglas Adair and John A. Schutz., eds., *Peter Oliver's Origin and Progress of the American Rebellion* (Stanford: Stanford University Press, 1967).

Rowe Anne Rowe Cunningham, ed. *Letters and Diary of John Rowe* (Boston: W. B. Clarke, 1903).

Sibley *Sibley's Harvard Graduates, 1642–1774* (Boston: Massachusetts Historical Society, 1933), vols. 12–18.

WAL *Warren-Adams Letters* (Boston: Massachusetts Historical Society, 1917), 2 vols.

Wells William V. Wells, ed., *The Life and Public Services of Samuel Adams* (Boston: Little, Brown, 1865), 3 vols.

WSA Harry Alonzo Cushing, ed., *The Writings of Samuel Adams* (New York: Putnam's, 1907), 4 vols.

CHAPTER I: TRULY THE MAN OF THE REVOLUTION

1 "Omissions": Marianne Moore, *The Complete Poems* (New York: Viking Press, 1968), vii.

1 "truly the man": Henry Randall, *The Life of Thomas Jefferson* (New York: Derby & Jackson, 1858), I:182.

1 the pipe-smoking farmers: The description is JA's, in retrospect, of a Shrewsbury visit, JA to Benjamin Rush, 21 May 1807.

1 "Shallow men": Samuel Adams Wells, Bancroft Collection, vol. 384, NYPL.

2 an original: JA to William Tudor, 5 June 1817.

2 "the cool voice": SA to AL, 14 February 1775, WSA III:180.

2 "all the smoke": PO, 9.

2 "He eats little": Joseph Galloway, *Historical and Political Reflections on the Rise and Progress of the American Revolution* (London: G. Wilkie, 1780), 67.

2 "Our friends are": SA to James Warren, 20 November 1780, WSA IV:221. Similarly, SA to John Winthrop, 21 December 1778, WSA IV:103.

2 "Happy is he": SA to Thomas Paine, 30 November 1802, WSA IV:413.

2 "Rulers should have": William Bentley, *The Diary of William Bentley* (Salem: Essex Institute, 1911), III:49.

2 "the odious hereditary": SA to EG, 19 April 1784, WSA IV:298.

3 "pomp and retinue": James Warren to JA, 7 June 1778, WAL II:20. The 11 March 1778 *Pennsylvania Ledger* has JH traveling "with all the pageantry and state of an

Oriental prince," attended by four superbly liveried servants on caparisoned horses and escorted by fifty horsemen with drawn sabers, half ahead of and half behind his carriage. See also Frank Moore, *Diary of the American Revolution*, II. Elsewhere it was "with the pomp and retinue of an Eastern prince."

3   "I glory in being": SA to EA, 24 November 1780, WSA IV:226.

3   greatest incendiary: TH to John Pownell, August 1771, version 1, CTH IV.

3   "A man wrapped up": the Marquis de Chastellux, *Travels in North America in the Years 1780, 1781, and 1782*, ed. Howard C. Rice Jr. (Chapel Hill: University of North Carolina Press, 1963), I:142. Chastellux continued: SA "never spoke but to give me a good opinion of his cause and a high idea of his country."

3   the Hutchinson interview: TH, *Diary and Letters*, I:157–80.

4   "the earliest, most active": TJ, cited in "Letter from Benjamin Waterhouse, 15 January 1819," J. Jefferson Looney, ed., *The Papers of Thomas Jefferson: Retirement Series*, XIII (Princeton: Princeton University Press, 2016), 578.

4   "Very few have fortitude": SA to AL, 2 January 1777, WSA III:339.

4   "The character of your": Josiah Quincy Jr. to Mrs. Quincy, 7 December 1774, *Memoir of the Life of Josiah Quincy, Jr. of Massachusetts Bay* (HardPress, 2019), 218.

4   "Without the character": JA to Tudor, 5 June 1817. On SA slipping out of the pantheon, then slipping some more: Bruce C. Daniels, "Samuel Adams's Bumpy Ride: Recent View of the American Revolution in Massachusetts," in *The Fragmentation of New England* (Westport: Greenwood Press, 1988), 45–67; Charles W. Akers, "Sam Adams—and Much More," *NEQ*, March 1974, 120–31; Pauline Maier, "Coming to Terms with Samuel Adams," *American Historical Review*, February 1976, 12–37; James M. O'Toole, "The Historical Interpretations of Samuel Adams," *NEQ*, March 1976, 82–96; *Boston Patriot & Daily Chronicle*, 29 July 1826.

4   "thoughts which breathe": Thomas Thacher, "A Tribute of Respect to the Memory of Samuel Adams" (Dedham: H. Mann, 1804), 14.

4   "Whatever becomes": JA to Tudor, 5 June 1817.

5   "I would mention": Life of Samuel Adams by Samuel Adams Wells, Bancroft Collection, vol. 384, 139, NYPL. Per Sibley, on John Avery: "Unquestionably someone removed from the manuscripts of Sam Adams the papers which showed the aggressive, opportunistic, irresponsible, and unprincipled conduct of the aggressive Whigs." If true, the sanitizing was incomplete. For more on the mutilated record: Wells I:ix–xi; Wells II:503; Maier, *The Old Revolutionaries*, 12; Samuel Adams Wells to TJ, 14 April 1819; JA to William Tudor, 5 June 1817.

5   "There ought to be": Conversation with Joseph J. Ellis, 10 December 2021.

6   "All good Americans": George Clymer to Josiah Quincy Jr., 29 July 1773, Quincy, *Memoir*, 119.

6   "pilloried in a manner" to "popular applause": Samuel Adams Wells, as "Historicus," *Boston Patriot & Daily Chronicle*, 8, 15, and 19 December 1818; *Boston Commercial Gazette*, 7 December 1818. In response, "Tempus," *Boston Patriot & Daily Chronicle*, 11 December 1818; "Philo Tempus," *Boston Patriot & Daily Chronicle*, 16 December 1818; "Tempus," 29 December 1818. Trumbull defended himself from

the critics, *New York Daily Advertiser*, 22 October 1818; "Detector" in the *National Advocate*, 20 October 1818. Benjamin Waterhouse reported in detail on the brouhaha, Waterhouse to TJ, 15 January 1819. Waterhouse was himself Tempus or Philo Tempus per Philip Cash, *Dr. Benjamin Waterhouse: A Life in Medicine and Public Service*. Also excellent on the imagery: Tanya Pohrt, "Reception and Meaning in John Trumbull's 'Declaration of Independence,'" *Yale University Art Gallery Bulletin*, 2013, 116–19; Helen A. Cooper, *Life, Liberty, and the Pursuit of Happiness* (New Haven: Yale University Press, 2008). JA too complained: "Where was Samuel Adams? Carefully stowed away into the most obscure corner of the gallery, scarcely visible to human sight." He could barely find him or JH, JA to Tudor, 24 June 1817. SA as "AB," Annotated papers of Dorr, *BG*, 17 May 1766, MHS. As SA's grandson wrote to TJ: Trumbull's canvas was likely to "have a tendency to obscure the history of the event which it is designed to commemorate."

7   Garry Wills, *Inventing America* (New York: Doubleday, 1978), 19.

7   "Probably no American": Morgan and Morgan, *Stamp Act Crisis*, 306.

7   "No one took": Gordon Wood, *Radicalism of the American Revolution* (New York: Vintage, 1993), 205.

7   "the premier leader": Murray Rothbard, "Modern Historians Confront the American Revolution," libertarianism.org, accessed January 2022. David Freeman Hawke credited SA with having done more than anyone to launch the American crusade; Vernon Louis Parrington deemed SA "the first of our great popular leaders"; Alfred Young dubbed him "the most thoroughgoing democrat of his generation."

7   "as astute a politician": Esther Forbes, *Paul Revere's Ride* (New York: Houghton Mifflin, 1999), 86. In the original the line reads: "As astute a politician as even America has ever produced," which I am assuming to be wide of Forbes's intent.

7   "the whole continent": TH to Unknown, 4 September 1774, Library of Congress, cited in Schlesinger, *Prelude*, 204.

7   too much credit: In various accounts he is responsible for the Stamp Act riots, the Tea Party, the Coercive Acts, *Common Sense*—and for luring Gage to Boston, where SA seems personally to have authorized every broken window. See also Bernhard Knollenberg, "Did Samuel Adams Provoke the Boston Tea Party and the Clash at Lexington?" *Proceedings of the American Antiquarian Society*, October 1960, 493–503. James P. Munroe held that there would have been no Revolution without SA, *Proceedings of the Lexington Historical Society*, 1910, 94.

7   "Is this exactly": TJ to SA, 29 March 1801.

7   "finessed out of": AL memoir, in *Life of Arthur Lee*, Richard Henry Lee., ed. (Boston: Wells and Lilly, 1829), I:244.

8   campaign of civil resistance: Alfred F. Young, *The Shoemaker and the Tea Party* (Boston: Beacon Press, 1999), x.

8   "Neither religion": SA to Paine, 30 November 1803, WSA IV:413.

8   "the best cause": SA to EA, 29 November 1776, WSA III:320.

8   the author of the Revolution: RHL to SA, 6 June 1779, SA Papers, NYPL.

8   "Scripture is brought in": HH to Unknown, 5 February 1770, HH, 229.

CHAPTER II: A VOICE IN THE DARKNESS, A KNOCK AT THE DOOR

For the night of 18 April 1775: Edmund Morgan, ed., *Paul Revere's Three Accounts of His Famous Ride* (Boston: MHS, 1968); Fischer's classic *Paul Revere's Ride*; Jonas Clarke *A Brief Narrative of the Principal Transactions of that Day* (Boston: James R. Osgood, 1875); "Journal of My Tour to the Camp," Jeremy Belknap, *Proceedings of the MHS*, 1858, 77–87; Force II:428; Andrews, 404; Mackenzie diary, in Vincent J-R Kehoe, *We Were There!: April 19th, 1775* (1975); "Gage's Answers to Chalmer's Queries," *Collections of the MHS*, 4th series, IV; Paul Revere's Depositions, Letter of PR to Jeremy Belknap, c. 1798, MHS; *London Gazette*, 10 June 1775; Pitcairn to Gage, 26 April 1775, Clements; Jonas Clarke Diary, P-072, MHS. Derek W. Beck is best on the tick-tock, "Dissecting the Timeline of Paul Revere's Ride," *Journal of the American Revolution*, 9 April 2014, and Beck, *Igniting the American Revolution* (Sourcebooks: Naperville, IL), 2016. On Gage, John Richard Alden, *General Gage in America* (New York: Greenwood, 1969) and John Alden, "Why the March to Concord?" *American Historical Review*, April 1944, 446–54. Henry W. Holland, "William Dawes and His Ride with Paul Revere" (Boston: John Wilson, 1878); William Gordon, *The North American's Almanack*, 1776; Clement C. Sawtell, ed., *The Nineteenth of April, 1775: A Collection of First Hand Accounts* (Lincoln, MA: Sawtells, 1968); Jeremy Belknap, "Journal of My Tour to the Camp," *Proceedings of the MHS*, 1858, 77–86; Harold Murdock, ed., *Late News of the Excursion and Ravages of the King's Troops on the 19th of April, 1775* (Cambridge: Harvard University Press, 1927).

9 "Everything in American affairs": TH, *Diary and Letters*, II:312.

10 For the wainscoting and the parsonage details: Samuel Adams Drake, *Old Landmarks and Historic Fields of Middlesex* (Boston: Roberts Brothers, 1888), 365–68; "Reminiscences by Gen. Wm. H. Sumner," *NEHGR*, 1854, VIII:187. PR and Joseph Warren both assumed the expedition was to arrest the two men. Jack Rakove, *Revolutionaries* (New York: Mariner, 2011) has PR heading off to warn them. So did the London papers: *Gazetteer and New Daily Advertiser*, 16 June 1775, which carried a letter from an officer in Percy's regiment; Robert Zeus Finkelstein, "Merchant, Revolutionary and Statesman: A Reappraisal of the Life and Public Services of John Hancock, 1737–1793," PhD dissertation, 1981, University of Massachusetts, 285–88. David Ammerman is especially good on Gage's calculations, *In the Common Cause: American Response to the Coercive Acts of 1774* (New York: Norton, 1974), 132–38. John Ferling thinks it was a two-objective sortie, *Almost A Miracle: The American Victory in the War of Independence* (New York: Oxford University Press, 2007), 29–30, as did E. S. Thomas, *Reminiscences of the Last 65 Years* (Hartford; Case, Tiffany, and Burnham, 1840), II:8. On Clarke: *A Brief Narrative of the Principal Transactions of That Day* (Boston: James R. Osgood, 1875). Richard P. Kollen, *The Patriot Parson of Lexington, Massachusetts: Reverend Jonas Clarke and the American Revolution* (Charleston, SC: History Press, 2016); William B. Sprague, *Annals of the American Pulpit* (New York: Carter & Bros.), 1859, 514–19. SA to Richard Henry Lee, 21 March 1775, WSA III:205–09.

11 "void of a spark": SA to AL, 4 March 1775, WSA III:195.

11 "is to foresee": SA to James Warren, 2 July 1775, MHS.

11 "that truly worthy": BG, 27 March 1775. The printer anticipated robust sales. For the panegyrics, *Royal American Magazine*, March 1775. Intercepted letters, 16 March 1775, CO 5/39, Kew.

11 "I doubt whether": TH to J. Pownall, early August 1771, version one, CTH IV.

11 "the black art": TH to FB, 10 May 1771, CTH IV.

12 "such arts as an oyster": PO, 96.

12 the anonymous letter: BEP, 19 September 1774.

12 "Tell Governor Gage": Samuel Adams Wells, vol. 382, 503, NYPL. There are hints in the Warren Papers, ms. N-1732, MHS, about various offers to buy off SA; mentions of the bribes and SA's inexorability surfaced later in eulogies to him; he wrote of bribes to the members of the Continental Congress to James Warren in July, 1778. John Kenneth Rowland, "General Thomas Gage, the 18th Century Literature of Military Intelligence, and the Transition from Peace to Revolutionary War," *Historical Reflections*, Fall 2006, 503–21, believes TG attempted to bribe SA soon after the Boston arrival.

12 "You are an incendiary": Rowe, 2 October 1768, 176. Joseph Warren had been jostled in the street and challenged by an officer. Church had been insulted around town and his house attacked, the windows broken in the night. Clarke says JH and SA had been frequently and publicly threatened, Jonas Clarke, "Fate of Bloodthirsty Oppressors and God's Tender Care of His Distressed People," Lexington sermon (Boston: Powars and Willis, 1776).

12 "to share the name": Samuel Adams of Truro to SA, 7 February 1775, American Philosophical Society.

13 in chains: *Virginia Gazette*, 19 May 1774. William Gordon, *The History of the Rise, Progress and Establishment of the Independence of the United States of America* (London: Charles Dilly, 1788), I:477.

13 as he saw it, forbidden: SA to James Warren, 28 December 1773, WAL I:20.

13 "I hear nothing": James Warren to SA, 1 January 1775, WAL II:407.

13 arrested en route to Congress: Joseph Hawley to JA, 25 July 1774.

13 "'endeavoring,' Adams wrote": SA to AL, 4 March 1775, WSA III:197.

14 "The people get": Gage to Dartmouth, 12 September 1774, CO 5/763, Kew.

14 "They had received notice": "Gage's Answers," *Collections of the MHS*, 1907, 372. FB had commented too on the uncanny flow of information.

14 the pewter-melter: Fischer, *Paul Revere's Ride*, 126.

15 "some evil design": Jonas Clarke, "The Fate of Bloodthirsty Oppressors," Lexington sermon, April 19, 1776. It seemed evident to all, wrote Clarke, that "under cover of darkness, sudden arrest, if not assassination might be attempted."

15 "and the whole people": *London Public Advertiser*, cited in *William Tudor, The Life of James Otis of Massachusetts* (Boston: Wells and Lilly, 1823), 184.

15 Gage's instructions: Dartmouth to Gage, 9 April 1774, *Correspondence of TG*, II:160.

15   "The first and essential": Dartmouth to Gage, 27 January 1775, in *Correspondence of TG*, II:181.

15   "by the hands": John Barker, 6 March 1775, *The British in Boston: The Diary of Lt. John Barker* (New York: Arno Press, 1969), 26. Similarly Alexander Leslie to the Earl of Leven, in Bunker, *Empire*, 297.

16   "I would wish": SA to Charles Thomson, 17 June 1774, in Arthur Bernon Tourtellot, *William Diamond's Drum* (New York: Doubleday, 1959), 207.

16   "that would be the last": Cited in *The Last Journals of Horace Walpole* (London: John Lane, 1910), I:459.

16   "a foppish pseudo-aristocrat": Harlow Giles Unger, *John Hancock: Merchant King and American Patriot* (New York: Wiley, 2000), 5. "I fear if you was to see my tailor's bill," wrote the twenty-three-year-old JH, "you would think I was not a very plain-dressing person." Similarly, Finkelstein, "Merchant, Revolutionary and Statesman," 87. Indeed JH's London 1760 tailor bill was greater than what Adams earned in five years. Very few of his contemporaries had a kind word to spare for JH. Nor would Sibley, on JH, 416–46.

17   "like the cuttlefish": PO, 40. PO spelled it "cuddlefish."

17   "Such a parcel": *BG*, 25 November 1771. A British major who led the 19 April expedition agreed: "I never was so plagued and distressed with such a set of profligate scoundrels in my life," he swore. He had no choice but to flog some of them each morning; he preferred to "live on bread and water than have the command of such people;" he cursed the ministry that had "sent such vagabonds." They were ill-disciplined, old, and puny. Pitcairn to MacKenzie, 16 February 1775, add. Ms. 39190, MacKenzie Papers, BL.

17   "mercenary, hackneyed": "Cosmopolitan Number IV to the Inhabitants of the American Colonies," *Massachusetts Spy*, 17 November 1775.

17   "I cannot yet believe": TH to TH Jr., 10 April 1775, in TH, *Diary and Letters*, I:428.

18   "One cannot foresee": SA to AL, 9 November 1773, WSA III:70.

18   "Are your letters": Benjamin Church to SA, 20 September 1774, NYPL.

18   "Noise! You'll have" to "afraid of him": William Monroe testimony, 7 March 1825, in Charles Hudson, *History of the Town of Lexington, MA* (Boston: Houghton, 1913), I:541.

19   "without bloodshed": Dartmouth to Gage, 27 January 1775, CO 5/765, Kew.

19   "God damn" to "brains out": Morgan, ed., *Paul Revere's Three Accounts*. In Elias Phinney, *History of the Battle at Lexington* (Boston: Phelps & Farnham, 1825), PR's bridle and saddle are cut to pieces.

21   "cleaning his gun": Mrs. Hancock to William H. Sumner, in "Reminiscences by Gen. Wm. H. Sumner," 187–88. *London Evening Post*, 22 April 1775; Ammerman, *In the Common Cause*, 137.

21   "That is not": "Reminiscences by Gen. Wm. H. Sumner," 187.

21   "The delight of the eyes," JA to Tudor, 1 June 1817.

21   burying the valuables: "Extracts from Letter of Miss Betty Clarke, Daughter of Rev. Jonas Clarke," *Proceedings of the Lexington Historical Society*, 1912, 91–93.

22 "to find" to "of musketry": Morgan, ed., *Paul Revere's Three Accounts.*

23 the breakfast: "Reminiscences by Gen. Wm. H. Sumner," 187–88. Abram English Brown, *Beneath Old Roof Trees* (Boston: Lee and Shepard, 1896), 56.

23 that bright spring day: SA to James Warren, 31 December 1776, WSA III:338.

23 "O! What a glorious": The line seems to have originated in William Gordon, *The History of the Rise, Progress, and Establishment of the Independence of the United States* (London: Charles Dilly, 1788), I:479. "The Revolutionary Journal of James Stevens of Andover," *Essex Institute Historical Collections*, 1912, 41–70.

23 "this important glorious crisis": SA to James Warren, 10 June 1775, WAL I:54.

24 "a thousand uncertain": Samuel Savage to John Scollay, 19 April 1775, Savage Papers, ms. N-885, box II, MHS. The countryside in motion: Hannah Winthrop to Mercy Otis Warren, May 1775, MHS website. Mercy Otis Warren has the two on the point of capture, *History of the Rise*, I:214; Force II:428; *Pennsylvania Ledger*, 1 May 1775, 6 May 1775; *New York Gazette*, 1 May 1775; *London Evening Chronicle*, 13 June 1775; Andrews, 403–05; Stiles, *The Literary Diary of Ezra Stiles* (New York: Scribner's, 1901), I:549; James Jeffry, "Journal Kept in Quebec in 1775, *Essex Institute Historical Collections*, 1914, 98–150.

24 appeared a deserter: JH to Committee on Safety, 24 April 1775, Force II:384.

CHAPTER III: THE GREAT TOWN OF BOSTON

25 "Security and leisure": Samuel Johnson, *Taxation no Tyranny: An Answer to the Resolutions and Address of the American Congress* (New Haven: Yale University Press), 451.

25 born a revolutionary: Despite an addiction to accuracy, JA was a continual backdater. In 1818 he and TJ attempted to work out between them when the Revolution began. JA proposed the arrival in America, JA to TJ, 29 May 1818.

25 the malt-making: The details derive largely from the work of Catherine S. Menand.

26 on the education: Kenneth Murdock, "The Teaching of Latin and Greek at the Boston Latin School in 1712," *Publications of the Colonial Society of Massachusetts*, 1930, 21–25; Robert Francis Seybolt, *The Public Schools of Colonial Boston* (Cambridge: Harvard University Press, 1935). There is some indication that SA Sr. had prepared for Harvard, then found himself unable to matriculate given family finances. Samuel Eliot Morison, *Three Centuries of Harvard* (Cambridge: Harvard University Press, 1936); Robert Brand Hanson, ed., *The Diary of Dr. Nathaniel Ames of Dedham, Massachusetts* (Camden, ME: Picton Press, 1998); *Boston Post-Boy*, 1 September 1740. Timothy Pickering on HC, Pickering Papers, MHS; Benjamin Pierce, *A History of Harvard University from its foundation in the year 1636 to the Period of the American Revolution* (Cambridge: Brown, Shattuck, 1883); Yuhtaro Ohmori, "The Artillery of Mr. Locke: The Use of Locke's 'Second Treatise' in Pre-Revolutionary America," PhD dissertation, Johns Hopkins, 1988.

27 the New England hierarchy: Nash, *Urban Crucible*, xiii; Gordon Wood, *The Creation of the American Republic* (Chapel Hill: University of North Carolina Press,

1998), 73–74; J. R. Pole, "Historians and the Problem of Early American Democracy," *American Historical Review*, 1962, 626–46. Adams would have ranked second had Harvard's president not manipulated the list. As no son of a governor or Council member matriculated that August, sons of two justices of the peace, neither in possession of a college education, would have headed the class. To preclude that indignity, President Wadsworth reversed the order; four prominent clergymen's sons preceded the justices' sons.

27   Franklin's rant: *New England Courant*, 14 May 1722. BF was sixteen.

28   it would be said: François Jean Chastellux, marquis de 1734–1788, *Voyage de M. le Chevalier de Chastellux en Amérique* (Cassel: 1785), 52. The translation is mine.

28   "contemptuous hallowing": Sibley, on Joseph Adams, 233.

28   oversleeping: The offense, from family recollections, left no trace in the Harvard records. An Adams was punished for drinking rum in March 1740, but there were two men named Adams on campus that year, Harvard University, Early Faculty Minutes 1725–1752, vol. 12, box 8. The claim that SA waited tables as a senior because of losses at home is likely false; that waiter was more likely Joseph Adams, '42, Early Faculty Minutes, UAIII 5.5, vol. 12, box 8, Harvard University Archives.

28   "It is my fate": SA to James Warren, 2 July 1775, MHS.

28   the mountain lion: *Boston News-Letter*, 15 December 1726.

29   "a happy young man": Cited in Wells I:4.

29   "He read theology": Davidson, *Propaganda*, 3.

30   more relaxed form of Puritanism: Wood, *Creation of the American Republic*, 418; Edmund S. Morgan, "The Puritan Ethic and the American Revolution," *WMQ*, January 1967, 3–43.

30   "It is your God-damned": Peter Edes, *A Diary of Peter Edes, the Oldest Printer in the United States* (Bangor: Smith, 1837), 1 July 1775.

30   "where every man": Gage to Hillsborough, 31 October 1768, Gage Papers, Clements. On New England and the law: Henry Hulton to Unknown, 5 February 1770, HH, 230; by 1788 a French visitor noted that it was "unhappily, one of the most lucrative" professions in Massachusetts, J.-P. Brissot de Warville, *New Travels in the United States of America* (London: 1794), 345. The call for honest lawyers, Randolph to Povey, 24 January 1687, in Thomas Hutchinson, *A Collection of Original Papers Relative to the History of the Massachusetts Bay* (Boston: Fleet, 1769), 557.

30   "not consonant": Samuel Adams Wells, *Life of Samuel Adams*, Bancroft Collection, vol. 384, NYPL.

31   "his whole soul": Cited in Wells I:12. Menand speculates that SA Sr. made the gift to shield the funds from Land Bank liabilities. The sum was colossal; TH had started out with only 500 pounds.

32   thesis subjects: Minor Myers Jr., "A Source for 18th Century Harvard Master's Questions, *WMQ*, April 1981, 261–67, is invaluable, as is Edward J. Young, et al., "Subjects for Master's Degree, 1655–1791," *Proceedings of the MHS*, 1881, 118–78. It would be thirteen years before another candidate explored whether resistance to a king could be justified.

33 "propensity to" to "to the law": *Independent Advertiser*, 11 January 1748. I am following Menand's lead in reading this as SA's thesis recycled.

34 "By fretting": SA to Lovell, 10 November 1783, NYPL.

34 "always great in proportion": SA to AL, 31 July 1771, WSA II:191.

34 "The censure": SA to EA, 13 December 1778, WSA IV:97.

34 peevish humors: SA to James Warren, 1 February 1777, WAL I:287.

34 "thinking aloud": SA to EA, 1 February 1781, WSA IV:244.

34 "You therein speak": SA to James Warren, 1 February 1777, WAL I:287.

34 "The cottager": SA to JA, 25 November 1780, WSA IV:351. The scoundrel,
Wells III:201.

34 "I am *in* fashion": Hannah Wells, cited in Wells I:217.

35 "What is life": SA to James Warren, 13 April 1772, WAL I:11.

35 "designed to complete": SA to Thomas Wells, 22 November 1780, WSA IV:224.
He had all the more reason to champion parity: The groom was engaged, as SA
phrased it, to "the dear girl whom I pride myself in calling my daughter."

35 "as much of the stern": SA to James Warren, 4 November 1774, WSA III:238. Mercy
Otis Warren commended the "Roman-like firmness" in *History of the Rise*, I:211.

35 For his looks: "Philo Tempus," *Boston Patriot & Daily Chronicle*, 16 December 1818.

36 "vast insinuation": Edward H. Tatum Jr., ed., *The American Journal of Ambrose
Serle* (San Marino: Huntington Library, 1940), 180. PO sniffed that Adams's
"power over weak minds was truly surprising."

36 on the New England accent: *The Journal of Nicholas Cresswell* (New York: Dial,
1928), 271; "Remembering Peter Faneuil: Yankees, Huguenots, and Ethnicity in
Boston, 1743–1900," Jonathan M. Beagle, *NEQ*, September 2002, 388–414; Dwight,
Travels in New England, 367–68. Richard W. Bailey, *Speaking American: A History of
English in the United States* (New York: Oxford University Press, 2012), 27–47;
Anders Orbeck, *Early New England Pronunciation* (Ann Arbor: Wahr, 1927).

36 "singing societies": PO, 41.

36 "speak better English": *The Journal of Nicholas Cresswell*, 271.

37 "Tell me what": TH to Leitch, 2 August 1773, TH letterbooks, vol. 25, box 5, ms.
N-1461, MHS.

37 pale and graceful Boston: Nathaniel B. Shurtleff, *A Topographical and Historical
Description of Boston* (Boston: City Council, 1871), 68. Also on Boston: Russell Bourne,
Cradle of Violence (New York: John Wiley, 2006), 153–54; Annie Haven Thwing,
Crooked and Narrow Streets of the Town of Boston (Norwood, MA: Marshall Jones, 1920);
"The Common British Soldier: From the Journal of Thomas Sullivan," S. Sydney
Bradford, ed., *Maryland Historical Magazine*, September 1767, 239–42; Abbé Robin,
New Travels Through North America (Philadelphia: R. Bell, 1783); G. D. Scull, ed., *Jour-
nal of John Montresor* (New York: Collections of the NY Historical Society, 1881);
Thomas Pemberton, "A Topographical and Historical Description of Boston, 1794,"
Collections of the MHS, 1794, 241–304; Jacqueline Barbara Carr, *After the Siege: A Social
History of Boston* (Boston: Northeastern University Press, 2005; Rev. Andrew Burn-
aby; *Travels through the Middle Settlements in North America in the Years 1759 and 1760*

(Ithaca: Cornell University Press, 1960); G. D. Scull, ed., *Memoir and Letters of Captain W. Glanville Evelyn of the Fourth Regiment* (Oxford: James Parker and Co., 1879); G. B. Warden, *Boston 1689–1776* (Boston: Little, Brown, 1970); Carl Bridenbaugh, *Cities in Revolt* (New York: Knopf, 1955); Charles H. Sherrill, *French Memories of Eighteenth-Century America* (New York: Scribner's, 1915); Mark Peterson, *The City-State of Boston* (Princeton: Princeton University Press, 2019). Justin Winsor, *The Memorial History of Boston* (Boston: Ticknor and Co., 1881), vols. II and III; Timothy Dwight, *Travels in New-England and New-York* (London: Baynes & Son, 1823), I:367–68. Philip Padelford, ed., *Colonial Panorama, 1775: Dr. Robert Honyman's Journal* (San Marino: Huntington Library, 1939); "Narrative of the Prince de Broglie," part IV, *The Magazine of American History*, 1877, 374–80; Baron Cromot du Bourg, "Journal de mon séjour en Amérique," *The Magazine of American History*, 1881, 205–14. Here especially I am grateful for the notes and unpublished manuscript of Catherine S. Menand.

37 "This is the most": Hugh Earl Percy to Henry Reveley, 8 August 1774, in Charles Knowles Bolton, ed., *Letters of Hugh Earl Percy from Boston and New York* (Boston: Charles E. Goodspeed, 1902), 30.

39 "Knowledge is probably": Dwight, *Travels in New-England*, I:465.

39 "Luxury and extravagance": SA to Samuel Savage, 6 October 1778, WSA IV:67.

39 "In short we are arrived": James Warren to SA, 30 March 1779, WAL II:97.

40 "A wretched condition": Robert Treat Paine to Elizabeth Freeman, 11 September 1758, in Stephen T. Riley and Edward W. Hanson, eds., *The Papers of Robert Treat Paine* (Boston: MHS, 1992), II:111.

40 on the faltering economy: G. B. Warden, "The Caucus and Democracy in Colonial Boston," *NEQ*, March 1970, 19–42; Belcher Papers, *Collections of the MHS*, 1893 and 1894, vols. VI and VII; Nash, *Urban Crucible*. T. H. Breen, *The Marketplace of Revolution: How Consumer Politics Shaped American Independence* (New York: Oxford University Press, 2004).

40 the Land Bank: Theodore Thayer, "The Land-Bank System in the American Colonies," *The Journal of Economic History*, Spring 1953, 145–59; Andrew H. Ward, "Notes on Ante-Revolutionary Currency and Politics," *NEHGR*, 1860, 261–63; Andrew McFarland Davis, "Legislation and Litigation Connected with the Land Bank of 1740, *Proceedings of the American Antiquarian Society*, April 1896, 86–123; Davis, "The General Court and Quarrels between Individuals Arising from the Land Bank," *Proceedings of the American Antiquarian Society*, April 1897, 351–68; Conrad Edick Wright and Kathryn P. Viens, eds., *Entrepreneurs: The Boston Business Community, 1700–1850* (Boston: MHS, 1997); *An Account of the Rise, Progress and Consequences of the Two Late Schemes, Commonly call'd the Land Bank or Manufactory Scheme and the Silver Scheme* (Prince Society, 1744), 238–349. TH HIST, I:392–402; Malcom Freiburg, "Thomas Hutchinson and the Province Currency," *NEQ*, June 1957, 190–208. George A. Billias, "The Massachusetts Land Bankers of 1740," *University of Maine Studies*, 74, 1959. Catherine S. Menand, "Shadow of Revolution: Massachusetts Politics and the Land Bank of 1740," and "The Massachusetts Land Bank of 1740 Revisited," private papers; I have benefited hugely from Menand's

notes and unpublished pages. "Belcher Papers," in *Collections of the MHS*, 1893 and 1894, vols. 6–7; BTR XII:119–23; *New-England Weekly Journal*, 16 September 1740; Articles of the Land Bank, Suffolk Deeds, vol. 60, fol. 21. In his diary JA dated SA's commitment to the cause of his country to 1741, 9 February 1772, *Diary of JA*, II:55.

41 "seemed to study": Belcher to Richard Waldron, 15 May 1740, Belcher Papers, VII:298.

42 "total subversion": Belcher to Lords of the Admiralty, 27 January 1741, ibid., 369.

43 "speedily and effectually" to "old shoes": Belcher to TH, 11 May 1741, CTH I:95.

44 "consternation and distress" to "suffer much by it": Shirley to Newcastle, 15 September 1742, in Charles Henry Lincoln, ed., *Correspondence of William Shirley* (New York: Macmillan, 1912), I:89–92.

45 "represented as a rude": Cited by Catherine S. Menand, from the 1747 *Independent Advertiser*.

45 "of low condition" to "principal merchants": TH HIST II:299–300.

46 "a peccadillo": TH to FB, 17 October 1769, CTH II:359. For the bank as a metric of discontent: AO to FB, 21 November 1769, Egerton ms. 2670, letterbook of AO, BL; TH to TH Jr., 29 May 1766, CTH I:434. Though happy to weigh in, JA had been five years old at the time.

46 "Let the people keep": SA to JA, 4 November 1783, WSA IV:288.

CHAPTER IV: THE VERY HONEST SAMUEL ADAMS, CLERK

47 "The blessed work": George Eliot, *Janet's Repentance: Scenes of Clerical Life* (New York: Munro, 1883), 55.

47 market clerk: Thomas Cushing Jr., John Singleton Copley, Benjamin Edes, and Oxenbridge Thacher all served as clerks of the market. On clerkships, Pemberton, "Description of Boston," 253–54; John L. Bell was supremely helpful with details of the post.

47 "a man who is not": Dwight, *Travels in New-England*, I:466.

48 on the Governor's Council: Francis G. Walett, "The Massachusetts Council, 1766–1774: The Transformation of a Conservative Institution," *WMQ*, October 1949, 605–27.

48 Knowles Riot: John Lax and William Pencak, "The Knowles Riot and the Crisis of the 1740s in Massachusetts" in *Contested Commonwealths* (Lehigh University Press, 2011), 3–52; Pauline Maier, "Popular Uprisings and Civil Authority in Eighteenth-Century America, *WMQ*, January 1970, 9; Hoerder, *Crowd Action*, 62.

49 "occasion of the late" to "upon the press": "Amicus Patria," "Address to the Inhabitants of the Province of the Massachusetts-Bay in New-England" (Boston: Rogers & Fowle, 1747).

49 "pompous promises" to "rouse them to pursue it": *Independent Advertiser*, 4 January 1748. The "haughty commander," *Independent Advertiser*, 8 February 1748.

50 "There is" to "promote its virtue": *Independent Advertiser*, 8 August 1748.

51 the honest, unlettered shoemaker: *Independent Advertiser*, 26 December 1748, 31 July and 11 September 1749.

51 The people owed: *Independent Advertiser*, 25 July 1748.

51 "a most lovely" to "upon their liberties": *Independent Advertiser*, 14 March 1748.

52 "the middle industrious": *Independent Advertiser*, 26 December 1748.

52 For Joseph Adams: Sibley, on Joseph Adams, 233–34.

53 The Checkleys: I am grateful to Tim Salls of the NEHGS for pages from the New South Church Record Book. "As sincere a friend": Adams Family Bible, NYPL. Betsy may have had some experience with disorderly accounts; though an accomplished preacher, her brother "neglected the keeping of church records to an almost criminal extent." Sibley, on Checkley Jr., 190. Penuel Bowen, *A Discourse Occasioned by the Death of Rev. Samuel Checkley* (Boston: Edes & Gill, 1770).

53 "There is hardly": *Independent Advertiser*, 5 December 1749.

54 "If they had" to "right to expect it," and the appearance before the LB committee: *BG*, 23 February 1756, 1 March 1756; TH to FB, 23 October 1769, CTH II:370. On the Town House: My thanks to Nathaniel Sheidley of Revolutionary Spaces for clarifications. SA Sr. too had squared off against sheriffs; the bravado seems inherited. On the defects of the LB resolution, Andrew McFarland Davis, "Legislation and Litigation Connected with the Land Bank of 1740," *American Antiquarian Society*, April 1896, and Davis, "The General Court and Quarrels Between Individuals Arising from the Land Bank," *Proceedings of the American Antiquarian Society*, April 1897.

56 selling off the estate: *BEP*, 28 February 1743.

56 tax-collecting: The revenue-producing is from Sibley, on AO, 456. Best on tax-collecting: Catherine S. Menand, "The Things That Were Caesar's: Tax-Collecting in 18th Century Boston," *Massachusetts Historical Review*, 1999, 49–77. Menand unpublished ms., 10:5–6; Merrill Jensen, *The Founding of a Nation* (Indianapolis: Hackett, 2004), 405. As for the salary, FB complained in 1766 that he could not live in one of the capital cities of America on a mere 1075 pounds a year. For the "natural aversion": Samuel Adams Wells, vol. 384, NYPL.

57 "Collecting taxes": JA, 1 March 1766, *Diary of JA*, I:301. The wealthy moaned that their assessments were absurd; they paid multiple times the tax they would have under any other government in any other town. Selectmen's Minutes, 1767, 20: 261. SA claimed it was impossible to so much as supply a list of his 1767 outstanding debts.

58 death of Elizabeth: There is no burial record of the first EA, presumably laid to rest in the Checkley family tomb at the Granary Cemetery.

58 "She ran" to "her graces": Adams Family Bible, NYPL. SA remained close to the family.

58 the call-and-response: *BEP*, 9 March 1752, 16 March 1752, 23 February 1756, 17 August 1758.

58 "any gentleman who": *BEP*, 16 March 1752; *Boston News-Letter*, 24 August 1758; *BG*, 27 October 1755. Greenleaf had himself amassed something of an estate; in the 1740s he designed a family crest. Sibley, on Greenleaf, 182–90.

60 SA's collecting: Jeffries Account Book, MHS, indicates that—at least through the first half of 1763—SA collected sums regularly. On the suits, Suffolk Court of Common Pleas. Also on SA's difficulties, Abner C. Goodell Jr., "The Charges Against Samuel Adams," *Proceedings of the MHS*, 1883, 213–26. I benefited from Menand's notes on SA's vexed career as a collector.

60 the distiller: *Boston News-Letter*, 27 July 1758. Wells had had thousands of pounds at his disposal in the 1740s, BTR XIV:283.

60 the fire and its aftermath: Pemberton, "Description of Boston," 270; John Boyle, *A Journal of Occurrences in Boston*, Houghton, I:20; *Boston Post-Boy*, 24 March 1760. William Pencak, "The Social Structure of Revolutionary Boston: Evidence from the Great Fire of 1760," *Journal of Interdisciplinary History*, Autumn 1979, 267–78. Sibley, on AO Jr., 457.

60 "it raged": SA petition to the town, 13 March 1769, WSA I:320; BTR XII:123.

61 indulging delinquents: *BG*, 3 June 1765, 20 May 1765; *BEP*, 12 September 1763. Warden theorized that SA rode to office on the tax abatements. He was not himself an overeager settler of accounts; a tax-collecting cousin swore that he knew no more vexing assignment than the extracting of monies from SA.

61 private collection: Andrew H. Ward, "Subscribers to Mr. Adams's Debt," *NEHGR*, 1860, 261–63. For another round-up of SA's tax travails, Bernhard Knollenberg, *Growth of the American Republic* (Indianapolis: Liberty Fund, 2003), 302–6.

62 the town meeting: Rowe, 13 March 1769, 183; SA petition to the town, 13 March 1769, WSA I:319–22; BTR XVI:271–73; Selectmen's Minutes, 14 February 1770. Sibley, on Foster Hutchinson, 238.

62 "rebellious herd": John Mein, *Sagittarius's Letters and Political Speculations* (Boston, 1775), 109.

62 "the very honest": Cited in Wells II:139.

63 a snide borrowing: Annotated papers of Dorr, *BG*, 17 April 1767, MHS.

63 "forfeited the good": Henry Hulton, "Some Account of the Proceedings of the People of New England," André De Coppet Collection, AM 15460, 121–22, Princeton University Library.

63 "a man of superior": Mein accused SA of having burned the LB records; he caricatured SA as the author of "some curious anecdotes relating to the Land Bank scheme," *Boston Chronicle*, 26 October 1769. SA was an embezzler pure and simple to PO, 41.

CHAPTER V: NOTHING COULD HAVE GIVEN GREATER DISGUST

65 "No great thing": Rebecca West, *The Young Rebecca: Writings of Rebecca West, 1911–17* (New York: Viking Press, 1982), 11.

65 On the disorder: Maier, "Popular Uprisings," 3–35; Gordon S. Wood, "A Note on Mobs in the American Revolution," *WMQ*, October 1966, 635–42; R. S. Longley, "Mob Activities in Revolutionary Massachusetts," *NEQ*, March 1933, 98–130; Philip G. Davidson, "Sons of Liberty and Stamp Men," *North Carolina Historical Review*, January 1932, 38–56; Arthur M. Schlesinger, "Political Mobs and the

American Revolution," *Proceedings of the American Philosophical Society*, August 1955, 244–50; and, especially, Colin Nicolson, "McIntosh, Otis & Adams Are Our Demagogues: Nathaniel Coffin and the Loyalist Interpretation of the Origins of the American Revolution," *Proceedings of the MHS*, 1996, 72–114.

65 as one woman deemed it: Ann Hulton to Elizabeth Lightbody, 8 July 1774, HH, 304.

66 "the little tattle": JA to Niles, 13 February 1818. Or as the *BEP* put it, the clubs allowed the political dabbler to say and write "whatever his shallow understanding or vicious passions may suggest against the wisest and best men," 14 March 1763.

66 "miserable, despicable": JO to JO Sr., cited in John J. Waters Jr., *The Otis Family in Provincial and Revolutionary Massachusetts* (Chapel Hill: University of North Carolina Press, 1968), 112. On JO: James Ferguson, "Reason in Madness: The Political Thought of James Otis," *WMQ*, April 1979, 194–214; Ellen Brennan, "James Otis: Recreant and Patriot," *NEQ*, December 1939, 601–725; Frances Bowen, *Life of James Otis* (Boston: Little, Brown, 1864); JA to Niles, 13 February 1818. William Pencak points out that natural rights were summoned for the first time now, *America's Burke: The Mind of Thomas Hutchinson* (Washington, D.C.: University Press of America, 1982), 26. At some point in Adams's tax-collecting odyssey, the town treasurer hired JO to prosecute; it is unclear if the treasurer—whose political opinions aligned with SA's—meant to do him a favor, Sibley, on David Jeffries, 174.

65 the quiver: Elan D. Louis, "Samuel Adams's tremor," *Neurology*, 2001, 1201–05, Louis email to author, 7 March 2019.

66 the smuggling: John W. Tyler, *Smugglers and Patriots: Boston Merchants and the Advent of the American Revolution* (Boston: Northeastern University Press, 1986).

68 "than from any other man": JA, 9 February 1772, from what appears to be a draft essay, *Diary of JA*, II:55.

68 "unremitting" to "jealousy among friends": SA to AO Jr., 7 April 1763, ms. N-2212, MHS. It was more complicated yet: Oliver's father-in-law and Adams's wife had been first cousins.

68 "that he would do all": *Boston News-Letter*, 7 April 1763. JO's biographers have disputed the line: See Bowen, *Life of James Otis*, 46. JA believed JO had said, "Hutchinson's appointment will set the province in a flame." There was no need for FB to honor an earlier governor's promise regarding the position, but TH struck some as "notoriously partial," per JA to Jedidiah Morse, 29 November 1815. For the writs, JA to Niles, 14 January 1818.

68 "but barking at the moon": *BEP*, 28 March 1763.

68 "and as soon as he": TH to David Chesebrough, 9 March 1763, CTH I:172–73. The non-shrugging: TH to Bollan, 11 April 1763, CTH I:174.

69 first man on the continent: JA, 17 March 1766, *Diary of JA*, I:306.

69 "Summa Potestatis": JA to Niles, 13 February 1818.

70 half the women: *BG*, 31 January 1763. "His beauty has captivated half the pretty ladies, and his finesse more than half the pretty gentlemen in the province."

70   writing the *History*: TH to Richard Jackson, December 1764, CTH I:242; to Ezra Stiles, 15 January 1765, CTH I:254. The wardrobe is from TH's correspondence with his tailor, MHS, and the 1765 household inventory, CTH I:325.

70   genuinely believed: TH to Bollan, 31 December 1765, CTH I:375.

70   "I found no part": Cited in Liam Riordan, "A Loyalist Who Loved His Country Too Much: Thomas Hutchinson, Historian of Colonial Massachusetts," *NEQ*, September 2017, 348. Riordan is especially good on TH's *History*.

70   "foolish internal": TH to Bollan, 11 April 1763, CTH I:174.

70   "I have no talent": TH to Ezra Stiles, 15 January 1765, CTH I:254. TH felt it required delicacy; he preferred to let facts speak for themselves.

70   "I hate the unholy": TH to Bollan, 15 November 1762, CTH I:166.

70   FB's arrival: *BEP*, 4 August 1760; *BG*, 4 August 1760; FB to Barrington, 7 August 1760, PFB I:48. AO Sr. had ridden to Rhode Island to meet FB; a great number of Boston gentlemen escorted him into town on a sultry August afternoon. Mary Caroline Crawford, *St. Botolph's Town* (Boston: L.C. Page, 1908), 346–47.

71   "told a thousand good": HH, 139. On FB, Mrs. Napier Higgins, *The Bernards of Abington and Nether Winchendon: A Family History* (London: Longmans, 1963), 2 vols. FB was partial to Handel; there were concerts at home, where each family member played an instrument, Higgins, II:74.

71   "a quiet" to "that I know": FB to Board of Trade, 18 August 1760, CO 5/891, Kew.

71   The subpar math: Grenville to Walpole, 8 September 1763, *The Grenville Papers: Being the Correspondence of Richard Grenville and Earl Temple* (London: J. Murray, 1853), II:114. A Maryland Crown official, Daniel Dulany, estimated in 1765 that the North American colonies produced a total revenue of 700 or 800 pounds a year; the cost of installing officers to collect that revenue amounted to 7,600 pounds per year.

72   "Let us now avail": Thomas, *British Politics*, 53. Allen S. Johnson, "The Passage of the Sugar Act," *WMQ*, October 1959, 507–14.

72   "treating them as" to "ought to think": BF to William Shirley, 4 December 1754. BF pointed out that the men dispatched to govern the colonies were not unfailingly "men of the best abilities and integrity." They were more interested in accruing profits for friends and dependents. The remarks were cheeky, addressed as they were to the sitting MA governor.

72   TH on taxation: TH to Ebenezer Silliman, 9 November 1764, CTH I:237–38; TH's report on the colonies, 11–23 July 1764, CTH I:216.

73   "polish and burnish": JA to Tudor, 7 March 1819. EG recalled that SA wrote papers for the House before he was yet a member; Bowen, *Life of James Otis*, 140. Bowen concedes that SA was the more correct writer, though "may have carried his emendations so far that it was sometimes necessary to make a fair copy of the document in his own hand-writing." Penmanship, he implied, blurred authorship.

73   "simplicity, purity": JA to Wirt, 7 March 1818.

73   golden eggs: FB to RJ, 7 January 1764, PFB II:29.

73 "For if our trade" to "obtain redress": SA for the House, May 1764, WSA I:1–7. The idea gained currency; PR would later paraphrase SA in a furious wartime letter to a cousin: "Now certainly if they have a right to tax one shilling from us without our consent, they have a right to all we possess." Cited in Robert Martello, *Midnight Ride, Industrial Dawn* (Baltimore: Johns Hopkins, 2010), 69.

74 "If a shilling" to "lawful authority": JO, "The Rights of the British Colonies Asserted and Proved," 1764.

74 "A slave cannot" to "abhorrent practice": Wells I:138. SA and slavery: Wells II:20–21; Wells III:185–87; Hugh Hughes to SA, 8 January 1776, NYPL; George Bryan to SA, 5 January 1780, NYPL; Townsend, "The Thought of Samuel Adams," 279. Both Adams Sr. and Wells had owned slaves. Adams sold his at an undetermined date, Wells under duress in 1758. Abigail Adams grew up with slaves; JO too was a slaveholder; by one estimate there were 2000 enslaved people in Boston at the time. Massachusetts abolished slavery formally in 1780. Wedding announcement: *BG*, 10 December 1764. The earlier petition: JHR, 10 June 1766.

75 "converse upon any": Samuel Adams Wells, Bancroft Collection, vol. 384, 215, NYPL.

75 the scissors: EA to SA, 12 February 1776, NYPL.

75 "You will allow me" to "never dies": SA to William Checkley, 16 March 1766, *NEHGR*, 1853, 45.

75 the giddy letter: May 1766, to William Checkley, Collection of Herbert R. Strauss, Newberry Library.

76 "a trick I cannot": SA to James Warren, 16 July 1772, SA transcriptions, vol. 2, NYPL.

76 "In them is to be seen": Abigail Adams to Mary Smith Cranch, 15 July 1766.

76 "Indeed my dear": EA to SA, 12 September 1774, NYPL.

76 "refined policy": JA, 23 December 1765, *Diary of JA*, I:271.

76 finest commencement speech: Hanson, ed., *Diary of Dr. Nathaniel Ames*, 153. Sibley, on Josiah Quincy, 479–80.

76 "was brought up": Coffin to Steuart, 24 August 1774, Steuart Papers, National Library of Scotland. On the recruiting, JA to Tudor, 9 February 1819. JA, 27 April 1766, *Diary of JA*, I:310. TH implied that SA had recruited Hawley, TH to FB, 26 June 1770, CTH III:281. Patterson, *Political Parties*, 57, suggests SA conscripted Mackintosh and Molineux.

76 "If in no other respect": Gordon, Patterson, *Political Parties*, 58. He was the "master of the puppets" to TH.

77 "has set people a thinking": JO, "Rights of the British Colonies."

78 Harbottle Dorr: Bernard Bailyn, "The Index and Commentaries of Harbottle Dorr," *Proceedings of the MHS*, 1973, 21–35; Barbara Ripel Wilhelm, "The American Revolution as a Leadership Crisis: The View of a Hardware Store Owner," *Studies in the Social Sciences*, West Georgia College, 1976, 43–53. Dorr's index would run to 133 pages and include 4,969 terms.

78 "The year 1765": JA, 18 December 1765, *Diary of JA*, I:263.

78 The Stamp Act: Generally, Morgan and Morgan, *Stamp Act Crisis*; Davidson, "Sons of Liberty," 38–56. The horse-shodding is from JA to Tudor, 21 August 1818.

78 "their infancy": Jared Ingersoll to Thomas Fitch, 11 February 1765, *Papers of the New Haven Colony Historical Society*, IX:307.

79 "The Act," he declared: TH to Jackson, 5 June 1765, CTH I:273.

79 "factious and insolent": FB to J. Pownall, 20 July 1765, PFB II:295.

79 "with libels of the most": FB to the Board of Trade, 15 August 1765, PFB II:301.

79 the effigy: Malcolm Freiberg, ed., "An Unknown Stamp Act letter, 15 August 1765, *Proceedings of the MHS*, 1966, 138–42; Rowe, 88–89; John Avery to John Collins, 19 August 1765, in Franklin B. Dexter, ed., *Extracts from Itineraries and Other Miscellanies of Ezra Stiles* (New Haven: Yale University Press, 1916), 436–37; Notebook of James Freeman, ms. S-578, MHS. The wording of the labels varies.

80 "Boyish sport": FB to Board of Trade, 15 August 1765, II:301; *BG*, 19 August 1765; *BEP*, 19 August 1765; TH to Jackson, 16 August 1765, CTH I:279–80.

80 the Hallowell encounter: JA, 16 January 1766, *Diary of JA*, I:295.

81 "by which I understand" to "continual danger": FB to Board of Trade, 15 August 1765, PFB II:303.

82 "as an early method": *BEP*, 19 August 1765. The crowd afterward made a half-hearted attempt to locate FB, FB to Board of Trade, 15 August 1765, PFB II:304.

82 "gentlemen actors" and "the curtain": FB to Board of Trade, 15 August 1765, PFB II:304, 308. By an anonymous note, FB was advised that the perpetrators "are in all respects as good and respectable men as the governor and Council." As JA explained later, no one was indicted for flattening the Stamp Act office "because this was thought an honorable and glorious action, not a riot. And so it must be said of several other tumults." JA as "Novanglus," 20 February 1775, *Papers of JA*, II:283.

82 the August 26 riot: *Deacon Tudor's Diary* (Boston: Wallace Spooner, 1896), 17–19; "An Unknown Stamp Act Letter," Malcolm Freiberg, ed., *Proceedings of the MHS*, 1966, 138–42; FB to Halifax, 31 August 1765, PFB II:338; TH HIST, 123–25; TH to Jackson, 30 August 1765, CTH I:291–94; TH to Loudoun, 10 November 1765, CTH I:344; JA to Niles, February 1818; Edmund S. Morgan, "Thomas Hutchinson and the Stamp Act," *NEQ*, December 1948, 459–92. Riordan, 372, for the footprints of the mob all over TH's manuscript pages. The mob may have been waiting for TH, who had returned only hours earlier from the country. One of the few who included himself in the events was Harbottle Dorr, a member of the Sons, who noted under a newspaper parody of the day: "This refers to the fresh stir we made in deed to oppose the Stamp Act, which forced A. Oliver to resign," Annotated papers of Dorr, *BG*, 19 August 1765, MHS.

83 morning after: John Osborne to TH, 28 August 1765, CTH I:289; Sibley, on Josiah Quincy, 480.

84 "My temper" TH to Jackson, 15 October 1770, CTH III:415.

84 mastermind: Sibley, on SA, 428.

84 "truly mobbish": SA to John Smith, 20 December 1765, WSA I:60.

84 "the most barbarous": TH to Jackson, 9 September 1765, CTH I:298.

85 "the nurseries": JA to Tudor, 24 July 1774, *Papers of JA*, II:114. In a letter to SA years later, he referred to them as virtuous clubs "such as we used to delight and improve ourselves in," JA to SA, 27 April 1785, *Papers of JA*, XVII:56. Here too SA got extra credit: In some accounts, he led the secret Long Room Club, established around 1762 and anti-imperialist from the start. Having hatched the Tea Party, it was said to have morphed into the provincial congress, Crocker, *Reminiscences and Traditions*, 66, 92N.

85 "felt an ambition": JA, "The Stamp Act, 1765," *Diary of JA*, III: 283. JA would later report that SA had borrowed his paragraphs, a chronological impossibility. He also remembered having encouraged SA to take a more radical stand.

85 "the inherent, inalienable": *BG*, 23 September 1765.

85 deceased representative: It was the amiable Oxenbridge Thacher, who nursed an immoderate hatred of TH. JA thought Thacher had been worn down by struggles to keep America's enemies at bay. He died of tuberculosis. SA was elected only on the second ballot, BTR XVI:157–58; Rowe, 15.

86 "general outlawry": FB in TH HIST, 129–130 and Appendix C, 467.

86 "adopting the follies" and "their business": FB to Henry Seymour Conway, 28 September 1765, PFB II:368–69.

86 "head and father" to "brink of a precipice": SA for the House, 23 October 1765, WSA I:20–21.

87 "more troublesome": FB to Richard Jackson, 22 October 1765, PFB II:383.

87 "ready cut and dried" to "come out of": FB to J. Pownall, 26 October 1765, PFB II:390. The statement suggests that FB could decipher pseudonyms; SA may have been less elusive to him than he is to us. Hinting that advantage had been taken of JO's absence, TH would say that the task was entrusted to SA, "for several years an active man in the town of Boston, always on the side of liberty," TH HIST, 133.

88 "Nothing could have given": SA to "GW," 13 November 1765, WSA I:35.

88 on the unanimity: JA said as much even two generations later, JA to Morse, 22 December 1815; JA to Morse, 5 December 1815. No religious or political issue had ever, he wrote, touched every class of people to the quick. Arthur M. Schlesinger, "The Colonial Newspapers and the Stamp Act," *NEQ*, March 1935, 63–83.

89 "such a thundering": SA as "AB," *BG*, 21 October 1765.

89 TH and the ill will: Despite a prodigious memory, he did not seem to recall that when his home had caught fire in 1749, some in the crowd outside had cheered: "Let it burn!" Malcolm Freiberg, "Thomas Hutchinson and the Province Currency," *NEQ*, June 1957, 190–208. On TH and his travails: John W. Tyler, "Thomas Hutchinson's Enemies List," *NEQ*, December 2020, 553–85; Tyler, "From First Citizen to Arch-Villain: The Downfall of Thomas Hutchinson," in *Colonial Society of Massachusetts*, vol. 84; CTH I:1–38; Bernard Bailyn, "Thomas Hutchinson in Context: 'The Ordeal' Revisited," *Proceedings of the American Antiquarian Society*, October 2004, 281–300; Riordan, "A Loyalist," 344–84; *Boston News-Letter*, 7 and 14 November 1765.

89 "artfully improved": TH to Lord Kinnoull 27 October 1765, CTH I:337.

89 "We are in such a state": TH to T. Pownall, 8 November 1765, CTH I:342.

90 "fell in their way": SA to John Smith, 20 December 1765, WSA I:59. The cause of the second riot was not known publicly, SA explained to a London correspondent. He then added obliquely: "Some persons have suggested their private thoughts of it."

90 "he would have thought": SA for the House, to Dennis De Berdt, 22 October 1766, WSA I:93.

90 Pope's Day: Hoerder, *Crowd Action*, is especially good, 73–74; FB to J. Pownall, PFB II:396; Notebook of James Freeman, MHS. Luke Ritter, "Pope's Day and the Language of Popery in Eighteenth-Century New England," *Journal of Religious History*, 16 January 2022; Alfred Y. Young, "George Robert Twelves Hewes: A Boston Shoemaker and the Memory of the American Revolution," *WMQ*, October 1981, 578; Tudor, *Life of James Otis*, 25–28. Young returns girls to the picture in Applewhite and Levy, eds., *Women and Politics in the Age of Democratic Revolution* (Ann Arbor: University of Michigan Press, 1993), 191.

91 "provided I don't": FB to the Board of Trade, 22 August 1765, PFB II:317.

91 "actually mad": FB to J. Pownall, 7 September 1765, PFB II:355. The trusted relative was Barrington, 23 November 1765, PFB II:413.

CHAPTER VI: ON THE BRINK OF A PRECIPICE

93 "I could never": Twain, "The Turning Point of My Life," in Phillip Lopate, ed., *The Glorious American Essay* (New York: Pantheon, 2020), 341.

93 "ill-dreaded": Diaries of Robert Treat Paine, 1 November 1765, ms. N-641, MHS. *Boston Post-Boy*, 4 November 1765; *BG*, 4 November 1765.

93 Bernard's surprise: FB to J. Pownall, 1 November 1765, PFB I:395–400; FB to J. Pownall, 26 November 1765, PFB II:422–24. Mackintosh had been arrested and tried for the 1764 Pope's Day rumble, at which the North End leader wound up so badly bludgeoned he remained unconscious for days. Several gentlemen arranged for his 1765 release, possibly fearful of what he might divulge, Hoerder, *Crowd Action*, 112–13; *BG*, 4 November 1765; TH HIST, 136.

94 masons and carpenters: TH to T. Pownall, 8 March 1766, CTH I:406.

94 "the lawless ravages" to "hypocritical": SA as "Britannus Americanus," *BG*, 4 November 1765. On Mackintosh: "Ebenezer Mackintosh: Stamp Act Rioter and Patriot," *Transactions of the Colonial Society of Massachusetts*, 1924, 15–64; TH to T. Pownall, 8 March 1766, CTH I:406; George P. Anderson, "Ebenezer Mackintosh: Stamp Act Rioter and Patriot," and "A Note on Ebenezer Mackintosh," in *Publications of the Colonial Society of Massachusetts*, vol. 26, 15–64, 348–61. Hoerder first noticed that SA may have manipulated Mackintosh, *Crowd Action*, 96.

95 Pandora's Box: *Massachusetts Gazette*, 7 November 1765.

95 "Let everyone study": SA as "Britannus Americanus," *BG*, 4 November 1765.

95 "political scribblers": FB to J. Pownall, 20 July 1765, PFB II:295.

95 "silent upon maxims": SA to "GW," 13 November 1765, WSA I:36.

96 the dinner: "Reminiscences by Gen. Wm. H. Sumner," 187–88, has JH behind it. *Boston News-Letter,* 14 November 1765. FB to J. Pownall, 26 November 1765, PFB II:423; TH to Jackson, 11 November 1765, and TH to BF, 18 November 1765, CTH I:345–47. Not everyone felt comfortable with his complicity. At least to FB's face, some afterward shamefacedly stammered regrets.

97 AO and the messenger: Leslie Thomas, "Partisan Politics," I:226; TH HIST, 139; AO to FB, 17 December 1765, PFB II:434–35. JA distinguished between the ignominy of being hanged in effigy and that of being paraded through town, 15 August 1765, *Diary of JA,* I:259–61.

98 deeply gratifying: Annotated papers of Dorr, *BG,* 23 December 1765, MHS.

98 "a very genteel supper": Henry Bass to Samuel P. Savage, 19 December 1765, MHS.

98 on the legal consultation: JA, 21 December 1765, *Diary of JA,* I:268–270.

99 particularly pleased: Henry Bass to Samuel Savage, 19 December 1765, in *Proceedings of the MHS,* June 1911, 659–705.

99 "more attentive to their liberties": JA, 18 December 1765, *Diary of JA,* I:263.

99 the female patriots: David Alan Richards, "New Haven and the Stamp Act Crisis of 1765–66," *Yale University Library Gazette,* October 1971, 78. My thanks to the author.

99 the servant: TH to Jackson, 26 February 1766, CTH I:396. The joke appears to have circulated; PO told it, too.

100 "Politicians all" to "artful pen": JA, 23 December 1765, *Diary of JA,* I:270–72.

100 "secret, invisible connections": JA, 4 January 1766, *Diary of JA,* I:286.

101 "the learning": JA to Tudor, 9 February 1819. He dated the recruiting from 1758.

101 Henry VIII: SA as "AB," *BG,* 30 December 1765.

102 "'til I was knocked": FB to J. Pownall, 1 March 1766, PFB III:105.

102 "to prevent the cunning": SA to the RI Sons, 4 April 1766, Rhode Island Historical Society.

102 "the inhabitants of the moon": SA as "Britannus Americanus," *BG,* 17 March 1766.

103 the lack of colonial coordination: Margaret Marion Spector, *The American Department of the British Government* (New York: Farrar, Straus and Giroux, 1976), is especially good, as are Thomas, *British Politics,* and Barbara Tuchman, *The March of Folly* (New York: Random House, 1984), 145–204. For the unfamiliarity with American law: Morgan and Morgan, *Stamp Act Crisis,* 54; Thurlow and Worcester, *The Last Journals of Horace Walpole* (London: Bodley Head, 1910), I:428; Barnard diary, in T. H. Breen, *American Insurgents, American Patriots* (New York: Farrar, Straus and Giroux, 2010), 39. "The outside": SA to McKean, 11 December 1800, Historical Society of Pennsylvania. JO mocked letters addressed to "the island of New England." "Jamaica lay": T. H. Breen, *The Marketplace of Revolution: How Consumer Politics Shaped American Independence* (New York: Oxford University Press, 2004), 83. TH to T. Pownall, 8 March 1766, CTH I:405. FB and the lack of definition: FB to Barrington, 23 November 1765, PFB II:414; FB to Conway, 28 February 1766, PFB III:98–99.

104 "innocent diversion": *BG*, 31 March 1766, and FB to J. Pownall, 31 March 1766, PFB III:132. The news was slowed by nonimportation, which reduced transatlantic crossings.

104 "Benevolence, gratitude" to "part of the town": *Boston Post-Boy*, 26 May 1766; *BG*, 26 May 1766.

105 A thank-you note: London letter of 20 March 1766, *BG*, 26 May 1766; Conway to FB, 31 March 1766, PFB III:134–35.

105 "haughty and disrespectful": SA for the town, to De Berdt, 22 October 1766, WSA I:90.

106 "not so void of understanding": SA as "Alfred," *BG*, 2 October 1769.

106 "into measures": Cited in Wells I:119.

106 "The press hath never": "A son of liberty" in *The New Hampshire Gazette*, 11 April 1766, cited in Schlesinger, *Prelude*, 82. On the papers: Eric Slauter, "Reading and Radicalization: Print, Politics, and the American Revolution," *Early American Studies*, Winter 2010, 5–40; Thomas C. Leonard, "News for a Revolution: The Exposé in America, 1763–1773," *Journal of American History*, June 1980, 26–40; Schlesinger, "The Colonial Newspapers," 63–83; Schlesinger, "Propaganda and the Boston Newspaper Press," *Transactions of the Colonial Society of Massachusetts*, 1937, 395–415; Neil L. York, "Tag Team Polemics: The 'Centinel' and his Allies in the 'Massachusetts Spy,'" *Proceedings of the MHS*, 1995, 85–114.

106 mere primitives: SA as "Alfred," *BG*, 2 October 1769.

106 "Power, once acquired": TH HIST, 148; "Power is intoxicating": SA as "Alfred," *BG*, 2 October 1769.

107 a resounding triumph: SA may have won voters with the half-hearted tax-collecting but seems not to have stooped to the tactics of the colleague who explained that—a few weeks before an election—he sent for the cooper to repair his casks, the mason to repair his chimneys, the carpenter to repair his roof.

107 on recruiting JH: Wells II:381–83. There are two versions: Gesturing toward the mansion, SA announced that the town had done a wise thing by electing JH that morning. "They have made that young man's fortune their own." Or he asked, his eye on the same prize: "Is there not another John that might do better?" JA to Tudor, 1 June 1817, for the "wise thing" variation; the better John: William Gordon, *The History of the Rise*, I:205.

107 more radical paper: Sibley, on Cushing, 383. For the halt mid-reading: TH to FB, 27 November 1769, CTH II:421.

108 the Land Bank year: TH to TH Jr., 29 May 1766, CTH I:434.

108 "No one has suffered": TH to TH Jr., 29 May 1766, MHS. TH felt forsaken by the British Ministry.

108 "a most nitreous": JA, 29 May 1766, *Diary of JA*, I:313. FB believed the speech wholly innocuous.

108 "At such a time" to "the most abject slaves": SA for the House, 3 June 1766, WSA I:76–86.

109 "unprovoked asperity of expression": SA for the House, 5 June 1766, WSA I:83.

109 "dangerous union": WSA I:81. The multiple offices: Hoerder, *Crowd Action*, 106N; Ellen E. Brennan, *Plural Office-Holding in Massachusetts* (Chapel Hill: University of North Carolina Press, 1945); Bailyn, *Ordeal*, 183–84.

109 "Why then won't you": FB to Shelburne, 24 January 1767, PFB III:316.

110 JA wishing TH dead: JA, 11 November 1766, *Diary of JA*, I:324.

110 "what they know": FB to J. Pownall, 6 June 1766, PFB III:159.

111 the conspiratorial overtones: Gordon S. Wood, "Conspiracy and the Paranoid Style: Causality and Deceit in the 18th Century," *WMQ*, July 1982, 401–41; Ira D. Gruber, "The American Revolution as a Conspiracy: The British View," *WMQ*, July 1969, 360–72.

111 "without reserve, in private": TH HIST, 134

111 "not always so much": TH to Unknown, 26 October 1765, CTH I:315.

111 "that if any person": FB to Gage, 2 July 1768, PFB IV:236.

112 "A governor of spirit": Samuel Hood to Grenville, 15 October 1768, *Grenville Papers*, 377.

112 frenzied delusion: FB to Jackson, 1 March 1766, PFB III:103. Many ventured the Salem comparison but FB came to it first. Whatever MA was brewing, Boston's Anglican minister wondered why no one noticed that delusion was careening into revolution.

112 "'which,' Bernard regretted": FB to Board of Trade, 18 August 1766, PFB III:204.

112 "That more pernicious": Cited in Hiller B. Zobel, *The Boston Massacre* (New York: Norton, 1970), 149.

CHAPTER VII: PERHAPS I AM CAPTIOUS

113 "Politics, as a practice": Henry Adams, *The Education of Henry Adams* (Boston: Houghton Mifflin, 1918), 7.

113 "the late times": SA for the House to De Berdt, 16 March 1767, WSA I:120.

113 the fishing and hunting: No one is better on the details than the gregarious John Rowe, in his diary. The Masonic rites: Wells III:200. As his family understood it, SA disapproved of secret societies. He left no thoughts on the subject but a contemporary did: Samuel Dexter griped that—members of a frivolous institution—Masons liked to display their "windy titles" in formal processions, while "covered with trinkets." Letter of the Hon. Samuel Dexter to the Grand Master of the Grand Lodge of Freemasons of Massachusetts, 1798.

114 "There is a set": SA for the town to De Berdt, 22 October 1766, WSA I:95.

114 "concealed and not noticed": SA to Gadsden, 11 December 1766, WSA I:109–10.

114 "Perhaps I am captious": SA to Gadsden, 11 December 1766, WSA I:111.

114 "the Sam Adams": On Gadsden, Richard Walsh, ed., *The Writings of Christopher Gadsden* (Columbia: University of South Carolina Press, 1966). Gadsden made SA seem mild-mannered; by 1773 he was ready to pick up his gun and march to New England, ibid., 92.

114 "I wish there was a union": SA to Gadsden, 11 December 1766, WSA I:110.

114 on the social clubs: Nicolson, "McIntosh, Otis, & Adams," 85; Hoerder, *Crowd*

Action, 93–96; Warden, "The Caucus and Democracy." JA counseled a young Bostonian to choose his clubs wisely; they could make or break a career. Warden alludes to another dimension: "A complete alcoholic history of colonial America remains to be written."

115 "threaten destruction": Coffin to Steuart, 22 May 1770, Steuart Papers, National Library of Scotland.

116 "a parcel of button-makers": Fragments of JO's speech, PFB IV:299N.

116 The gallery and "bringing the government": FB to Board of Trade, 7 July 1766, PFB III:175; FB to Shelburne, 21 January 1768, PFB IV:73; TH to Jackson, 16 November 1766, CTH I:470; TH to Williams, 7 December 1766, CTH I:485. SA as "AB," *BG*, 17 February 1766. To PO the gallery was the address where SA and his confederates assembled their "Mohawks and Hecubites," PO, 110. Adams floated the idea in the 17 February 1766 *BG*, as tribes margins "AB": Was this not an ideal moment for constituents to listen in on House debates? In his margins, Dorr reported that the gallery was complete by the following May.

116 "I am the worst paid": FB to J. Pownall, 10 March 1766, PFB III:110.

116 "good men and bad": FB to Conway, 25 November 1765, PFB II:421.

116 "the low and ignorant": FB to Board of Trade, 7 July 1766, PFB III:175.

116 "creatures of the people": FB to Shelburne, 28 March 1767, PFB III:346.

116 baldly informed: TH to Mauduit, 20 November 1766, CTH I:477.

117 "the greatest instance": FB to Shelburne, 24 August 1767, PFB III:384.

117 "enjoyed every honor": SA for the House, 16 March 1767, WSA I:129.

117 Hutchinson's offices: JA, 15 August 1765, *Diary of JA*, I:260. JA and SA compiled their inventories separately and at different times; SA got so carried away he nearly forgot to mention that AO and TH were brothers-in-law. SA to AL, 31 October 1771, WSA II:265–66. As of the mid-1760s TH was captain of the Castle guard as well. The many offices "were frequently clashing and interfering with each other," JA as "Novanglus," 20 February 1775, *Papers of JA*, II:278. JA in partic-ular resented TH's charm. As he saw it, the governor had suborned three of his closest friends.

117 "to make all offices": TH cited in Pencak, *America's Burke: The Mind of Thomas Hutchinson* (Washington, DC: University Press of America, 1982), 4.

118 "the greatest and best": JA, 17 March 1766, *Diary of JA*, I:306

118 "amazing ascendancy": JA, 15 August 1765, *Diary of JA*, I: 260.

119 "a talent of artfully": TH HIST, 295.

119 the indemnification: TH to T. Pownall, 8 December 1766, CTH I:487. In mid-May the Privy Council invalidated the Indemnity Act. MA had overreached: The col-ony enjoyed no power to grant pardons, a Crown prerogative. The news horri-fied FB. The monies had already been distributed. Would he need to demand refunds from the victims? Events eclipsed the issue.

119 "only a warm" to "of his countrymen": SA for the House, 16 March 1767, WSA I:114–30; JHR 43, part 2:231–33; FB to Shelburne, 7 February 1767, PFB III:323; TH HIST, 175–77.

119 the cruel rejection: FB to Shelburne, 7 February 1767, PFB III:323.

120 "In short it looks": TH to Bollan, February 1767, CTH II:44.

120 "long-continued ill": TH to Bollan, 2 June 1767, CTH II:63. Dr. Warren treated TH in May and daily through July 1767, Joseph Warren account books, I, ms. N-2074, MHS.

120 "lately been ill" to "oak among them": FB to Jackson, 9 May 1767, PFB III:359.

120 "I really believe" to "be recovered": FB to Shelburne, 24 January 1767, PFB III:316.

121 humoring a spoiled child: FB to Barrington, 20 May 1767, PFB III:363.

121 "inconsistency, inability, and concession": Whately to Grenville, 5 August 1769, *Grenville Papers*, IV:435.

121 "because his virtues": *BG*, 27 April 1767. SA's view, SA to EG, WSA III:247.

122 "almost every person": FB to Shelburne, 27 July 1767, PFB III:379.

122–23 on the Townshend Acts: Robert J. Chaffin, "The Townshend Acts of 1767," *WMQ*, January 1970, 90–121.

123 "the sooner": SA as "Determinatus," *BG*, 21 September 1767.

124 silk and snuff: The agreement avoided mention of the duties themselves and neatly sidestepped the taxed items. On the effort: FB to Shelburne, 30 October 1767, PFB III:416–18.

124 "There is not": FB to Shelburne, 30 October 1767, PFB III:417.

124 without affront: There were a few insulting posters, as well as buttons that read "Liberty Property and no Commissioners." See Wallace Brown, "An Englishman Views the American Revolution: The Letters of Henry Hulton," *Huntington Library Quarterly*, February 1973, 4. At least one sign calling for resistance disappeared before Greenleaf could remove it.

125 "Is hunger the cause": "Simple Sammy," *BG*, 11 January 1768.

125 "You say you" to "his *reviling*": SA to JH, 11 May 1770, WSA II:9.

126 "indefatigable zeal" to "sacred flame": Dickinson to JO, 5 December 1767, WAL I:3.

126 "the Parliament": FB to J. Pownall, 9 January 1768, PFB IV:63.

126 "the cold regions": Dickinson to JO, 25 January 1768, WAL I:5.

127 "humble supplications" to "faithful subjects": WSA for the House, WSA I:162–66. "Letters from Andrew Eliot to Thomas Hollis," *Collections of the MHS* (Boston: Little, Brown, 1858), Eliot to Thomas Hollis, 27 September 1768, 427. TH sniffed that it was "quite a modern thing" for a colonial assembly directly to approach a secretary of state. By circumventing FB, the House committed a breach of protocol, which allowed the Crown to reject the document.

127 "It will, my dear": James K. Hosmer, *Samuel Adams* (Boston: Houghton Mifflin, 1885), 105. There is a variation: "This is a humble, dutiful petition to the King, and it will I suppose have the honor of being kicked by the royal toe." Samuel Adams Wells, Bancroft Collection, vol. 381, NYPL.

127 "But it is my private" to "in this letter": SA to De Berdt, 30 January 1768, WSA I:178.

128 "the messages": FB to Shelburne, 5 March 1768, PFB IV:112.

128 "brought on consequences": TH HIST, 186.

128–29 the *BG* attack: Joseph Warren, as "True Patriot," 29 February 1768. "No mobs": SA as "Populus," *BG*, 14 March 1768.

129 the jury tampering: TH fumed that "the honest and independent grand jurors" had become a toast among the Sons, TH to Jackson, 23 March 1768, CTH II:151–52.

129 Warren nursing TH: Joseph Warren account books, ms. N-2074, MHS.

129 "bankrupt in reputation" to "kind of gentry": FB to Hillsborough, 19 May 1768, PFB IV:162. Jonathan Sewall, 30 May 1775, in Haldimand, additional ms. 21695, BL, blamed the disappointed ambition of one man "of great influence and no principle or public or private virtue." Which is how the opposition as a whole viewed SA.

130 "a disposition among the people": SA to De Berdt, 14 May 1768, WSA I:217.

130 the true friends: *BG*, 21 March 1768.

130 "treated with sneer": SA as "A Puritan," *BG*, 4 April 1768, WSA I:201.

131 "By Popery": Annotated papers of Dorr, *BG*, 4 April 1768, MHS.

131 Turkish despots: Sheldon S. Cohen, "The Turkish Tyranny," *NEQ*, December 1774, 564–83. TH could not have overlooked the parallels. As transgressions increased at the college, its president disengaged. In his absence, young tutors disciplined harshly and arbitrarily.

131 "indefatigable in mischief": FB to Hillsborough, 19 May 1768, PFB IV:161.

131 the House maneuver: TH, 26 May–7 June 1768, CTH II:167–75. The merciful creditors: TH to Grant, 27 July 1768, CTH II:192.

132 Calvin and Luther: JA to Morse, 5 December 1815.

132 "two chief heads": FB to Hillsborough, 30 May 1768, PFB IV:167. One ill-wisher hoped that JO would "burst like a toad with his own venom:" Peter Livius to his brother, 18 October 1768, ms. Am 811 (41), Houghton.

132 by the coattail: Andrew Ward, *NEHGR*, XIV, "Notes on Ante-Revolutionary Currency and Politics," 262–63. Bowen, *Life of James Otis*, 68, has a different coattail custodian, with equally poor results.

133 "scarce short of madness": FB to Hillsborough, 18 June 1768, PFB VI:209.

133 "covertly influenced": Catherine Barton Mayo, ed., "Additions to Thomas Hutchinson's 'History of Massachusetts Bay'," American Antiquarian Society, 1949, 38.

133 on Bowdoin: Francis G. Walett is best, "James Bowdoin, Patriot Propagandist," *NEQ*, September 1950, 320–38, and Walett, "The Massachusetts Council." See also Gordon E. Kershaw, *James Bowdoin: Patriot and Man of the Enlightenment* (Brunswick, ME: Bowdoin College, 1976). On Hawley: E. Francis Brown, "The Law Career of Major Joseph Hawley," *NEQ*, July 1931, 482–508, and William Tudor, *The Life of James Otis*, 260; TH to Bollan, 22 November 1766, CTH I:477. On Cooper: Charles W. Akers, *The Divine Politician: Samuel Cooper and the American Revolution in Boston* (Boston: Northeastern University Press, 1982); John G. Buchanan, "The Justice of America's Cause: Revolutionary Rhetoric in the Sermons of Samuel Cooper," *NEQ*, March 1977, 101–24.

133 "their political dictator": HH, 136.

133 "secret influence": AO to Jackson, 1 March 1769, Egerton ms. 2670, BL.

133 "cool, abstemious": JA to Morse, 5 December 1815.

133 Otis discouraged: TH, Writings and Correspondence, ms. 51665, CHS.

133 "It might be expected": Mayo, "Additions," 38.

134 the June delegation: Rowe, 14 June 1768; Leslie Thomas, II:516; FB to Hillsborough, 16 June 1768, PFB IV:208.

134 Otis's rant: FB to Hillsborough, 25 June 1768, PFB IV:221, 299N.

135 Adams beaming: TH to Bollan, 14 July 1768, CTH II:186. By the end of the year, every colony except NH had approved the letter.

135 SA on the Circular Letter: SA as "Candidus," *BG*, 9 September 1771, WSA II:209, and *BG*, 16 September 1771.

135 "The most respectable" to "public tranquility": SA for the House to Hillsborough, WSA I:221–29.

135 "desperate faction": SA for the House to Hillsborough, 30 June 1768, WSA I:228–29. He mocked FB to Hillsborough of 22 April 1768, PFB IV:150.

136 "direct and peremptory": SA for the House to FB, 30 June 1768, WSA I:230.

136 New Jersey: FB to Barrington, 29 June 1768, PFB IV:233.

136 "To give it to" to "which I please": FB to Hillsborough, 9 July 1768, PFB IV:244.

137 "a variety of sedition": FB to Hillsborough, 18 July 1768, PFB IV:262.

137 "swarms of bloodsucking": TH to Jackson, 16 June 1768, TH II:178.

137 "Animated by his": SA as "Determinatus," *BG*, 8 August 1768, WSA I:236–40.

138 "a frolic of a few": FB to Hillsborough, 9 July 1768, PFB IV:243.

138 on the vermin: FB to Hillsborough, 11 June 1768, PFB IV:186, 189; SA, WSA I:416.

138 "a great number": FB to Shelburne, 19 March 1768, PFB IV:130.

138 "a few disorderly": SA for the House to De Berdt, 10 October 1768, WSA I:244.

138 "Whether this lady": *Appeal to the World* WSA I:401.

139 "in antipodes" to "at variance": JA, "First Residence in Boston, 1768," *Diary of JA*, III:287–88.

139 laws against: TH believed nonimportation illegal to begin with. As John Tyler explains, the very idea reeked of conspiracy. Bullying tactics aside — no group of businessmen should enjoy the power to dictate to another what goods it might sell. Email to author, 8 April 2022.

139 "the most violent" to "to make bricks": FB to Hillsborough, 9 September 1768, IV:295–98.

140 "any sense" to "ductile dupes": SA as "Determinatus," *BG*, 8 August 1768, WSA I:240.

140 special messenger: Gage to FB, 31 August 1768, PFB IV:290–91.

CHAPTER VIII: IT IS DANGEROUS TO BE SILENT

141 "I agree with you": JA to TJ, 29 May 1818.

141 He shuddered: FB to HB, 9 September 1768, PFB IV: 296–97.

141 "And no wonder": *Appeal to the World*, WSA I:429.

142 "with a duplicity" and "artful ambiguity": Ibid., 432.

142 flustered FB: FB to Gage, 5 September 1768, PFB IV:293. FB claimed he had been partly packed since 1765.

142 "as if they were acting": FB to Hillsborough, 16 September 1768, PFB IV:319. The hothead appears in the same letter, as do the firearms. SA, *Appeal to the World*, WSA I:434; PFB VI: Appendix IV, 309; TH HIST, 205; *Boston Post-Boy*, 19 September 1768; BTR XVI:259–61. TH muttered that the convention was a House of Representatives in all but name, something FB alone had the authority to convene, TH to Tryon, 21 Nov 1773, CTH V. Samuel Cooper disapproved of the town vote to arm itself but believed the gathering legal. Cushing too squirmed at the vote to arm.

142 "tools of the faction": FB to Hillsborough, 23 September 1768, PFB IV:332.

143 the convention: Best on the convention are John C. Miller, "The Massachusetts Convention," *NEQ*, September 1934, 445–74, and Richard D. Brown, "The Massachusetts Convention of Towns, 1768," *WMQ*, January 1969, 94–104. Peter Livius to his brother, 18 October 1768, ms. Am 811 (41), Houghton. The number of towns varied: the *BG* reported on more than seventy; the petition was from ninety-six; SA said ninety-nine. The number of attendees and the number of towns represented were not identical, which in part explains the discrepancy. "Letters from Andrew Eliot," 27 September 1768, 428. SA for the convention, to De Berdt, *BG*, 10 October 1768, WSA I:241–47. On 23 October 1775 a London letter to TH appeared in the *BG*, denouncing the convention and reporting that if TH could report that the malefactors were seized, his correspondent could assure him they were hanged. The letter may have been spurious, Mauduit to TH, *BG*, 26 September 1768. Cushing to De Berdt, 19 January 1969, in Letters of Thomas Cushing, *Collections of the MHS*, IV:352–53. Also excellent on the convention: Owen R. Stanley, "Samuel Adams: A Case Study in the Strategics of Revolution," PhD dissertation, Washington State University, 1975, 203–29.

143 "dreadfully precarious" to "good order": Convention petition to FB, *BG*, 26 September 1768.

144 "I will stand": Wells I:217.

144 "While we quite transported": *BG*, 26 September 1768. Livius too mentions the song, 18 October 1768 letter to his brother, Houghton.

144 shock waves: Whately to Grenville, 27 October 1768, *Grenville Papers*, IV:389–90.

144 "like a herd": John Mein, *Saggitarus's Letters of Political Speculators* (Boston, 1775), 81. Also Hood to Grenville, 15 October 1768, *Grenville Papers*; J. Pownall to FB, 19 November 1768, PFB IV:120. Causation is difficult to establish. There was no question as to how the administration would paint the coincidence, however. TH had earlier predicted of the faction chiefs: "Upon the least appearance of danger they would flee, or renounce their principles," TH to RJ, 20 October 1767, CTH II:93. The transcription reads "principals," presumably not what TH meant. Again, my thanks to John Tyler for parsing.

144 Commodore Hood's opinion: Hood to Grenville, 15 October 1768, *Grenville Papers*, IV:373–79. On wishing him gone years earlier: "Letters from Andrew Eliot," Eliot to Hollis, 10 July 1769, 442.

145 "bear the smell": *BG*, 19 September 1768.

145   the landing: J of O, 5; *Virginia Gazette*, 27 October 1768; *BEP*, 3 October 1768, *Massachusetts Gazette*, 19 September 1768; *Deacon Tudor's Diary*, 30 September to 1 October 1768, 27–28; Joseph Allen 1768 diary, American Antiquarian Society, 271125.

145   "You are a very": PO, 71. Others too noted the precipitous end of bravado; Boston was mocked throughout the colonies. One Tory deemed the convention a scarecrow "afraid of its own shadow."

145   "cannibals nor street": Hood to Grenville, 15 October 1768, *Grenville Papers*, IV:378.

146   "Some men": *Appeal to the World*, WSA I:430. One informer told FB that uniforms had been distributed to encourage the people to rise up in rebellion.

146   "a new and intolerable": SA to De Berdt, 3 October 1768, WSA I:249.

146   incredulity re quartering: Dalrymple to Gage, 2 October 1768, Gage Papers, Clements.

146   the strategy on quartering: "Letters from Andrew Eliot," 17 October 1768, 429–34; AO to John Spooner, 28 October 1768, letterbook of AO, Egerton ms. 2670, BL; FB to Hillsborough, 23 September 1768, PFB IV:332. At the Castle twelve men shared an eighteen-square-foot room. The responsibility for quartering indeed fell squarely on the Americans.

147   "in consequence of": Why was the governor so intent on lodging troops among the inhabitants? asked the paper. It seemed a disagreeable and dangerous step, designed only to gratify the customs men, tired of their Castle stay, *Virginia Gazette*, 27 October 1768.

146   On quartering: FB to Hillsborough, 23 September 1768, PFB IV:331; FB to Hillsborough, 1 October 1768, PFB V:63–68.

147   the Manufactory House: *BEP*, 3 October 1768; *BEP*, 24 October 1768; *BG*, 24 October 1768; FB to HB, 1 November 1768, PFB V:97; J of O, 16–17; TH HIST, 214–15. On quartering, James C. Brandow and William Senhouse, "Memoirs of a British Naval Officer at Boston 1768–1769," *Proceedings of the MHS*, 1993, 74–93. For Gage's frustration with FB, Gage to FB, 2 October 1768, Gage Papers, Clements. Some Bostonians profited handsomely from the impasse: Canny Molineux leased his sugar house and warehouse for 30 pounds a month, at a time when SA was making 90 pounds a year. FB acknowledged that he was stretching the law a bit: The building was provincial property, but in appropriating it he acted without the authority of his Council.

148   "the first open": *Appeal to the World*, WSA I:440.

148   "No man can": SA, unsigned piece, *BG*, 17 October 1768, WSA I:252.

148   "spirit-stirring": JA, "1768–1770," *Diary of JA*, III:289–90. Best on these taut weeks: John Shy, *Toward Lexington: The Role of the British Army in the Coming of the American Revolution* (Princeton: Princeton University Press, 1965); "Letters from Andrew Eliot," *Collections of the MHS*, 1858.

149   the whipping reprieve: Wells I:223.

149   "on pretense of preserving": J of O, 31. Alexander is especially good on J of O authorship, *Samuel Adams*, 345–46N. FB to Hillsborough, 25 February 1769, PFB V:216; TH to Mauduit, 5 December 1768, CTH II:226; Schlesinger, "Propaganda

and the Boston Newspaper Press"; TH on the J of O, TH HIST, 225. At least eleven other papers in America and three in Great Britain ran the entries in some form, Schlesinger, *Prelude*, 313.

149   Rowe insulted: Rowe, 2 October 1768, 176.

149   entirely new propaganda: James Green email to author, 18 May 2021.

150   "either absolutely": TH to Williams, 26 January 1769, CTH II:244.

150   "Adams and his assistants" to "in this paper": FB to Hillsborough, 25 February 1769, PFB V:216. The situation was the more frustrating, fumed Dalrymple, as a prosecution would only promote the paper. It left him with a difficult card to play, Dalrymple to Gage, 25 September 1769, Clements.

151   "a greater collection": FB to Hillsborough, 25 February 1769, PFB V:216.

151   "This being": FB to Hillsborough, 25 February 1769, PFB V:217.

151   the lieutenant colonel: Dalrymple to Gage, 25 September 1769, Clements.

151   Bowdoin and the Council: Bowdoin caviled with FB's assertion that he directed the Council; reason and the Massachusetts charter alone did. The Council had "neither leaders nor fondness for dictators, in which character Bernard seems lately to be acting," Bowdoin elucidated that winter.

151   "One of the first": J of O, 42–43.

152   the desertions: "Letters from Andrew Eliot," Eliot to Hollis, 29 January 1769, 434–41; Shy, *Toward Lexington*, 303–13; J of O, 95. As whoever wrote JH's 1775 Massacre oration had it: Standing armies tended to consist of men whose allegiance was for sale, "and who had not only given up their own liberties but envied those who enjoyed theirs." By September 1768 Gage suggested to Dalrymple that he discourage desertions with promises of rebels' estates, Hinderaker, *Boston's Massacre*, 75. A year later Dalrymple wrote Gage in embarrassment; he had run out of room in which to imprison deserters, Dalrymple to Gage, 24 September 1769, Clements.

152   villain and scoundrel: *Boston Post-Boy*, 29 May 1769.

152   "that Boston is": J of O, 231–32; SA as "Vindex," *BG*, 5 December 1768.

153   "great art, and little truth": TH HIST, 225. No J of O outrage left a trace in the Boston court records.

153   "though upon a near" to "greatness": J of O, 144. *Deacon Tudor's Diary*, 6 October 1768, 28. Reframed, the picture was moved upstairs in Harvard Hall and placed under lock and key, Harvard University Corporation records, 25 November 1768, UAI 5.30, box 2, Harvard University Archives.

154   "which is repugnant" to "of the administration": J of O, 104. Submitting the names: TH HIST, 221. All was a replay of what Governor Shirley had recommended after the Knowles Riot. It was time to disperse the mob, seize its leaders, and reestablish authority.

154   the statute of Henry VIII: Hillsborough to FB, 30 July 1768, PFB IV, 272, 275N. Some pointed out that the law was meant for regulating treason within the province; it did not permit the Crown to send for subjects to stand trial outside of it. It existed before the colonies had. It could moreover be used only for high treason, of which there remained, at every turn, insufficient evidence. As "Shippen," SA

reminded Bostonians how difficult it would be to make charges stick, *BG*, 30 January 1769. TH agreed and cast about for other ideas. Colin Nicolson disagrees with me about the queasiness. In his view the statute was simply impractical on many levels; it would be difficult to obtain witnesses willing to testify against the radicals. And there was no political appetite, in Nicolson's opinion, for such an explosive measure, email to author, 28 December 2021. TH HIST, 223, allowed that no one really took the idea seriously, and that the statute "became a subject of contempt and ridicule." Whately to TH, 11 February 1769, CTH II:259–60.

154 on Silvester's affidavit: 23 January 1769, Bancroft volume 159, F207–09, NYPL. The surprising calm in Boston: Alexander Mackay to Gage, 5 July 1769, Clements. I am indebted to Lindsay Fulton at the NEHGS for additional Silvester details.

154–55 "If you are men" to "his head cut off": Silvester deposition, 23 January 1769, CO 5/768, Kew. In January 1770 Silvester was appointed to a minor post in the customs commission, presumably not a coincidence. And TH would attempt again, out of sympathy, to find him a position later. Dr. Warren burned his papers when he heard of Silvester's report; another of Adams's confederates evidently attempted to extract the original of one of his *BG* essays from its editors. Already there were men in Boston prepared to resist to the last drop of blood. SA was not among them.

154 "An attempt to seize": Chatelet to Choiseul, 28 January 1769, cited in George Bancroft, *History of the United States* (Boston: Little, Brown, 1852), VI:200.

155 "the reproach": Whately to Grenville, 4 August 1768, *Grenville Papers*, IV:322. Similarly, Cushing to De Berdt, 19 January 1769, "Letters of Thomas Cushing," 353; MacKay to Gage, 5 July 1769, Clements. In London even members of Parliament conceded that the redcoats had been dispatched carelessly, to spare all concerned the reproach of having done nothing. As SA observed, troops could not even suppress a riot without orders from 3000 miles away.

156 "the greatest personage": J of O, 104.

156 "the most wicked": TH to Mauduit, 5 December 1768, CTH II:226. Now that punishment seemed imminent, TH felt almost tenderly; he pitied the incendiaries their fate, TH to Williams, 26 January 1769, CTH II:244.

156 the frustration: TH HIST, 223–24.

157 SA and the idea of independence: JA supposed the idea close to SA's heart from the landing of the troops, JA to Benjamin Rush, 21 May 1807; he based the claim not on anything he had personally heard or observed. Rush would quote SA as saying he had labored for independence for two decades, which placed the dividing line in 1756. Maier wrangles most eloquently with the 1768 date and its proponents in "Coming to Terms with Samuel Adams," 19. Gordon Wood dates the conversion to 1768, as does John Miller; Alexander is excellent on the subject, 83. SA would be one of the rare players who never identified a Rubicon. "was settled in Boston": PO, 148; FB to Shelburne, 14 September 1767, PFB III:404. The girl in the closet: Elbridge Henry Goss, *The Life of Colonel Paul Revere* (Boston: Cupples,

1891), I:113. The word "independency" turns up in SA's writing mostly, in 1769, as a concept from which Great Britain should shrink, SA as "Alfred," *BG*, 2 October 1769, WSA I:387, or "Shippen," *BG*, 30 January 1769, WSA I:297. He warned repeatedly of self-fulfilling prophecies. As Rakove has it, *Revolutionaries*, 17: "With the possible (and doubtful) exception of Samuel Adams, none of those who took leading roles in the struggle actively set out to foment rebellion or found a republic. They became revolutionaries despite themselves." John Tyler, email to author, 18 January 2021, thinks SA engaged, from 1765 to 1776, in a series of carefully calculated chess moves to his end.

157 on Queue: Wells II:21. For a variation: Sibley, on SA, 434.

158 "the incessant motion" to "against the Tories": Wells I:202–03. The watchman: WAL I:337.

158 "the only way": Alexis de Tocqueville, *Democracy in America* (New York: Penguin, 2003), 600. That was one view. TJ provided another. "Nothing can now be believed which is seen in a newspaper," he wrote in 1807, decrying the extent of "misinformation."

158 on the *Boston Gazette*: Miller, *Sam Adams*, 138; Robert G. Parkinson, *Thirteen Clocks: How Race United the Colonies and Made the Declaration of Independence* (Chapel Hill: University of North Carolina Press, 2021), 13–35; The *BG* was also one of the few papers read outside Boston.

158 "never awe a sensible": SA as "Vindex," *BG*, 12 December 1768, WSA I:267.

158 "intended to bring" to "rights and liberties": SA as "Shippen," *BG*, 30 January 1769, WSA I:299.

159 "*a secret intention*": SA as "EA," *BG*, 27 February 1769, WSA I:318.

159 the pseudonyms: Wells attempts a list, I:445. Menand did, too. See also James Francis Timon Jr., "Samuel Adams's Contribution to American Independence: An Analysis of his Writings, Speeches, and Activities," BA thesis, Boston College, 1923, 12. A full list will no doubt elude us, as it did Harbottle Dorr, whom we have to thank for having identified several pseudonyms. The symbolism too baffles: It is easier to understand why SA wrote as "Determinatus" than as "Alfred." Eran Shalev is especially good on the names, "Ancient Masks, American Fathers: Classical Pseudonyms during the American Revolution and Early Republic," *Journal of the Early Republic*, Summer 2003, 151–72, as is Sandra M. Gustafson, *Eloquence Is Power: Oratory and Performance in Early America* (Chapel Hill: University of North Carolina Press, 2000). See also "A Note on Certain of Hamilton's Pseudonyms," *WMQ*, April 1955, 282–97; Davidson, *Propaganda*; Philip Hicks, "Portia and Marcia: Female Political Identity and the Historical Imagination," *WMQ*, April 2005, 265–94; Michael P. Marden, "Concealed Authorship on the Eve of the Revolution," University of Missouri, Columbia, MA thesis, 2009. SA and JO also identified their antagonists with difficulty, Bowen, *Life of James Otis*, 133.

160 "A Letter from the Country": 28 December 1772, NYPL. Among other grievances, SA stressed the shocking new power granted to customs commissioners. What were they doing in Boston in the first place?

161 for the newsroom: Jeffrey L. Pasley, *The Tyranny of Printers: Newspaper Politics in the Early American Republic* (Charlottesville: University of Virginia Press, 2001), and Joseph M. Adelman, *Revolutionary Networks* (Baltimore: Johns Hopkins, 2019).

161 "Discerning readers": FB to Hillsborough, 21 February 1769, PFB V:209. One pseudonymous author challenged his critic: I'll reveal my name when you reveal yours, *Boston Post-Boy*, 11 September 1769.

161 "freedom and property": "Pervidus," *BG*, 16 March 1772.

161 the 1770 parody: "His rebel dictates/all the Sons of Liberty obey," wrote the satirist. With thanks to the Historical Society of Pennsylvania.

161 "barefaced chicanery": FB to Hillsborough, 1 July 1769, PFB V:297.

162 "Mr. Adams's attention": TH HIST, 413.

162 the linguistic adaptations: Alexander, *Samuel Adams*, 95, 154; TH HIST, 413–14. Benjamin Rush on the sensitivity to language and SA's gift for connecting words with emotions, Rush to JA, 8 August 1812. Probably in 1768, SA had substituted "calamities" for the "horrors of a civil war."

162 "anything with the appearance": TH to Hillsborough, 29 May 1772, CTH IV.

163 the August 14 celebration: TH to FB, 11 August 1769, II:308; Rowe, 14 August 1769; *Diary of JA*, I:341–42; *BG*, 21 August 1769; *BEP*, 21 August 1769; Wells I:270, for the full list of attendees, *Proceedings of the MHS*, August 1869, 140–42. BC evidently wrote a "Liberty Song" sung at these dinners; Sibley, on Church. For the toasts, *BEP* and *BG*, 21 August 1769.

163 trifling details: SA to James Warren, 20 October 1778, WAL II:57.

163 the malfunction: "Boyle's Journal of Occurrences in Boston," 14 August 1773, NEHGR, 1930.

163 "For they tinge": JA, 14 August 1769, *Diary of JA*, I:341.

164 "Whatever his reception": J of O, 229. For the 27 June 1769 petition, with SA's obsessive notes in the margin, Sabin 49222, NYPL.

164 "stood more in need" to "designing men": TH to J. Pownall, 25 July 1769, CTH II:296.

164 "I tremble": TH to Unknown, 1 September 1769, CTH II:322.

165 "the true daughters": J of O, 215. SA was well aware of the toll war had taken: women in Boston far outnumbered men.

165 "every master of a sloop": TH to FB, 8 August 1769, CTH II:303.

166 TH referencing the Land Bank: TH to FB, 26 August 1769, CTH II:318; FB to TH, 17 November 1769, PFB VI.

166 on Mein: John Eliot Alden, "John Mein: Scourge of the Patriots," *Publications of the Colonial Society of Massachusetts*, 1942, 571–99; George Mason to Joseph Harrison, 20 October 1769, Sparks ms. 10, Chalmers Papers, III, Houghton. SA attempted to debunk each of Mein's claims: Those imported British linens were nothing but 100 pieces of perfectly permissible Russian duck cloth.

166 "this overzealous" to "determined continent": SA as "Populus," *BG*, 28 August 1769, WSA I:380.

166 "cooking up": JA, 3 September 1769, 113, *Diary of JA*, I:343.

167 "superlative blockheads" to "his hand": JO, in *BG*, 4 September 1769.

167 "The most talkative" to "ridiculing": JA, 3 and 4 September 1769, *Diary of JA*, I:343.

167 on the challenge and the scuffle: Coffin to Steuart, 4 September 1769, Steuart Papers, National Library of Scotland; Tudor, *Life of James Otis*, 361; JO in *BG*, 4 September 1769; *BG*, 4 September 1769; *Boston Chronicle*, 11 September 1769; *BG*, 11 September 1769; *Massachusetts Gazette*, 11 September 1769. Gridley's very different account: *BG*, 18 September 1769. For TH on the ploy: TH to FB, 5 September 1769, CTH II:325–26; Leslie Thomas, "Partisan Politics," I:651–54; Dalrymple to Gage, 25 September 1769, Clements. SA as "An Impartialist," *BG*, 25 September 1769, WSA I:381, for the getaway vessels. SA seems to have particularly enjoyed torturing Robinson. On 5 October 1769 Robinson complained that some of his correspondence had been conveyed to Candidus, who printed it. He railed against the temper of a man "so rancorous and malevolent not only towards myself but every other servant of the Crown in this place." SA seemed intent on destroying the customs board.

168 Were Otis to hang himself: TH to Unknown, 11 September 1769, CTH II:333.

168 "trash, obsceneness" to "distraction": JA, 16 January 1770, 116. SA and respect: SA to AL, 9 April 1773, NYPL. The *Boston Patriot*, 29 July 1826, credits SA with the "constant guardianship" of JO.

169 Mein and the Land Bank: John Mein, *Sagittarius's Letters*. Mein offers another take on Adams elsewhere. He was the principal man among the faction, "once our tax gatherer, and spent about 2000 pounds lawful money belonging to the town; but he was forgiven this and made Representative, and Clerk to the House of Representatives, on account of his seditious writings."

169 The Mein mauling: Coffin to Steuart, 30 October 1769, Steuart Papers, ms. 5025–31, National Library of Scotland; TH HIST, 259–60; TH to and about Mein, 28 to 31 October 1769, CTH II:379–89. He declined to supply the armed guard that Mein frantically requested: George Mason to Unknown, 28 October 1769; Mein to Joseph Harrison, 5 November 1769; Sparks 10; Chalmers III; Houghton; *BEP*, 30 October 1769. Mein also left Boston without an opposition paper. On the damages: Had JO mauled Robinson in the same way, howled TH, the jury would not have granted his victim a shilling.

170 "small statesmen": *BEP*, 7 December 1767; "reptiles": *BEP*, 21 December 1767; "execrable set": *BEP*, 7 Dec 1767. The two sides blasted even each other's grammar: *BG*, 22 January 1770; "splashed and splattered": *BG*, 29 December 1766.

170 "to feast and fatten": SA as "Alfred," *BG*, 2 October 1769, WSA I:389.

170 "How much longer": Ibid., WSA I:395.

170 "And what return": SA as "Populus," *BG*, 1 February 1768.

171 a whole continent: *Appeal to the World*, WSA I:441. In London the MA agent had five hundred copies printed and distributed among members of the House of Lords and Commons. Even SA's bitterest detractors conceded the piece was masterly. For the reverse image of the *Appeal*, FB's "State of the Disorders,

Confusion, and Misgovernment in Massachusetts Bay," PFB VI:300. Dalrymple vowed to blunt its assertions: Dalrymple to Gage, 12 November 1769, Clements. For more on the power of SA's language, Patrick Samuel Loebs, "An Appeal to the World: The Controversial Rhetoric of SA," University of Memphis, PhD thesis, 2013. Nicolson believes the *Appeal* written by committee, PFB VI:64.

171 "shamefully evasive": TH to FB, 27 October 1769, CTH II:375.

172 "Independent we are": TH HIST 265; also TH to Mackay, 15 August 1771, CTH IV; TH HIST, 222.

172 out of sight: As TH wrote in, then omitted from, his *History*: "The earlier it should be known the easier it would be to counteract it. The leaders strove to keep it out of sight," Mayo, "Additions," 23.

172 "Britain may fall" to "children's children": SA to De Berdt, 6 November 1769, WSA I:446–47.

CHAPTER IX: AN EXASPERATED PEOPLE

173 "Is there not": Henry David Thoreau, *On the Duty of Civil Disobedience* (London: The Simple Life Press, 1903), 23.

173 He was pleased: SA to De Berdt, 6 November 1769, WSA I:446.

173 "all the abusive": For the epitaphs, Gage to Hillsborough, 12 November 1770, CO 5/88, Kew; Hoerder, *Crowd Action*, 298. The hissing: TH HIST, 270. TH acknowledged that the soldiers were themselves "very abusive," also that while Preston had not meant for his men to fire, "they are in general such bad fellows in that regiment that it seems impossible to restrain them from firing upon an insult or provocation given them," TH to Mackay, 12 March 1770, CTH III:318. After it was too late, Gage sniped that the people of Boston remained as lawless after troops had disembarked as they had been before.

174 He took a shot: SA as "Vindex," *BG*, 8 January 1770, WSA II:3.

174 JO's family: His wife was a Tory; their daughter would marry a British officer. JO was jealous too of rising legal stars like JA: AO to FB, PFB VI:60N; Rowe, 16 March 1770, 22 April 1770. "the man I love": SA to AL, 9 April 1773, NYPL.

174 On the sympathy: JA to Tudor, 11 March 1818. For the "banter and ridicule" of SA: Mayo, "Additions," 51.

175 "the affair of the lewd": Sibley, on SA Jr., 344.

175 "I am sure you": SA to Josiah Williams, 23 November 1770, NYPL.

175 the conversation at the window: *BG*, 22 January 1770; *Pennsylvania Chronicle*, 5 March 1770. TH HIST, III:44N "When I was attacked": Thomas Young to Hugh Hughes, 29 January 1770, cited in Ray Raphael, *Founders: The People Who Brought You a Nation* (New York: The New Press, 2009), 82. The regret: TH HIST, 267.

176 "persons of character" to "towards man": *BG*, 29 January 1770; TH to Unknown, nd, CTH III:50; TH to Hillsborough, 24 January 1770, CTH III:55.

177 "have talents beyond": TH to Gage, 24 January 1770, CTH III:52.

177 "our madmen": TH to FB, 1 February 1770, CTH III:60.

177   the nonsubscribing Scot: Elia Lyman Magoon, *Orators of the American Revolution* (New York: Baker & Scribner, 1848), 107–09.

177   "God perhaps might": Proceedings of the Town Meeting at Faneuil Hall, 4 October 1769; Sparks Papers 10; Chalmers 3; Houghton. Friends took him to task on occasion for his excessive zeal; he could be impatient with those who deviated on a single detail. In 1773 a colleague begged SA not to be narrow-minded and paint him as a Tory just because he failed to support one particular measure, John Pickering to SA, 5 July 1773, NYPL.

178   "save this abused country": *BG*, 12 February 1770; *Massachusetts Gazette*, 1 March 1770.

178   "people who contend so": *Boston News-Letter*, 11 January 1770.

179   on Richardson: Sons of Liberty photocopies, ms. N-1827 vol. 1, MHS. Richardson's name alone could summon a mob, JA to Morse, 20 January 1816. *Massachusetts Spy*, 4 November 1773. The hatchet is from Tyler, *Smugglers & Patriots*, 39. SA for the town, to De Berdt, SA I:96; TH to Hood, 23 February 1770, III:89; TH to Gage, 25 February 1770, III:91. One George Mason deserves credit for much of the detail, at least some of it accurate, Sparks 10, Chalmers 3, Houghton. An informer could count on making about twice as much as a market clerk.

179   Seider's death: *BG*, 12, 19, 26 February and 5 March 1770; TH HIST, 268–69; Rowe, 26 February 1770; Archer, *As If an Enemy's Country*, 178–81; *Massachusetts Gazette*, 1 March 1770; *BEP*, 26 February 1770.

179   "A grand funeral": TH HIST, 269.

179   "this little hero": *BG* and *BEP*, 26 February 1770.

179   Adams complained: SA to Sayre, 16 November 1770, WSA II:60. The "bird of darkness": *Massachusetts Spy*, 4 November 1773.

180   "but would have chosen": TH, Almanac, cited in Zobel, *The Boston Massacre*, 178.

181   For the Massacre: Hinderaker's excellent and essential *Boston's Massacre*; Zobel, *The Boston Massacre*; *Legal Papers of JA*, III. Zobel notes that the Twenty-Ninth were a predominately Irish, older, Roman Catholic regiment; Jesse Lemisch, "Radical Plot in Boston: A Study in the Use of Evidence," *Harvard Law Review*, December 1970, 490, points out that at least three of the soldiers who fired had been involved in earlier incidents, as had at least three of the victims. Preston would say the entire episode took place in twenty minutes. Hoerder, *Crowd Action*, 223–30. Bowdoin *et al.*, *A Short Narrative of the Horrid Massacre in Boston* (Boston: Edes & Gill, 1770). Preston's account, *BG*, 25 June 1770. "it was apprehended": TH HIST, 271. SA as "Vindex," *BG*, 24 December 1770, WSA II:92; *Pennsylvania Chronicle*, 26 March 1770; *BEP*, 4 February 1771; *BG*, 12 March 1770. Gage to Hillsborough, 10 April 1770, *Correspondence of TG*, I:248–51; TH to Gage, 6 March 1770, CTH: III:102–03; TH to FB, 12 March 1770, CTH III:117; TH to Hillsborough, 12 March 1770, TH III:120. It was rare to go for more than a season or two without a late-night cry of fire. AO Jr. to Lynde, 6 March 1770, in *The Diaries of Benjamin Lynde* (Boston, 1880); FB to TH, 27 April 1770, PFB VI:122–23. According to Peter Messer, "A Scene of Villainy Acted by a dirty Banditti, as must astonish the Public: The Creation of the Boston Massacre," *NEQ*, December

2017, 510, the ropewalk fight never appeared in the paper, omitted, explained Edes and Gill in the 5 November *BG*, for "want of room." Gage would report later ("Gage's Answers," *Collections of the MHS*, 370) that every straggling soldier—and many sentinels—were beaten. For a comparison of the Boston Massacre with Kent State, nearly two hundred years later to the day, Peter Stone, "Afraid of Revolution?" *New York Times*, 3 October 1970.

182 the arrival of TH: TH to Gage, 6 March 1770, CTH III:102–03; TH to FB, 12 March 1770, CTH 117–19; TH to FB, 22 May 1770, CTH III:239. Bailyn, *Ordeal*, 157–58. L. H. Butterfield, ed., *Legal Papers of JA* (Cambridge: Harvard University Press, 1965), III:80–81, 87–88; *Deacon Tudor's Diary*, 5 March 1770, 31–32; TH to Hillsborough, 12 March 1770, CTH III:120; TH to Gage, 18 March 1770, CTH III:134.

183 the Black sailor: Attucks's mother was Wampanoag Indian, his father a Black enslaved man; the *BG* identified him as "a mulatto man." The supine figure on his back in the foreground of the engraving may well be Attucks, though is neither Black nor markedly a sailor.

183 "with guns loaded": SA as "Vindex," *BG*, 28 January 1771, WSA II:154–55. That morning FB sat down to write TH about repeal. Some insisted that it was "not consistent with the policy, dignity, or honor of Great Britain to give way to the obstinacy of America."

184 the evacuation orders: TH to Hillsborough, 12 March 1770, CTH III:120–24; TH HIST, 273–74. The accounts differ.

184 on the room: JA to Tudor, 29 March 1817. On the showdown: JA to Tudor, 15 April 1818; *Pennsylvania Chronicle*, 26 March 1770; *BG*, 12 March 1770; Rowe, 6 March 1770, 198; Dalrymple in "An Anecdote," *Independent Chronicle*, 31 March 1794. There are discrepancies among the versions; PO reported that it had taken place the night of the riot and collapses the two appeals into one. I have tried to return them to their original sequence, bearing in mind that decades elapsed before JA committed his heart-stopping account to paper. TH barely mentions SA in his various letters, though everyone else does. AO account, 6 March 1770, Co/759, f 114, from vol. 2, K. G. Davies, *Calendar*; TH HIST, 274; TH to Gage, 6 March 1770, CTH III:102–03; TH to Hillsborough, 12 March 1770, CTH III:120; TH to FB, 18 March 1770, CTH III:132–33; TH to Gage, 18 March 1770, CTH III:134–36; Tudor, in Robert N. Linscott, ed., *State of Mind: A Boston Reader* (New York: Farrar, Straus, 1948), 90–92; Nina Moore Tiffany, ed., *Letters of James Murray, Loyalist* (Boston: Gregg Press, 1972), 162–65; BTR XVIII:2–4; Richard Frothingham, "The Sam Adams Regiments in the Town of Boston," *Atlantic Monthly*, November 1863. Dalrymple was little impressed with TH's resolve, Dalrymple to Gage, 9 October 1769, Gage Papers, Clements. TH account book, Egerton ms. 2666, BL; Samuel Adams Wells, Bancroft Collection, vol. 384, 62, NYPL.

185 "when his deeper": JA to Tudor, 15 April 1818.

185 "discretion, his ingenuity": JA to Morse, 1 January 1816.

186 "weak as water": JA to Morse, 5 January 1816.

186 "I observed his knees": SA to James Warren, 25 March 1771, WAL I:9.

186   he seriously doubted: TH to Unknown, 5 March 1770, CTH III:125. Hallowell wrote three years later that "that shameful retreat is dreadful to think of," Hallowell to Mauduit, 5 December 1773, MHS. FB would alert TH to the censure he received in the London press, 13 May 1770, PFB VI:127.

186   "with the utmost difficulty": SA as "A," *BG*, 19 July 1773. The worst night: TH to FB, 18 March 1770, TH III:132. TH HIST, 275; TH to Hillsborough, 12 March 1770, CTH III:121.

186   "gave greater assurances": TH HIST, 276–77.

186   the militia: Selectmen's Minutes, 7 March 1770, 57.

187   JA and the portraiture: JA to Tudor, 15 April 1818. He thought it would be as difficult to do the moment justice "as to paint an Apollo; and the transaction deserves to be painted as much as the surrender of Burgoyne."

187   TH's agony: JA to Morse, 20 January 1816. JA has TH on a different occasion flattened between the terror of his Crown responsibilities and Boston unpopularity.

187   the Gage portrait: On the resemblance, "Reminiscences by Gen. Wm. H. Sumner," 187–88. For Copley, Jane Kamensky, *A Revolution in Color: The World of John Singleton Copley* (New York: Norton, 2016), 174–75. Copley also painted James Murray, a prominent Loyalist, with a scroll in his right hand. Murray prefers an underhanded grip; in his hand the document is not a lethal instrument. The JH portrait is dated 1765.

187   on the portrait: For the most lavish collection of the Boston cast, Carrie Rebora et al., eds., *John Singleton Copley in America* (New York: Metropolitan Museum of Art, 1995). For the portrait details I am in debt to the immensely generous Erica Hirshler at the Museum of Fine Art. She dates the picture to 1770–72, email to author, 29 March 2022.

187   "Moses with his tablets": Wills, *Inventing America*, 18.

187   "the progress of liberty": TH HIST, 277.

188   the evacuation: SA for the town to BF, 13 July 1770, WSA II:18; *BG*, 12 March 1770; BTR XVIII:4. "to protect them": JA to Tudor, 15 April 1817; Hoerder, *Crowd Action*, 233. From London FB wrote TH: No one could understand how six hundred regulars had capitulated to three thousand civilians, "who they say would not have dared to attack them if they had stood their ground," 28 April 1770, PFB VI:124. Dalrymple hesitated to remove troops out of concern for the customs officials.

188   "'Thus,' groaned Andrew": AO Jr. to Benjamin Lynde, 6 March 1770, in Lynde, *Diaries*, 227–28. FB reported that TH was harshly treated in the British press for his role on 6 March, FB to TH, 13 May 1770, PFB VI:127.

188   "horrid massacre": The term was used as early as the next day, in the official report of the town meetings that requested removal, BTR XVIII:4. TH at the time talked of "the action of the last evening." "the unfortunate event": Hillsborough to Gage, 12 June 1770, CO 5/88, Kew. PO preferred "the Boston riot"; by 9 April the *BG* used "the late terrible massacre." TH complained that with his "Vindex" pieces SA kept the word alive.

188 "In short": Preston's massacre account, 13 March 1770, *BEP*, 25 June 1770.

189 either by Bowdoin: Sibley, on Bowdoin, 528: He credits Bowdoin, who had yet more animus against the customs officials than did SA. Bowdoin evidently cringed even at the mention of TH's name, Sibley, on Bowdoin, 535. TH reported later that Bowdoin headed the committee to draw up the narrative, TH to Williams, 10 December 1770.

189 "Every funeral": TH to Gage, 18 March 1770, CTH III:136. Rowe, 17 March 1770, 199.

189 "two balls entering": *BG*, 12 March 1770. In 1773 JA would use "Crispus Attucks" as a pseudonym. The woodpile: *Legal Papers of JA*, III:192. Lemisch on Zobel's demonizing of SA, "Radical Plot," 485–504.

190 "as truly as if you": Pelham to Revere, 29 March 1770, cited in Louise Phelps Kellogg, "The Paul Revere Print of the Boston Massacre," *Wisconsin Magazine of History*, June 1918, 385. Revere signed his work, as Pelham had not. Hinderaker is excellent on the engraving, *Boston's Massacre*, 227–31.

191 "a settled plot": Committee to Pownall, 12 March 1770, from the London *Gentleman's Magazine*. Hinderaker points out that it is unlikely but not impossible that customs agents fired. They were equally besieged, *Boston's Massacre*, 216.

191 the narrative: Messer, "A Scene of Villainy." Some papers held off as evidence was being gathered. The *BG* forged ahead on March 12, though made no mention of customs commissioners, preconcerted plots, Otis, or Seider, all attached later.

191 Robinson departure: Samuel P. Savage diary, P-363, reel 5, MHS. For the best chronology of the reports: Editor's Note, CTH III:199

191 "a preconcerted conspiracy": Tobias Smollett, *The Critical Review, or, Annals of Literature* (London: Simpkin and Marshall, 1817), May 1770, 390.

192 "restless adversaries": SA to BF, 13 July 1770, William B. Wilcox, ed., *The Papers of Benjamin Franklin* (New Haven: Yale University Press, 1973), XVII:187–93.

192 the plank-in-hand version: *Gazetteer and New Daily Advertiser* (London), 30 April 1770. Hints of the same surface in *Legal Papers of JA*, III:275.

192 the timing of the trials: TH HIST, 285; SA for the town, to TH, 19 March 1770, WSA II:7–8; TH to FB, 25 March 1770, CTH III:150–52; TH to Gage, 9 April 1770, CTH III:169; *Legal Papers of JA*, III:14; TH to Hood, 7 April 1770, CTH III:164–65. FB to TH, 26 April 1770, PFB VI:121. SA reported that Preston insinuated the town had designs on the customs money; those hints prejudiced the town against him, SA to BF, 13 July 1770, WSA II:15.

193 the intimidation of judges: TH to FB, 25 March 1770, PFB VI:150; TH HIST, 285; *BG*, 5 June 1775; *Legal Papers of JA*, III:3; PO, 88; "Letters from Andrew Eliot," Eliot to Hollis, 28 June 1770, 451; Gregory Townsend to Jonathan Townsend, 15 March 1770, MHS.

193 "a profound secret": TH to Greenleaf, 22 June 1770, CTH III:277.

193 on the Preston visit: SA to BF, 13 July 1770, WSA II:15. For the lying: Zobel, 236. Preston declined to engage further. He was depressed, did not appreciate the town deputations, and had no ink. SA saw to it that a letter went to him: Could

Preston offer a shadow of proof for the barbarous accusation that there had been a preconcerted plan? London *Public Advertiser*, 25 August 1770, WSA II:14.

193 "malice and guile": Preston's response from Boston jail, 12 March 1770, in *Transactions of the Colonial Society of Massachusetts*, 1902, 20.

193 misery of TH: TH to Gage, 18 March 1770, CTH III:135; TH to Unknown, nd, CTH III:139. The tied hands: TH to Hood, 7 April 1770, III:165; TH HIST, 280.

194 "met with opposition": TH HIST, 293.

194 "but the determined spirit" to "their estates": TH HIST 295.

194 days of witchcraft: TH to FB, 30 March 1770, CTH III:159.

194 Nothing intimidated: TH to FB, 25 March 1770, CTH III:150.

195 the letter of resignation: TH HIST, 267. As Dorr saw it, TH wrote London desiring not to be made governor while simultaneously aiming at the governorship.

195 "wish for nothing" to "the inhabitants": TH to Whately, 30 April 1770, CTH III:202.

195 the 1770 commencement: *Boston Post-Boy*, 23 June 1770. The overheard remarks: Mayo, "Additions," 26.

196 the carriage ride: JA, 27 June 1770, *Diary of JA*, I:352

196 the judicial assignments: Aghast, Quincy's father asked if his son, an SA acolyte, really intended to "become an advocate for those criminals who are charged with the murder of their fellow-citizens." Quincy retorted that even alleged murderers were entitled to legal counsel. And for the record, he took the case only after prominent Sons—SA first among them—insisted, 26 March 1770, in Quincy, *Memoir*, 26–28. Wells has SA conferring with Quincy at the Adams home, Wells I:329. Quincy had also defended Richardson, an equally unpopular assignment. He would help prepare Preston's case but argued only for the soldiers. For the prosecution team: Molineux to RTP, 9 March 1770, MHS. JA would write that he took the case under heartrending circumstances: Tears streaming down his face, a Tory merchant had paid him a call on March 6. No one in town would defend Preston. JA leapt to the rescue. If Preston did not believe he could expect a fair trial without his assistance, well, then Preston would have it. JA's high-mindedness met its match in his pathological sensitivity to criticism. The high-mindedness also dated from three decades later.

196 the opprobrium: Noted JA in 1822, *Legal Papers of JA*. "We heard our names execrated in the most opprobrious terms whenever we appeared in the streets of Boston." Quincy, *Memoir*, 29N.

196 "the greatest humanity": SA as "Vindex," *BG*, 31 December 1770, WSA II:112. Some would claim that the pages had by no means been withheld but scattered industriously throughout NY and the other colonies. They sat on the table in the courtroom, "Philelutheros," *New York Gazette*, 4 April 1774.

197 "he would sit": SA to Sayre, 16 November 1770, WSA II:59.

197 the clashing testimony: TH to Gage, 28 October 1770, CTH III:437; TH to HB, 30 October 1770, III:439. Both TH and FB feared an acquittal would trigger violence.

197 "brought truth": TH to HB, 30 October 1770, CTH III:441. We have no explanation for the absence of the faction leaders from the courtroom during the Preston trial.

197 "preferred their own": *BG*, 1 January 1770.

198 torn to pieces: *BEP*, 30 July 1770.

198 each other's throats: TH to FB, 20 December 1769, CTH II:451; TH to FB, 20 October 1770, CTH III:425; TG to Barrington, 8 September 1770, in Gage, *Correspondence of TG*, II:556–57.

198 "To see eight": SA as "Vindex," *BG*, 17 December 1770, WSA II:83; Lemisch, "Radical Plot," 500. The disjointed notes: *Papers of Robert Treat Paine*, c. December 1770, P-392, Reel 14, MHS.

199 "inspire a glow": Quincy opening argument, 29 November 1770, *Legal Papers of JA*, III:167.

199 "a motley rabble": *Legal Papers of JA*, III:266. The 1747 Knowles Riot had been blamed on "foreign seamen, servants, Negroes, and other persons of mean and vile condition."

199 "Every species of rubbish": *Legal Papers of JA*, III:268. The record is shoddy and defective even where it is not. JA found the stenographer's work riddled with errors. He did not feel the trials could ever "be truly, impartially and faithfully represented to posterity," JA to Jedidiah Morse, 5 January 1816.

199 "that they fight": *Legal Papers of JA*, III:262. SA to RTP, 29 November 1770, 4 December 1770. Colin Nicolson and Owen Dudley Edwards are superb on the trial, *Imaginary Friendship in the American Revolution: John Adams and Jonathan Sewall* (London: Routledge, 2019), 91–94.

199 "Noble, fine-looking": JA in 1822, cited in Quincy, *Memoir*, 29. The departure from court: *BG*, 17 December 1770.

199 "There certainly is": TH to J. Pownall, 5 December 1770, CTH IV. Or as SC put it, they were not so violent and bloodthirsty a people as to stand in the way of justice, SC to T. Pownall, 2 January 1771, "Letters of Samuel Cooper to Thomas Pownall," *The American Historical Review*, January 1903, 323–24.

199 "pretty good distinctions": TH to FB, 10 December 1770, CTH IV.

200 resurrected "Vindex": "Letters from Andrew Eliot," Andrew Eliot to Thomas Hollis, 26 January 1771, 458.

200 asked Paine: SA to RTP, 30 December 1770, Papers of Robert Treat Paine, P-392, MHS. SA did not want to publish without it.

200 "If these are not" to "innocence": SA as "Vindex," *BG*, 10 December 1770, WSA III:81–82. On numerous points SA baldly argued the opposite of what JA had in court.

200 "this very bayonet" to "in the street": SA as "Vindex," *BG*, 17 December 1770, WSA III:88.

201 the Roman Catholic: SA as "Vindex," *BG*, 24 December 1770, WSA III:91. The notorious tale-spinner: SA as "Vindex," *BG*, 7 January 1771, WSA III:132. He had a higher opinion of another slave who had testified differently, WSA II:146.

201 "It is, I am apt": SA as "Vindex," *BG*, 7 January 1771, WSA III:132. His master had
weighed in: It was true that the enslaved man had a lively imagination, but he
had provided an identical account of the evening minutes after it had happened.
Were the townspeople to blame? They were indeed, he had replied. Two Black
slaves and one free Black pastry cook testified for the defense, Zobel, 259.

201 the command: SA as "Vindex," *BG*, 14 January 1771, WSA III:138–39.

202 Philanthrop: Sewall stepped in to defend trials he should in all rights have conducted; he had preferred to make himself scarce, JA to Jedidiah Morse, 5 January
1816. SA picked up a defender in the *BEP*, who signed himself "Detector." Probably erroneously, Sewall assumed Detector was SA under another name.

202 "to whom even": SA as "Vindex," *BG*, 21 January 1771, WSA III:150–51.

203 "It is really necessary": TH to Williams, 10 January 1771, CTH IV. Similarly, TH
to HB, 17 January 1771, CTH IV. In a subsequent dustup Sewall took it upon himself to remind Adams that the *Massachusetts Gazette*, in which he parried, "is
esteemed a very good paper by those who are *really* the better sort of people in
the province."

203 The dioramas: *BG*, 11 March 1771; "Journal of Thomas Ainslee," 5 March 1776,
Sparks Papers I, Houghton. The idea was to keep people's minds focused, as SA
saw it, or to keep their minds in a state of constant agitation, as TH did. SA was
manipulating the past as he went along.

203 Malignus: TH to Unknown, 31 January 1771, CTH IV.

204 "by everybody" to "promising genius": JA to Jedidiah Morse, 5 January 1716. On
the power of the celebrations: PO, 95.

204 "ought to be solemnized": JA to Abigail Adams, 3 July 1776.

204 "the fairest and most": TH HIST, 336.

CHAPTER X: I SHALL STAND ALONE

205 "No man lives": Thomas Carlyle, review of *Memoirs of the Life of Sir Walter Scott,
Baronet, London and Westminster Review*, January 1838, 158.

205 "gnash their teeth": PO, 95–96. The sense in London: Walter Logan to FB, 18
November 1770, PFB VI:182–84. Parliament did not discuss America in 1770,
Bunker, *Empire*, 90.

205 the cool reception: TH HIST, 334–35. TH suspected the long arm of SA, TH to
Williams, 7 March 1771, CTH IV. The resignation arrived in London two weeks
after he was named governor.

206 the election: *Boston Post-Boy*, 22 April 1771, for election results. The vote was 1,123
to 467.

206 "like dung-hill cocks": JA, 2 May 1771, *Diary of JA*, II:10.

206 JO's conversion: TH HIST, 339; TH to Unknown, 5 June 1771, CTH IV.

206 "next freak of": SA for the House, 3 August 1770, WSA II:27; JHR, 29 May 1772.
On the inconvenience, Joseph Hawley to his daughter, 3 April 1770, Hawley
Papers, ms. Coll. 1360, box 1, NYPL.

207 "they rather make": SA to James Warren, 25 March 1771, NYPL. What appears to be "faithful" in the original is "fretful" in the published edition, WAL I:9.

207 "the rugged path": SA to AL, 19 April 1771, WSA II:164.

207 Some wondered: JA, 28 June 1771, *Diary of JA*, II:43. On the same visit JA says he has been fully convinced for a decade of TH's insidious motives.

207 "The opinion of": SA to William Checkley, 14 December 1772, WSA II:381.

207 "to disturb": SA as "Candidus," 10 June 1771, WSA II:172.

207 "whose works": SA as "Candidus," 23 September 1771, WSA II:229.

208 "content to be": SA as "Candidus," 16 December 1771, WSA II:294.

208 "slanderous" through "a governor": SA as "Candidus," 30 September 1771, WSA II:237. He was quoting himself when he announced that FB had "played the part of a pimp rather than a governor."

208 "Our incendiaries": TH to Williams, 7 March 1771, CTH V.

208 the mob: Rowe, 24 July 1771, 218.

208 "surrounded with dying": SA to AL, 31 July 1771, WSA II:189.

208 The patronage: TH acknowledged the patronage system but assumed the malice derived from the disappointments of those shut out of posts in his new administration. In October 1771, inventorying TH family appointments, SA wound his way to a new prediction: "The eldest son of the governor will probably soon be appointed a justice of the same court in the room of his uncle advanced to the superior bench."

209 "had learning": SA as "Candidus," *BG*, 14 October 1771, WSA II:252. For JA on the subject, 13 June 1771, *Diary of JA*, II:33–35.

209 any Parliamentary law: SA as "Candidus," *BG*, 20 January 1772, WSA II:319.

209 "I have often": SA as "Candidus," *BG*, 16 September 1771, WSA II:220.

209 "This is a sudden" to "despaired of": SA to AL, 27 September 1771, WSA II:234.

209 "the chief incendiary": TH to Jackson, 9 October 1771, CTH IV.

210 "The Devil himself": TH to FB, 21 January 1772, CTH IV.

210 "would push the": TH to J. Pownall, 17 October 1771, CTH IV.

210 TH's calculations: TH to HB, 25 August 1771, TH to HB, 10 September 1771, CTH IV; Peter Kalm, *Peter Kalm's Travels in North America* (New York: Wilson-Erickson, 1937) I:190; Benjamin L. Carp, *Defiance of the Patriots: The Boston Tea Party and the Making of America* (New Haven: Yale University Press, 2011), 250N. Elsewhere TH put the figure at 100,000 pounds.

210 "Mr. Hutchinson": Cited in Joseph J. Ellis, *First Family* (New York: Knopf, 2010), 24.

211 splitting worship: FB had encouraged him to make the change. For the sake of his political fortune, TH would be better off with a foot in each camp. SA did not touch that decision, unless he was "A Bostonian" in the *BG*, 14 June 1773: What could one say of someone who betrayed the church of his youth? If he was not constant in his religion, was a man likely to stand firm in any realm?

211 putty in Adams's hands: TH to FB, 26 June 1770, PFB VI.

211 especially when the British Ministry: Annotated papers of Dorr, *BG*, 20 April 1767, MHS. Abigail Adams to JA, 25 July 1775, *Adams Family Correspondence*, I:260–64.

211 Church informing, and TH chipping away at the faction: TH to FB, 29 January 1772, CTH IV.

211 The boasting: TH to Unknown, 24 January 1772, TH to FB, 29 January 1772, CTH IV. TH would explain that JH had sworn off public business having come to understand—or having been led by TH to understand—the toll it took on his private ventures. He was not wrong about the bribes; they had produced briga-dier generals and attorneys general, JA to Morse, 22 December 1815.

212 "It must be something": TH to T. Pownall, 22 June 1772, CTH IV.

212 "because he uses": Sewall as "Philanthrop," *Massachusetts Gazette*, 9 April 1772.

212 "the disinterested": *Massachusetts Gazette*, 19 March 1772. TH was pleased with the piece, which he thought silenced the opposition, TH to FB, 23 March 1772, CTH IV.

212 "The tears of sincere friendship": SA to James Warren, 13 April 1772, WAL I:11.

213 "stirred by others": SA memorandum, 18 December 1771, WSA II:296–97.

213 "So long the idol": AO to Gambier, 8 May 1772, letterbook of AO, Egerton ms. 2670, BL. JH and SA each had his partisans, TH to Gage, 1 December 1771, CTH IV.

213 JH's cadets: Unger, *John Hancock*, 159, has JH dreaming of stylish uniforms and advertising for fifers, 12 May 1772. SA was incensed: It was not up to TH to hand out commissions. The men chose their officers!

214 "the art and insidiousness": TH to J. Pownall (unsent), 15 June 1772, CTH IV; JHR, 29 May 1773, 49:11–12. On the Cambridge address: Donald C. Lord and Rob-ert M. Calhoon, "The Removal of the Massachusetts General Court from Bos-ton," *The Journal of American History*, March 1969, 735–55.

214 "the poison": TH to FB, 29 May 1772, CTH IV.

214 "I doubt whether": TH to J. Pownall, early August 1771, CTH IV.

214 "conclusion to me": SA to James Warren, 16 July 1772, in transcriptions of SA papers, II, NYPL.

214 "coarse, illiberal": TH to J. Pownall, 15 June 1772, CTH IV; JHR 49:10–12.

215 Moses himself: TH to Wentworth, 7 November 1772, CTH V. TH compared the Sons to the Kohathites who led a rebellion against Moses—and afterward dis-appeared into a crevice.

215 "It has been his": SA to Sayre, 23 November 1770, WSA II:67–68.

215 "and with all his art" to "country's rights": SA to James Warren, 9 December 1772, WAL I:8.

215 "flattered by ideas": Mercy Otis Warren, *History of the Rise, Progress, and Termina-tion of the American Revolution* (Boston: E. Larkin, 1803), I:214.

215 "and the wrath": Mayo, "Additions," 43. Either too painful or too undignified, it was another line he excised.

215 "By a scurvy" to "duty to do so": SA to AL, 12 April 1773, cited in Wells I:470. JA on the expert brand of TH courtship, reasoning, flattering, frightening, overawing: *Works of JA*, X:194–95. SA did not understand how the administration could gloat about having suborned JO given the joy they took in harping on his lunacy.

215 The reconciliation: SA correctly surmised that TH attempted to bribe JH only after orders from London.

215 The portrait: Wells dates the portrait to 1772: Wells I:475–76; Wells II:211.

215 "like thunder": SA as "Candidus," *BG*, 12 April 1773, WSA III:30. The pensioners seemed to multiply like locusts, devouring everything in sight, wrote SA as "Valerius Poplicola."

216 "would complete": SA for the Committee of Correspondence to BF, 31 March 1774, 85, NYPL.

216 "I have heard": AO to FB, 31 August 1772, letterbook of AO, Egerton ms. 2670, BL.

216 "We are brewing": Thomas Young to Hugh Hughes, 31 August 1772, misc. bound mss., MHS. On Young: Pauline Maier, "Reason and Revolution: The Radicalism of Dr. Thomas Young," *American Quarterly*, Summer 1976, 229–49; "Memoir of Dr. Thomas Young," *Publications of the Colonial Society of Massachusetts*, December 1906, 1–44.

216 "Let us converse": SA as "Valerius Poplicola," *BG*, 5 October 1772, WSA II:334–37.

216 "I wish": SA to Gerry, 27 October 1772, WSA II:339.

216 a friend pointed out: James Warren to SA, 8 November 1772, WAL II:399.

216 "a plan of opposition": SA to EG, 5 November 1772, WSA II:347. He persisted in his belief that the committees would work a contagious magic, that as soon as the country towns knew one another's minds, "that spirit which is necessary will not be wanting," SA to James Warren, 4 November 1772, WAL I:12.

217 "Where there is a spark": SA to James Warren, 9 December 1772, WAL I:14.

217 "to circulate the most": SA to Thompson, 30 May 1774, WSA III:123. The true design: SA for the Boston Committee, to the other committees, 21 October 1773, WSA III:65. Assemblies and associations should form in all towns, to promote their union, and to share intelligence, he wrote RHL six months later. Elsewhere SA explained that the committees would inspire the public, redirecting "their views to great objects." By early 1774 they had "wonderfully enlightened and animated" the colonies, SA for the Committee to BF, 31 March 1774, WSA III:88. On who precisely founded the committees, Bancroft vigorously fended off assertions they were anyone but SA's. See also Samuel Adams Wells to TJ, 14 April 1819, and TJ to Wells, 12 May 1819. As "Novanglus," JA proved the point on 6 February 1775, when he wrote of "a certain masterly statesman" who had invented the Boston Committee, immediately copied throughout the continent as "the happiest means of cementing the union and acting in concert." Papers of JA, II:248. On the committees: Edward D. Collins, "Committees of Correspondence of the American Revolution," *American Historical Association*, 1901, 245–71.

217 the cold-shouldering: SA to AL, 3 November 1772, WSA II:344. SC described the sidling off to BF, 15 March 1773. Hoerder, *Crowd Action*, 142, points out that two of the committee's twenty-one initial members were also members of the Loyal Nine. The committee for the most part met weekly, early in the evening, at Faneuil Hall, where the meetings grew longer and longer.

217 "most formidable": JA to Morse, 22 December 1815. Edmund S. Morgan deemed them "the most effective means yet discovered" for mobilizing public opinion in the colonies, *The Birth of the Republic* (Chicago: University of Chicago Press, 2013), 56; Galloway, *Historical and Political Reflections*, 62–63. Those who reached for superlatives at the time did so in different terms. A writer in the 1775 *Massachusetts Gazette* had a few choice comments for this "new unheard-of mode of opposition": It was "the foulest, subtlest, and most venomous serpent that ever issued from the eggs of sedition." JA, Works of John Adams, X:197 for "dangerous machines"; "What an engine!" JA marveled elsewhere. SA believed no measure so unsettled America's enemies; small wonder they attempted to destroy the committees, SA to JO, 19 March 1773, WSA III:2.

218 "the grand committee": Mayo, "Additions," 51.

218 "as black-hearted fellows": TH to J. Pownall, 10 November 1772, CTH V.

218 "moping about": JA, 27 October 1772, *Diary of JA*, II:66.

218 the hair-splitting: SA to AL, 31 November 1772, WSA II:380.

218 a scoundrel: SA as "Vindex," BG, 30 November 1772, WSA II:374–79.

218 the authorship: TH erroneously assigned the parts. I am following John Tyler's lead in his annotation, TH letter to Unknown, 8 December 1772, CTH V. Bailyn, *Ordeal*, 206, believed SA wrote most of the *Votes and Proceedings*. See also CTH I:27.

219 "to doze": Committee to the other towns, 20 November 1772, WSA II:372.

219 not worth the postage: TH to Jackson, 8 December 1772, CTH V.

219 JA's report on the SA home: JA, 30 December 1772, *Diary of JA*, II: 74.

220 "intemperate and furious": TH to HB, 29 May 1772, CTH IV.

220 JA and the Massacre oration: JA, 29 December 1772, *Diary of JA*, II: 73–74. JA could still recall the stigma of having defended the soldiers fifty years later, JA to Pickering, 6 August 1822. Given the taunts and reproaches, he believed the assignment the most difficult of his career.

220 to the different actors: TJ overheard by Nicholas P. Trist, cited in "Mr. Trist's Memoranda," Henry S. Randall, *The Life of Thomas Jefferson* (New York: Derby & Jackson, 1858), I:182; Trist also heard TJ proclaim that "If there was any Palinurus to the Revolution, Samuel Adams was the man."

221 TH's speech and fallout: TH HIST, 372; JA to Tudor, 8 March 1817. TH to Dartmouth, 7 January 1773, CTH V; TH to Gambier, 19 February 1773, CTH V; SC to BF, 15 March 1773.

221 "elementary principles" to "his infant": JA to Tudor, 8 March 1817. JA amused himself a little by quoting from an obscure text familiar only to him. He knew no Crown officer would ask about it, lest JA produce it, to their detriment.

221 "Bowdoin's genius" to "of Parliament" TH to FB, 23 February 1773, CTH V. Similarly TH to FB, 10 March 1775, PFB VI:241.

222 "great deal of low": TH to Mauduit, 20 February 1773, CTH V.

222 Hutchinson believed: TH to J. Pownall, 24 February 1773, CTH V.

222 amused Adams: SA for the House, to TH, 2 March 1773, WSA II:431–54.

222 "far above the reach": TH to Dartmouth, 9 March 1773, CTH V.

222 "of so little discernment": SA for the House, to TH, 2 March 1773, WSA II:454.

222 "open every" to "haughty power": SA to RHL, 10 April 1773, WSA III:25.

223 the election: In 1769, he received 503 of 508 votes; in 1773, 413 of 419, *Boston Post-Boy*, 3 May 1773.

223 the purloined letters: BF to Cushing, 2 December 1772; BF to Galloway, 18 February 1774. BF had mailed them in January. JA indicated they arrived on March 22; TH seems to suggest they had arrived earlier, TH HIST, 395. JA to David Hosack, 28 January 1820; SC to BF, 15 June 1773; JHR, 2 to 23 June 1773.

224 "It is a pity": SA to AL, 17 May 1773, WSA III:40.

224 the TH correspondence: And for as many years TH had been pleading that his letters be kept secret. The number of letters varies: TH says seventeen. On their origins, BF to Galloway, 18 February 1774. Only three people, SC assured BF, 10 November 1773, knew their source.

224 "of a conspiracy": TH HIST, 395. The reaction, Andrews, 323; JA to D. Hosack, 28 January 1820; *Diary of JA* 22 March 1773.

224 "bring many dark": *Massachusetts Spy*, 3 June 1773; *BG,* 7 June 1773.

224 on the drama: TH HIST, 400–02; TH to FB, 29 June 1773, CTH V. *Massachusetts Spy*, 3 June 1773; *BG,* 7 June 1773.

225 "There must be": TH to Whately, 20 January 1769, CTH II:242, TH had written "what is called English liberty"; his words were twisted to "are called English liberties." SA's name appears first among the eighty-two yeas. There were twelve nays, *Boston Post-Boy*, 21 June 1773. SA knew he was grandstanding; he could have expected neither for the king to answer their petition nor for him to recall TH.

225 "The world": TH to Unknown, 14 June 1773, CTH V. Before they proceeded, TH requested a transcript of their 2 June proceedings. The House complied—on the condition that in exchange TH submit copies of the rest of his correspondence.

225 JH's stroll: TH to Tryon, 6 July 1773, and to Jackson, 12 August 1773, CTH V; TH HIST, 403.

226 "to raise their own fortunes": SA for the House, to King George, 23 June 1773, WSA III:45; SA to AL, 14 June 1772, MA 554.8, Morgan Library. Harbottle Dorr raged in the margins of his copy, interspersing refutations with "'Traitor!" and "Oh, the villain!"

226 appeared flustered: SA to AL, 28 June 1773, WSA III:49. SA would say later that he could forgive the previous two royal governors, but not TH.

226 "a standing army": SA as "A," *BG,* 26 July 1773.

226 such villainy: TH to J. Pownall, 3 July 1773, CTH V.

226 the abridgement remark: TH to Unknown, 27 Oct 1773, editor's note, CTH V; though TH's words were twisted, his meaning was not entirely contorted. Bailyn, *Ordeal*, 246, 250–51. TH had said something very similar in the House a year earlier without anyone batting an eyelash. SA as "An American," *BG*, 4 October 1773.

227 Was it unreasonable: TH to Crosse, late August 1773, CTH V.

227 preferred to listen: TH to Jackson, 12 August 1773, CTH V.

227 "From a natural obstinacy": TH to Dartmouth, 9 October 1773, CTH V.

227 the three essays: SA as "A," *BG*, 9 August, 13 September, 20 September 1773. Further parsing the letters, SA added that TH had inveighed against "the control of a few ignorant leaders of the Boston town meetings," called for punishment of those who subscribed to an illegal boycott, and advocated for urgent, severe measures.

228 "cakes and sugarplums": SA to Hawley, 4 October 1773, WSA III:57.

228 "a few ignorant leaders": SA as "A," *BG*, 9 August 1773.

228 "do twenty other" to "own purposes": SA to Hawley, 13 October 1773, WSA III:63.

228 origin of the letters: The search continues: Bernhard Knollenberg, "Benjamin Franklin and the Hutchinson and Oliver Letters," *Yale University Library Gazette*, vol. 47, July 1972, 1–9. BF to Galloway, 18 February 1774.

228 the East India Company: SA for the Boston Committee, 21 October 1773, WSA III:67. By mid-month, two Philadelphians and a New Yorker had also advocated for resistance to the Tea Act.

CHAPTER XI: A REMARKABLE INSTANCE OF ORDER AND JUSTICE AMONG SAVAGES

229 "We have too many": Abigail Adams to JA, 16 October 1774.

229 any means possible: SA to Hawley, 4 October 1773, WSA III:52–58. SA wrote a series of particularly invigorating letters that season.

229 plot against America: As Oxenbridge Thacher pieced it together well before the Stamp Act, TH and AO, the Crown officers in America and their British counterparts, together engaged "in a deep and treasonable conspiracy to betray the liberties of their country, for their own private personal and family aggrandizement." Thacher issued regular, unbridled philippics on the subject. They particularly disconcerted TH as Thacher was in all ways a mild man, with—unlike Adams or Otis—no ulterior motive. By March 1774, JA had taken to calling TH one of the "original conspirators" against the public liberty. Elsewhere TH was one "of the family who are planning our destruction," *Diary of JA*, 6 March 1774.

230 "extravagant absurdities": Wedderburn, "Final Hearing," 29 January 1774.

230 did not ask: JA, *Diary of JA*, 14 February 1771, II:5.

230 the pale liquid: PO, 73.

231 "An Old Prophet": *Rivington's*, 9 December 1773.

231 on the preparations: Winthrop, Frothingham, et al., "Tea-Party Anniversary," *Proceedings of the MHS*, 1875, 151–216.

231 "They are much more" to "common enemies": Warren and Adams for the Boston Committee of Correspondence (BCC), Wells II:97–99; WSA III:62–67.

231–32 the anonymous letters and the Clarke visit: TH to Tryon, 21 November 1773, CTH V; *Boston News-Letter*, 30 December 1773; TH to Dartmouth, 4 November 1773 Dossier 406, F2089, Parliamentary Archives; TH HIST, 423–25; *Massachusetts Spy*, 4 November 1773.

232 the goose chase: BTR XVIII:145–46. There was a skirmish afterward about whether or not the town should extend special thanks to JH, the meeting's moderator. For the assassination rumors: HH, 18 November 1773, 155.

232 "brandishing their naked": SA as "Determinatus," *BG*, 8 November 1773.

232 the alarm system: "The pretense is that they are sickly and require such exercise, but why then are they to be thus armed?" asked SA. SA for the BCC, 21 September 1773, ms. collection 343, box 1, NYPL.

233 "It's impossible": TH to Tryon, 11 November 1773, CTH V.

233 "One cannot foresee": SA to AL, 9 November 1773, WSA III:70.

233 "You rascals" to "brains out": *BG*, 13 December 1773.

233 "I am in a helpless": TH to Tryon, 21 November 1773; TH to Unknown, 24 November 1773, CTH V.

233 "When once they have": SA for the BCC, 23 November 1773, Wells II:109.

234 "That worst of plagues": TH HIST, 429N.

234 could not trust: Cited in Hoerder, *Crowd Action*, 261–62. For the next days generally: Hoerder; Carp, *Defiance*; SC to BF, 17 December 1773; L F S. Upton, "Proceedings of Ye Body Respecting the Tea," *WMQ*, 1965, 287–300; David Black testimony, 19 February 1774, F 89, CO 5/763, Kew; Bromfield letterbook, letter of 25 October 1773, ms. 644, NEHGS; Bunker, *Empire*, 187–235; Rowe; TH HIST; Winthrop, Frothingham, et al., "Tea-Party Anniversary"; Andrews, 324–26.

235 howling political tempest: Upton, *Proceedings*, 291. Rotch's difficulties could not much have bothered JH; rivals in trade, the two had double-crossed each other for years.

235 patrolled the wharf: SA to AL, 31 December 1773, WSA III:76; HH to Unknown, 2 December 1773, HH, 289; TH to Dartmouth, 14 December 1773, CTH V. TH was not alone in believing that the watch constituted a violation of imperial authority, Force I:37.

235 "for his part": Upton, *Proceedings*, 294. *Massachusetts Gazette*, 9 December 1773.

235 Admiral Montagu: Montagu to the Lords of the Admiralty, 8 December 1773, CO 5/120, Kew; TH to Tryon, 1 December 1773, vol. 267, TH Papers, Bancroft Collection, NYPL.

236 the insult to TH: Alexander Leslie to Barrington, 6 December 1774, Dossier 407, PARL; TH to Dartmouth, 14 December 1773.

235–36 Greenleaf's visit and "a *representation* of *majesty*": Upton, *Proceedings*, 292–93. Already word circulated that TH would be sailing home, news that may have incited SA.

236 Rowe's suggestion: TH knew what most in the room did not: Rowe was playing both sides. Simultaneously he attempted to arrange for duties to be paid. He would find himself swept up in an enthusiasm he did not share: To his horror,

Rowe was placed alongside SA and JH on a committee to alert Great Britain that no more tea would be imported until repeal. He knew he had been manipulated but dared not object.

236 reputable tradesmen: Thomas Danforth to Dartmouth, 28 December 1773, Dartmouth Papers, Staffordshire.

237 sole member and TH's suspicions: TH to Montagu, 28 December 1773, vol. 267, TH Papers, Bancroft Collection, NYPL; CTH V; TH HIST, 433.

237 a more stubborn spirit: By the end of the month someone argued, as "Oliver Foresight," that this was the thin edge of the wedge: After tea would come salt, cider, and windowlight—followed by the inevitable tax on land, *Massachusetts Spy*, 23 December 1773.

237 "he would be willing": TH to Unknown, 3 December 1773, CTH V.

237 pistol for purchase: Andrews, 325.

237 had assumed direction: TH to Dartmouth, 14 December 1773, CTH V.

237 "usurpers of government": TH to FB, 1 January 1774, CTH V; TH HIST, 431.

238 Rotch's mission: BG, 20 December 1773, 27 December 1773. SA to AL, 31 December 1773, WSA III:74–75. Even hours before: TH to Montagu, 28 December 1773, TH to Mauduit, 28 December 1773, CTH V. John Tyler links TH's intransigence in 1773 to his concession in 1770 in "Hutchinson's Enemies List," 563.

238 limb from limb: Ann Hulton to Elizabeth Lightbody, 25 November 1773, HH, 287.

238 the Castle: Hulton to Unknown, 2 December 1773, HH, 288. Friends suggested that TH seek refuge at the Castle as well. It was cold and everyone slept two to a room, but the cannon reassured.

238 the Salem analogy: HH to Unknown, 8 January 1774, HH, 292.

238 "Sprung from the soil": Jonathan Odell, *The American Times: A Satire in Three Parts* (London: Richardson, 1780), 8.

239 the Rotch interview: SA to AL, 31 December 1773, WSA III:75; TH to EIC, 19 December 1773, CTH V; TH to Mauduit, 28 December 1773, CTH V; TH HIST, 436; Hoerder, *Crowd Action*, 261–62. Leslie had a regiment poised to take up arms. He awaited only orders from TH, paralyzed without his Council.

239 Rotch and the tea agents: Consignees to EIC Directors, 17 December 1773, dossier 408, F 2272, PARL. Rotch and Hall to the consignees, 7 December 1773, BCC, box 8, misc. correspondence, NYPL.

239 "a lawless": TH to FB, 1 January 1774, CTH V. On quitting with honor: TH to Gambier, 2 August 1773, CTH V.

239 "They have run": Colonel Leslie to General Haldimand, 16 December 1773, in G. D. Scull, ed., *The Montresor Journals* (New York: Collections of the New York Historical Society, 1881), 531.

240 "sitting upon thorns": *Rivington's*, 23 December 1773.

240 "That there is no animal": Samuel Adams Wells, Bancroft Collection, vol. 384, 134, NYPL.

240 "They had now": Upton, *Proceedings*, 297. Also on Rotch's return: *New York Journal*, 23 December 1773; BG, 20 and 27 December 1773. Andrews, 325. Benjamin Woods

Labaree for the prearranged signal: *The Boston Tea Party* (New York: Oxford University Press, 1964), 141; BCC, 17 December 1773, box 1, vol. 6, 468, NYPL.

241 "make—or be desired": Upton, *Proceedings*, 298. Samuel Savage, of Weston, served as moderator. Some at the Castle believed an out-of-towner was chosen strategically, to distance him from responsibility. Savage was the father-in-law of Henry Bass, a close SA associate.

241 "in case any should": Upton, *Proceedings*, 298.

241 "as remarkable an event": SA to AL, 31 December 1773, WSA III:73–74.

242 on the destruction: Andrews, 325. Tidesmen: Customs House men to Committee of Customs, Dossier 408, F2306–20, PARL; Young, "George Robert Twelves Hewes," 561–623. Hewes reported that men little known in town had specifically been chosen to lead the parties. They were about thirty in all, a figure that tallies with SA's estimate; a larger group, in more improvisatory disguises, appears to have joined them. "Opposition by the town of Boston," HH, 157; Danforth to Dartmouth, 28 December 1773, Dartmouth Papers, Staffordshire; Frothingham offset, 177; *Boston News-Letter*, 30 December 1774; *Salem Gazette*, 24 September 1833. JA to James Warren, 17 December 1773; *Deacon Tudor's Diary*, 19 December 1773, 44–45; Upton, *Proceedings*, 298–99; SC to BF, 17 December 1773; Samuel Savage diary, P-363, reel 5, MHS; *Rivington's*, 23 December 1773; "Destruction of the Tea in the Harbor of Boston," *Collections of the MHS*, 1858, 373–89; "Minutes of the Tea Meetings," *Proceedings of the MHS*, 1883, 1–36; SC to BF, 17 December 1773; Bromfield to Flight and Halliday, 17 December 1773, Bromfield letterbook, ms. 644, NEHGS; BTR XVIII:141–47; Winthrop, Frothingham, et al., "Tea-Party Anniversary"; Francis S. Drake, *Tea Leaves: Being A Collection of Letters and Documents Relating to the Shipment of Tea* (Detroit: Singing Tree Press, 1970); George R. T. Hewes, *Retrospect of the Tea Party* (New York: S. S. Bliss, 1834); Benjamin Thatcher, *Traits of the Tea Party, Being a Memoir of George R.T. Hewes* (New York: Harper, 1835); Carp, *Defiance*; Montagu to Philip Stephens, 8 December 1773, 17 December 1773, CO 5/760, Kew; CO 5/160, FF 1–15, Kew; CO 5/153, I 89–90; Summary of the intelligence on the tea, box 2, F 695, CO 5/7, Kew; Labaree, *The Boston Tea Party*.

242 "Perhaps never was": Danforth to Dartmouth, 28 December 1773, Lord Dartmouth Papers, Staffordshire. Savage timed the incident to 100 minutes, Samuel P. Savage diary, P-363, reel 5, MHS.

242 "remove the causes": JA, 17 December 1773, *Diary of JA*, II:86.

242 "a remarkable instance": SC to BF, 17 December 1773. In the *New York Journal* they were described as "men of sense, coolness, and intrepidity," in no way a mob, 23 December 1773.

243 transacted no business: The Committee noted as much on December 12 and again both on the morning and evening on December 14. No such notation occurs at any other time, BCC, box 1, ms. coll. 343, vol. 6, NYPL.

243 master list: It is reprinted in Harlow Giles Unger, *American Tempest: How the Boston Tea Party Sparked a Revolution* (New York: Da Capo, 2011), 247–51. Edes's son

would remember a list locked in his father's desk and removed decades later, after his death, by a colleague, for security's sake. "Letter of Peter Edes," *Proceedings of the MHS*, 1873, 174–82. At least one person who had destroyed TH's house was on the wharf per Carp, *Defiance*. SC, in his 17 December letter to BF, said two hundred to three hundred persons had destroyed the tea. He may have inflated the number to diffuse the blame.

243 "as one man": *Rivington's*, 23 December 1773. On the dress, Danforth to Dartmouth, 28 December 1773, Dartmouth Papers, Staffordshire. Carp, *Defiance*, 146–160, is especially fine on the symbolism of the disguise.

244 "his chickens": Cited in Young, *Liberty Tree*, 343. Mackintosh had become a talkative man. Coincidentally, he also left Boston for NH early in 1774, when rumors circulated of his death, a convenient untruth. Four years earlier it had been suggested that he be arrested, shipped to Great Britain, and made to divulge the faction's secrets.

244 the preconcerted signal: The idea traces back at least to Schlesinger, "Political Mobs and the American Revolution," 245.

244 "The questions proposed": Testimony of Andrew Mackenzie, CO 5/763, F 89, Kew.

244 SA hindering no one: Sibley, on Gordon, 64. Montagu on JH and SA: Montagu to Philip Stevens, Secretary of the Admiralty, 17 December 1773, P-165, Kew.

244 "I was there": Thomas Fletcher to SA, 7 March 1795, NYPL. Fletcher reminded SA that he was as familiar with SA's movements and character as anyone.

244 "It cannot therefore": SA to AL, 31 December 1776, WSA III:76. The town had taken every possible measure to protect the shipment, night after night, for twenty nights. They had labored around the clock to resolve the impasse, *BG*, 27 December 1773.

245 record-shattering time: Adelman, *Revolutionary Networks*, 107, points out that Philadelphia heard the news from NY on Christmas Eve, or twice as fast as usual.

245 "a number of people": SA for the BCC, 17 December 1773, WSA III:72.

245 "Immediately thereupon": TH to Dartmouth, 17 December 1773, CTH V. Neither SA nor TH mentioned indigenous peoples in their initial accounts. Everyone would say disguised; not everyone would say disguised as Indians. Perhaps the most accurate description was men "painted and disfigured, assuming the name of Indians." The deed rested on a crude caricature of Native Americans, "Indians" in these pages because they appear as such in the contemporaneous accounts.

245 "The spirit" to "interesting event": SA to the committees, 17 December 1773, WSA III:72–73.

245 "our opposition": SA to James Warren, 31 March 1774, WAL I:24. The 27 December 1773 account in the *BG* omits the destruction entirely, ending with the dissolution of the meeting, all options having been exhausted.

245 "sneer and ridicule": SA to James Warren, 31 March 1774, WAL I:24. It is "scorn and ridicule" in WSA III:93.

245 "late frolic": JA to James Warren, 22 December 1773. In Merry Otis Warren's 1805 history they were a number of people "clad like the aborigines of the wilderness, with tomahawks in their hands and clubs on their shoulders."

246 "There is a dignity": JA, 17 December 1773, *Diary of JA*, II:85–86. The grandeur of the event: JA to James Warren, 17 December 1773.

246 "You cannot imagine": SA to AL, 31 December 1773, WSA III:76.

246 "disappointed, disconcerted": SA to AL, 31 December 1773, WSA III:76; Andrews, 325.

246 coffee prices: BG, 20 December 1773. By the end of the century, coffee would supplant tea as the beverage of choice.

246 "and in a very little": SA for the BCC, to NYC and Philadelphia, 17 December 1773, box 7, BCC papers, 343, NYPL.

246 "Samuel Adams and his": PO, 104.

246 "supposed to be the": BG, 20 December 1773. There was some fuzziness on timing. In that paper those "assumed to be the aboriginal natives" appeared before the meeting dissolved, while, in another column in the same issue, the "brave and resolute men" appeared after it had.

246 "copper countenances": Andrews, 18 December 1773, 326.

246 blame-shiftings: The "Mohawk warriors" took their place in the long history of deplorables, "persons of mean and vile condition," as it was said after the Knowles Riot. They included liquorish boys, foreign sailors, and Blacks—even when no rioter at hand answered to those descriptions. At the same time there was some proud appropriation: Late in November, when a New Yorker wanted to send up a warning—he intended to pay an unwelcome visit to any ship carrying EIC tea to American shores—he signed himself "The Mohawks." As early as 1765, Harbottle Dorr noted that a Son of Liberty had watched AO "humble himself in the biting wind and rain before Samuel Adams and his Mohawks."

247 "highly extolled": BG, 3 January 1774. Half-holding to a fiction to which no one subscribed at the time, JA would allow a half-century later: "You may depend upon it, they were no ordinary Mohawks," JA to Niles, 9 May 1819.

247 "a number of persons": SA to James Warren, 10 January 1774.

247 "Even our enemies": SA to Plymouth Committee, 17 December 1773, box 1, ms. collection 343, BCC papers, NYPL.

247 Rowe's opinion: Rowe, 16 and 18 December 1773, 258.

247 Montagu watching: Montagu to Lords of the Admiralty, 17 December 1773, CO 5/120, Kew.

248 Admiral Montagu stomping: *Salem Gazette*, 24 September 1833. Rowe too found him very angry, Rowe, 7 January 1774, 259.

248 gloomily conceded: TH HIST, 429, 437. TH to Dartmouth, 24 December 1773, CTH V; JA to James Warren, 22 December 1773; SA to AL, 31 December 1773, WAL III:77.

248 "I cannot find": TH to Dartmouth, 24 December 1773, CTH V. Most newspapers reported there had been at least seven thousand people present.

248 It annoyed Hutchinson: TH to J. Pownall, 7 January 1774, CTH V.

249 "Adams never was": TH to Mauduit, 28 December 1773, CTH V.

249 singing to the deaf: TH to Montagu, 28 December 1773, CTH V.

249 "for indeed": JH to Jonathan Barnard, cited in Unger, *John Hancock*, 174. Similarly Rowe, 18 December 1773, 258; the Letters of Reverend William Gordon, *MHS*

Proceedings, June 1930, 595–600. The evening was designed with sufficient secrecy that JA would write nearly fifty years later: "I know not the name of one man concerned in it," JA to Niles, 10 May 1819. No one publicly admitted responsibility until some five decades afterward.

249 "I think we have put": SA to James Warren, 28 December 1773, WAL I:20.

249 Admiral Montagu's question: TH to Williams, 23 December 1773, CTH V.

249 "A sachem": Bolton's lampoon, Wells II:139. Thomas Bolton, *An Oration: Delivered on March 15th, 1775, at the Request of a Number of the Inhabitants of the Town of Boston* (New York: James Rivington, 1775).

249 the table-turning: SA to James Warren, 28 December 1773, WAL I:20. SC noted that TH and the tea agents "seemed to choose that the tea should be destroyed." *Pennsylvania Gazette*, 5 January 1774; *Massachusetts Spy*, 23 December 1773.

249 indemnification: SA to AL, 25 January 1774, WSA III:79.

250 "You must strive": TH to IW, cited in Sibley, on Israel Williams, 313. Even some Tories blamed the consignees and suspected TH would be recalled for having failed to protect the tea. Many—including a previous MA governor—believed he should have called in the military.

250 "With great regularity": BCC to Sandwich, 9 March 1774, BCC papers, IX, 729, NYPL; Thomas Newell diary, 7 March 1774, Sparks ms. 47, Houghton. TH in his HIST suggested that the owners of the vessel were complicit in the destruction. The March evening too was written down, with invisible quotation marks, to the Narragansetts.

250 "if they could find": TH to Dartmouth, 9 March 1774, CTH V.

250 the Plymouth visit: Ann Hulton to Elizabeth Lightbody, 31 January 1774, HH, 297.

250 "the approbation and applause": Colrain to the Committee, 7 January 1774, BCC papers, I:7, NYPL; Gorham, 10 February 1774, BCC papers, I:7, NYPL. It could seem as if every town clerk and the moderator of every MA meeting had discovered a copy of the colonial charter in a desk drawer.

251 "on tiptoe": JA to James Warren, 22 December 1773, *Papers of JA*, II:3.

251 the half-chest: *BEP*, 3 January 1774.

251 "every Rational": Concord, 24 January 1774, BCC papers: 3, NYPL.

251 "taken from all": Medfield, 4 January 1774, BCC papers I:6, NYPL.

251 the dissonant tones: Charles Thomson to SA and JH, 19 December 1773, NYPL. Thomson denounced the monopoly but disapproved of a colonial rupture.

252 "the boldest stroke": TH HIST, 439.

252 "the most worthy": *BG*, 20 December 1773.

252 JA on the punishment: JA to James Warren, 17 December 1773, *Papers of JA*, II:1–2. Similarly HH to Jacob Preston, 19 January 1774, HH, 292; TH HIST, 439.

252 "frightful list": James Warren to JA, 3 January 1774, WAL I:23. SA to James Warren, 31 March 1774, WSA III:93.

252 "rationally destroying": SA to EG, 25 March 1774, WSA III:83.

252 acted their consciences: SA to James Warren, 31 March 1774, WAL I:24.

253 "an electrical shock": AL to SA, 31 January 1774, NYPL.

253 no retreat: Along with PO, TH believed that if they had not just crossed a Rubicon, they never would. In Plymouth, James Warren agreed.

253 "the great" to "extravagant absurdities": Wedderburn, "Final Hearing Before the Privy Council Committee for Plantation Affairs," 29 January 1774.

253 BF in the cockpit: Bunker, *Empire*, is especially good, 243–55. In the audience, Gage wondered how BF managed to continue to stand upright, Gage to Haldimand, 2 February 1774, Haldimand Papers, add. ms. 21665, BL. There was some irony in the fact that SA would be slow to trust BF, who returned to Philadelphia later in the year; SA thought him insufficiently revolutionary. TH Diary, 5 January 1779, Egerton ms. 2665, BL.

253 "I almost envy": Gadsden to SA, 23 May 1774, NYPL.

254 the treason investigation: CO 5/160, FF 1–15; CO 5/763, FF 77–85, Kew; Bunker, *Empire*, 245–75.

254 ice-cold logic: BF to Cushing, 22 March 1774.

254 "I cannot enough": AL to SA, 16 February 1774, NYPL.

254 his daughter: Wells II:138.

255 anti-slavery petition: SA to Pickering, 8 January 1774, WSA III:78. On hints that the petition may have been drafted with SA's assistance, Brown, *Revolutionary Politics*, 173. Benjamin Rush would inscribe a copy of his 1773 anti-slavery pamphlet to SA.

255 "The colonies must": SA to James Warren, 31 March 1774, WAL II:25.

255 "Adams and all his": PO, 107; TH HIST, 443; TH to Dartmouth, 14 February 1774, CTH V. PO was unapologetic: Given the expense of traveling the circuit, the stipend was insufficient. The House doorkeeper outearned him. The salary was 400 pounds, paid from the tea duty.

255 the impeachment: JA, "Independence of the Judges, 1773–1774," *Diary of JA*, III:297–302. JA to Tudor, 15 February 1791, 24 January 1817; *BG*, 7 March 1774; TH to the House, 26 February 1774; TH HIST, 453–54; PO, 111. Juries refused to serve under Oliver, which, according to TH, left the course of the law "wholly stopped." Oliver accused SA of spearheading that action—and of inciting the gallery to attack him if he so much as appeared in court. He learned of his impeachment from "one of Mr. Adams's right hand men," who delivered a document signed by SA, and which the messenger abjectly apologized for having to submit. The messenger believed PO's life in danger, PO, 110–111.

256 political distress: TH to Mauduit, 23 August 1773, CTH V; TH to FB, 9 March 1774, CTH V.

256 the funeral: Rowe, 265.

256 "rule and overbear": JA, 6 March 1774, *Diary of JA*, II:90. JA shrugged: Another Oliver would become lieutenant governor, and the two families would rule as usual. The funeral occasioned a tussle between JH, who insisted that his cadets honor Oliver, and SA, who preferred the cadets boycott the burial; Adams in no way acknowledged the debt of years earlier, when Oliver had underwritten his tax-collecting. Hancock

prevailed: He and his honor guard headed the cortege and fired three volleys at the grave, though a hooting crowd also interrupted the procession. Cheers went up as the lieutenant governor's coffin was lowered into the ground.

256 "the most malicious": TH to Williams, 23 February 1774, CTH V.

256 "Such a mixture": TH to FB, 9 March 1774, CTH V.

257 "what was still called": TH HIST, 457.

257 Cynics suggested: Noah Webster to E. L. Thomas, 29 July 1840, Norcross ms. TH 97269, MHS.

257 the oration: JA, 5–7 March 1774, *Diary of JA*, II:89–91; TH HIST, 457; Rowe, 264. Sibley, on SC, 202, credits SC with having written the address. Others were skeptical. The editors of JA's diary note that SA reported the bulk of the work was Church and Warren's; elsewhere SA and SC together received credit. It no doubt helped that a victim of the evening sat in the audience. "A shocking monument to that horrid transaction," he languished still from the bullet that had entered his lungs four years earlier. The town took up a collection for him.

258 "that great" to "for American freedom": SA to Dickinson, 21 April 1774, WSA III:104.

258 Boston alone: As Lord North saw it, all colonial disturbances originated in Boston, to be credited with seven years of "riot and confusion," *Northampton Mercury*, 21 March 1774.

258 As Franklin noted: BF to Cushing, 22 March 1774. The king was deeply pleased with the act. It was time to make an example of Boston, from which no one had heard a syllable of remorse.

258 itself objectionable: SA to AL, 18 May 1774, WSA III:119.

259 "'The King,' Lord Dartmouth": Dartmouth to Gage, 9 April 1774, *Correspondence of TG*, II:161.

259 Thurlow and Wedderburn: Robert Gore-Brown, *Chancellor Thurlow: The Life and Times of an XVIIIth Century Lawyer* (London: Hamish Hamilton, 1953), 86. Donoghue, *British Politics*, 21–6, is best on the London fallout.

259 "flagrant injustice" to "malignant design": SA to AL, 18 May 1774, WSA III:117.

CHAPTER XII: THIS IMPORTANT GLORIOUS CRISIS

261 "The hero is": Ralph Waldo Emerson, *The Complete Works of Ralph Waldo Emerson* (Boston: Houghton, 1904), V:77.

261 "Outrages have been": SA to James Warren, 14 May 1774, WSA III:112.

261 "the most favored": BG, 23 May 1774.

262 the landing: BG, 23 May 1774; *Boston Post-Boy*, 16 May 1774; *Draper's*, 19 May 1774. Gage preferring more submission: Gage to Hillsborough, 12 June 1774, Haldimand Papers, add. ms. 21665, BL. The diluted welcome: 9 June 1774, *Papers of Robert Treat Paine*, oversized box 1, folder 2, ms. N-641, MHS.

262 "to distress the trade": SA to Gadsden, 18 July 1774, WSA III:142.

262 the Boston bullies: Gage to Barrington, 12 November 1770, *Correspondence of TG*, II:564.

263 the four regiments: Gage's estimate was a frank critique of TH's administration. King George to Lord North, 4 February 1774, in *Correspondence of King George the Third from 1760 to December 1783* (London: Macmillan, 1928), III:59.

263 stationed friends: Harrison Gray, *A Few Remarks Upon Some of the Votes and Resolutions of the Continental Congress, Held in Philadelphia in September* ("The Grey Maggot"), Boston, 1775, 7. A sizeable party supported reimbursement, Joseph Warren to SA, 15 June 1774, NYPL.

263 "When the righteous": *BG*, 30 May 1774.

263 "'Adams,' reported the colonel" to "his neighbors": James Robertson to Haldimand, May 1774, Haldimand Papers, add. ms. 21666, f 282, BL.

263 "It is hard": SA to Thomson, 30 May 1774, WSA III:122.

264 "Nothing can ruin": SA to James Warren, 21 May 1774, P-164, MHS.

264 "barbarous beyond" to "so much dreads": SA to Checkley, 1 June 1774, WSA III:127–28.

264 "I verily believe": SA to RHL, 15 July 1774, WSA III:137.

264 "I can live happily": SA to Checkley, 1 June 1774, III:128.

265 increased Crown control: The recommendations began early and escalated in the wake of the Land Bank scandal: Shirley to Lords of Trade, 7 November 1743, Charles Henry Lincoln, ed., *Correspondence of William Shirley* (London: Macmillan, 1912), I:108; Gage to Barrington, 8 September 1770, *Correspondence of TG*, II:556–57. TG continued to sound the same notes through 15 April 1775.

265 "The people have done": Rowe, 2 June 1774, 274. On his departure TH expected the damages to be repaid. A revision of the charter, he immediately grasped, precluded any reconciliation. With dread, he ended the *History* there.

265 "Where is your leader" to "part of the House": Wells II:173. The legislature had barely assembled when SA pointed out that their new address violated the charter. While it empowered TG to move the House, it nowhere empowered London to instruct TG to move the House.

265 "outguards to watch": SA to Thomson, 30 May 1774, WSA III:123.

265 the sternness: John Pitts to SA, c. 1774, NYPL; John Pickering to SA, 5 July 1773, NYPL. "to encounter" is from SA to James Warren, 25 March 1771, WAL I:9.

266 the Leonard maneuver: Edward W. Hanson, ed., *The Letters of Robert Treat Paine* (Boston: MHS, 2005), II:545. Leonard should have had his suspicions, having served on committees with SA since 1773. In 1766 Leonard had lamented that those who wrote on politics sacrificed their reputations. "Everyone who does is a dirty fellow," he sputtered, thinking of JO and SA, whom he believed merited prosecution. Also on Leonard: JA X:194. JA could not forgive TH for having suborned Leonard, initially a zealous patriot.

266 on calling the congress: Ammerman, *In the Common Cause*, 20, is especially good on the decision, so swift and synchronized it is impossible to credit a single organizer. NY very much wanted the congress there, Alexander McDougal to SA, 25 June 1774, NYPL; Adams very much wanted it in Philadelphia, SA to Charles Thompson, 30 June 1774, NYPL. *Boston Post-Boy*, 5 December 1774.

267 the locked door: *Massachusetts Gazette*, 23 June 1774.

267 the Solemn League: Coffin to Steuart, 6 July 1774, Steuart Papers; Percy to his father, 27 July 1774, in Charles Knowles Bolton, ed., *Letters of Hugh Earl Percy from Boston and New York* (Boston: Goodspeed, 1902); Andrews, 329–36. SA as "Candidus," *BG*, 27 June 1774.

268 eliminating the committee: James Warren to SA, 10 July 1774, NYPL. HH to Unknown, 6 July 1774, HH, 304; *Rivington's*, 7 July 1774; *Draper's*, 30 June 1774; *Massachusetts Spy*, 30 June 1774. BTR XVIII:177–78; Coffin to Steuart, 6 July 1774, F 226, Steuart Papers, National Library of Scotland. "The better sort": Gage to Dartmouth, 5 July 1774, *Correspondence of TG*, I:358. Patterson, *Political Parties*, is best on the meeting, 82–5.

269 "you may as well": Andrews, 336.

269 the donations: Richard Price Letters, *Proceedings of the MHS*, May 1903; John Winthrop to Price, 10 April 1775, 283–86; Andrews, 336; *Rivington's*, 12 September 1774. Breen, *American Insurgents*, is especially good on the WPA program, as is Brown, *Revolutionary Politics*, 221–22. "Donations to Boston during the siege," *Collections of the MHS*, 1822, 158–66. Boston Committee of Donations, ms. N-2038, MHS. As SA put it, the donations allowed Boston to "smile with contempt on the feeble efforts of the British administration" to subjugate a proud colony.

269 the "inextinguishable": Cited in Wells II:265.

269 "unexpected union": SA to RI IL, 15 July 1774, WSA III:137.

270 "a triumph to the faction": Dartmouth to Gage, 9 April 1774, in Davies, *Documents of the American Revolution*, VIII. On the statute: *Sir Henry Cavendish's Debates of the House of Commons*, 1841, I:207–15. The law, argued some in Parliament, was "a disgrace to the statute book." How could it apply to colonies that had neither existed nor even been imagined? Dartmouth to Gage, 15 April 1775, *Correspondence of TG*, II:196.

270 from headquarters: Hawley to JA, 25 July 1774.

270 "*good* sense, *great* abilities": Andrews, 340. Emphasis in the original.

270 "various artifices": Ann Hulton to Elizabeth Lightbody, 8 July 1774, HH, 304.

270 "a poor contemptible fool" to "desperate fortune": Captain Evelyn to his father, 18 February 1775, *Proceedings of the MHS*, 1879–1889, 289.

270 "a poor man": Colonel Robertson to Dartmouth, 5 July 1774, Dartmouth Papers, Staffordshire.

271 "I depended" to "very strange": TH, *Diary and Letters*, I:164, 171.

272 "The ultimate wish": Andrews, 340. Dartmouth called on TH in London on August 3. While he did not thirst for blood, he did want JH and SA to suffer the punishment they deserved.

272 "a complete suit": Wells II:208, for one version; Andrews, 340, for the other.

272 "It is not easy": SC as "Amicus," to SA, 5 September 1774, NYPL.

273 "a more extensive" to "upon the continent": JA, 20 and 25 June 1774, *Diary of JA*, II:96.

273 "In solid abilities": JA to Abigail Adams, 3 August 1776.

273 the speed of the fury: Gage to Dartmouth, 17 February 1775, in K. G. Davis, *Calendar*, IX. Best on the response, David Ammerman, *In the Common Cause*. Some fathomed the phenomenon perfectly well: The new lieutenant governor, Thomas Oliver, believed the people putty in the thrall of a few wicked men, "who in form of committees of correspondence, and under the name of patriots, were propagating treason and rebellion through the country."

273 "an inseparable band": SA to Gadsden, 18 July 1774, WSA III:142.

273 the instructions: In a secret 18 April 1775 message, Church reported to Gage that in SA's absence, Warren would be in charge "who has particular direction from him [SA] how to act," Clements. Young and the Committee to SA, 19 August 1774, NYPL.

274 "alive by adjournment": Selectmen's Minutes, 13 August 1774, 225.

274 "chicane, elude": Gage to Dartmouth, 27 August 1774, CO 5/763, Kew.

274 the Philadelphia departure: Andrew Oliver, ed., *The Journal of Samuel Curwen, Loyalist* (Cambridge: Harvard University Press, 1972), 8.

275–78 "the grandest" to "allure the taste": The Philadelphia trip draws primarily from JA, 10 to 29 August 1774, *Diary of JA*, II:97–115. The three-hundred-mile ride that took PR a matter of days took the delegates fourteen. See also *Papers of Robert Treat Paine*, III:44; Frank Moore, *Diary of the American Revolution*, I:74. Not every aspect of the travail was as appealing as the NY menu: The best policy was often to search your bed before diving in, where you were as likely as not to meet an extended family of bedbugs, William Ellery, "Journal of Route," *Pennsylvania Magazine of History and Biography*, XI:190–99. SA to Livingston, 21 November 1774, WSA III:164; JA to AA, 17 June 1775; Hawley to JA, 25 July 1774. Mifflin had advised SA to arrive early, to take the temperature of the town. Georgia absented itself from the meeting.

276 Demosthenes: Clawing back New England eminence decades later, JA would assert that if Henry were Demosthenes and Lee Cicero, then JO was Isaiah and Ezekiel combined.

277 "four poor" to "vulgar for his living": JA to Pickering, 6 August 1822.

278 Carpenter's Hall: Charles E. Peterson, "Carpenter's Hall," *Transactions of the American Philosophical Society*, 1953, 96–128; Peter Thompson, *Rum Punch and Revolution: Taverngoing and Public Life in 18th Century Philadelphia* (Philadelphia: University of Pennsylvania Press, 1998), 148–70. For Philadelphia: *Caspipina's Letters* (London: Dilly, 1777), I:1–31; David Hawke, *In the Midst of a Revolution* (Philadelphia: University of Pennsylvania Press, 1971). For these weeks: William Hogeland, *Declaration: The Nine Tumultuous Weeks When America Became Independent* (New York: Simon & Schuster, 2011); Wills, *Inventing America*; Benjamin H. Irvin, "Representative Men: Personal and National Identity in the Continental Congress," Brandeis University, PhD dissertation, 2004. SA was described at the time as "a mobster by profession, now the principal delegate at the grand American Congress," cited in Sigmund Diamond, "Bunker Hill, Tory Propaganda, and Adam Smith," *NEQ*, XXV:369.

278 "You may have been taught": JA, 17 November 1782, *Diary of JA*, III:55.

279 "the most cautious": Galloway, *Historical and Political Reflections*, 109. For the "milksops": William B. Reed, ed., *The Life and Correspondence of Joseph Reed*

(Philadelphia: Lindsay and Blakiston, 1847), 75. The radicals, noted Caesar Rodney, all seemed to hail from VA and SC. Gage worried that—from what he had heard—the MA delegates wielded an outsized influence in Philadelphia, Gage to Barrington, 2 November 1774. Gadsden made SA seem mild-mannered, Walsh, 92. Thomson had written a long letter to the BCC at the end of December 1773; his ideas on resistance were entirely consonant with SA's.

280 working behind the scenes: SA to AL, 20 September 1774, in James Curtis Ballagh, ed., *Letters of Richard Henry Lee* (New York: Macmillan, 1911), I:124. JA to Pickering, 6 August 1822; JA to Tudor, 29 September 1774.

280 "a prayer from a gentleman": Wells II:223; *BG*, 26 September 174. The account derives from JA.

280 "masterly stroke": Reed, cited in *Journals of the Continental Congress*, I:27. SA reported on the minor coup to James Warren, who published it in the *BG*, to reassure their Episcopalian brethren; they were entitled to a free exercise of their religious rights. SA fared less well with another sect. In mid-October a Baptist delegation registered complaints against the MA ecclesiastical establishment which, for nearly an hour, SA argued did not exist. The Baptists had no cause for complaint. He left his callers deeply unsatisfied.

281 some feared: Reed to Dartmouth, 25 September 1774, in William B. Reed, ed., *Life and Correspondence of Joseph Reed* (Philadelphia: Lindsay and Blakiston, 1847). Powder Alarm: Paul H. Smith, ed., *Letters of Delegates to Congress*, I:75–86.

281 happily noted: SA to Charles Chauncy, 19 September 1774, WSA III:156.

281 "was that they came": Gray, "The Grey Maggot," 9.

282 SA was pleased: SA to Young, 17 October 1774, WSA III:163. For the deliberations: SD, "Silas Deane Reports on the Continental Congress," *CHS Bulletin* XXIX, January 1964, 1–8. JA to Tudor, 14 September 1774.

282 "we are a hardy": SA to Joseph Warren, 25 September 1774, WSA III:158.

282 "by the united" to "never eradicate": SA draft for the CC to Gage, October 1774, WSA III:159–62. The toning down: Ammerman, *In the Common Cause*, 77.

282 "Adams, with his crew": Maryland merchant to a Philadelphia friend, 28 January 1775, Force I:1194.

282 "It was this man": Galloway, *Historical and Political Reflections*, 67.

283 the foremost politician: Josiah Quincy to Mrs. Quincy, 7 December 1774, *Memoir of the Life of Josiah Quincy, Jr.*, 218.

283 "I doubt not but": Cited in Winthrop Sargent, *The Life and Career of Major John André* (New York: W. Abbatt, 1902), 72.

283 "they have declared": Dartmouth to TH, 1 November 1774, cited in TH, *Diary and Letters*, I:284.

283 "vain enough": Coffin to Steuart, 20 July 1774, Steuart Papers, National Library of Scotland.

283 "It is somewhat surprising": Gage to Dartmouth, 20 September 1774, CO 5/763, Kew.

283 on the resistance: Force I:802; Andrews, 355. The fire: *Journal of Samuel Curwen*, 31 May 1775, I:14; the sheep: Winsor, *Memorial History*, III:80. Deborah Cushing to

TC, 19 September 1774, Cushing Family Papers, ms. N-1072, MHS, for the cannon. Gage was ultimately forced to import carpenters and bricklayers from Nova Scotia to outfit barracks, given the "mulish" Bostonians. On the cannon, see J. L. Bell, *The Road to Concord: How Four Stolen Cannon Ignited the Revolutionary War* (Yardley, PA: Westholme, 2016). For details on occupied Boston, "Diary of Ezekiel Price," *Proceedings of the MHS*, 1863, 185–262.

284   the September proposal: *BEP*, 19 September 1774.

284   Dyer testimony: Dyer deposition, CO 5/760, F 307–08; CO 5/120, F 251–52; Gage to Dartmouth, 30 October 1774, Kew; Diary of TH, 4–5 August 1774, Egerton ms. 2662, BL; Andrews, 377; TY to SA, 11 October 1774, NYPL; J. Pownall to Dartmouth, 4 August 1774, *The Manuscripts of the Earl of Dartmouth*, II:220.

284   The lumpy currency: *Diary of Jonathan Sayward*, 31 December 1775, ms. N-888, NEHGS. For the attack, Gage to Dartmouth, 30 October 1774, Dartmouth Papers, Staffordshire; Andrews, 378; TY to SA, 11 October 1774, NYPL; SA to Young, 17 October 1774, WSA III:162; Montagu to Stephens, 1 August 1774 and F306–8, CO 5/760, Kew; Gage to Dartmouth, 30 October 1774, CO 5/92, Kew. Dyer claimed to have returned with letters from AL to JH and SA which—should their recipients have been murdered—he was to burn. He boasted that he could handily entice 100 soldiers to desert.

285   target practice: Andrews, 372.

285   the regimental jacket: Dalrymple to Gage, 25 September 1769, Clements.

285   the wilting ardor: Pitts to SA, 16 October 1774, NYPL.

285   "I can't help observing": Richard Price Letters, Proceedings of the MHS, Charles Chauncy to Price, 10 January 1775, 276.

286   "with becoming patience": SA to Curtenius, 9 January 1775, WSA III:166.

286   "for the inspection": SA, as committee chairman, *BG*, 26 September 1774.

286   "to be in a state": SA to AL, 29 January 1775, WSA III:169.

287   forty or fifty men: Harrison Gray would sputter that "they have reduced the number of those that were concerned in the destruction of the tea to 30 or 40, when it is very evident that 2000" were involved, "The Grey Maggot," 10.

287   "Be prepared" to "in danger": SA for MA, to the Mohawk Indians, March 1775, WSA III:213.

287   the officers' antics: Andrews, 348, 368–400.

287–88 the oration, and "to beat up": SA to RHL, 21 March 1775, WSA III:206. "It was thought best": SA to AL, 4 March 1775, WSA III:196. SA's tangle with the officer: *Rivington's*, 9 March 1775, Force II:106; WSA III:199N. Wringing the nose: Andrews, 400; "A British Officer in Boston in 1775," *The Atlantic Monthly*, April 1877, 390–401, May 1877, 544–54; *Rivington's*, 23 March 1775; The toga: *Rivington's*, 16 March 1775. Elizabeth Ellery Dana, ed., *The British in Boston: Being the Diary of Lt. John Barker of the King's Own Regiment from November 15, 1774 to May 31, 1776* (Cambridge: Harvard University Press, 1924), 26; Eran Shalev, "Dr. Warren's Ciceronian Toga," *The Journal of Early American Life*, January 2007. Hinderaker deems the toga nonsense, at best a metaphor, *Boston's Massacre*, 251. Warren wrapped himself in it as did SA in Roman virtue.

288   "Put your enemy": SA to RHL, 21 March 1775, WSA III:206. The officers in atten-
      dance could not have been happy to hear Britons described as ruffians, poised to
      pounce on American property.

289   the pandemonium: Lister is best, "A British Officer in Boston in 1775," *The Atlan-
      tic Monthly*, April 1887, 397; *Rivington's* reported that the Bostonians "swarmed
      down the gutters, like rats, into the street," 16 March 1775; Moore's *Diary of the
      Revolution*, I:34–35; Force, II:212, Force, II:121. For SA's understated version, WSA
      III:199. "not a man of them" to "dagger in her heart": SA to RHL, 21 March 1775,
      WSA III:206–09. In his address Warren conjured up widowed mourners and
      orphaned babes, neither of which 5 March had produced.

289   "rather than precipitate": SA to Gadsden, 12 March 1775, WSA III:200.

290   "a rude rabble" to "determined part": Dartmouth to Gage, 27 January 1775, cited
      in K. G. Davies, *Documents of the American Revolution, 1770–1783*, vol. 9.

290   "not to be the aggressors": SA to AL, 29 January 1775, WSA III:171. On the minute-
      men: John R. Galvin, *The Minute Men: The First Fight: Myths and Realities of the
      American Revolution* (Lincoln, NE: Potomac Books, 1996).

290   "rashness and imprudence": Thomas Gage, "A Circumstantial Account of an
      Attack that Happened on the 19th of April 1775," www.masshist.org/database
      /viewer.php?item_id=498&pid=2. On the MHS copy is a note that appears to be in
      Dr. Warren's hand: "The people say the troops fired first and I believe they did."
      On the retreat, Reverend Samuel West, memoir, P-363, MHS. There were no scalp-
      ings, as the papers claimed, but there were threats, dead livestock, and looting of
      meetinghouse silver.

291   "an unnatural and unprovoked": Gage to Dartmouth, 15 May 1775, CO 5/769, F
      284, Kew. The theory does not hold up entirely, as an informer had written Gage
      on 3 April that should troops march out of Boston the country was to be alarmed;
      Gage's orders to his men seem not to have addressed that eventuality either.
      Gage never explained how he had landed on a raid in Concord rather than an
      arrest in Lexington. On the fugitive cannon: J. L. Bell's excellent *The Road to
      Concord*. Many criticized TG for not having made arrests sooner. Had he done so,
      insisted the Anglican minister in December 1774, the town would be perfectly
      quiet, Henry Caner to TH, 22 December 1774, in Kenneth Walter Cameron, ed.,
      Letter Book of the Reverend Henry Caner (Hartford: Transcendental Books, 1972).
      Ammerman on the disconnect in the orders: *In the Common Cause*, 137.

291   the patriot propaganda: *London Morning Chronicle*, 13 June 1775; "An American,"
      letter of 28 April 1775, Force II:428.

291   "to seize a quantity": Lieutenant John Barker Diary, *The British in Boston*, in
      Kehoe, 113. Gage knew at the end of March that most stores had left Concord. He
      also knew that—should he move a body of troops out of Boston—the country-
      side would be "called together to oppose the march to the last extremity."

292   "expressed himself": William Samuel Johnson Papers, series III, box 11, folder 10,
      ms. 22977, CHS.

292 "the instruments of warfare": JA, "Novanglus Papers, 1774–1775," *Diary of JA*, III:314. Best on the spread of the news, Adelman, *Revolutionary Networks*, and Frank Luther Mott, "The Newspaper Coverage of Lexington and Concord," *NEQ*, December 1944, 489–505. The news made its way through New England in five days, into at least sixteen publications as far south as Williamsburg by month's end. It arrived in London eleven days before Gage's account.

292 "famed in the history": SA to James Warren, 10 June 1775, WAL I:54.

293 "and robbed the mails": Gage to Barrington, 13 May 1775, *Correspondence of TG*, II:388; Gage to Colden, 4 May 1775, Clements; June 1 "Letter from London," *BG*, 7 August 1775. For London accounts of the alleged atrocities, see, for example, *London Evening Post*, 13 June 1775; *Gazetteer and New Daily Advertiser*, 16 June 1775; *London Morning Chronicle*, 13 June 1775. On the concern that Congress would not approve, JA to James Lloyd, 24 April 1815.

293 "I was with my friend" to "memorable battle": SA to Purviance, N-2390, box 36, MHS.

293 announced TH: TH to Dartmouth, 29 May 1775, F 1278, Dartmouth Papers, Staffordshire.

293 judged them indecent: SA to James Warren, 11 February 1777, P-164, MHS.

294 the NYC entrance: JA to AA, 8 May 1775, *Adams Family Correspondence*, I:195; SD to Elizabeth Deane, CHS Collections, II:222, 7 May 1775. JH reported that he appealed to several prominent New Yorkers to intervene. Under no circumstance would he allow such a tribute, "not being fond," he claimed, "of such parade," JH to Dolly Quincy, 7 May 1775, ms. N-2390, box 36, MHS. The distaste for pageantry aside, the account may have been true. "If you wish": Wells II:300. It was a dizzying trip: On 7 May, SA initially wrote EA that they would proceed to New York, where he had just spent the night. The delegation also crashed a wedding along the way.

294 one associate: SD to Mrs. Deane, 21 January 1776, *Collections of the Connecticut Historical Society*, II:349–51.

294 "The accounts of": JA to Abigail Adams, 8 May 1775, *Adams Family Correspondence*, I:196.

295 "rolling and gathering": SD to Elizabeth Deane, 12 May 1775, *Collections of the Connecticut Historical Society*, II:226–29. To SD it felt like "a march in state for over 200 miles."

295 "They are a most rude": HH to Robert Nicholson, 20 June 1775, HH, 329. "Jewish obstinacy": HH to Nicholson, 7 May 1775, HH, 321.

296 "the principal spring": "Remarks by Mr. Robert C. Winthrop Jr.," *Proceedings of the MHS*, February 1898, 140.

296 "nursed their tender" to "private virtue": Jonathan Sewall, 30 May 1775, Haldimand add. ms. 21695, BL.

296 "I believe it has": TH to Hardwicke, 17 July 1775, add. ms. 35427, BL.

296 "There is no instance": Boston letter of 23 June 1775, *London Evening Post*, 25 July 1775.

297 "'so that,' one assured Adams": Samuel Hodgdon to SA, 20 May 1776, NYPL.

297 "Mobs, or rather two": Serle, *American Journal*, 149.

297 "not the despicable": Gage to Dartmouth, 25 June 1775, in Davies, *Documents of the American Revolution*, IX.

297 The proclamation: Gage credited "well-known incendiaries and traitors" with having suppressed the truth, hijacking the press to nefarious ends.

298 "Damnation" and the saucy child: Edes, *Diary*, July 1775.

298 Samuel Adams Jr: There were three surgeons of the same name in New England military service; the record is hopelessly tangled.

298 Boston conditions, and the rats: Timothy Newell, "A Journal Kept during the Time that Boston Was Shut Up," ms. 261076, 48, MHS; Sibley, on TH Jr., 294; EA to SA, 12 February 1776, NYPL. Gage took a census that week: Half the town was missing.

299 "What punishment": SA to EA, 30 July 1775, WSA III:223.

299 "I wish": Gage to Barrington, 26 June 1775, *Correspondence of TG*, I:687.

299 "cool water": SA to EA, 28 September 1778, WSA IV:65.

299 "looked as blooming": James Warren to SA, 9 July 1775, NYPL.

299 "sister delegate" to "her companions": Abigail Adams to JA, 25 July 1775; similarly EG to SA and JA, 3 August 1776. The steadiness: Amos Adams to SA, 18 July 1775, NYPL.

299 the rifts in the delegation: Charles J. Stillé, *The Life and Times of John Dickinson* (Philadelphia: Historical Society of Pennsylvania, 1891), 172; RTP to James Warren, 1 January 1776, and RTP to Hawley, same date, *Papers of Robert Treat Paine*, III; Wells II:384–85.

300 "a certain eminent": SD to Elizabeth Deane, 21 January 1776, *Collections of the Connecticut Historical Society*, II:350.

300 the GW appointment: JA, "In Congress, June and July 1775," *Diary of JA*, III:321–24.

300 Benjamin Church: A J of O collaborator and an original member of the BCC, Church had been involved in every patriot effort. SA had recommended him to confederates as "a gentleman of ingenuity and integrity," SA to De Berdt, 20 April 1768, New Hampshire Historical Society. "dishonest designs": SA to James Warren, 13 October 1775, WAL I:141. The payroll: John Kenneth Rowland, "General Thomas Gage, the 18th Century Literature of Military Intelligence, and the Transition from Peace to Revolutionary War," *Historical Reflections/Réflexions Historiques*, Fall 2006, 506. For want of evidence, Church was never convicted.

301 "He who is void" to "public men": SA to James Warren, 4 November 1775, WSA III:236–37.

301 "I have long" to "it to others": SA to EA, 30 July 1775, WSA III:221–22. He all the same said something similar to James Warren.

301 "the pure motive": SA to EA, 20 October 1775, WSA III:228.

302 the riding lessons: JA to James Warren, 17 September 1775, *Papers of JA*, III: 158–59. For a few days one imperfection remained: SA mounted and dismounted only with the help of two servants. JH had courted Dolly since early 1771. Her flirtation with Aaron Burr evidently expedited the wedding.

302 "produce the grandest": SA to James Warren, 4 November 1775, WSA III:234. I have removed a wayward "s" from "revolutions."

303 most influential: See for example Wills, *Inventing America*, 19; JA to Pickering, 6 August 1782.

303 "I hope to hear": James Warren to SA, 14 February 1776, NYPL.

303 "Men of moderate": SA to James Warren, 4 November 1775, WSA III:235. TJ reported that SA was the second-oldest at the congress. He underlined "founding empires."

303 the evening debate: JA, 24 September 1775, *Diary of JA*, II:182.

303 "so rigorously logical": TJ to Samuel Adams Wells, 12 May 1819.

305 the discussion with BF: SA to JA, 15 January 1776, WSA III:259–60.

305 "the effect of which": SA to James Warren, 12 December 1776, WAL I:280.

305 "We have been afraid": Eliot cited in Sibley, on Andrew Eliot, 154.

305 the evacuation: Thomas Sullivan's journal, *Maryland Historical Magazine*, 241–53; Newell, "A Journal Kept during the Time that Boston Was Shut Up in 1775," *Collections of the MHS*, 1852, 261–76; Carr, *After the Siege*; Sibley, on Andrew Eliot; "Diary of SC," *The American Historical Review*, January 1901, 338; Isaac Cazneau letter, 4 April 1776, in Walter K. Watkins, "How the British Left the Hancock House," in *Old-Time New England*, April 1923, 194–96; Eldad Taylor, "Evacuation of Boston by an Eyewitness," NEHGS, 1854, 231–32; James Murray to D. Forbes, 14 February 1776, EF to Mrs. Barnes, 17 April 1776, in Nina Moore Tiffany, ed., *Letters of James Murray, Loyalist*, 235–52; William Davis to SA, 22 April 1776, NYPL; TG to Dartmouth, 20 August 1775, *Correspondence of TG*, I:414. "the removal": SA to Palmer, 2 April 1776, WSA III:273.

306 "It requires time": SA to SC, 20 April 1776, WAL III:384.

306 the hesitation: Secret intelligence from Philadelphia, 17 November 1775, F 44, CO 5/93, Kew; SA to SC, 3 April 1776, WAL III:276.

306 "The child independence": SA to James Warren, 16 April 1776, WAL I:225.

306 "Thank God": Credited to William B. Reed, *Army and Navy Chronicle*, 2 January 1840, vol. 10, #1, 13.

306 "Our petitions": *Journals of the Continental Congress*, VI:1075.

307 SA's speech: Samuel Adams Wells, Bancroft Collection, vol. 384, 161, NYPL. Wells to TJ, 14 April 1819, and TJ to Samuel Adams Wells, 12 May 1819, on restoring accuracy to that July.

307 "and a question": SA to James Warren, 6 June 1776, WAL I:255. JA to William Tudor, 28 March 1813.

307 the signing: As John Trumbull fairly warned, *New York Daily Advertiser*, 22 October 1818: "The journals of Congress are silent—it would be dangerous to trust the memory of any one." For the quiet around the Declaration: Howe to Lord Germain, 6 July 1776, box 2, Co 5/93, Kew.

307 "But what does it avail": SA to RHL, 15 July 1776, WSA III:297.

307 a "catalogue" to "good men": SA to Pitts, 17 July 1776, WSA III:301. Relatively little attention was paid at the time to what that August still passed for "the

proclamation of independence," Rowe, 316; Wills, *Inventing America*, 340. With New England loyalty, JA would assert in time that the Declaration's essence derived from JO's 1763 pamphlet, "pruned and polished by SA." JA to Pickering, 6 August 1822. PO would say that independence had been declared in 1776 but decided in 1768 by SA and his junto, PO, 148, or Adams and his posse, PO, 146.

308   "he had labored": Galloway, *Historical and Political Reflections*, 110. Galloway would also say that SA so incited colleagues against him that Galloway feared assassination. On the revolution in thinking: JA to McKean, 26 November 1815; JA to J. Morse, 29 November 1815; JA to TJ, 24 August 1815.

308   "among all the young": Serle, *American Journal*, 168.

308   "the first wish": Rush to JA, 12 May 1807.

308   Purchase Street destruction: Wells II:380. Most everyone returned to wreckage. SC had been robbed of all his furniture; the home of JH's beloved aunt was in shambles. Copley's JH and SA portraits survived, having been removed from the Hancock home.

308   "We must": SA to EA, 7 November 1775, WSA III:239.

308   "the best cause": SA to EA, 29 November 1776, WSA III:320.

309   "Was there ever" to "to perfection": SA to Kent, 27 July 1776, WSA III:304–05.

309   "contracted no alliance": Tocqueville, *Democracy in America* (New York: Adlard and Saunders, 1838), 52.

CHAPTER XIII: THE BEST CAUSE THAT VIRTUOUS MEN CONTEND FOR

311   "History's what": Hilary Mantel, *Giving Up the Ghost* (New York: Picador, 2004), 144.

311   "I am apt to be": SA to RHL, 15 July 1777, WSA III:387.

311   "But I get out": SA to James Warren, 1 February 1777, WSA III:353.

311   "I possess": SA to RHL, 15 July 1777, WSA III:387. "As I am not a judge": SA to JA, 17 December 1780, IV:233. He wound up arranging for the congressional reception of America's first foreign emissary. Was it not astonishing, he asked James Warren, that one who was so little a "man of the world as I should be joined in a committee to settle ceremonials"?, SA to Warren, 15 July 1778.

311   "I wish for retirement": SA to James Warren, 3 November 1778, WSA IV:90.

312   "he would have been": Cited in Wells III:338.

312   the Baltimore bliss: SA to James Warren, 16 January 1777, WSA III:347.

312   the spurs: McKean to JA, 20 November 1815, Historical Society of Pennsylvania.

312   "such idiots as": SA as "An American," BG, 30 December 1776.

312   "ancient purity": SA to Elbridge Gerry, 29 October 1775, WSA III:231.

312   "ill adapted": Luzerne, cited in John Durand, *New Materials for the History of the American Revolution* (New York: Holt, 1889), 240. SA seemed to glory, observed one, "in forming a party of opposition." "Mr. SA delights in trouble and difficulty," reported another Frenchman, Barbé-Marbois to Vergennes, 13 March 1782. Having forsaken his principles, SA had "become the most arbitrary and despotic man in the Commonwealth," wrote James Warren to JA, 18 May 1787, WAL II:293.

312 "and it is generally": SA to James Warren, 1 February 1777, WAL I:287.

313 "fortitude of mind": SA to James Warren, 29 October 1777, WAL I:376.

313 the trips north: SA to JA, 8 December 1777, WSA III:416–17. JA, 17 November 1777, *Diary of JA*, II:268. A Rhode Islander who crossed paths with both contingents remarked upon the "triumphant satisfaction" with which JH pranced through the country. A week later he met the Adams men; they turned back to their inn so they might eat bread and butter together, William Ellery, "Diary of Hon. William Ellery," *Pennsylvania Magazine of History and Biography*, October 1887, 323, 327. Finkelstein, "Merchant, Revolutionary and Statesman," 331; *Pennsylvania Ledger*, 7 January 1778; James Lovell to SA, 1 January 1778; *Independent Chronicle*, 21 November 1777; The Deane Papers, *Collections of the New York Historical Society*, 1887, II:467, 482.

313 the pageantry: *Pennsylvania Ledger*, 11 March 1778; James Warren to JA, 7 June 1778, has "the pomp and retinue of an Eastern prince," WAL II:20.

313 the stinging censure: SA to James Warren, 25 May 1778, WAL II:12.

313 "Mr Hancock never": SA to EA, 1 February 1781, WSA IV:246.

314 the feather in JH's hat: "A Querist," *Massachusetts Centinel*, 25 March 1789. For rumors that he had attempted to expel JH from Congress, *Middlesex Journal*, 26 December 1776.

314 "Ay, I remember": William Gordon to JA, 19 October 1780.

314 "to the shrine": James Warren to SA, 31 May 1778, WAL II:14.

314 "The history of mankind": SA fragment vindicating AL, 1779, NYPL.

314 "certainly equals him": James Warren to SA, 18 August 1778, WAL II:41.

314 "to arrest the course": James Warren to SA, 25 August 1778, WAL II:44. Tories stoked the antipathy. When a letter to Betsy fell into enemy hands, SA was mocked in the press for the formal tone in which he addressed his wife.

314 the toasts: SA to James Warren, 20 October 1778, WAL II:57.

315 "either real or": SA to Savage, 1 November 1778, WSA IV:87. JA wrote a similar letter when Rush suggested settling his differences with TJ, 25 December 1811. Some believed SA had moved in Congress for the expulsion of JH.

315 "'No man,' he swore": SA to Savage, 1 November 1778, NYPL.

315 the feuds: He was understood to be more antipathetic to France with each passing day, Henri Doniol, *Histoire de la participation de la France à l'établissement des Etats-Unis d'Amérique* (Paris: Imprimérie Nationale, 1888), IV:89. Over and over the French found him obstructionist; SA worried an infant republic could be overturned by Royalists.

315 Gadsden: Gadsden to SA, 4 April 1779, in Walsh, *Writings of Christopher Gadsden*, 164.

315 the calumny: SA to Warren, 20 November 1780, WAL II:148–49. To some his role seemed to consist of "censor to the failings of the human race," Sibley, on William Ellery, 141.

316 "Mr. Adams's principal": Benjamin Waterhouse to Christopher Champlin, 7 February 1783, in Philip Cash, *Dr. Benjamin Waterhouse: A Life in Medicine* (Sagamore Beach: Boston Medical Library, 2006), 459.

316 the Massachusetts Constitution and "passions and whims": Chastellux, *Travels*, 160–62.

316 "It has not always": AL to James Warren, 8 April 1782, WAL II:171.

316 "the few" to "by the few" SA to RHL, 3 December 1787, WSA IV:324–25. TH's son would manage to publish the final volume of the *History* only in 1828. At TH's death not a foot of American land remained to him.

317 the reassurance: SA to EA, 24 November 1780, WSA IV:225–26.

317 on JH: William Gordon to JA, 22 July 1780, *Papers of JA*, X:20–22; Abigail Adams to Lovell, 14 July 1781, *Adams Family Correspondence,* IV:176–78. "lived and entertained": Waterhouse, in Wells III:331. "Persons who relish flattery," SA feared, "will forever be deceived by those who design to deceive them." He was frankly astounded that his countrymen should install as their first elected governor someone variously described as "all caprice, incapacity, and indolence," "a man of straw," a purveyor of "quackery and exaggeration," "a court sycophant," "one of the most egregious triflers I know." Everyone from Mercy Otis Warren to James Madison thought JH a courtier.

317 "have had his name dinged": William Gordon to JA, 22 July 1780, *Papers of JA*, X:21. A magnanimous man, JH was also one who liked to be thanked.

317 "the administration of government": SA to Warren, 24 October 1780, WSA IV:213. When the American Academy of Arts and Sciences was founded that year, SA's name preceded JH's. JH protested. The bill was reworked, the names placed in alphabetical order, William Gordon, in *Proceedings of the MHS*, LXIII:445–46.

317 "I know it is very hard": SA as "An American" to the Earl of Carlisle, WSA IV:25–29.

318 "the man who had": James Warren to SA, 2 November 1780, WAL II:145.

318 "the fascinating charms": Catherine Macaulay to SA, 1 March 1791, NYPL. SA reported that the luxury was already unimaginable.

318 Winter Street: It was fitted with Loyalist furniture, much of which migrated to plundered rebel homes. Wells III:333; John Jay diary, 14 November 1790. The house had been confiscated from Sylvanus Gardiner; initially SA rented the home of Robert Hallowell, a customs comptroller.

318 the marital advice: SA to Thomas Wells, 22 November 1780, WSA IV:223.

319 "It is difficult": SA to JA, 13 January 1780, WSA IV:178.

319 "sink into insignificancy": *Letters of Capt. W.G. Evelyn*, 343.

319 the Cincinnati: Wells, III:201–02. Captain Thomas Wells, a nephew of EA's, was a member of the Society, Charles Chancey Wells and Suzanne Austin Wells, *Preachers, Patriots, and Plain Folks* (Oak Park, IL: Chauncey Park Press, 2004), 125.

319 one brand of nobility: SA to JA, 25 November 1790, WSA IV:351.

319 "times change": SA to RHL, 24 August 1789, WSA IV:335.

319 "I am, my dear Sir": SA to JA, 17 April 1797, NYPL.

320 "would travel fifty": In William E. Nelson, "Emerging Notions of Modern Criminal Law in the Revolutionary Era: An Historical Perspective," *NYU Law Review*, 450 (1967), 471. Samuel Teagers made the remark, for which he would be tried, convicted, and exiled.

320   on Loyalists: The stand set SA at odds with many, including Alexander Hamilton, Benjamin Waterhouse to TJ, 15 January 1819. And it drew down on SA, Waterhouse continued, "the hatred of their descendants, the high-toned Federalists of Boston, and of the whole state." Already the shunting aside had begun: Boston commissioned a fine marble sculpture of JA but made no nod to SA.

320   "we are safe": SA to Noah Webster, 30 April 1784, WSA IV:305.

320   the non-radical revolutionary: The point is William Appleman Williams's, "Samuel Adams: Calvinist, Mercantilist, Revolutionary," *Studies on the Left*, Winter 1960, 53.

320   "I confess": SA to RHL, 3 December 1787, WSA IV:324. C. Gore to Rufus King, 6 January 1788, in *The Life and Correspondence of Rufus King*, Charles R. King, ed. (New York: Putnam's, 1900), 311–12; Josiah Quincy to Thomas Armory, 20 February 1857, James Sullivan Papers, ms. N-997, MHS. For a violent reaction to SA's bill of rights, Jeremy Belknap to Paine Wingate, 29 May 1789, BPL. Belknap was scornful of the protections: If a man expressed his devout wish that someone not break into his house, it seemed fair to suspect that he viewed that individual as a burglar.

320   "odious, abhorrent": Merrill Jensen, ed., *Documentary History of the Ratification of the Constitution*, VI:1358. On SA's opposition to the Constitution, Josiah Quincy to Thomas Armory, 20 February 1857, James Sullivan Papers, ms. N-997, MHS.

320   Legend has it: Cited in Wells III:261; Samuel Hanson to Henry Knox, 4 June 1788, in Dorothy Twohig et al., eds., *The Papers of George Washington* (Charlottesville: University Press of Virginia, 1997), VI:40.

321   "So in despotic" to "is a crime": December 1789, SA Papers, NYPL.

322   John advised: JA to SA, 5 April 1783, *Papers of JA*, XIV:386. Similarly JA to Abigail Adams, 28 March 1783, *Adams Family Correspondence*, V:107–11.

322   the pained reading: Belknap to E. Hazard, 18 July 1789, "Extracts from Dr. Belknap's Notebooks," *Proceedings of the MHS*, 1876, 95–96. Only Paine fared worse with posterity.

322   "Whose heart is not" to "from antiquity": Rush to JA, 24 February 1790. SA on reading Gordon: SA to RHL, 29 August 1789, WSA IV:337. Among attempts to return SA to the founding fold: Edward G. Porter, *An Address on the Life and Character of Samuel Adams Delivered in the Old South Church*, 16 October 1884 (Boston: Clapp, 1885); Samuel Adams Wells to TJ, 14 April 1819. SA figured among the subscribers to Gordon's 1788 history, volumes that soon turned out to have been partly plagiarized. Gordon seems never to have let a rumor, an insinuation, or an occasion to ingratiate pass him by.

322   the GW visit: As one visitor remarked, JH's gout provided an ever-convenient excuse. The same visitor observed that enlightened Bostonians preferred Bowdoin, the people JH: J.-P. Brissot de Warville, *New Travels in the United States of America*, I:119. GW recorded the Boston slight but mentioned neither Adams, *The Diaries of George Washington*, V:473–76.

322   "Behold three men" to "damper on that": JA to Abigail Adams, 1 November 1789.

323   "be one continued lie": JA to Rush, 4 April 1790; Doniol, *Histoire*, III:263N. "more than Patrick": JA to Waterhouse, 30 January 1818. "the most disinterested": JA to Tudor, 1 June 1817; "I shall not attempt": JA to Tudor, 5 June 1817. The life of SA would require a volume, argued JA, to Niles, 13 February 1818. Already by 1815 JA believed the history hopelessly corrupted. Even the congressional speeches on paper differed from what he had heard.

323   JH's death: He died in debt and without having signed his will.

323   "has waded through": Cited in Alexander, *Samuel Adams*, 299. Similarly, William Davis to Samuel Pitts, 31 March 1796, Pitts Family Papers, ms. N-726, MHS.

323   "that pure unspotted": Dwight to Timothy Sedgwick, 19 April 1794, ms. N-851, MHS. Antiquated though he was, no one could argue with his integrity. See, for example, "A Countryman," *Independent Chronicle*, 11 December 1788; "A Voter," *Independent Chronicle*, 6 March 1794. For the "independent farmer": *Independent Chronicle*, 6 March 1794. Some defended him stoutly when it came to the 1796 gubernatorial election: SA had put all on the line in 1775, when "those pygmies who now bark at him were afraid to show their heads," William Davis to Samuel Pitts, 31 March 1796, Pitts family papers, ms. N-726, MHS.

323   the ghosts: *Federal Orrery*, 4 April 1796.

324   Even JA: "I wish the old fellow was a little more national, but he cannot do much harm and will not last long," JA wrote Abigail Adams, 26 January 1794. Seccombe, "From Revolution to Republic," is superb on the politics of these years.

324   "I respect his virtues": Abigail Adams to JA, 29 January 1797. To the end AA believed SA's principles pure.

324   "He always had": JA to Abigail Adams, 2 February 1796. SA's spartan values, JA seems to have concluded, came before the public good.

324   the stumble: Loring Andrews to Theodore Sedgwick, 13 February 1797, Sedgwick personal and professional correspondence, ms. N-851, MHS. As Leslie Thomas has pointed out, it was somehow appropriate that the highest office SA held represented the lowest point in his career.

324   "who used to boast": James Warren to Henry Warren, 5 June 1794, Mercy Otis Warren Papers, ms. N-17, MHS.

324   "superannuated": John Singleton Copley Jr. to his mother, cited in James H. Stark, *The Loyalists of Massachusetts* (Boston: W.B. Clarke, 1910), 219. Elizabeth Cady Stanton suffered a similar fate when the feminist movement took a turn for the more conservative and she did not.

324   "a grief and distress": JA to TJ, 16 July 1814. SA's mind had gone, leaving him "in the imbecility of second childhood," *Independent Chronicle*, 2 July 1823.

325   the funeral and eulogies: Young is particularly good on the details, *Shoemaker*, 116. *Independent Chronicle*, 10 and 31 October 1803; *Boston Transcript*, 6 October 1890; *Massachusetts Spy*, 19 October 1803; William Bentley, *The Diaries of William Bentley* (Salem: Essex Institute, 1911), III:50. "Called upon by the occasion to say something, he could not say less," reported the *Independent Chronicle* of SA's eulogist, 31 October 1803. Some twenty thousand had turned out for JH's funeral.

325 "No man contributed": William Bentley, *Diary*, III:49.

325 "The truly virtuous": SA to JA, 25 November 1790, WSA IV:353.

326 the papers: JA to Tudor, 5 June 1817. Some were evidently used as kindling by an unsuspecting servant. Others "were lost or submitted to improper hands and never returned," Wells II:391.

326 Boston Tea Party: the destruction became a party only as of 1826; proper Bostonians continued for some years to fit quotation marks around the three words. For Alfred Young on the evolution, *Liberty Tree*, 300, and *Shoemaker*, 193.

326 one historian: Linda Kerber, cited in Young, *Liberty Tree*, 301.

326 "a systematic course": JA to James Monroe, 19 June 1819. The "merits, services, sacrifices, and sufferings" of SA, wrote JA — the order is poignant — "are beyond all calculation." Also on the excising, *Boston Patriot*, 29 July 1826.

326 "great man [who]": *Independent Chronicle*, 2 July 1823. The quote continues: "and without whom that illustrious General would have remained only the most respectable gentleman planter, or farmer in America." It was hoped someone would erect a SA statue, which required another fifty years.

326 earliest politician: Jack Rakove compares SA to Madison; of the entire cast, they are the two founders who most lived for politics. Conversation with the author, 24 February 2022.

326 "the anxious days" to "come out pure": TJ to SA, 26 February 1800.

327 "Is this exactly" to "approve of it": TJ to SA, 29 March 1801. For a close, earthbound reading of TJ's canny inaugural, Joseph J. Ellis, *American Sphinx* (New York: Knopf, 1996), 214–21.

327 earliest, most active: TJ to Waterhouse, 15 January 1819. Annette Gordon-Reed has diagnosed TJ with a serious case of New England envy — the town meetings! The education institutions! — which in part explained the embrace.

327 his blessing: SA to TJ, 24 April 1801, WSA IV:410.

SELECTED BIBLIOGRAPHY

Alexander, John K. *Samuel Adams: The Life of an American Revolutionary*. Lanham, MD: Rowman & Littlefield, 2011.

Archer, Richard. *As If an Enemy's Country: The British Occupation of Boston and the Origins of the Revolution*. New York: Oxford University Press, 2010.

Bailyn, Bernard. *The Ordeal of Thomas Hutchinson*. Cambridge, MA: Harvard University Press, 1974.

Brown, Richard D. *Revolutionary Politics in Massachusetts: The Boston Committee of Correspondence and the Towns, 1772–1774*. New York: Norton, 1976.

Bunker, Nick. *An Empire on the Edge: How Britain Came to Fight America*. New York: Vintage, 2014.

Carter, Edwin Clarence, ed. *Correspondence of General Thomas Gage with the Secretaries of State, 1765–1775*. 2 vols. New Haven: Yale University Press, 1931.

Cary, John. *Joseph Warren: Physician, Politician, Patriot*. Urbana, IL: University of Illinois Press, 1961.

Chernoweth, Erica. *Civil Resistance: What Everyone Needs to Know*. New York: Oxford University Press, 2021.

Davidson, Philip. *Propaganda and the American Revolution*. Chapel Hill: University of North Carolina Press, 1941.

Donoughue, Bernard. *British Politics and the American Revolution*. London: Macmillan, 1964.

Fischer, David Hackett. *Paul Revere's Ride*. New York: Oxford University Press, 1994.

Forman, Samuel A. *Dr. Joseph Warren*. Gretna, LA: Pelican, 2017.

Fowler, William M., Jr. *Samuel Adams: Radical Puritan*. New York: Addison-Wesley, 1997.

Hinderaker, Eric. *Boston's Massacre*. Cambridge, MA: Harvard University Press, 2019.

Hoerder, Dirk. *Crowd Action in Revolutionary Massachusetts, 1765–1780*. New York: Academic Press, 1977.

Hutchinson, Peter O., ed. *Diary and Letters of His Excellency Thomas Hutchinson*. 2 vols. New York: Burt Franklin, 1971.

Maier, Pauline. *From Resistance to Revolution*. New York: Knopf, 1972.

———. *The Old Revolutionaries: Political Lives in the Age of Samuel Adams*. New York: Norton, 1990.

Miller, John C. *Sam Adams: Pioneer in Propaganda*. Stanford: Stanford University Press, 1964.

Morgan, Edmund S. and Helen M. Morgan. *The Stamp Act Crisis: Prologue to Revolution*. Chapel Hill: University of North Carolina Press, 1995.

Nash, Gary B. *The Urban Crucible*. Cambridge, MA: Harvard University Press, 1979.

Nicolson, Colin. *The "Infamas Govener": Francis Bernard and the Origins of the American Revolution*. Boston: Northeastern University Press, 2001.

Patterson, Stephen E. *Political Parties in Revolutionary Massachusetts*. Madison: University of Wisconsin Press, 1973.

Schlesinger, Arthur M. *Prelude to Independence*. New York: Vintage, 1965.

Seccombe, Matthew. "From Revolution to Republic: The Later Political Career of Samuel Adams." PhD dissertation, Yale University, 1978.

Thomas, Leslie Joseph. "Partisan Politics in Massachusetts during Governor Bernard's Administration." PhD dissertation, University of Wisconsin, 1960, 2 vols.

Thomas, P. D. G. *British Politics and the Stamp Act Crisis*. Oxford: Clarendon Press, 1975.

Townsend, Charles Ray. "The Thought of Samuel Adams." PhD dissertation, University of Wisconsin, 1968.

Yodelis, Mary Ann. "Boston's Second Major Paper War: Economics, Politics, and the Theory and Practice of Political Expression in the Press, 1763–1775." PhD dissertation, University of Wisconsin, 1971.

Young, Alfred F. *Liberty Tree: Ordinary People and the American Revolution*. New York: New York University Press, 2006.

INDEX

ILLUSTRATION CREDITS

Map of Boston: Norman B. Leventhal Map & Education Center, Boston
   Public Library.

Parisian print shop: Sarin Images / Granger.

Governor Frances Bernard: By permission of the Governing Body of
   Christ Church, Oxford.

Thomas Hutchinson: © Massachusetts Historical Society / Bridgeman
   Images.

Hutchinson's mansion: Granger.

The Town House: Collection of the Massachusetts Historical Society.

John Adams by Copley: Shawshots / Alamy Stock Photo.

Abigail Adams: Collection of the Massachusetts Historical Society.

Mercy Otis Warren: *Mrs. James Warren (Mercy Otis) c.1763* (oil on canvas),
   Copley, John Singleton (1738–1815) © 2022 MFA, Boston. All rights
   reserved. / Bequest of Winslow Warren / Bridgeman Images.

James Otis: Courtesy of Historic New England. Gift in memory of
   Gertrude and Carlos Hepp, 2017.148.1AB.

John Hancock: Photograph © (2022) Museum of Fine Arts, Boston.
   Deposited by the City of Boston L-R 30.76d.

Joseph Warren: National Portrait Gallery, Smithsonian Institution.

Samuel Adams by Copley: Photograph © (2022) Museum of Fine Arts,
   Boston. Deposited by the City of Boston L-R 30.76c.

Thomas Gage by Copley: Yale Center for British Art, Paul Mellon
   Collection.

The Year 1765: Collection of the Massachusetts Historical Society.

Stamp Act funeral: Courtesy of the John Carter Brown Library.

Tea-Tax-Tempest: Courtesy of the John Carter Brown Library.

Killing of Christopher Seider: Woodcut from *The Life, and Humble Confession, of Richardson, the Informer,* Historical Society of Pennsylvania.

Musket balls: Collection of the Massachusetts Historical Society.

Revere's Massacre engraving: Yale University Art Gallery.

Boston Tea Party: Americans throwing the cargoes of the Teaships into the river, at Boston, 1789. Photograph. https://www.loc.gov/item /2002718863/.

Boston blockaded: Collection of the Massachusetts Historical Society.

Faneuil Hall: Collection of the Massachusetts Historical Society.

Daughter of Liberty: Granger.

Watertown envelope: Manuscripts and Archives Division, The New York Public Library. "Watertown" The New York Public Library Digital Collections. 1773–1774. https://digitalcollections.nypl.org /items/ae2b5cd0-d722-0132-8849-58d385a7b928.

James Bowdoin: Collection of the Massachusetts Historical Society.

Paul Revere by Copley: Photograph © (2022) Museum of Fine Arts, Boston; Gift of Joseph W. Revere, William B. Revere and Edward H. R. Revere 30.781.

Hancock parsonage: The Print Collection, The New York Public Library.

Battle of Lexington: Connecticut Historical Society.

Samuel Adams statue: Latitude Stock / Alamy Stock Photo.

Endpapers: Paul Revere's engraving of the 1768 occupation of Boston, designed "for supporting the dignity of Britain and chastising the insolence of America," as Revere insolently labeled the work. Boston Athenaeum.

ABOUT THE AUTHOR

Stacy Schiff is the author of *Véra (Mrs. Vladimir Nabokov)*, winner of the Pulitzer Prize; *Saint-Exupéry*, a Pulitzer Prize finalist; *A Great Improvisation: Franklin, France, and the Birth of America*, winner of the George Washington Prize and the Ambassador Book Award; *Cleopatra: A Life*, winner of the PEN/Jacqueline Bograd Weld Award for biography; and most recently, *The Witches: Salem, 1692*. Schiff has received fellowships from the Guggenheim Foundation, the National Endowment for the Humanities, and the Center for Scholars and Writers at the New York Public Library. Awarded an Academy Award in Literature in 2006, she was inducted into the American Academy of Arts and Letters in 2019. She has written for, among many other publications, the *New York Times, The New Yorker,* and the *New York Review of Books*. Named a Chevalier des Arts et des Lettres by the French government, she lives in New York City.